Culture in Mind

Culture in Mind

Toward a Sociology of Culture and Cognition

EDITED BY
Karen A. Cerulo

Routledge
New York   London

Published in 2002 by
Routledge
29 West 35th Street
New York, NY 10001

Published in Great Britain by
Routledge
11 New Fetter Lane
London EC4P 4EE

Routledge is an imprint of the Taylor & Francis Group.

10 9 8 7 6 5 4 3 2 1

Library of Congress Cataloging-in-Publication Data

Culture in mind : toward a sociology of culture and cognition / edited by Karen A. Cerulo
    p. cm.
  Includes bibliographical references and index.
  ISBN 0-415-92943-1—ISBN 0-415-92944-X (pbk)
  1. Cognition and culture—Congresses.   I. Cerulo, Karen A.

  BF311. C85   2001
  153—dc21   2001019757

Printed on acid-free, 250-year life paper.
Manufactured in the United States of America.

For Joseph and Edna Nicastro,
bright and warm in my heart

Contents

Section III: Representation and Integration

Section IV: Storage and Retrieval

Section V: Building Bridges

Appendix: Mapping the Field

Acknowledgments

The papers that constitute this volume were originally presented at a conference entitled "Toward a Sociology of Culture and Cognition," held at Rutgers University in November 1999. I am grateful not only to this volume's contributors, but to all those who presented their work at that event. These participants are all significant to the establishment of a new and exciting intellectual agenda.

I take this opportunity to acknowledge gratefully the many sponsors that made this project possible: the American Sociological Association's Funds for the Advancement of the Discipline, the Rutgers University Center for the Critical Analysis of Contemporary Culture, the Rutgers University Research Council, the Rutgers University Institute for Health, Health Care Policy, and Aging, and Rutgers University's Vice President of academic affairs, Dean of Social Sciences, Graduate School, and Department of Sociology.

Special thanks go to my research assistant Ruth Simpson, who contributed significantly to the conference organization and provided insightful feedback on sections of this volume. Ruth also designed the wonderful Web site that accompanies both of these efforts. This collection also greatly benefited from Lyn Spillman's careful and constructive review of the original proposal. I am grateful as well to Paul DiMaggio, Allan V. Horwitz, Magali Sarfatti Larson, Janet Ruane, Robert Wuthnow, and Eviatar Zerubavel for their intellectual and collegial support during various phases of this project. Finally, thanks go to my wonderful editor Ilene Kalish and the equally wonderful staff at Routledge (especially assistant editor Kimberly Guinta and production editors Tom Wang and Hope Breeman) for their help in bringing this project to fruition.

CHAPTER 1

Establishing a Sociology of Culture and Cognition

Karen A. Cerulo

What is thought . . . and how does one come to study and understand it?

Plato was among the first to grapple with the issue. "Thinking," he argued, " is the talking of the soul with itself."[1] With such ideas the philosopher established what, for centuries, proved the reigning image of thought—one that stressed the private, the contemplative, the solitary nature of human cognition. In thinking, it was argued, human beings sustain their secrets and bring their fantasies to life. Planning, analysis, self-reflection, and reasoning all begin in the seclusion of the mind. In Plato's imagery—indeed, in the images forwarded by so many artists and humanists that followed him—thinking embodied one of the most personal activities in which human beings engage.[2]

The "personalized model" of human cognition dominated public discourse for centuries. Medieval and Renaissance theologians, Romantic visionaries, psychoanalysts, and modern behaviorists all placed the intersection of personal experience and private reflection at the heart of human thought. The late twentieth century, however, brought the first sustained challenge to such visions of the mind. In the 1950s, cognitive science[3] burst onto the intellectual scene. The field grew rapidly, and as it did, the discipline triggered a revolution in definitions of thinking.[4]

With the advent of cognitive science, concerns with "the mind" gave way to the study of "the brain." Activities such as "thought" and "reflection" were reconceptualized as "information processing." "Individualistic" elements of thinking became secondary to "universal" cognitive mechanisms. With the dawn of cognitive science, the human mind ceased to be viewed as an amorphous component of the self. Rather, the mind emerged as a mechanical device—one unique to a species. It became structurally divisible, with the process of cognition mapped and coded according to a series of natural stages and operations: sensation, attention, discrimination, classification, representation, integration, storage, retrieval, and so forth.

Cognitive science has made many impressive discoveries regarding the act of thinking. The field has taught us, for example, about the electrochemical and cerebral processes that accompany the apprehension and initial processing of information. Studies have also identified several of the mental mechanisms involved in organizing, representing, and storing sensory stimuli. In addition, research has uncovered many of the precepts, the semantic and syntactic rules, that enable symbolic communication among humans. And the literature illustrates ways in which thinking and remembering can be adversely affected by sensory and cognitive overload. In light of these and many other important findings, it would be difficult to challenge the value of the field. Yet for all of the virtues and strengths of cognitive science, the discipline's commitment to studying universal elements of human thought, its emphasis on mind as an information processor, leaves us with many unanswered questions. Can cognitive science tell us all we need to know about thinking?

For example, cognitive scientists carefully analyze attention systems of the brain, exploring both the conscious and unconscious elements of the process. Researchers chart the specific areas of the brain involved in attention; they document the brain's ability to attend simultaneously to multiple stimuli, to shift attention, or habituate to stimuli. Such studies are undeniably important. Yet they tell us little about broader, socioculturally based patterns of attending. For despite growing knowledge of the brain's natural capacity, we still cannot explain the role of factors such as social background, institutionalized scripts of action, or situational context in establishing the parameters of conscious awareness. Similarly, cognitive scientists scrutinize the ways in which human beings discriminate and classify stimuli. Researchers explore processes such as concrete comparison, analogical thinking, and metaphoric thinking tracing these skills to infancy. In exploring the neural mechanics of such sorting processes, however, current studies fail to explain the variable salience of mental categories and classes. The literature neglects the ways in which criteria of sameness and difference can vary across cultural communities. Now consider cognitive scientists' work on the integration of sensory input. Studies document the tools that enable the positioning and interpretation of information—tools such as concepts, frames, formats, and schemata.[5] And yet, beyond the basic operations of these organizational tools, the field tells us little about the variable ways in which such tools are applied. We have still to discover the factors that drive human groups to invoke specific concepts and frames, or to withhold certain formats and schemata at different historical moments or within divergent social situations. Finally, consider cognitive scientists' work on storage and retrieval. The literature distinguishes long-term and short-term memory structures and identifies the neurocognitive processes involved at each juncture. Yet for all of its strengths, this research cannot address the sociocultural dimensions of memory construction. Such studies fail to explain, for example, how or why certain events take precedence over others in the building of a particular individual's or group's historical narrative.

Clearly, there are important gaps in our current knowledge of thought. It is these gaps that beckoned *Culture in Mind*. I conceived the book not as a challenge to the cognitive science literature. Rather, it is designed as a much-needed complement to that body of work. In assembling this collection, my goal is to move beyond issues of cognitive universals and toward a deeper engagement of cognitive difference and distinction. I hope to move beyond the neurological details of mental processing, opting instead to locate and analyze cognition in its sociocultural context. To accomplish these tasks, I have assembled a distinguished array of scholars—authors who direct their readers to an analytic "middle ground."[6] Each contributor treats cognitive patterns as neither general to the species nor specific to the individual. Rather, each author considers cognition as an act of social beings—an act both enabled and constrained by one's position in the complex web of social and cultural experience. Using this perspective, contributors temporarily background concerns for the routine neuromechanics of thinking. They focus instead on the very different places that these routine processes can lead.

Logic of the Volume

In analyzing thought, cognitive scientists typically invoke a series of sequential stages. These stages include the human brain's *sensation and attention* to sensory stimuli, its ability to *discriminate and classify* such input, the ways in which the brain *represents and integrates* information, and finally, its ability to *store and retrieve* data. From the cognitive scientist's perspective, understanding these stages, including the specific operations that occur at each stage, holds the key to comprehending fully the process of human thought.

These four sequential stages provide a useful organizational frame for *Culture in Mind*. Using them, we can embark on an intellectual journey that takes us from the very sparks of a thought to its long-term development. Yet as authors direct us to the various phases of cognition, they will raise a set of issues that cognitive scientists have heretofore ignored. Authors will not dissect the moment-by-moment of cognition; they will not link thinking to specific brain structures. Rather, each chapter of *Culture in Mind* will consider the ways in which sociocultural conditions temper and amend the cognitive experience. The road to this goal is straightforward. Each contributor will lead readers to a different social setting: the negotiation of intimate relationships, medical decision making, economic rivalry in the market, the construction of political villains, and so on. Using setting as a vehicle, authors will document the ways in which cognition varies across different cultural contexts. They will illustrate as well the ways in which cognitive processes become institutionalized dimensions of these settings. And the articles to follow will also explore the ways in which institutionalized cognitive processes can direct social action.

The first section of this volume examines *sensation and attention*, the initial stage of thought. Contributors explore the specific processes that characterize this phase of mental activity. Chapter 2, for example, considers "focusing," and "denial." For cognitive scientists, focusing involves the selection and centering of specific environmental stimuli. The process allows the brain to "lock in" certain stimuli, thus rendering them the sole point of concentration. Denial, in contrast, occurs when something blocks or inhibits the connection between specific stimuli and brain receptors. The phenomenon is typically explained as the product of either a physiological abnormality or a psychological trauma. Author Eviatar Zerubavel locates focusing and denial at the heart of his work. But in contrast to cognitive scientists, Zerubavel directs his efforts to the sociocultural foundations of these processes. The author argues that the stimuli to which we attend, as well as those that we ignore, are influenced by existing social agendas—agendas that define relevance on the basis of cultural criteria. In support of his argument, Zerubavel takes readers to a variety of social settings. At each site, he accents the explicit and implicit cultural norms that can block information from entering our awareness.

Chapter 3 continues the emphasis on sensation and attention, exploring a process known as "signal detection." Among cognitive scientists, signals constitute special environmental stimuli that target and excite key receptors within the human brain. Those studying signals typically search for factors that can increase the detection of these stimuli. In this regard, researchers gauge the impact of factors such as signal strength or observer expectancy. In Chapter 3, however, Diane Vaughan suggests a broader approach to the issue of signal detection. Vaughan's research takes us to three different sites: couples in deteriorating intimate relationships, managers and engineers at NASA making assessments of technical components of the space shuttle, and air traffic controllers reading information on radar screens. In each case, the author focuses her readers on the ways in which individuals interpret and respond to signals of potential danger. By studying danger signals in context, Vaughan provides a fresh insight on signal detection, one that highlights the sociocultural aspects of the process. Specifically, Vaughan demonstrates that the social location of individuals, as well as the organization of the social contexts in which individuals interact, proves crucial to discovering both those signals that are sufficiently strong to stimulate attention, and those that fail to enter our awareness.

The next section of the volume is devoted to *discrimination and classification*. Here, contributors dissect the mental mechanisms by which human beings establish similarity, difference, and relativity. Chapter 4, for example, examines the process of "concrete comparison." Among cognitive scientists, concrete comparison constitutes an evaluative strategy. When engaged in the process, human beings search the environment, looking for cues and criteria by which to make relative assessments. As such, objects, actions, and events are defined vis-à-vis a network of relevant entities. In considering concrete comparison, Wendy Espeland alerts readers to a sociocultural variant of the process. Her article explores "commensuration," an institutionalized method that guides societal level comparisons. According to Espeland, commensuration allows societies to transform different qualities into a common metric. It is a process that guides the establishment of things such as pricing, cost-benefit ratios, utility functions, and the quantitative ranking of goods and services. In Chapter 4, Espeland documents commensurative practices across a wide variety of contexts. She also highlights the ways in which the process can change that to which societies attend, that which they value, and the rules of value-based interaction. Such work holds broad implications for those engaged in social science analysis. The study of commensuration provides vital insight on the organization and sustenance of social hierarchies, social networks, and social settings.

Chapter 5 directs readers to "metaphoric thinking," another critical tool of discrimination and classification. Cognitive scientists define metaphoric thinking as a process of creative substitution. When engaged in this process, human beings speak of or treat an entity as if it were something else. Typically, cognitive scientists study metaphorical thinking as it occurs among very young children (between the ages one to six). They argue that a child's ability, for instance, to turn a finger into a gun or a cardboard box into a castle is critical to cognitive development, for such metaphoric thinking ultimately advances intellectual skills, creativity, and imagination. In Chapter 5, Nicole Isaacson stresses the importance of metaphoric thinking as well. However, her work takes us beyond the minds of children or the realm of the individual. Isaacson situates metaphoric thinking within a growing American controversy—distinguishing the premature baby from the human fetus. Using medical writings produced over the last two decades, she documents a growing trend toward treating the ever-younger fetus as premature. Isaacson discusses the social tensions that accompany this classification shift, and she notes the ways in which the application of metaphors often reduces these tensions. Her work provides numerous examples of situations in which metaphors are systematically invoked in order to foreground the fetus's babylike characteristics. In so doing, Isaacson demonstrates that metaphoric thinking at the macro level can redefine both the nature of the fetus and the point at which life begins.

Chapter 6 provides an innovative synthesis of the concepts presented heretofore. In a quintessential sociological analysis, Harrison White brings signaling, denial, and concrete comparison to the economic marketplace. White contends that such cognitive processes form "the drive-train of any social vehicle" (see White, p. 101), and he highlights signaling, denial, and comparison as institutionalized dimensions of production markets. In support of these claims, White charts the evolution of production markets as signaling mechanisms. He analyzes market action in terms of social comparisons and the rivalry profiles that such comparisons generate. Finally, he considers economic theorists' denial of markets in favor of optimal cost schedules, and he notes the ways in which this denial has impeded the scholarly understanding of economic structures.

Discriminatory practices operate in conjunction with other cognitive skills. As human beings sort information, they must symbolize it and reconcile it with an existing stock of knowledge and core expectations. The third section of this volume takes up these issues, addressing the *representation and integration* of information. The section begins by focusing readers on mental "concepts."

According to cognitive scientists, concepts are abstractions that represent some part of the world; they describe the properties common to a class of objects or ideas. Invoking concepts allows human beings to symbolize and interpret new stimuli and information; these abstractions help human beings locate new material within a broader mental scheme. In studying concepts, cognitive scientists have been particularly interested in concept formation. Some argue that concepts are acquired via a continual process of association; others contend that concepts are formed through an elaborate process of hypothesis testing. Cognitive scientists have also been concerned with the structure of concepts. Here, four competing models drive the dialogue. The "classical view" posits that concepts are structured around defining features—features that are singly necessary and jointly sufficient to define the concept. The "prototype view" is more flexible, suggesting that concepts represent a "best example"; they summarize the most common features among a concept's instances. The "exemplar view" provides a highly concrete model, arguing that concepts consist of extremely similar or exemplar instances. Finally, the "theory dependence view" contends that concepts are inextricably tied to broader theories and knowledge bases.[7]

Exploring the formation and structure of concepts is undeniably important. At the same time, such an agenda excludes equally critical research issues. For example, what can concept structure tell us about the impact of concepts? Can the origins or characteristics of concepts help us to understand the ways in which their application shapes and limits shared definitions of reality or patterns of social action? Keeping these questions in mind, the chapters of Section III explore contexts in which specific concepts (and the broader structures they constitute) can encourage narrow and sometimes misleading perceptions of the world. In Chapter 7, for example, Robert Wuthnow considers the sociological study of morality. Wuthnow contends that such moral inquiry has been unduly restrictive. This is because conceptions of morality have been limited by a few "exemplar" works, works described as models of moral inquiry. Wuthnow argues that these exemplars, in addition to limiting conceptions of morality, have spurred a false conceptual dichotomy. The false dichotomy is between value-laden and value-free inquiry, between normative and empirical, between pre-scriptive and positivist, or between moral and amoral. In Chapter 7, Wuthnow revisits the exemplars of moral inquiry. In so doing, he reconsiders the idea that "only a few sociologists really do moral inquiry, while the majority of sociologists are engaged in "hard-nosed (soulless) empirical investigations" (see Wuthnow, p. 130). This exercise, according to Wuthnow, directs us to a true dichotomy that deserves our emphasis, one that contrasts autonomous and embedded selves. Further, the author suggests ways in which this true dichotomy might broaden sociological treatments of morality.

In Chapter 8, I too examine the ways in which concepts can restrict collective per-ceptions. My inquiry addresses conceptualizations of social relations. Traditionally, social theorists and other analysts have adopted certain "theory-dependent" concepts to describe social relations: *Gemeinschaft* versus *Gesellschaft, mechanical* versus *organic solidarity, primary* versus *secondary relations*, and so on. The analytic models that have emerged from these concepts suggest that social relations evolve in a linear fashion. As the argument goes, societies such as the United States experience a shift from the "we-ness" of civic community to the "me-ness" of individualism—a shift that is the unfortunate yet inevitable price of a fully developed, complex, and highly modern society. Over the past several years, I have studied social relations relative to historical data on social behaviors, attitudes, cultural products, and images (U.S. circa 1850–1990). These data fail to confirm the much touted march from "we" to "me" relations. Indeed, these data suggest that the concepts typically applied to the study of social relations may be blinding us to certain realities of social and cultural life. Knowing this, my work poses a critical question. What sustains analytic con-cepts that no longer apply to the conditions at hand? In the hopes of answering this question, Chapter 8 examines the role of both cultural practices and specific social events in the creation and sustenance of lapsed concepts.

Beyond concepts, one can identify broader mental structures that function to rep-resent and integrate information. "Frames," "formats," and "schemata" are the three most important of these structures. According to cognitive scientists, "frames" are static constructs; they are models that allow human beings to represent stereotyped interactions or situations. With experience, human beings develop a repertoire of frames—play frames, work frames, danger frames, intimacy frames, and so on—creating a structured set of expectations within which new situations are evaluated. By invoking frames, human beings can place daily encounters in perspective; they can impose meaning on experiences that emerge with each new day. While cognitive scientists emphasize the static nature of frames, social scientists view these constructs in more dynamic terms. In Chapter 9, David Altheide illustrates this tradition, highlighting the distinctive dimensions that a sociocultural approach brings to frame analysis. Specifically, Altheide rejects the notion of frames as static entities—innate constructs that lie ready, waiting to be tapped. Rather, he conceives of frames as dynamic social constructs that are differentially applied in the service of social interaction. Using media news as the context for his inquiry, Altheide analyzes the ways in which media narrators invoke certain frames to construct actively a "discourse of fear." In tracking this discourse over time, Altheide demonstrates that the public's fears are not necessarily tied to real risk. Rather, he shows that the framing of the news shapes audience understandings and expectations of what to fear and how to avoid it.

"Formats" constitute another central tool of representation and integration. While frames help human beings to process actual experience, formats help human beings to process reports and descriptions of experience. For example, formats can help the brain to distinguish entertainment from news, factual from fictional accounts. Formats can differentiate public discourse from private or intimate discussion. In studying formats, cognitive scientists typically explore the ways in which humans acquire knowledge of formats; they also study human beings' ability to recognize and distinguish formats. But in Chapter 10, William Gamson broadens the parameters of such inquiry. His work examines the institutionalization of formats—the systematic pairing of certain themes with particular information arrangements. Gamson is especially concerned with the institutionalized formats that guide policy discourse. Like Altheide, he chooses media news as the context for his inquiry, and he explores the media's formatting of stories on abortion. Analyzing stories on both sides of the debate, Gamson shows that a "personalization format" has come to dominate abortion policy discourse. He also notes that abortion discourse is not unique in this regard. Indeed he suggests that personalization, a format formerly reserved for private exchange, has become a regular feature of media policy coverage. In Chapter 10, Gamson explores the reasons behind this unexpected format transfer. But more important, he explores the ways in which the media's application of the personalization format can empower its audience.

Beyond concepts, frames, and formats lie the broadest of representation and integration structures—the "schema." According to cognitive scientists, schemata are metaconcepts; they represent various types of knowledge, including basic knowledge such as the shape of the number "1," and complex knowledge such as intricate mathematical equations. Cognitive scientists tell us that schemata can be linked and configured, forming broad mental constructs. For example, the schema for "child" may be linked to those representing "parent" or "sibling"; the schema for "a burger" may be linked to those representing "fries" and "a Coke." When schemata are linked, the brain typically organizes them hierarchically, creating elaborate, nested constructs. In this way, a high-level, general schema such as "the nuclear family" encompasses lower-order, specific schemata such as "parent," "child," and "siblings";

a general schema such as "fast food" encompasses specific schemata such as "a burger," "fries," and "a Coke." Like the cognitive tools heretofore discussed, schemata influence the ways in which new information is represented and integrated. But from the cognitive scientist's perspective, the most important aspect of schemata is the role that these structures play in information *storage and retrieval*. This issue, then, provides the focus for the volume's fourth section.

Cognitive science has taught us much about the ways in which schemata enable information *storage and retrieval*. For example, when storing newly acquired information, schemata render data abstract and general. These structures allow the brain to exclude the specific details of a new experience and retain only the generalities that liken the event to other experiences in one's past. In this way, schemata filter new data, allowing the brain easily to incorporate new information with prior knowledge. Schemata behave similarly when invoked for information retrieval. Studies show that in remembering, the brain normalizes representations to fit an active schema. Discrepant features of one's memories are adjusted or omitted so that information conforms to the schema in use.

Cognitive scientists restrict their interest in schemata to the internal workings of the brain. But some contend that schemata play an equally important role in the external world—specifically, in the construction of collective memory. In Chapter 11, Barry Schwartz and MiKyoung Kim explore this idea. They examine schematic representations of national identity, the cultural contexts in which these schemata develop, and the role that identity schemata play in the construction of national memory. Schwartz's and Kim's study addresses two very different national cultures: the United States and South Korea. Their research presents readers with the historical reflections of more than one thousand American and Korean undergraduates. Specifically, students in the study were asked to name the events in their respective nations' histories that elicited the greatest pride or invoked the greatest shame. Schwartz and Kim then analyzed students' reasons for selecting specific events. Findings reveal that students' answers are patterned in accord with the specific cultural themes that comprise each group's national identity. Schwartz and Kim argue that these cultural themes function as "priming" schemata which, in turn, direct Americans' and Koreans' memories of the past. By identifying these priming schemata and tracking their influence, Schwartz and Kim illustrates the ways in which sociocultural context can configures a nation's history.

Gary Allan Fine is interested in collective memory construction as well. In Chapter 12, he pursues the issue with a special eye toward historical narrative. According to Fine, historical narrative presents a special type of schema. Such narrative consists of "a set of linked reputations . . . a sequential pageant of individuals, each defined as being 'the cause' or engine of events" (Fine, p. 227). In this way, great figures—the heroes of a culture—provide a lens through which a collective body assesses its past and configures its present. The stories of heroes filter the people, places, and events that drive the evolution of a group. While heroes are important to the construction of both collective memory and collective consciousness, they represent only part of any collective's story. To fully examine collective memory and its impact on present perception, Fine contends that one must examine the villains of historical narrative as well. Like heroes, these evildoers establish behavioral boundaries and, thus, contribute to collective definitions of moral order. Villains can also increase collective cohesion as members join in opposition against them. And a collective often invokes evildoers to stigmatize undesirable actions and images. In this way villains, too, are a critical part of the collective's self-reflective lens. To explore fully the role of evildoers in collective memory and current consciousness, Fine examines a particularly striking case study of evil. Specifically, his project explores historical narratives and current assessments of Adolf Hitler, the Nazis, and the Holocaust. In probing accounts of these persons and events, Fine lays the groundwork for a broader theory addressing evil exemplars and their impact on the construction of the past.

In previewing this volume, I have contrasted each chapter with cognitive scientists' approach to the issues at hand. In so doing, I hoped to emphasize the unique contributions that sociologists can make to studies of thought. Yet identifying the differences between cognitive science and sociology raises important questions. Is there common ground within these two disciplines? Can an interdisciplinary dialogue offer something of value to those working in each tradition? Three scholars address these questions in the final section of *Culture in Mind*. In Chapter 13, psychologist Jerome Wakefield presents an interdisciplinary analytic model that he calls "the Foucault Sandwich." To illustrate the workings of the model, Wakefield directs readers to the concept of "mental disorders." When analyzing mental disorders, Wakefield suggests that certain essentialistic assumptions must provide the "meat" of one's inquiry. One must accept "mental disorders" as a concept that is representative of a true dysfunction—a real breakdown in natural mental functioning that has little or nothing to do with social structure. Yet Wakefield's model is not essentialist in toto, for the author argues that certain sociocultural questions must form the "outer crust" of one's analysis. In analyzing mental disorders, one must ask: Why is this concept salient at a particular time or in a particular culture? Why does this concept rather than another come into prominence, organizing thought and action? How is the deployment of this concept in classificatory judgments manipulated for purposes of power? According to Wakefield, only when one stands at the intersection of the essential and the constructed will culture's impact on cognition fully emerge.

In Chapter 14, sociologist Allan Horwitz "answers" Wakefield's proposition. The author builds on Wakefield's effort, forging new issues for the sociological study of mental disorders. Horwitz begins with a statement of support for Wakefield's universalistic definition of mental disorders. He argues that conceptualizing mental disorders as a harmful internal dysfunction provides both a solid basis for reevaluating and improving current diagnostic techniques, and a standard means for comparing mental disorders across differing cultural contexts. At the same time, Horwitz notes some specific ways in which culture must amend Wakefield's discussion. According to Horwitz, "culture has a critical role in structuring the symptoms through which internal dysfunctions become manifest. Unlike physical illnesses, where symptoms are usually indicators of underlying disorders, the symptoms of mental disorders are symbolic representations of underlying vulnerabilities that are structured to fit dominant cultural models of "appropriate" disorders in particular times and places. In this sense, the symptoms of mental disorders are part of "cultural tool kits" no less than language, fashion, and musical or culinary tastes" (Horwitz, p. 268).

Cultural sociologist Paul DiMaggio provides still a third proposal for the interdisciplinary study of thought, one that elegantly intertwines current ideas on culture, cognition, and action. In Chapter 15, DiMaggio focuses readers on several key issues within the cognitive science literature. These topics include debates surrounding the differences in deliberative and automatic cognition, discussions that distinguish "hot" and "cold" cognition, and research establishing domain independence. DiMaggio suggests specific ways in which these various lines of inquiry both support and extend sociological visions of culture—visions that depict culture as a malleable entity differentially applied across different social situations. Further, he suggests ways in which these lines of inquiry might directly feed new sociological theories of action. By exploring the convergence of cognitive science and cultural sociology, DiMaggio delineates a strong foundation for exciting intellectual collaboration.

Maximizing the Value of this Book

Culture in Mind presents the core concerns of a rapidly growing sociological area— the field of culture and cognition. The collection delivers the most recent works of several well-established culture and cognition scholars. It also presents the initial excursions of several prominent sociologists who are "newcomers" to this field of specialization. Taken together, the volume's fourteen original essays provide a critical resource for those drawn to this burgeoning area of inquiry.

In order to maximize the utility of *Culture in Mind*, I have added two important elements to the book's fourteen essays. First, I have prefaced each section of the book with a general discussion of relevant cognitive science literature. Knowing where cognitive scientists have been, intellectually speaking, helps us to appreciate better the new and exciting destinations forwarded by each of the volume's authors. Second, I have supplemented each section in the volume with suggestions for further study. In the "Mapping the Field" appendix, I provide readers with a pointed list of bibliographic materials that will guide readers as they explore each new topic presented in this book. These additions are designed to establish the parameters of the culture and cognition discipline. In this way, *Culture in Mind* provides a solid foundation for those planning to embark on the sociocultural study of thought.

Mapping the Field

As *Culture in Mind* unfolds, readers will quickly see the unique contributions that sociologists of culture bring to the study of thought. But many individuals may also find it useful to position the sociological perspective within the broader field of cognitive studies.

At present, cognitive science dominates the study of thought. As such, it is a literature with which any student of the mind will want to become familiar. Several sources can furnish readers with a detailed background of the cognitive science agenda. For example, Harold Gardner's *The Mind's New Science: A History of the Cognitive Revolution* (New York: Basic Books, 1987) provides a lively history of the field. Similarly, Karl H. Pribram reflects on the essence of cognitive science in his article "The Cognitive Revolution and Mind/Brain Issues" (*American Psychologist* 41:507–20, 1986). And for a good review of critical differences between cognitive science and its intellectual predecessor, behaviorism, consult Bernard J. Baars's *The Cognitive Revolution in Psychology* (New York: Guilford Press, 1986). Two additional works provide readers with a sense of the field's current controversies and future trajectories. Peter Baumgartner and Sabine Payr have edited a wonderfully engaging set of interviews entitled *Speaking Minds: Interviews with 20 Eminent Cognitive Scientists* (Princeton, NJ: Princeton University Press, 1996). Here, cognitive scientists provide candid commentary on some of the field's most central issues. Cognitive scientists' perspectives on the future can be found in *The Science of the Mind: 2001 and Beyond*, a collection of essays edited by Robert L. Solso and Dominick W. Massaro (New York: Oxford, 1995).

While cognitive scientists consider the internal workings of the brain, the sociologists contributing to this volume consider the ways in which extramental components shape processes of thought. It is important to note that social psychologists were among the first to encourage this extramental agenda. George Herbert Mead's *Mind, Self, and Society* (Chicago, IL: University of Chicago Press, 1934) provided the theoretical engine for much of this work. A number of now-classic experimental works also dramatically underscored social situation's impact on thought. Muzafer Sherif, for example, documented the influence of group norms on the perception of environmental stimuli ("An Experimental Approach to the Study of Attitudes" *Sociometry* 1:90–8, 1937). Philip Zimbardo's prison study demonstrated that situations, and the social roles embedded within them, can alter key elements of thought and behavior (*The Stanford Prison Experiment*, Stanford, CA: Philip G. Zimbardo, Inc., 1972). Also relevant is the work of Shelly Taylor and Susan Fiske, who studied the ways in which social settings influence the perceptual salience of various stimuli ("Point of View and Perceptions of Causality," *Journal of Personality and Social Psychology* 32:439–45, 1975). H. Markus and Robert B. Zajonc offer a good review of relevant works in this area; consult "The Cognitive Perspective in Social Psychology" (pp. 137–230 in G. Lindzey and E. Aronson, eds., *The Handbook of Social Psychology*, New York: Random House, 1985). Nobert Schwartz offers another important review of this literature in "Warmer and More Social: Recent Developments in Cognitive Social Psychology" (*Annual Review of Sociology* 24:239–64, 1998).

Sociologist Paul DiMaggio reflects on the recent convergence of cognitive science and cultural sociology. In his essay "Culture and Cognition: An Interdisciplinary Review," DiMaggio highlights the many important elements that sociologists can garner from the cognitive science literature (*Annual Review of Sociology* 23:263–87, 1997). This insightful work is a must-read for those pursuing the culture and cognition agenda.

Endnotes

1. See Plato's *The Republic* ([1951] 1973).
2. Plato was among the first to establish the brain as the locus of knowledge. His contemporary, Aristotle, believed that knowledge was localized in the heart. Aristotle's position may have originated with the Egyptians, as ancient hieroglyphics frequently linked thought to the heart.
3. When I use the term "cognitive science," I cast my definitional net broadly, encompassing the work of cognitive psychologists, developmental psychologists, neuroscientists, Chomskian linguists, and students of artificial intelligence.

4. Many would argue that the seventeenth-century rationalists provided the seeds for the cognitive revolution. In emphasizing reason over experience, the rationalists implied the existence of essential principles of thought. Descartes's, Spinoza's, and Leibniz's discussion of the "axiom," or Kant's discussion of the "a priori proposition" provide examples of these essential principles. By the twentieth century, some psychologists were equating essential principles of thought with the existence of innate mental structures. Indeed, decades before the cognitive revolution swept the academic world, both Edward Tolman and Sir Frederick Bartlett proposed two such structures: the "cognitive map" and the "schema." Tolman's (1932) work emerged from animal learning studies; he described cognitive maps as internal representations that allowed rats and other animals to amend performances in accord with new contexts. Bartlett (1932) introduced the concept of schema in conjunction with his work on memory. He defined the schema as an organizational frame that influenced the character and content of an individual's remembrances. By formalizing the search for innate mental structures, Tolman and Bartlett laid critical groundwork for the cognitive revolution.

5. Sociolinguist Deborah Tannen (1993, chap. 1) offers some interesting reflections regarding the various ways in which cognitive scientists apply and interchange these concepts.

6. The papers that constitute this volume were originally presented at a conference entitled "Toward a Sociology of Culture and Cognition," held at Rutgers University in November of 1999. The work of the conference continues in "The Culture and Cognition Network," an extension of the ASA's Culture Section. The network's Web site can be accessed at http://sociology. rutgers.edu/cultcog/. There one can find abstracts from papers presented at the 1999 conference, instructions for joining an online discussion group, a list of the network's upcoming activities, and bibliographic material in the culture and cognition area.

7. In the Introduction to Section III, I will explore these intricate ideas in greater detail.

References

Bartlett, F. C. 1932. *Remembering: A Study in Experimental and Social Psychology*. Cambridge, England: Cambridge University Press.

Plato. [1951] 1973. "The Republic," Pp. 236–386 in *Dialogues of Plato*, edited by J. D. Kaplan. New York: Pocket Books.

Tannen, D. 1993. "What's in a Frame?: Surface Evidence for Underlying Expectations." Pp. 14–56 in *Framing Discourse*, edited by D. Tannen. New York: Oxford University Press.

Tolman, E. C. 1932. *Purposive Behavior in Animals and Man*. New York: Appleton-Century.

SECTION I

Sensation and Attention

Sensation and Attention: An Introduction

Thinking begins when information enters the mind. Such information may enter through our eyes or ears; it may enter in the form of a scent or a touch; it may even present itself as an idea or a memory. Yet for thinking to ensue, the brain must detect "data"; it must take hold of the data and center it in conscious awareness. Cognitive scientists describe the detection of information as *sensation*, and they refer to the centering of that information as *attention*. Together, these processes initiate the act of thinking.

Cognitive scientists pose several key questions in studying sensation and attention. They ask: What are the sensory mechanics behind information detection—that is, how are the eyes, ears, and so on structured? Once detected by sensory organs, why do some objects or events take precedence over others in conscious awareness? And why does the brain seemingly ignore certain environmental stimuli? For cognitive scientists, answering these questions requires, in part, a detailed picture of brain activity. They believe that a true understanding of sensation and attention demands that one "take the brain apart," so to speak, and learn how it works. The neurocognitive branch of the discipline leads the way in this regard. Via technologies such as the CAT scan,[1] the PET scan,[2] and the MRI,[3] neurocognitionists actually observe the brain as it encounters and processes new stimuli or previously stored material. Such observations form the basis of several fascinating theories on sensation and attention.

Francis Crick (1994), for example, explains sensation and attention as a function of neuron activity. Neurons are specialized cells that transmit information through the nervous system.[4] Crick argues that each object or event we encounter, whether in the environment or in memory, activates a specific network of neurons. As the neurons of a network fire, information is carried throughout the nervous system. When a neural network's activity is especially concentrated, the network can direct or focus the brain on the specific stimulus that triggered the activity. According to Crick, every human being possesses thousands of neural networks. Further, he argues that these neural networks operate competitively—that is, the firing of one neuron network can suppress the firing of another. This competition, according to Crick, may help to explain why human beings focus their attentions on certain stimuli while seemingly ignoring or denying others. For Crick, the particular network that apprehends the stimuli may ultimately determine its fate. Specifically, his work suggests that stimuli apprehended by powerful or dominant neural networks take precedence in conscious awareness. When stimuli move through networks suppressed by the activity of others, those stimuli fail to garner the active attention of the brain.

Many believe that neuron activity offers only a partial explanation of sensation and attention. Experimental psychologists such as David Broadbent (1958) or Anne Triesman (1969) have long argued that neural transmissions operate in conjunction with selective filters in the brain—innate structures activated in response to an abundance of incoming stimuli. According to these theorists, selective filters quickly sort incoming stimuli. In so doing, they exclude irrelevant information from further mental analysis, and they preclude irrelevant information from being stored in long-term memory. At the same time, attention filters help to centralize relevant stimuli, allowing them to dominate conscious awareness and ultimately be processed, integrated, and stored in memory.

If the brain does indeed filter irrelevant from relevant material, one must then inquire as to what makes stimuli relevant. Robert Shepard (1995), a perceptual psychologist, links relevance to "mental universals"—psychological laws that underlie all forms of mental processing. For Shepard, mental universals are the cognitive counterpoints to laws of the physical world, laws such as Newton's "laws of motion" or Einstein's "theory of relativity." He argues that these laws are evolutionary in origin and develop via the brain's response to nonarbitrary features of the physical environment such as gravity, reflected light, temperature fluctuations, and so forth. Shepard contends that mental universals are deeply internalized, perhaps genetically engrained, within members of the human species. As such, they powerfully shape the brain's cognitive capacities. Mental universals make the brain more susceptible to certain cues than others and more attracted to certain stimuli than others. These laws of thinking determine those cues to which we attend as relevant versus those that we dismiss.

Relevance and subsequent attention have also been explained with reference to stimuli characteristics. Developmental psychologist Evgenii Sokolov (1963), for example, examined the attention patterns surrounding "unfamiliar" (novel or unusual) versus "familiar" (recognized via prior experience) stimuli. He argued that unfamiliar stimuli are more likely to be centered in conscious awareness. According to Sokolov, each stimulus encountered by the brain is subjected to a rapid matching process; it is quickly compared to those acquired during past experience. If the brain fails to match an incoming stimulus to previously acquired data, an "orienting reflex" ensues, thus focusing the brain on the new stimulus at hand. If, however, a match occurs (or if a new stimulus is repeated over and over again), the brain "habituates" to the stimulus.[5] It dismisses it and fails to center the stimulus in conscious awareness.[6]

Of course, the familiarity of a stimulus cannot be considered in isolation. Research shows that the "energy" of a stimulus may also play a role in assessments of relevance and subsequent attention. Wilson Tanner Jr. and John Swets (1954) studied this topic extensively, developing a set of ideas to which cognitive scientists refer as "signal detection theory."[7] Tanner and Swets uncovered an amazing similarity between radar signal detection equipment and the signal detection apparatus of the human brain. Via experimental work, they established that the brain is most likely to attend to strong signals from the environment. In contrast, it tends to ignore signals that are weak or unclear. But Tanner and Swets showed that certain criteria can mediate the impact of signal strength on attention. For example, the brain's attention to a signal can be influenced by the brain's state of readiness. If the brain has been primed or alerted to the potential for a particular signal (a signal of danger, attraction, and so on), signals of weak or moderate strength may be successfully apprehended. Similarly, if the "payoff" for accurate signal detection is high (for instance, a life is saved, or the observer garners financial reward), then too, signals of weak or moderate strength may be successfully apprehended.

In reviewing these excursions on sensation and attention, it is important to note the following. For cognitive scientists, activities such as signal detection and the focusing of attention constitute normal brain operations. In turn, the failure to execute these processes represents serious dysfunction. Cognitive scientists treat such failures as distinct neural malfunctions or disruptions. Thus they write of "blindsight" (an inability to detect certain stimuli), "attention deficit disorder" (an inability to concentrate attention), "amnesia" (an inability to access previously stored information), or "denial" (the repression of apprehended information), typically attributing such conditions to irregularities that reside within the individual—biological deficiencies, physiological injuries, or psychological traumas. In addressing such conditions, many prescribe specific treatments or adaptive strategies—coping mechanisms for those inflicted with the dysfunction.

To be sure, sensation and attention are inextricably tied to the internal workings of the brain. Yet considering these processes solely in terms of the brain's normal capacities and standard operating procedures fails to address the full scope of these cognitive experiences. For example, we know that normal brains can sometimes encounter strong sensory signals and yet fail to detect them; the brain can be primed to certain signals and yet fail to apprehend them. In the absence of neural abnormality, why do such "oversights" occur? And what explains the fact that such oversights are often systematically concentrated in certain social settings and cultural contexts? Similarly, we witness normal brains bracket the environment in ways that defy neurological expectation. The brain may focus attention on the seemingly obscure while it ignores the obvious; it may foreground the familiar while it backgrounds the novel. In the absence of cognitive dysfunction, why do such "errors" ensue? And why are such errors often systematically located in specific types of interactions and situations?

Answering these questions requires a broader consideration of sensation and attention. We must move beyond issues of brain capacity and explore the extraneural factors that govern the initial stages of thought. Toward that end, the authors included in this section of *Culture in Mind* suggest that sensation and attention may be as much socioculturally scripted as they are innately inscribed. In Chapter 2, for example, author Eviatar Zerubavel considers oversights and omissions—that which is deliberately excluded from conscious awareness. Zerubavel suggests that ignoring, denying, and overlooking are not always the mark of a dysfunctional brain. Rather, these processes can be guided by sociocultural norms of attention. To support this position, Zerubavel takes readers to a variety of contexts and settings. In each location, he highlights the ways in which norms both explicitly and implicitly block information from active attention. Zerubavel's observations establish a basis for a sociocultural theory of attention, for his work suggests that social and cultural standards of operation can encourage normally functioning individuals to ignore the perceptually obvious.

Author Diane Vaughan continues this probe of sensation, attention, and their sociocultural foundations. In Chapter 3, she directs readers to the contextual aspects of signal detection. Specifically, Vaughan analyzes danger signals as they emerge in three very different interaction sites. First, she explores signals that warn of the impending breakup of intimate relationships. Next, she examines signals warning of technological failure—in this case, the failure of the "O rings" during the launch of the *Challenger.* Finally, she studies signals that alert air traffic controllers to potential traffic collisions. While acknowledging the importance of factors such as signal strength or state of readiness (factors stressed in the cognitive science literature), Vaughan demonstrates that the successful detection of danger signals is also powerfully tied to the "structured predispositions" that characterize different sociocultural contexts. As Vaughan's study unfolds, we learn that each of the contexts she researched displayed institutionalized "ways of seeing"—systems of "cognitive and motivating structures" that enhanced actors' sensitivity to some stimuli while diminishing their sensitivity to others. Based on these findings, Vaughan argues that the signal detection involves factors beyond the brain or the signal itself. Detection is also contingent upon a context's ability to direct and delimit an actor's vision in systematically patterned ways.

Endnotes

1. CAT stands for "computerized axial tomography."
2. PET stands for "positron emission tomography."
3. MRI stands for "magnetic resonance imaging."
4. For more on neural networks, see Kandel et al. (1991).
5. While the basic ideas behind Sokolov's notions of "orienting reflex" and "habituation" are still embraced, his work has been challenged for locating this process in the cortex. Recent studies suggest that these processes may occur at the subcortical level. See, e.g., Graham et al. (1978).
6. Triesman (1964) notes one important exception to the "rules" of stimulus familiarity. Her work demonstrates that the brain actively attends to personally important stimuli (e.g., the uttering of one's name or the cry of one's child) despite the familiarity of such stimuli.
7. John Swets continued to develop this line of research. See, e.g., Swets (1996).

References

Broadbent, D. E. 1958. *Perception and Communication.* London and New York: Pergamon Press.
Crick, F. 1994. *The Astonishing Hypothesis: The Scientific Search for the Soul.* London: Simon and Schuster.

Graham, F. K., L. A. Leavitt, B. D. Strock, and J. W. Brown. 1978. "Precocious Cardiac Orienting in Human Anencephalic Infants." *Science* 199:322–24.

Kandel, E. R., J. H. Schwartz, and T. M. Jessell. 1991. *Principles of Neural Science.* New York: Elsevier.

Shepard, R. N. 1995. "Toward a Twenty-First Century Science of Mental Universals." Pp. 50–62 in *The Science of the Mind: 2001 and Beyond*, edited by R. L. Solso and D. W. Massaro. New York: Oxford University Press.

Sokolov, E. N. 1963. *Perception and the Conditioned Reflex.* New York: Macmillan.

Swets, J. A. 1996. *Signal Detection and ROC Analysis in Psychology and Diagnostics: Collected Papers.* Mahwah, NJ: Lawrence Erlbaum Associates, Inc.

Tanner, W. P. and J. A. Swets. 1954. "A Decision-Making Theory of Visual Detection." *Psychological Review* 61:401–09.

Triesman, A. 1964. "Monitoring and Storage of Irrelevant Messages in Selective Attention." *Journal of Verbal Learning and Verbal Behavior* 3:449–59.

———. 1969. "Strategies and Models of Selective Attention." *Psychological Review* 76:242–99.

CHAPTER 2

The Elephant in the Room

NOTES ON THE SOCIAL ORGANIZATION OF DENIAL

Eviatar Zerubavel

This chapter looks at a somewhat unusual aspect of cognition, namely that which does not enter our awareness. I am referring here to that which, at least potentially, could have entered awareness yet nevertheless does not. Furthermore, I am referring to that which is deliberately left out of our consciousness. In other words, I am talking about the active process of blocking certain information from entering our minds. In that respect, I follow Sigmund Freud's critical distinction between that which we simply forget and that which we actively repress from our awareness, thereby regarding ignoring as an active process of deliberately not noticing.

Let me add here that I do not intend to discuss the physiological level of perception. I will not address, for example, the natural constraints affecting what enters our visual field. That is something on which psychologists and biologists are much more qualified to comment. By the same token, I do not intend to address the physiology of other senses, such as hearing, taste, or smell, the disruption of which certainly blocks the flow of information into our minds. I also will ignore the individual dimension of perception and attention. I shall therefore refrain from addressing strictly psychological phenomena such as self-numbing or dissociation, which have to do with the way individuals manage to block certain information from entering their consciousness. Though absolutely fascinating, they are quite irrelevant to my distinctly sociological concern with cognition.

As I have demonstrated elsewhere,[1] cognitive sociology addresses cognitive matters at a level that both cognitive individualism and universalism leave untouched between them. I am therefore particularly interested in the *social* organization of attention, a topic I first addressed in a 1993 article I wrote on horizons,[2] further developed in a chapter of *Social Mindscapes* titled "The Social Gates of Consciousness,"[3] and am now expanding into a book. At the heart of this book lies a phenomenon I call "the elephant in the room." I regard it as the sociological equivalent of what psychologists call "denial."

What makes the metaphor of "the elephant in the room" so evocative is the choice of such a large animal. Unlike a grasshopper on a twig, which we are unable to notice because it is so well camouflaged that its outlines practically blend with the surrounding background, the elephant has a commanding visual presence that is objectively unavoidable. Thus if we manage not to notice it, it can only be as a result of a deliberate act of ignoring, since naturally it would be practically impossible not to notice it! Not noticing an elephant, in other words, involves blindness to the obvious.

Notice the visual aspect of ignoring in this case. What is so striking about the elephant is not its smell (as it would have been had I used the metaphor of a skunk), but its visual presence. Not noticing the elephant in the room is thus the equivalent of being blind (which might explain the particular choice of punishment that Oedipus inflicted upon himself). Note, in this regard, the abundance of unmistakably visual metaphors related to denial: having a "tunnel vision," wearing "blinders," turning a "blind eye" to the obvious, or "looking the other way." Consider also statements such as "this time I'll overlook what you just did," or the way we seem so much more easily to ignore that which is not in the "spotlight," not to mention the "blind spots" we all seem to have in certain areas!

Yet as we come to focus on the proverbial monkey who "sees no evil," let us not forget his colleagues who hear and speak no evil. The conditions of being deaf or mute certainly complement the picture we begin to get when addressing the phenomenon of mental "blindness." And I definitely see the sociology of ignoring as complementing the sociology of silence as well as the sociology of secrecy, first introduced by Georg Simmel ninety years ago.[4] Secrets, as we very well know, certainly help solidify structures of denial and ignorance.

As someone who grew up in a household where every single room housed several such elephants, I think that I have developed a particular sociological sensitivity to instances where the obviously present nonetheless remains publicly unacknowledged or even actively denied. Yet I also believe that I am pointing here to a critical generic social phenomenon which sociologists in general cannot afford to ignore. Can you imagine, for example, formal, official, social life without the mental process of relegating the "informal" and "unofficial" to the domain identified by Erving Goffman as the "out of frame"?[5] By the same token, can you envision everyday social interaction without the element of tact, which presupposes a display of what he called "civil inattention,"[6]—that is, assigning certain aspects of the situation an "unfocused" status so as to allow the interaction to flow more "smoothly"?[7]

Blocking certain information from entering our awareness (not to mention from allowing it to circulate among different individuals' awarenesses) is often done quite blatantly. Christopher Columbus, for example, actually threatened to cut out the tongue of any participant in his second voyage to the Caribbean who would not testify back home that Cuba was indeed part of the mainland![8] Similarly, God banished Adam and Eve from the Garden of Eden for tasting from the Tree of Knowledge.

Consider also, in this regard, judges' explicit instructions to court stenographers actually to strike certain statements from the official record, or the invention of the eraser, identified by my 14-year-old son last year as "the most deadly weapon of denial."

Yet blocking certain information from entering our awareness is also done in a more subtle manner. Consider the way in which Captain Jeffrey Purdie (the watch commander of the Secret Service uniformed division), referring to an incident when President Clinton's mistress angrily stormed out of the White House, instructed one of his subordinates: "As far as you're concerned, this never happened" (*New York Times*, September 12, 1998, p. B7). And note the striking contrast between this explicit denial of what he had experienced only a few hours earlier and what actually precipitated that statement, namely the way in which the president himself had told him earlier, "I hope you use your discretion" (*New York Times*, September 12, 1998, p. B7), which is only an implicit invitation to forget. I am sure that at least some readers have been in situations where they were practically told by a superior, referring to what they were actually in the middle of doing, "This conversation never happened."

From a sociological perspective, of course, it is even more striking when even such "subtle" statements need not be uttered at all because it is implicitly quite clear to all participants that they are not "supposed" to know what they clearly do know! This is the basis of the fascinating social phenomenon commonly known as a "conspiracy of silence." The difference between explicit "hushes" and such subtle conspiracies of silence is analogous to the difference between a direct order actually to remove a particular passage from the next edition of an official history textbook and the implicit manner in which traditional historiography, until quite recently, has ignored the role of women in human history. It is the difference between deliberate, active repression and more passive negotiation of "blind spots."

As demonstrated by Freud in his writings on denial, as well as by Simmel in his discussion of the blasé attitude often displayed by dwellers in large cities,[9] blocking certain information from entering our awareness seems to serve some obvious psychological functions. Yet the common saying that "ignorance is bliss" has a rather significant social dimension as well. After all, in an effort to avoid internal turbulence, many social systems are quite willing to ignore any "inconvenient" information that might possibly generate such turbulence. That is why women who are well aware of the horrendous fact that their own daughters are being sexually molested by their husbands or boyfriends, for example, nonetheless often choose to overlook such disquieting information and, in a manner somewhat evocative of the proverbial ostrich, try to pretend that such abuse is not really taking place, thereby inevitably "enabling" its persistence. The very same phenomenon is also evident, of course, when, in the name of the survival of the organization as a whole, fellow workers often choose to ignore obvious injustices inflicted upon one of their members, particularly when he or she is structurally located at the bottom of the organizational totem pole.

Needless to say, such "conspiracies of silence" obviously have some very significant moral undertones, particularly when the act of ignoring inevitably allows—or even encourages—the perpetuation of some clear abuse of power. Hence the distinctive moral role of those stubborn disturbers of silence we call "whistle-blowers," whether at the level of the family (such as neighbors in the case of child abuse), the organization (such as workers who take the courageous step of filing a grievance against an abusive boss), or even the nation as a whole (such as Emile Zola or Anita Hill).

In order to appreciate fully the social aspect of the way in which our attention is organized, we need to focus on the normative dimension of such organization. As I have argued elsewhere, there are some unmistakably social *rules* of focusing our attention.[10] A classic example is what Goffman called "rules of irrelevance,"[11] one of the most obvious manifestations of which is the way in which we "downplay" various aspects of situations in order to conduct what we consider "fair" competition. As Kristen Purcell has demonstrated in her work on the sociomental organization of such competition,[12] entire aspects of competitive situations are often treated as socially irrelevant and, as such, officially bracketed and thereby systematically ignored. Statutes of limitations, of course, have the same effect by curbing our historical attention, so that certain "prehistorical" elements are bracketed out of our official awareness.[13] Note also the social rules of establishing agendas of meetings, which include formal articulations of what is "on the table" and what is not, as manifested in the distinction between that which does or does not enter the official minutes of meetings.

Consider also various rules of etiquette, many of which involve tact-related ethical obligations to "look the other way" and ignore things we otherwise most likely would have noticed about others around us. As if to underscore the way in which ignoring complements secrecy, normative prohibitions against not being "discreet" are often complemented by similar prohibitions against being too "nosy." Hence the rules of "civil inattention," whereby we learn to be like those monkeys who see and hear no "evil." And when we do see or hear it, we are expected to pretend we didn't, so as to save the face of others with whom we interact, as evident within families of stutterers, alcoholics, or the terminally ill. This, mind you, involves not just individual "niceness" but actual social, normative pressure to be "tactful."

As Hans Christian Andersen reminds us in his delightful sociological parable "The Emperor's New Clothes," the only one who did see the emperor's naked body was the young boy who had still not learned how not to notice embarrassing things about others! In other words, not noticing involves learning, as it is obviously part of a process I call "optical socialization,"[14] as when we teach children how not to look too attentively at people who have physical deformities. By the same token, one needs to learn what to ignore officially when taking the minutes at a faculty meeting.

Such optical socialization is often done explicitly. In sharp contrast to professions that train their members to try to notice "everything" to the point of being deliberately "nosy" (police detectives, journalists, psychotherapists, insurance claim investigators), there are others that try systematically to regulate what enters their members' awareness. Note, for instance, the way lawyers are specifically trained to focus just on that which is legally "relevant" to their case, or the way scientists are taught to control in their research designs the variables they plan to examine in their experiments. In the same way that Betty Edwards has been training artists how not to focus on objects so as to be able to notice the spaces between them,[15] Wayne Brekhus is now trying to train sociologists how not to focus on politically sensitive topics so as to be able to research the socially mundane.[16] As Ludwig Fleck noted with regard to microbiologists looking through a microscope, one needs to learn how to focus in order to notice anything.[17] Yet as Ruth Simpson is showing in her current study of the transition from miasmatic to bacteriological theories of disease, medical practitioners also had to learn how to ignore the communal dimension of epidemics in order to be able to "see" how diseases spread through germs.[18] In order to notice things, one needs to also learn first what not to notice! As the judge instructs the jury in Billy Wilder's *Witness for the Prosecution*: "You must shun out from your minds everything except what will take place in this court." In other words, only by becoming partly blind can we come to see anything in a "focused" manner.

Yet part of such "optical socialization" is also done implicitly. By merely noticing on what the camera focuses, young television watchers also learn what society normally ignores! The media, of course, are not the only agents of such tacit process of delineating our horizons. By hearing our parents sum up in two minutes how we spent an entire day together, we also learn from a very young age that which merits social attention and that which can actually be ignored.

As I have shown elsewhere, this also applies to our concern.[19] The striking manner in which our social environment leads different individuals to place the limits of their concern at the same place, which is often quite different from where members of other social environments place them (contrast, for example, meat-eaters' and vegans' respective spheres of moral concern) suggests a certain social "calibration" of concern. And the differences are not just between cultures or subcultures but also between different historical periods within each of those. My blindness as a child in the fifties toward the very existence of Arab-Israelis living only a few miles away from me is certainly not as widely shared by children growing up in my hometown Tel Aviv today.

And what is true of concern also applies to curiosity.[20] Consider, for example, the social organization of reading. The social curbing of our curiosity is quite evident in any reading list for doctoral comprehensive exams, as well as in the inevitably parochial academic pattern of citing only sources lying within the essentially conventional confines of supposedly discrete bodies of "literature."

Such references to curiosity and concern clearly underscore the implicit tension between the sociological and psychological perspectives on the mental processes of attending and ignoring. Yet I believe that we should acknowledge the inherent differences between those two perspectives and not treat those processes as lying exclusively within the psychologist's domain, as they traditionally have been until now. The fact that someone represses the memory of a particular traumatic experience because it is too painful to remember certainly belongs within the domain of the psychology of denial. Yet when a superior tells a subordinate "this conversation didn't happen," it clearly calls for a *sociology* of denial. Similarly, when Kathryn Harrison describes in her book *The Kiss* the way she tried to numb her awareness of the sexual relations she was having with her father by making various attempts at a "selective self-anesthesia" that "leaves me awake to certain things and dead to others,"[21] she is referring to mechanisms of denial that are clearly *intra*psychic. Yet when she describes how her boyfriend, himself threatened by such forbidden relations, colludes with her in such process of joint forgetting,[22] we are dealing not just with denial but also with "codenial," which is an *inter*psychic process, thereby acknowledging the social dimension of ignoring.

Only when both psychologists and sociologists turn their attention to the mental processes of attending and ignoring can we have a truly comprehensive understanding of those processes. That, of course, is one of the principal intellectual missions of cognitive sociology.

Endnotes

1. Zerubavel (1997).
2. Zerubavel (1993).
3. Zerubavel (1997:35–52).
4. Simmel ([1908] 1950).
5. Goffman (1974:201–46).
6. Goffman (1963:83–88).
7. Goffman (1959:229–37).
8. Zerubavel (1992:90).
9. Simmel ([1903] 1950).
10. Zerubavel (1997:13–22, 50–51).
11. Goffman (1961:19–26).
12. Purcell (1996).
13. Zerubavel (1997:84–85).
14. Ibid., 32–33, 46–51.
15. Edwards (1979:98–113; 1986:155–65).
16. Brekhus (1998).
17. Fleck ([1935] 1981:90–93).
18. Simpson (1999).
19. Zerubavel (1997:39–40, 43, 45).
20. Ibid., 42–43, 52.
21. Harrison (1997:137).
22. Ibid., 74. See also 86, 176.

References

Brekhus, W. 1998. "A Sociology of the Unmarked: Redirecting Our Focus." *Sociological Theory* 16:34–51.

Edwards, B. 1979. *Drawing on the Right Side of the Brain: A Course in Enhancing Creativity and Artistic Confidence*. Los Angeles, CA: J. P. Tarcher.

———. 1986. *Drawing on the Artist Within: A Guide to Innovation, Invention, Imagination, and Creativity*. New York: Simon and Schuster.

Fleck, L. [1935] 1981. *Genesis and Development of a Scientific Fact*. Chicago, IL: University of Chicago Press.

Goffman, E. 1959. *The Presentation of Self in Everyday Life*. Garden City, NY: Doubleday Anchor.

———. 1961. "Fun in Games." Pp. 17–81 in *Encounters: Two Studies in the Sociology of Interaction*. Indianapolis, IN: Bobbs-Merrill.

———. 1963. *Behavior in Public Places: Notes on the Social Organization of Gatherings*. New York: Free Press.

———. 1974. *Frame Analysis: An Essay on the Organization of Experience*. New York: Harper Colophon.

Harrison, K. 1997. *The Kiss*. New York: Avon.

Purcell, K. 1996. "In a League of Their Own: Mental Leveling and the Creation of Social Comparability in Sport." *Sociological Forum* 11:435–56.

Simmel, G. [1903] 1950. "The Metropolis and Mental Life." Pp. 409–24 in *The Sociology of Georg Simmel*, edited by Kurt H. Wolff. New York: Free Press.

———. [1908] 1950. "The Secret and the Secret Society." Pp. 307–76 in *The Sociology of Georg Simmel*, edited by Kurt H. Wolff. New York: Free Press.

Simpson, R. 1999. "Microscopic Worlds, Miasmatic Theories, and Myopic Vision: Changing Conceptions of Air and Social Space." Presented at the Annual Meeting of the American Sociological Association, Chicago, IL.

Zerubavel, E. 1992. *Terra Cognita: The Mental Discovery of America*. New Brunswick, NJ: Rutgers University Press.

———. 1993. "Horizons: On the Sociomental Foundations of Relevance." *Social Research* 60:397–413.

———. 1997. *Social Mindscapes: An Invitation to Cognitive Sociology*. Cambridge, MA: Harvard University Press.

CHAPTER 3

Signals and Interpretive Work

THE ROLE OF CULTURE IN A THEORY OF PRACTICAL ACTION

Diane Vaughan

In their introduction to *The New Institutionalism in Organizational Analysis* (1991), Paul DiMaggio and Walter Powell consider the possibility of a microsociological supplement to the macrosociological focus on structure, order, and persistence that has so far dominated research and theory in the new institutionalism. Searching for some answers, they analyze transformations in sociological theory since Parsons' theory of action, transformations that offer alternatives to the Parsonian emphasis on norms and roles. DiMaggio and Powell suggest that elements necessary to a "theory of practical action" compatible with the new institutionalism can be found in the more recent cultural turn in contemporary social theory. This cultural turn: (1) "emphasizes the cognitive dimension of action to a far greater extent than did Parsons'"; and (2) "departs from Parsons' preoccupation with the rational, calculative aspect of cognition to focus on pre-conscious processes and schema as they enter into routine, taken-for-granted behavior (practical activity)" (1991:22). DiMaggio and Powell conclude that ethnomethodology (Garfinkel 1967) and phenomenology (Berger and Luckmann 1966), in combination, offer an alternative, but one that leaves important questions unanswered. Specifically, how do the microprocesses of these theories produce social order? What is the role of interests and intentionality?[1]

DiMaggio and Powell then consider three theorists whose work deals with the problem of social order in a way that gives some insight into microlevel sources of macrolevel stability: Giddens on structuration, Goffman on ritual order, and Collins on interaction ritual chains. Noting that, in common, these theorists make gains by maintaining the importance of cognition and revealing more of the noncalculative, routine elements of practical reason, DiMaggio and Powell still find gaps. Chief among them is the failure to complete the macro-micro link: What, specifically, is the analytic equivalent of Parsons's notion of the role system as a connector between individual behavior and social structure? They suggest that Bourdieu's (1977) theory of the *habitus*, with its attention to the taken-for-granted aspects of social action and practical consciousness, may be the most viable candidate.

Although many theorists have explored the connection between structure and agency, strikingly absent is empirical work that specifically attempts to test the various possibilities about macro-micro connections that these theorists have presented. This paper is an empirical exploration into the microsociology of a theory of practical action, with particular attention to the relationship between culture and cognition. Thus this inquiry follows Zucker (1977), who argued that: "Without a solid cognitive, microlevel foundation, we risk treating institutionalization as a black box at the organizational level, focusing on content at the exclusion of developing a systematic explanatory theory of process . . . neglecting institutional variation and persistence." In order to pursue this question, the new institutionalists' traditional focus on organization fields must be supplemented by empirical work that exposes processes. In this paper, I examine three case studies of signal detection and decision making in naturalistic settings: couples in deteriorating intimate relationships (Vaughan 1986), managers and engineers at NASA making assessments of technical components of the space shuttle (Vaughan 1996), and air traffic controllers reading information on radar screens (Vaughan, unpublished data).

These cases are analyzed as situated action. A situated-action approach is built on the sociological understanding that a full theoretical explanation of the action of any social actor needs to take into account, to the greatest extent possible, the fact that individual activity, choices, and action occur within a multilayered social context that affects interpretation and meaning at the local level (Vaughan 1998b; cf. Suchman 1987). Using a situated-action approach for a comparative case analysis of decision making in naturalistic settings is a particularly advantageous methodology for considering macro-micro connections. Whenever the research focus is kept on situated interpretation and the dynamics of interaction, the microlevel focus and point of entry will allow us to observe the situational logic and contingency that marks a situation while at the same time broadening our vision to encompass macro and mesolevel factors, enabling us to examine the linkage between environment, organizations, and individual action and meaning. Methodologically, this situated-action approach is consistent with the theoretical perspectives of Jepperson (1991), who emphasizes the connection between constructedness at the microlevel and higher-order effects (but does not explicitly consider the mesolevel), and Friedland and Alford (1991), who do include the mesolevel by emphasizing the interconnection between individual, organization, and society.

In the next section of this paper, I briefly introduce the method of analogical theorizing in order to explain the logic on which the case comparisons are based. Next, I establish the comparability of the three cases by summarizing the substantive findings about decision making, signal detection, and interpretive work for each case analysis. Then I examine how the social context affected the interpretive work and decision making that went on in the three cases, analyzing the data by its appropriateness to the categories of environment, organization, and individual cognition/choice in order to attend to the macro, meso, and microlayers of situated action. Finally, I reflect on the theoretical significance of this analogical comparison for understanding the relationship between culture and cognition in general and what it suggests about a microsociological theory of practical action in particular.

Methodology: Analogy, Cases, and Comparative Social Organization

The logic of comparing intimate relationships, a flawed space shuttle launch decision, and air traffic controllers doing routine work may not be immediately apparent. What follows is the briefest possible exegesis. Extended explanations are in Vaughan (1992) and Vaughan (2001, in preparation); for recent examples in addition to those mentioned in this paper, see Vaughan (1998a; 1999).

Analogical theorizing is a heuristic, theory-generating, comparative method using qualitative data (e.g., comparative historical, ethnography, interviews). It relies on selecting cases on the basis of some event, activity, or phenomenon of theoretical or substantive interest, and then comparing it with another example or examples that appear, hypothetically, to share that feature. However, in contrast to the more conventional approach of comparing similar units of analysis (all families, all social movements, all nation-states), analogical comparison is made between socially organized settings that vary in size, complexity, and function. The point is then to proceed with comparison in a discovery-oriented yet systematic way that identifies both the similarities and differences between cases, which then (depending upon the findings) may aid in the development of general theory across cases. The method draws from Blumer on sensitizing concepts (1969) and from Glaser and Strauss on grounded theorizing and comparison (1967), but it is explicitly different in its requirement of comparing different units of analysis. The precedent for selecting cases based on analogous circumstances occurring in different social settings finds legitimacy in Georg Simmel's formal sociology and his argument that the distinctive task of the sociologist is to discover essential social forms—commonalities of structure and processes that exist despite the appearance of difference in events, activities, and phenomena (1950). His best-known illustration, used to demonstrate the search for form across social settings, is that sociologists ought to be able to study both marital conflict and martial conflict and find characteristics in common.

He did not leave a road map for how to proceed, but implicit in what he said is the legitimacy of comparing similar events, activities, or phenomena despite variation in the unit of analysis. Neither did he provide a methodological rationale for proceeding in this way. I suggest that the methodological rationale for doing so rests in analogy of another sort: Socially organized settings, despite differences in size, complexity, and function, do have generic structures and processes in common that make them comparable in fundamental ways—division of labor, socialization, culture, hierarchy, conflict, power, environments, network ties, and so forth (Vaughan 1992:179–80). Thus when we select cases on the basis of some dependent variable (X), qualitative data tend to offer a window into the relation between some of these generic structures and processes and X, allowing comparison across cases on those conditions. The primary goal must be to explain the substantive problem first. This strategy produces a rich, complex analysis in each instance that brings the details of each case to the fore. Thus the differences between the cases (the substantive detail, analysis, and theoretical explanations) become salient to the researcher, controlling for possible bias in comparison (1992:195–99). What is to be gained? In my experience of developing theory with this method since 1980, I have found that comparing different units of analysis enhances the potential for theory generation in two ways: (1) shifting units of analysis yields different kinds of data, making it possible to study new aspects of some phenomenon; and (2) sometimes when we shift units of analysis, we simultaneously shift levels of analysis, allowing insights into the microelements of a macrolevel explanation, or vice versa (1992:182–84). The comparisons in this paper fulfill both of these promises; thus we are able to reflect upon the connection between culture and cognition and the possibility of *habitus* as a microsociological complement of the new institutionalism.

How these cases were selected needs explanation. Initially I had no plan for a coordinated project entailing a three-case comparison on signals and interpretive work, the title of this paper. My work on intimate relationships and the *Challenger* case each began as an investigation of a unique substantive question. The only connection I saw between them was that, conceptually, I was treating both the dyad and NASA as organizations. Using analytic induction and other strategies that force the analysis toward differences (Vaughan 1992:195–99), the fact that signals, interpretive work, and mistake were part of the explanation of both projects became apparent to me only midway through the second project. Despite their many differences, both cases, I realized, were studies of decision making in which mistakes were made in the interpretation of information, with signals and interpretive work essential to the explanation. Spence's (1974) theory of market signaling, which was central to the explanation of uncoupling, also became critical for understanding what happened at NASA and so serendipitously became part of the analogical theorizing project (Vaughan 1998a). Whereas the first two cases in this comparison were chosen by virtue of serendipitous discovery, in fall of 1998 I initiated the air traffic control study with the express purpose of making a comparison with the other two. This third case was selected on the basis of *difference* in order to explore the "flip side" of what I had found about signals, interpretive work, and mistake.

Both previous cases showed that the crisis was preceded by a long incubation period filled with early warning signs, clear in retrospect, that were ignored or misinterpreted at the time decisions were made. Because signals of potential danger were misinterpreted in both preceding studies, mistakes were made. I wanted a project that allowed me: (1) to examine the relationship between social context and cognition in a circumstance in which early warning signs are detected; and (2) to be present in the decision-making context *as decisions were being made*, rather than analyzing cognitive processes retrospectively, as was the case with both previous projects. Air traffic control is ideal because, first, air traffic controllers seldom make mistakes; they have the ability to recognize anomalies early, responding to correct errors and thereby avoid collisions. Second, the problems of retrospective analysis are eliminated; interviews and observations of air traffic controllers on the job are possible.

Advantages accrue from both the analogies and the differences between the cases being compared. In each case, the substantive focus is on how social actors interpret and respond to signals of potential danger; the analytic focus is on decision making and choice within social context. Substantively, the three cases have in common: (1) decisions that are being made about objects and issues that are high on uncertainty and therefore, interpretive flexibility (Pinch and Bijker 1984)—the quality of an intimate relationship, the performance of an unprecedented large-scale technology for which the sky is the laboratory, and the position of aircraft in space without direct observation or evidence; (2) the decision process involves some risk of harmful consequences if mistakes are made; and (3) the decision-makers are involved in the social construction of meaning. The analytic focus on signals that warn of risk, mistake, and the possibility of harmful outcomes is a particular advantage given our stated interest in the taken-for-granted and prerational aspects of choice, because mistake, when recognized and defined as one, causes taken-for-granted assumptions to surface in the minds of people who hold them, calls them into question, and allows people to articulate what otherwise remains unquestioned and thus invisible.

Case differences are also helpful. In analogical comparison, the differences in the cases throw similarities and differences in structure and process into broad relief. Here, the variation in substantive content evidenced in the three cases—that is, the distinctive categories, beliefs, and motives created by specific institutional logics—allows us to examine the link between institutions and their relationship to organizations and individuals (Friedland and Alford 1991:251). The organizational settings vary in size, complexity, formalization, and function. The strategy of varying the units of analysis has benefits because the data from each case provide new insights not available in the others. Moreover, the variation in the organizational forms being studied (a social group and two complex organizations) varies the degree of institutionalization. Thus we are able to consider the relationship between microprocesses, change, and the production of social order—key issues in institutional theory.

A final methodological note on situated action: For the NASA research and the air traffic control project, all three layers of situated action were part of the original explanations, because the projects were designed specifically to investigate the links between macro, meso, and microlevels of analysis. However, my 1986 research on uncoupling was social-psychological in orientation. This paper is based on a rereading and reanalysis, done in order to pay new attention to data that reflect on the macrolevel contingencies of choice and action, thus allowing a comparison between the three cases on the three levels of analysis. A reconsideration of that (1986) work is particularly suitable for a discussion of a microsociological component of institutional analysis, because the original theoretical framing of the problem was Berger and Kellner's (1964) "Marriage and the Construction of Reality." Preceding Berger and Luckmann (1966), who argued that shared cognitive systems come to be viewed as objective and external structures defining social reality, Berger and Kellner showed how in marriage the more institutionalized the cognitive categories and belief systems, the more the actions of partners are defined by a widening sphere of taken-for-granted routines. *Uncoupling* analyzed the reverse of this process, showing lower-level processes that counter higher-order institutional effects.

It is first necessary to establish that the three cases are comparable at the microlevel on the substantive topic of signals and interpretive work in order to proceed with the more detailed analysis of similarities and differences, as they pertain to the theoretical issues that are the topic of this paper. Differences at the meso and macrolevels will become clear as the comparison proceeds.

Signals and Interpretive Work: Three Cases

UNCOUPLING

The research problem was to understand the process that occurs when intimate relationships break up. The data were interviews with married and cohabiting couples, both gay and straight. I collected oral histories of their experience of their relationship.[2] I began with the question; "Tell me about your relationship from the moment you first realized something was seriously wrong." They began a chronological autobiographical account. The main finding was that uncoupling happens in a patterned way. It is not a sudden chaotic break, as people tend to experience it, but a social process, a gradual transition with an identifiable pattern that has as its core a process of redefinition of self, other, and relationship. That pattern has one person, whom I called the "initiator," beginning to leave the relationship socially and social psychologically before the other. By the time the partner being left behind realizes something is seriously wrong, the initiator has been in transition for some time, making the relationship difficult to retrieve. Typically, partners being left behind experience grief and shock, saying "I didn't even know anything was seriously wrong," while initiators say they had been "yelling and screaming about the quality of the relationship for years." Soon, however, the partner redefines the relationship as seriously troubled and begins going through the same social transition that the initiator began long before. Both people make the same transition, but it starts and ends at different times for each. The question remaining to be answered was this: In an intimate relationship, the smallest organization we create, how is it possible for one person to get so far away without the other person noticing and acting to forestall the transition? Returning to my interview transcripts, I found that the answer lay in information and how it was interpreted: how the unhappy initiator signaled his or her discontent to the partner, and how the partner interpreted those signals.

In early stages of the transition, for complicated reasons, the initiator does not send clear, strong signals of discontent. As the initiator's discontent grows and she or he sends more frequent and stronger signals, the initiator still refrains from giving direct signals, instead (again for very complicated reasons) relying on indirect methods. Nonetheless, the landscape of the relationship is littered with warning signs. However, the partner does not define the relationship as a serious problem because the salience of these signals is reduced by the social context and the patterns of information. Rather than strong signals that the relationship is in serious trouble (the initiator's point), the partner confronts signals that are mixed (an argument, a signal that the relationship might be in trouble, is followed by a blissful making-up, a signal that all is well); signals that are weak (the initiator starts working late; the initiator says "I'm unhappy in this relationship" but doesn't say "I'm unhappy—and I'm seeing someone else"); and signals that become routine (sleeping in separate beds; arguing). Only when the initiator is socially and psychologically ready to go does that person send a clear, strong signal (a direct confrontation; leaving) that the partner cannot miss or reinterpret in a way that reduces its salience. Then, alone, the partner is able to look back and see clearly the meaning of the warning signs that were there all along.

THE CHALLENGER LAUNCH DECISION

The research problem was to understand why NASA managers had launched the *Challenger* in January 1986 despite a recommendation by contractor engineers that the mission be delayed because of unprecedented cold temperature predicted for launch time. My data were original documents stored at the National Archives, Washington, DC; interviews; the published volumes of two official investigations; and other materials.[3] The analysis showed a decision-making pattern that was fundamentally like the pattern that occurs in the demise of intimate relationships. The demise of the *Challenger* was preceded by a long incubation period filled with warning signs that something was seriously wrong with the technology. In the eight years prior to that flawed launch decision, NASA and the contractor made repeated decisions to launch space shuttles despite frequent in-flight anomalies on the solid rocket boosters—the very component responsible for the *Challenger* accident. In this project I also treated information as signals, but here I identified them as "signals of potential danger." One key research question was to determine how it was that, despite repeated signals of potential danger in the years preceding the *Challenger* accident, the managers and engineers of NASA and contractor organizations who did the hands-on engineering work continued to make official launch recommendations to their superiors based on engineering analyses indicating that the technical component was (in NASA language) an "acceptable risk" for flight.

Analogical with the pattern in uncoupling, as incidents occurred, the managers and engineers did not define the technical design as a serious problem because the social context and patterns of information affected interpretive work: As decisions were being made, signals of potential danger appeared mixed, weak, and routine. Mixed signals were information indicating something was wrong followed by information indicating all was well. For example, the first incident of a technical anomaly on the solid rocket boosters (a signal of potential danger) was examined, the cause identified, and the problem corrected. Then for five subsequent flights, there were no anomalies on the boosters (signals that all was well). A weak signal was one that at the time had no apparent clear and direct connection to risk and potential danger, or one that occurred once but the conditions that created it were viewed as rare and unlikely to occur again. Routine signals were anomalies that occurred repeatedly, but were expected and predicted as a consequence of a new safety procedure, and that engineering analysis supported as tolerable. Analogically, like the person left behind in an intimate relationship, only after the disaster were the managers and engineers able to look back and see clearly the meaning of the signals of potential danger that were there all along.

DEAD RECKONING: TECHNOLOGY, CULTURE, AND COGNITION IN AIR TRAFFIC CONTROL

The advantage of a long incubation period is that it increases the possibility that intervention might occur early, staving off a harmful outcome. The air traffic control research is multifaceted in the questions being asked; for this paper, however, I address only the question of how signals of potential danger are recognized and small mistakes corrected before they turn into big mistakes with harmful outcomes. The study is a comparison of three air traffic control facilities that vary in size, architecture, amount and kind of technology, type of aircraft, traffic patterns, and traffic responsibilities. Still in progress, it combines ethnography and interviews in three settings: a small tower that handles takeoff and landing with primarily Visual Flight Rule traffic, a large tower and approach that handles national and international traffic, and a large radar facility that directs traffic at high altitudes. The findings I report here are from the radar facility only. My data include observations of controllers and supervisors making decisions about aircraft while on position at the radar screen; the data also include exchanges between pilots and controllers that I listened to while wearing a headset with controllers on the job. Finally, the data provide informal conversations with controllers and supervisors on break and interviews with facility directors and Traffic Management Unit personnel.

Explaining Decision Making and Cognition within Social Context

Having established the logic of this comparison based on the centrality of signals and interpretive work in the three cases, we now turn to the explanations of decision making in each setting. Why were signals of potential danger misinterpreted and mistakes made that resulted in harmful outcomes in the first two cases, and why not in the third? What aspects of situated action explain the process of signal detection in each of the three settings? To organize the data and the discussion within a situated-action framework, thus forcing attention to three levels of analysis, I artificially divide social context into individual, organizational, and environmental levels of analysis. Although creating these boundaries breaks up and contradicts the reality of everyday lived experience, it helps to set the stage for our later discussion on the relation between culture and cognition and the potential for a microsociological theory of practical action.

UNCOUPLING

Individual Cognition and Choice

The analysis showed that the long incubation period preceding a breakup is linked to the quality and quantity of the signals that the initiator gives the partner. However, we are primarily interested in explaining the partner's contribution: how that person interprets the warning signs that something is wrong. Typically, despite the initiator's display of discontent, the partner still finds that the relationship, warts and all, affirms identity and definition of self. Consequently, the partner interprets the array of information from the initiator within a frame of reference, or "worldview," that all is well in the relationship. The partner's worldview is developed from practical activity: It is comprised of taken-for-granted assumptions about the relationship that result from the partner's history and experience in the social world. These taken-for-granted assumptions constitute the frame of reference against which the partner decides what is normative and what is anomalous in the relationship.

The breakup itself is a strong signal that contradicts the partner's worldview, challenging many of the taken-for-granted assumptions that comprise it. The realization of mistake (the partner recognizes, in retrospect, the warning signs that had been there all along) has cognitive consequences. The crisis makes the partner *aware* of his or her assumptions, forcing the partner to confront them. Therefore, partners are able to articulate and thus make visible to others the cognitive components of worldview that usually guide the construction of meaning and choice invisibly. Interview data indicate that the sources of the partner's worldview are layered and that they arise from history and experience linked to that person's social location in: (1) the organization (i.e., the relationship), and (2) the environment. Initiators are exposed to these same influences, yet interviews with initiators show that in order to make the break, they shift to a different frame of reference/worldview from that of the partner. This aspect of the initiator's transition bears importantly upon the question of institutional persistence and change, and will be addressed in the concluding section of this paper.

Organization

At the mesolevel, partners' experiences in their own relationship generate taken-for-granted assumptions about what is possible in it. These taken-for-granted assumptions originate in practical activity that creates and recreates routines and rituals that constitute aspects of the culture of the relationship. These routines and rituals have symbolic meaning that typify the culture of a relationship: the words "I love you," holidays, good sex, mediocre sex, meal and shopping rituals, styles of talk, fighting, the routine exchange, "How was your day?" These routines and rituals come to represent the relationship. For the partner, they are themselves signals that indicate the well-being of the relationship. Their repetition constitutes and affirms the partner's definition of the situation, reinforcing the partner's worldview that all is well and affecting the partner's interpretation of the initiator's signals as follows.

The initiator's signals occur within the context of cultural patterns with established meaning for the partner. Consequently, the partner's reliance on daily rituals and routines to define the relationship tends to obscure change. The partner's frame of reference includes expectations about the range of signals that the initiator might convey based on the past. Change happens gradually. As the initiator's transition progresses and signals incrementally increase, becoming frequent and repeated, they tend to become part of the culture of the relationship (routine signals), rather than a sign of impending demise. If all signals occurred in a very condensed time frame, they would dramatically reorder the daily routine and thus surely would create a strong, attention-getting signal. However, uncoupling is a transition, not a sudden split. A new signal interjected into a daily schedule or a conversation style with taken-for-granted meaning that reinforces the partner's definition of the situation becomes simply a break in the pattern of information the partner normally takes into account (a mixed signal), rather than a challenge to worldview.

Signals that fall outside the partner's worldview (weak signals) may not be taken seriously, may be denied, or may be reinterpreted to fit within the partner's experientially defined understanding of what is possible in the relationship. For example, the partner may interpret signals that deviate from expectations as perhaps temporary anomalies that will go away "when the job crisis is over," or as a signal that the initiator is biologically or psychologically not himself or herself, but not as signals that the relationship is seriously troubled. The partner's interpretation is further complicated by the fact that even late in the uncoupling process, the initiator continues to participate in established rituals and routines, reproducing the culture of the relationship. The partner interprets these activities as signals that all is well. Thus at the same time as the initiator is signaling discontent, that person is affirming the taken-for-granted assumptions of the partner and therefore sustaining the partner's worldview.

Environment

The partner's worldview also is comprised of institutionalized beliefs about relationships in general that originate in the partner's history and experience outside the relationship. Zucker (1977:85) points out that when acts are institutionalized, they have ready-made accounts. Identifiable in interviews with both married and cohabiting partners are three institutionalized cultural beliefs about marriage, family, and partnership. First, partners articulate their belief in the institution of marriage, family, and/or togetherness, affirming the social expectation that people belong in couples—that they should come in pairs, like the animals of Noah's Ark. Second, they also articulate social expectations about the duration of the relationship: Partners comment, "I believed that once you're married, you're married"; "The idea of divorce never occurred to me"; "The holy sacrament of marriage is binding until death"; or "I was sure we would be together for the rest of our lives." Third, they express allegiance to a reinforcing set of institutionalized assumptions about gender roles that proscribe the division of labor in and commitment to the intimate dyad as taking priority over the individual. Partners articulate the belief that if things get tough, the tough stay put: "It was my job to make sure it worked and keep us all together"; "I stayed for the sake of the children"; or "A man has a responsibility to support his family."

Finally, partners' accounts assert an allegiance to institutionalized beliefs about the quality of relationships once we are settled in them. These taken-for-granted cultural assumptions have a folklore-like quality: "All marriages have trouble. Ours wouldn't be normal if we didn't"; "After a while, all couples lose their interest in sex"; "We had some arguments, but, you know, all couples have their arguments." As the initiator's signals of discontent increase (withdrawal, abuse, repeated absence, cheating, lack of interest in sex, complaining), the quality of the partner's experience in the relationship changes. Yet typically partners do not immediately react by redefining their relationship as at a danger point. Instead, within the context of these cultural scripts about what can be expected in relationships in general, partners tend to view their own relationships as merely visited by normal, natural trouble. Their accounts reflect classificatory principals about the quality of relationships in general, derived from history and experience, as in this woman's statement:

> Why in the world, even though if one looked one might see that I was not happy, why in the world would I ever want to change that? I mean, I never saw my mother happy. Why should I assume that I should be happy? You know. Happy, what's that? (1986:104)

In sum, then, the partner's interpretation of early warning signs is shaped by a worldview, comprised of nested cultural beliefs from history and experience that derives from social location in the environment and the relationship (i.e., the organization): Macrolevel institutionalized beliefs of the larger society about the value of relationships, the socially expected duration of relationships, gender and commitment, the priority of the group over the individual, and typifications about the quality of established relationships; and mesolevel taken-for-granted assumptions about what is possible in their own relationship, measured by culturally embedded expectations based on routines and rituals of everyday life past. This worldview or frame of reference influences the partner's construction of the meaning of the relationship, the partner's interpretation of the initiator's signals, and consequently, choice and action.

THE CHALLENGER LAUNCH DECISION

Individual Cognition and Choice

The research showed that the long incubation period (1981 to 1985) preceding the midflight breakup of the *Challenger* was typified by in-flight anomalies—early warning signs that presented an opportunity to intervene and possibly avoid the loss. Because formal organizations keep records, because engineers write everything down, and because the official investigations of the accident made all materials available to the public, I was able to trace design decisions made about the solid rocket boosters (SRBs) (the technical cause of the accident) during the developmental stage of the space shuttle program. I also traced all decisions, including each of the 25 launch decisions, made for the space shuttle once the program was operational. The analysis showed that in the years before the *Challenger* launch, managers and engineers in the work group assigned to the SRBs repeatedly made official, written recommendations in formal launch decisions that the design was an "acceptable risk," despite recurring anomalies.[4] The explanation for these official decisions is "the normalization of deviance": The process by which anomalies (technical deviations from performance predictions) that engineers and managers first interpreted as indicative of escalated risk (a signal of potential danger) after an examination of the evidence and engineering analysis were subsequently officially and formally found to be an "acceptable risk" by the work group. The normalization of technical deviation is an institutional and organizational construct: Macro and mesolevel factors shaped cognition and choice.

Analogous with uncoupling, the data indicated that sources of the work group's pattern of decisions officially to recommend launch in formal prelaunch decision making were layered and that they arose from history and experience linked to environmental and organizational influences on cognition and choice. Also analogous, the sources of the work group's frame of reference were identifiable because the demise of the *Challenger* was, in retrospect, a mistake: the strong signal that contradicted the taken-for-granted assumptions on which the launch decision was based enabled people to articulate those assumptions. Moreover (and in contrast to the previous case), written records existed that showed how these taken-for-granted assumptions operated in participants' logic as decisions were being made prior to the accident and the official investigation. Thus what people said in the aftermath of the tragedy could be evaluated against what they wrote, said, and did at the time. These data allowed a reconstruction of interpretation and meaning to insiders as meanings developed and were negotiated, maintained, and changed.

Organization

History and experience in the organization generated cultural understandings against which signals of potential danger were evaluated. As partners in intimate relationships weigh their assessment of signals of potential danger coming from initiators against taken-for-granted assumptions about what is normal and routine within the organization culture, so did the SRB work group. Organization culture contributed to the normalization of technical deviation in formal launch decisions via: (1) the uncertainty of technology itself as a context of decisions, and (2) the space agency's culture of production, with its triumvirate of cultural imperatives. In combination, the two provided a social context in which proceeding with official launch decisions despite the repeated anomalies became institutionalized at NASA.

Technological uncertainty created a situation where having problems and anomalies on the shuttle was itself a taken-for-granted aspect of NASA culture. The shuttle technology was of unprecedented design, so technical deviations from performance predictions were expected. Also, the forces of the environment on the vehicle in flight were unpredictable, so anomalies on returning space flights were frequent on every part of every mission and therefore routine and normal. Within this context of taken-for-granted problems, having problems on the SRBs was not a deviant event— problems were normal and expected. Changes in the quality and quantity of the problems on the SRBs occurred over several years, introduced gradually into a cultural context where problems and change were taken for granted. Had all the damage to the boosters occurred on one mission or on a series of missions in close succession, the sudden change might have been the attention-getting strong signal necessary to produce an official redefinition of the situation that the booster design was not an "acceptable risk." As it was, signals of potential danger occurred in an ongoing stream of problems that tended to obscure change. History and experience mattered to the frame of reference the work group brought to the interpretation of information in a second way. The engineering rationale developed to justify the first anomaly became the precedent for accepting anomalies in the future. That first engineering risk assessment was foundational, for the first technical analysis was elaborated in greater detail with tests and analysis each time, so that the past and past decisions became the basis for subsequent analysis and launch decision making. The technical rationale for launching with anomalies was reinforced and made stronger in the process.

The space agency's culture of production was the second mesolevel factor contributing to the normalization of technical deviation in official launch decisions at NASA. The culture of production maintained and sustained the definition of the situation that was developing at the microlevel. The culture of production was comprised of the original technical culture of NASA's successful Apollo era, political accountability, and bureaucratic accountability. Political accountability made cost and schedule a priority. Postaccident investigations uniformly showed that pressures to stick to the launch schedule permeated the culture. As one engineer said: "When people are working evenings and weekends, no one has to tell you that schedule is a priority. You know." Dramatic post-Apollo increases in bureaucratic accountability at NASA multiplied requirements for the agency to follow rules and procedures in making technical decisions, ordering hardware, reporting contractor performance, and conforming to industry and government regulations. This greater preoccupation with rules and procedures had a cognitive consequence: Rule-following was accompanied by the cultural belief that if all rules were followed scrupulously in launch decision making, safety was as sure as they could make it, given the unprecedented, unpredictable technology. Finally, a main tenet of NASA's original technical culture valorized quantitative information above hunch, intuition, and subjective feelings.

In combination, technological uncertainty and these cultural imperatives affected decision making, contributing to the normalization of technical deviation in official launch recommendations in the years preceding the *Challenger* launch. Within this culture, compromise, both in design and in performance, was normative; flying with hardware that frequently deviated from design predictions was normative; and proceeding with the schedule despite flying with flaws that had engineers worried was normative, because engineers were conforming to cultural imperatives about rule-following, the production schedule, and the validity of quantitative evidence over hunch and intuition.

Environment

Brint and Karabel stress that institutional analysis must include the "power structures and opportunity fields in the larger society that shape organizational possibilities" and "the efforts of organizational elites to take advantage of the environment to further their own interests as well as those of their organizations" (1991:345). NASA's internal culture of political accountability and bureaucratic accountability resulted from elite decisions conceived to aid agency survival in a post-Apollo environment of scarcity and competition. Faced with reduced consensus and resources for its mission, NASA officials engaged in political bargains with Congress, compromising the shuttle's technical design, purpose, and excellence. Further, to mitigate competitive pressures, NASA officials began "contracting out" work that used to be done in-house, which initiated the emphasis on bureaucratic accountability that was exacerbated by actions of the White House. These elite decisions trickled down through the agency, altering the taken-for-granted understandings of the original technical culture by introducing political accountability and bureaucratic accountability: bringing business interests front and center, emphasizing procedural regularity and schedule to the detriment of safety.

These three cultural imperatives of the NASA organization culture gained in strength because they were reinforced at the macrolevel by institutionalized belief systems of the engineering profession in general and the aerospace industry in particular. In *Craft and Consciousness* (1991), Bensman and Lilienfeld show the relationship between worldview and the occupational technique and methodology of many occupations and professions that they argue, create habits of mind that give each occupation its distinctive character. Engineering as a craft and as a bureaucratic profession contributed to the work group's normalization of technical deviation in official launch decision making venues by providing basic assumptions that were elaborated in the NASA organization culture. These, too, originated in history and experience and manifested in daily engineering practice. Among them are the following.

First, engineers hold the belief that technology is messy and unpredictable in large-scale technical systems; therefore making judgments under conditions of uncertainty is normal (Wynne 1988). Engineering decision rules are based on experience with the technical object, and those rules change as understandings of the technology changes. So changing the rules for what was acceptable to encompass each succeeding anomaly was not procedurally deviant but normal engineering practice in the work group, under those governing professional beliefs. Second, the social administrative arrangements of engineering also contain cultural scripts that are integral to the occupational worldview. Engineers typically work in bureaucracies guided by the principals of capitalism. They are prepared for this existence in colleges and technical schools, where they not only learn engineering but are prepared for work in production-oriented organizations where cost, efficiency, and schedule are valorized. They learn: (1) their place in the hierarchical system of these organizations and the importance of conforming to bureaucratic rules and procedures; (2) satisficing, rather than optimizing, in engineering design and practice; and (3) that cost and safety are in constant competition.[5] Third, at NASA science is used in service of technology, and engineers as a profession develop a set of beliefs about science and technology as truth-finding endeavors and about the methods on which truth is based. "Trust in numbers" (Porter 1995) dominates scientific practice, giving it legitimacy. Truth is revealed in the use of methods that quantify, such that proof is in mathematics, not intuition, observation, or tacit understandings.

These three institutional logics of the profession were taken-for-granted aspects of the SRB work group's worldview. They were cultural scripts that preexisted engineers' entry into the NASA workplace and were reproduced in the organization, elaborated upon, and materialized in the cultural triumvirate that existed after Apollo.

DEAD RECKONING: TECHNOLOGY, CULTURE, AND COGNITION IN AIR TRAFFIC CONTROL

Located in Nashua, NH, Boston Center is an en route center responsible for regulating all air traffic for upper altitudes (14,000 feet and higher) in the New England region, which includes the New England states, most of New York, northeastern Pennsylvania, plus 200 miles out to sea. The center has 280 controllers monitoring 30 radar positions around the clock, handling an average of 5,000 flights a day. The controllers' two main tasks are: (1) to direct traffic movement within their airspace and coordinate traffic between their airspace and other regions and between facilities within their own region that direct traffic at lower altitudes; and (2) to direct traffic safely, avoiding mistake and the ultimate harmful outcome—collision. In 1999, despite the annually expected increase in air traffic, no collisions of commercial aircraft occurred. Figures for 1999 at Boston Center are not yet available, but the number of aircraft handled during 1998 was 1,944,583. How is it that air traffic controllers are able to recognize signals of potential danger early, so that anomalies are identified and corrected?

When asked what the most important characteristics of air traffic controllers are, controllers recite individual characteristics. They stress the importance of vision and hearing, intelligence, the ability to do many things at once, the need for lots of stimulation and activity, excellent memory, and finally, "common sense." Common sense is, to them, the ability to avoid "messes." A mess happens because of an anomalous incident, bad weather, a technical problem. Common sense, they say, helps them avoid a mess in the first place by planning ahead, and helps get out of a mess "whatever way you can." Because getting out of messes is how they avoid mistakes, common sense is what we will examine.

Geertz (1983:73–93) writes that common sense is a loosely connected body of belief and judgment rather than just what anybody properly put together cannot help but think. He argues that common sense is a cultural system, a frame of mind, that both differs from place to place and yet takes a characteristic form. Controllers state that "much of traffic management is rote"; it "becomes second nature." It becomes second nature because their cognitive activity is embedded in a cultural system of knowledge from which decisions can be made and coordination effected without thinking. Common sense, for air traffic controllers, is a frame of mind and capacity to act shaped by: (1) institutionalized formal rules governing the air traffic system; (2) local knowledge gained in the facility to which they are assigned; and (3) tacit knowledge. Institutionalized formal rules, local knowledge, and tacit knowledge are overlapping and mutually reinforcing meaning systems. In combination, these three comprise a system of taken-for-granted understandings that enable radar controllers: (1) to make sense of what they see on the screen; and (2) to identify signals of potential danger early, so corrections can be made before small deviations turn into big mistakes.

Below, I treat the air traffic system as the environment and the air traffic management facility where the controllers work as the organization.[6] Because the project is in its early stages at this writing, here I define environment narrowly (cf. Brint and Karabel 1991). The data nonetheless yield insights about the connection between macrolevel institutionalized rules and the cognition and action of individuals. In contrast to the previous two cases presented, I reverse the order of the situated-action categories used to organize the case comparison, so that we first consider environment, then organization, and then individual cognition and choice. The reversal not only follows the explanation inductively derived from the case study data but also provides the clearest explanation of this case for the reader.

Environment

In the air traffic system, institutionalized formal rules and practices exist nationally and internationally to effect global coordination. All air traffic operates on Greenwich Mean Time, for example, and English is the common language for pilots and controllers. Other rules and regulations fill volumes. Controllers learn these formal rules and practices in four-month training schools covering Letters of Agreement, which are rules about transferring traffic between sectors and facilities; the Book of Phraseology, a common language for communication within the system between pilots and other controllers; air traffic routes—highways in the sky, with names and named intersections; types of aircraft equipment; and how to calculate the position of an aircraft. Controllers report struggling to learn these rules as students because they are tested under stressful conditions on their ability to memorize and reproduce rules and procedures. Standardization is the core of the system. These institutionalized formal rules are learned, but they become taken-for-granted understandings that guide cognition prerationally.

Organization

Geertz (1973:4) writes that "the shapes of knowledge are always ineluctably local, indivisible from their instruments and their encasements." After four months of formal training, controllers are assigned to a facility. Added to the formal rules of the air traffic system are sets of organizational procedures and practices that are peculiar to that facility and its distinctive traffic: "This is how we do it here." As one controller said, "You have to learn the facility—what are the patterns—before you can start paying attention to other things, like talking to people in the room, being able to cooperate with them, share tasks, do the job." Local knowledge comes from both experience at the facility and over-the-shoulder supervision by the trainer.

Local Knowledge Acquired from Experience. Airspace is divided into sectors. Each sector has its own name, different physical characteristics, traffic patterns, aircraft, winds, and connections with other air traffic facilities that controllers must master. Sectors are also typified by highways with named intersections, terrain, radar beacons, and Tower and Approach facilities. Standardized departure and destination points give each sector its own traffic patterns that cross the sector in predictable ways. The amount of sector traffic is also patterned; quiet times and busy times vary by day of the week, by season, by holiday. In the facility, controllers also learn from the performance capability of equipment in a sector and how responsive that equipment is under different conditions—which aircraft are hard to turn in certain winds and which are sluggish climbing in the summer.

Local Knowledge Acquired from Trainers. Senior controllers are assigned as trainers during the three years in the facility that are designated as developmental years prior to a controller being certified as a "full performance level" controller. Local knowledge learned from trainers is enacted in subtleties of traffic management skills that are not visible to the outsider observing controllers at work but can be seen in on-the-job training sessions with trainers. Other knowledge learned from trainers is observable in variations in the styles of talk controllers use with pilots—how crisply and briskly they use the official phraseology, the rhythms of routine commands and responses, and distinctive ways of using the technology to practice traffic management.

Individual Cognition and Choice

Formal rules are institutional; local knowledge is organizational. They are taught, memorized, and practiced. Experience in doing the work builds upon this foundation, adding an intuitive component to cognition: Controllers develop tacit knowledge. Polanyi (1958) describes tacit knowledge as "our ability to perform skills without being able to articulate them," making the further observation that skills involve "the observance of a set of rules which are not known as such to the person following them." Nelson and Winter (1982, chap. 3) make the point that in the exercise of a skill, choice is highly automatic, occurring without deliberation. Choice is, they argue, *suppressed* by its preconditions—routines and programs confine behavior to well-defined channels, reducing option selection. The making of a controller happens when "the light bulb goes on," as one said, enabling them to move beyond thinking and calculating based on many individual rules to an integrated cognitive approach to traffic management that enables decisions to be made without thinking. The "light bulb goes on" as a result of practical activity—history and experience as controllers work at regulating air traffic in simulators during training and on-the-job training experience in their facilities. The result is a cultural system of knowledge consisting of scripts that minimize choice, making air traffic control "common sense," in their view, and explaining why they say: "much of it is rote."

How does common sense as a cultural system affect controllers' ability to make sense of what they see on the screen? To the uninitiated, the radar scope is a screen crammed with disorganized data. Airplanes on a radar scope are represented by a square of flight data identifying an aircraft by number, equipment, altitude, airspeed, and so on. The number of planes in a sector may be as high as 20 to 30. Radar scopes also indicate the highways and intersections of the sector. But controllers do not see separate bits of information and individual flight paths, they see a gestalt. Controllers view activity on the scope with a frame of mind and capacity to act shaped by common sense as a cultural system. Cognition is an activity embedded in history and experience and grounded in institutionalized formal rules, local knowledge, and tacit knowledge. Common sense as a cultural system enables controllers to have foresight. They can be *proactive*: to plan ahead and avoid messes, to correct small mistakes, thereby avoiding big ones, and to get out of messes when they happen.

Foresight is possible because formal rules, local knowledge, and tacit knowledge enable controllers to predict the flight path of an aircraft in the sector and get it through past the other aircraft. The relationship between institutionalized rules and habits of mind is best illustrated by the cardinal concern for controllers: the Rules of Separation. These rules dictate the required distance between aircraft that controllers' must maintain in order to avoid collisions. At Boston Center and other high-altitude facilities, the Rules of Separation require a five-mile radius between aircraft and 1,000-foot clearance above and below. Maintaining separation requires calculation based on airspeed, equipment capabilities, and wind. But the calculation of these multiple factors becomes automatic, a habit of mind that becomes prerational, manifesting in this visualization: Controllers at Boston Center envision a plane as a block moving through space, having a destination from the moment it enters their airspace. The ability to convert a flat radar screen into three dimensions is not simply an innate cognitive skill, but reflects the connection between institutionalized formal rules and cognition. Controllers report that this visualization is due to the Rules of Separation. The assertion about the conversion of multiple formal rules into a habit of mind that enables them to make decisions without thinking is supported by data from a small facility handling takeoff and landing. There the task is different, so the rules of separation are different. Controllers are concerned with sequencing aircraft one at a time for takeoffs and landings. The Rules of Separation call for sequencing with 3,000 feet between aircraft, with pilots sharing responsibility for visual separation. In this setting, controllers report visualizing aircraft as "a string of pearls," not a block flying through space, reflecting the Rules of Separation that are particular to their task and that guide their work practice.

Common sense is a cultural *system*, however. Institutionalized formal rules upon which foresight (done without thinking) is based include standardized flight data that tell controllers of departure and destination points, and formalized highways that give guidelines by which traffic patterns can be predicted. Local knowledge sharpens foresight, because controllers are familiar with refinements in patterns. Foresight helps them develop a plan early and move traffic so that no crisis develops. They describe their work as a series of "moves." A new plane on the scope alters the plan, so the controller has to make adjusting moves with other aircraft. Experience with equipment capability and airspeed allows them to avoid collision:

"Here are two flights, a jet and a prop, on the same altitude, but they are distant now. It looks like they would violate the Rules of Separation, but airspeed means they will clear by five miles."

These sense-making processes are fundamental to directing traffic. How, then, do controllers recognize signals of potential danger? They are able to respond early to a deviation/anomaly by selective attention to a problem that gets identified as a problem by the cognitive frame, comprised of common sense as a cultural system. Some signals of potential danger are clear, strong signals that take no special skills to recognize—bad weather; aircraft emergency; failure of controller technology. But others are recognized only because institutionalized formal rules, local knowledge, and tacit knowledge form a base from which controllers are able to notice deviations from the expected. Taken-for-granted assumptions about traffic mean easy monitoring of most traffic. Controllers do not watch everything equally; normally they pay more attention to the planes that seem to be the most important to follow.

Some concrete examples from field observations: An aircraft following a standard traffic pattern but using a "strange approach" (e.g., "Lear jets don't normally fly that way"); traffic taking the wrong route to a known destination; rule violations by pilots; pilots procedurally reading back controllers' directions but making an error in the response (e.g., 20,000-foot altitude may be read back as 21,000 feet); pilots using correct phraseology and procedures, but deviations in speech characteristics draw attention (tone of voice, weak phraseology, foreign accent, hesitation, long periods of silence, rapid talk with elevated pitch—a sign of crisis). Like uncoupling and NASA's tragedy, decision making for controllers also has an incremental quality, although the sequence of decisions culminating in some final outcome is in seconds or minutes compared to the possibility of years in the other two. Nonetheless, the incremental character of controllers' work is an acknowledged part of their practical activity. On monitoring the progress of an aircraft across the radar scope, one controller observed: "There are many mistakes that get identified and corrected before the final decision (two aircraft clearing each other, within the Rules of Separation)."

In sum, in air traffic control cognitive practice is embedded in an intricate, overlapping system of formal rules, local knowledge, and tacit knowledge, which provides the standardized frame of reference against which even small anomalies (what in other decision contexts might appear as weak signals that did not attract attention) stand out as strong signals, enabling controllers to recognize early warning signals and take corrective action, thereby preventing small deviations and errors from turning into mistakes with harmful outcomes.

A Microsociology for Institutional Theory: The Role of Culture in a Theory of Practical Action

What are the implications of this three case comparison for: (1) the connection between culture and cognition, and (2) the potential of Bourdieu's theory of *habitus* as a microsociological supplement to institutional theory?[7] The comparison shows patterns common to the three cases that shed some light on: (1) the complex, layered connection between structure, culture, and cognition, (2) institutional processes of variation and persistence, and (3) *habitus*.

CULTURE AS MEDIATOR BETWEEN INSTITUTIONS AND COGNITION

In each case analysis, cultural understandings and scripts played a major role in the interpretation of signals of potential danger; they did so by establishing the preconditions of choice. Scott observed that: "Perhaps the single most important contribution of institutional theorists to the study of organizations is their reconceptualization of the environments of organizations . . . to include a neglected facet: Institutionalized beliefs, rules, and roles" that comprise shared cognitive systems (1991:165). In each case, the analysis showed sets of organizing assumptions—prerational, cultural, and layered—that permeated nested structures, shaping individual cognitive processes. Because each case in the comparison was originally investigated in order to find an explanation of its own substantive problem, I identified these taken-for-granted assumptions differently in each: worldview in uncoupling; institutionalized cultural beliefs at NASA; common sense as a cultural system in air traffic control. Although named differently, all three cases were typified by distinctive sets of institutional values, and culture was the medium through which they were expressed. All cases show culture at work cognitively in the nexus of information, schemata, and larger symbol systems. DiMaggio (1997:277) distinguishes between "logics of action," or constraints that influence action in a given domain, and more recently identified "institutional logics," emphasizing the cultural aspects of the connection between institutional requirements and mental structures:

> Friedland and Alford (1991:248–49) provide the most thorough exposition and definition, describing "institutional logics" as sets of "material practices and symbolic constructions" that constitute an institutional order's "organizing principles" and are "available to organizations and individuals to elaborate."

Confirming Friedland and Alford, the data for each of my three cases showed how institutional logics were comprised of material practices and symbolic meanings that guided decision making and consequently action. The comparison demonstrated empirically the overlapping, layered character of these organizing principles. Each case verified a trickle-down effect wherein institutional logics originating in the environment (professions, industries, American society) affected practical activity and were reproduced in the course of that activity. These institutionalized cultural beliefs were elaborated upon by organizations and individuals, such that they were transformed into substantively crafted, situation-specific scripts that derived from one's history and experience in that organizational setting. At the macrolevel in uncoupling, partners held taken-for-granted assumptions about marriage and cohabitation; at NASA, institutional logics about engineering as both a craft and a production-oriented bureaucratic profession were part of the work group's interpretive frame; in air traffic control, institutional logics about science, technology, and standardized rules framed the interpretive process.

Local variations on these larger institutional themes are identifiable at the mesolevel: In uncoupling, institutional beliefs about marriage and relationships were a foundation for more detailed cultural scripts idiosyncratic to the specific relationship; at the space agency, institutional logics surrounding the profession and craft of engineering were elaborated into cultural beliefs about cost/safety trade-offs, bureaucratic rules, and technical practices that were peculiar to the NASA organization; in air traffic control, taken-for-granted assumptions at the institutional level were refined by local, organizationally based cultural scripts grounded in history and experience at the air traffic facility. Each cultural layer was in many ways distinctive, but in each case, aspects of one layer carried over and interpenetrated the next. They were mutually reinforcing systems of meaning that contributed to and stabilized individuals' definitions of the situation, narrowing choice.

INSTITUTIONAL PROCESSES: VARIATION AND PERSISTENCE

The variation in the three cases compared offers some insight into reproduction and the problem of macrostability and change. Institutionalists argue that routines and scripts, not norms and values, are the source of macrostability. They stress the structuring quality of rules, routines, scripts, and frameworks. Although they make room for both agency and change, most of the empirical work has focused on fields rather than microlevel bases of institutional processes such as variation and persistence. The most extensive research into these issues at the microlevel has been through the laboratory experiments conducted by Zucker (1977). She concluded that her settings varied in the degree to which acts are institutionalized. In contrast, the three cases of decision making compared in this paper allow examination of the effects of the natural setting. They, too, vary in the degree to which acts are institutionalized. Whereas in all three cases, cultural scripts originating in the environment played a role, permeating and being elaborated in more immediate organizational settings, a major difference is at the mesolevel of analysis: The decision making takes place in a social group and two complex organizations. This condition allows us to consider variation in institutionalization and cultural persistence in natural settings.

The formal organization, Jepperson writes, is a "packaged social technology, with accompanying rules and instructions for its employment and incorporation in a social setting" (1991:147). Zucker hypothesized that an act being performed by the occupant of an office in a formal organization will have a high degree of institutionalization, whereas an act being performed by actors exercising personal influence (i.e., not acting through an office) will be low in institutionalization. She also hypothesized that the degree of institutionalization would affect the resistance of those cultural understandings to change. These case comparisons verify Zucker on the relationship between institutionalization and change.

Suppose we array our three organizational settings on a hypothetical continuum by degree of institutionalization. As a social group, the intimate dyad would be at the left, indicated as low institutionalization, and the two complex organizations toward the right, indicated as high institutionalization. However, variation exists between kinds of intimate dyads. *Uncoupling* was based on interviews with both married couples and couples living together, gay and straight. Marriage being the more highly institutionalized of the three, it would be placed between the complex organizations and the other dyads on our hypothetical continuum. Variation also exists between the two complex organizations. (This, too, is consistent with Zucker, who allowed for variation in institutionalization between formal organizations.) Microactivity in air traffic control is more highly institutionalized than activity in the solid rocket booster work group at NASA, because all air traffic controllers' choices are based on institutionally and organizationally programmed routines and scripts (a skill; see Nelson and Winter 1982) to make the *same* kinds of decisions about the *same* objects every day, whereas the engineering decisions of the SRB work group were more discretionary, based on universalistic guidelines rather than the particularistic ones used in air traffic management. Therefore, air traffic control would be on the far right of the hypothetical continuum.

The cases show the expected variation in cultural persistence. The greater the degree of institutionalization, the greater the cultural persistence, the greater the resistance to change. In directing aircraft, air traffic controllers reproduce nearly exactly common sense as a cultural system: the institutionalized formal rules of the system and the local knowledge gained at the facility, with tacit knowledge the only decipherable source of variation. Choices are made without thinking. As controllers say, much of it is "rote" and "common sense." As they direct traffic and identify anomalies, air traffic controllers' decision making and choice are so narrowly channeled that the adjective "determined" may be more appropriate than the softer term, "constrained." Training is intensive and repeated at intervals; innovation is minimal. To deviate from the layered system of rules that guided traffic management can lead to loss of one's job and being immediately and publicly responsible for the loss of the lives of others. The high costs of deviation all but eliminate resistance to institutional scripts. Ritualistically, the practical activities of air traffic controllers feed into cultural persistence and the reproduction of institutional rules about controlling traffic.

In the comparatively less institutionalized environment of NASA in which the SRB work group was making decisions, there was an effort to initiate change by challenging the official (and long-standing) documentation establishing "acceptable risk" of the solid rocket booster design with a "no launch" recommendation on the eve of the *Challenger* accident. The work group's official definition of the technical components of the SRBs had become institutionalized within the organization, reinforced by layered meaning systems of the culture of production that originated in the environment. But that night, the engineering protest contradicted the culture of production. Nonetheless, as they discussed the technical issues about the *Challenger* launch that were on the table, their construction of meaning and interpretation of signals were shaped by history and experience—past decisions on the SRBs, and the technical engineering rationale for proceeding that had been developed over many years.

Even as contractor engineers in the work group argued against the launch in the short run, cultural persistence was reinforced in the long run because all participants exactly followed the dictates of the culture of production, reproducing the shared symbol systems that guided their actions. Taken-for-granted assumptions about hierarchy, schedule, satisficing, quantitative data versus intuitive data, and rule-following were reenacted, affecting the proceedings, with the result that participants once again followed precedent. The official outcome was to expand the bounds of "acceptable risk" yet another time. Their behavior was to a great extent scripted, conforming to institutionalized cultural beliefs and thereby reproducing them.

Perhaps the strongest case for demonstrating variation and cultural persistence in institutionalization is in the data on deteriorating intimate relationships. First, the analysis showed that the relationships of heterosexual and homosexual couples living together are less stable and more likely to breakup than those of married couples. This is not because of either less commitment or greater promiscuity. Rather, these relationships are more precarious because of the lack of institutional support. Of the marriages that do break up, the behavior of the initiator who eventually leaves the relationship is the source of several insights about variation in cultural persistence. First, in contrast to the other two cases we are comparing, change happens; individual actors who become initiators do make choices and take actions that contradict layered, taken-for-granted assumptions about marriage, family, and gendered relations that their partners still hold. How does this change come about?

Friedland and Alford (1991) posit that contradictions between institutional logics can precipitate change. In the married initiator's transition, one such clash is between the cultural beliefs in the institution of marriage versus the democratic value of individual freedom. Initiators who uncouple make a shift from the former to the latter. The high degree of institutionalization of marriage is demonstrated by the fact that uncoupling is a gradual transition that takes time; the analysis reveals the lower-level processes that counter higher-order institutional effects. Uncoupling takes time because in order to make a transition out of the relationship, the initiator must redefine taken-for-granted assumptions about self, the partner, and relationship. One of the redefinitions necessary is that the individual takes primacy over the group. This switch to a different set of cultural assumptions is a slow process, because the initiator has to change social locations (i.e., *habitus*; see discussion below) in order to make the switch. The initiator gradually shifts ties from the partner and those coupled friends who reinforce and objectify the relationship to others who share this alternative worldview: the single, the divorced. Change does happen, as the divorce rates indicate, but the prevalence of remarriage among the divorced attests to cultural persistence of marriage as an institution. The ideological shift is necessary to uncouple, but for most initiators it is temporary. As initiators state after they have recoupled: "Nothing is wrong with marriage, only the marriage I was in."

HABITUS

DiMaggio and Powell (1991), searching for a microlevel solution to the problem of macrolevel stability, suggested Bourdieu's notion of *habitus* as the analytic link that connects individual behavior and social structure. Bourdieu, explaining the social construction of reality, asserts that the principle of that construction is *habitus*: A system of dispositions, acquired through experience and thus variable from place to place and time to time, that allows for agency without turning actors into rational calculators. These acquired dispositions function on the practical level as categories of perception and assessment or as classificatory principles, as well as being the organizing principles of action; as such, they portray the social agent as the "practical operator" of the construction of objects (Bourdieu 1990a:12–13). This system of dispositions generates strategies that can be directed toward certain ends, but those strategies are "neither unconscious calculation nor obedience to a rule" (Bourdieu 1990a:9–10). Bourdieu's notion of strategy is key to understanding agency within his perspective. Strategy is:

> ". . . the product of the practical sense as the feel for the game, for a particular historically
> determined game—a feel which is acquired in childhood by taking part in social activities
> . . . [it] presupposes a permanent capacity for invention, indispensable if one is to be able
> to adopt to indefinitely varied and never completely identical situations . . . this freedom of
> invention and improvisation which enables the infinity of moves allowed by the game to be
> produced . . . the *habitus* as the feel for the game is the social game embodied and turned
> into a second nature. (1990a:62–3)

Institutions are integral to this perspective because of their connection to the distribution of dispositions. Constituted in the course of an individual history, *habitus* makes
it possible to inhabit institutions, to draw on them practically, enacting their organizing
principles and thus reproducing them but at the same time allowing for revision and
transformation (Bourdieu 1990b:57). Rational strategies of action, in this view, themselves are institutionalized, shaped by standard rules and structures and reflected in
standardized cultural forms such as accounts, typifications, and cognitive models.

This three-case comparison affirms Bourdieu's notion of *habitus* as a microsociological complement to institutional theory. Affirming DiMaggio and Powell (1991),
it could serve as the analytic equivalent of Parsons's role system as a connector
between individual behavior and social structure. However, some new insights and
questions grow out of the comparison. Clear in each of the decision-making cases
compared was the operation of structuring predispositions—a system of cognitive
and motivating structures. Decisions were made in a practical world of already-
realized ends—procedures to follow, paths to take—that drew on existing regularities
that were institutionalized and became the basis of "the schemes of perception and
appreciation through which they were apprehended" (Bourdieu 1990b:53–54).
Although not discussed here due to space limits, the cases also show the role of
agency, as actors enacted a variety of strategies within the constraining predispositions. Each case showed decision-making processes as they unfolded, with multiple
small decisions made incrementally, demonstrating the indeterminacy people face on
a daily basis in the lived life. But exercise of agency was a matter of invention within
limits.

Invention within limits was visible in all three cases: In air traffic controllers'
enactment of tacit knowledge against a background of institutionalized formal rules
and local knowledge from the facility; in partners in relationships who turned
"detective" as signals of potential danger accumulated; in engineers at NASA who
used memos and informal conversations to express increasing concerns, even as they
continued officially to recommend launching shuttles. But also evident was the
capacity for invention of larger scale. Bourdieu asserts the importance of the "contingency of the accidental," positing that the act arises from "the unpredictable confrontation between the *habitus* and an event" (1990b:55). Institutional contradiction
at the microlevel does seem to initiate change. The contingency of the accidental
manifested in the initiator's uncoupling, in changes in the partner's worldview at the
realization that the relationship was seriously troubled, in the shattering of the institutionalized cultural belief in "acceptable risk" when *Challenger* was transformed
into a ball of fire and smoke clouds in the sky. In each of the cases, challenges to
taken-for-granted assumptions required a reconstruction of the immediate reality—a

redefinition of self in relation to the world—but that redefinition nonetheless went on within the parameters already set by institutional arrangements.

What becomes more explicit as a result of the case comparisons is how social choices are shaped, mediated, and channeled by institutional arrangements. The cases verify that the repetitive quality of much organized life cannot be explained by a consequentialist rational actor model, but by the preconditions of choice. The persistence of practices lies in their taken-for-granted quality and their reproduction in structures that are, to a certain extent, self-sustaining: "Institutional arrangements constrain individual behavior by rendering some choices inviable, precluding particular courses of action. . . ." (DiMaggio and Powell 1991:9–10). Also more explicit as a result of the case comparisons is the role of culture in organizing social reality. Culture becomes the medium through which institutional values and beliefs are both conveyed and enacted, and then reproduced. The nesting of institutional logics has a stabilizing effect. People are the carriers of culture, enabling institutional environments to penetrate organizational settings, where they are elaborated by organizations and individuals, shaping worldview and thus categories of structure, action, and thought. Both uncoupling and *Challenger* exemplified how schemas and scripts lead decision makers to resist new evidence. In all three cases, cultural categories shaped the rules by which rationality is perceived and experienced (Friedland and Alford 1991:247).

What also emerges from these comparisons is new insight into the complex way the distribution of dispositions is tied to social location. Bourdieu states that *habitus* is a product of history that produces more history. He argues that it is a "present past," acquired through experience that enables coordination of activities and macrolevel stability. People have the same history, thus behavior can be coordinated without thinking, without any conscious reference to a norm or calculation. His discussion (1990b:58–61) centers around group or class *habitus*, contrasting it with individual *habitus*. He acknowledges the importance of individual experience and the variation that implies, concluding that each individual is a "structural variant" of the social conditions producing the class *habitus*. He acknowledges the singularity of an individual's position within a class system of dispositions that are common, but nonetheless the result is common schemes of perception, conception, and action. However, most of his discussion is about class dispositions and the common experiences that shape them.

This empirical analysis suggests the importance of the mesolevel of analysis in a theory of practical action. The mesolevel of analysis focuses on the immediate social setting—the social group, the formal organization, the professional association—within which cognition and action take place. What this analogical comparison reveals is how organizational settings build upon and vary schemas derived from institutional logics, such that they become specifically tailored to practical activity in everyday life, reproducing universalistic symbol systems in the environment but elaborating them locally in particularistic ways. This finding about the role of the mesolevel of analysis suggests that instead of identifying *habitus* as social location, defined as history and experience shared by the same class, research and theory might better posit *habitus* as a product of *social location(s)*: positions in multiple structures that cut across class as well as the trajectory of time, space, and history that typifies individual experience. Understanding cognition sociologically requires taking into account the fact that individuals belong to multiple organizations, both sequentially and simultaneously: labor unions, families, gangs, business organizations, churches, sports teams, political groups, and so forth. This three-case comparison shows that the social setting can reproduce collective beliefs to a greater or lesser extent. Different organizational settings are likely to vary in degree of institutionalization, allowing closer examination of variation and cultural persistence and therefore the potential for agency and change.

Incorporating the mesolevel renders Bourdieu's notion of the "system of dispositions" empirically more complex. For developing further a theory of practical action, taking the mesolevel of analysis into account could be used productively to refine knowledge relevant to organization fields: How microprocesses produce social order and social change; the role of interests and intentionality; the nested relationship between culture, cognition, and practical activity. As a research strategy, a situated action approach, using qualitative methods and joining macro, meso, and microlevels of analysis could explore several issues relevant to institutional theory.

First, studying interpretation, choice, and action in naturalistic settings provides the opportunity to view both the macrolevel and mesolevel contexts of choice as they play out in individual and collective decision making. Second, it allows closer examination of activities of the elites—administrators and professionals—who use their power to determine the interests of the organizations they control. The *Challenger* data made possible not only situating the case within the larger economy and polity but also attending to the "organization-enhancing behaviors of administrators," "opportunity fields," and "mental sets of organizational elites" (Brint and Karabel 1991:345–52). Third, DiMaggio (1997) suggests that understanding the relationship between culture and cognition would be enhanced by work that distinguishes between socialization, experience, and history. These case studies suggest that the three are interconnected and difficult to separate analytically. Research at the mesolevel in naturalistic settings that specifically tries to untangle these connections while still acknowledging the role of larger symbol systems could be beneficial. Finally, a situated-action approach that directs attention to the three levels of analysis could enable understanding of change, because organizations sharpen and refine institutional logics. Disputes are a window into the social. By taking the organizational locus of practical activity into account, empirical work may begin to expose the contradictions both within and between organizational settings that Friedland and Alford posit are the source of change.

Endnotes

1. DiMaggio and Powell review Garfinkel's ethnomethodology and Berger's and Luckmann's phenomenology, two perspectives that began to shift social theory toward the link between culture and cognition. Garfinkel contradicted Parsons's imagery of rational, reasoning individuals, instead explaining social order through the operation of cognitive processes that are preconscious, demonstrated in practical knowledge governed by rules evidenced only when breached, the ability of individuals to sustain encounters under difficult conditions, and retrospective interpretive capacity that orders and justifies actions after the fact by drawing on legitimating cultural accounts. Berger and Luckmann, in contrast to Garfinkel, connect individual cognition and meaning to institutions, both in the construction of institutions by

individuals and the reciprocal relation between institutions and individuals that leads to habitualized actions.
2. For details of the methodology, see Vaughan (1986: "Introduction" and "Postscript").
3. For details, see Vaughan (1996: Chapter 2 and Appendix C).
4. This is a formal safety status for each technical component that must be conferred prior to each launch, based on engineering procedures that conform to NASA's "Acceptable Risk Process." See Hammack and Raines (1981).
5. Scott brings to our attention the important but neglected work of Berger, Berger, and Kellner (1973), in which they note that knowledge systems and cognitive styles' association with bureaucratic administration include "beliefs in delimited spheres of competence, the importance of proper procedure, and impersonality" (1991: 166).
6. The logic of analogical theorizing legitimizes shifting units of analysis in this manner. See Vaughan (1992).
7. A requirement of analogical theorizing is that each case be analyzed, searching for a full explanation of the phenomena of interest. Then the analyst compares the findings with some guiding theory or concepts that initially framed the investigation to see what has been clarified, discounted, or elaborated in the process. However, the role of culture in a theory of practical action was not a "guiding theory" behind the initiation of either of these projects. Instead, this question is imposed retrospectively.

References

Bensman, J. and R. Lilienfeld. 1991. *Craft and Consciousness: Occupational Technique and the Development of World Images*. New York: Aldine de Gruyter.

Berger, P. L. and H. Kellner. 1964. "Marriage and the Construction of Reality." *Diogenes* 46: 1–25.

Berger, P. L. and T. Luckmann. 1966. *The Social Construction of Reality*. New York: Doubleday.

Berger, P. L., B. Berger, and H. Kellner. 1973. *The Homeless Mind: Modernization and Consciousness*. New York: Random House.

Blumer, H. 1969. *Symbolic Interactionism: Perspective and Method*. Englewood Cliffs, NJ: Prentice-Hall.

Bourdieu, P. 1977. *Outline of a Theory of Practice*. Cambridge, England: Cambridge University Press.

———. 1990a. *In Other Words: Essays Towards a Reflexive Sociology*. Stanford, CA: Stanford University Press.

———. 1990b. *The Logic of Practice*. Stanford, CA: Stanford University Press.

Brint, S. and J. Karabel. 1991. "Institutional Origins and Transformations: The Case of American Community Colleges." Pp. 337–61 in *The New Institutionalism in Organizational Analysis*, edited by W. W. Powell and P. J. DiMaggio. Chicago, IL: University of Chicago Press.

DiMaggio, P. 1997. "Culture and Cognition." *Annual Review of Sociology* 23:263–87.

DiMaggio, P. and W. W. Powell. 1991. "Introduction." Pp. 1–41 in *The New Institutionalism in Organizational Analysis*, edited by W. W. Powell and P. J. DiMaggio. Chicago, IL: University of Chicago Press.

Friedland, R. and R. R. Alford. 1991. "Bringing Society Back In: Symbols, Practices, and Institutional Contradictions." Pp. 232–66 in *The New Institutionalism in Organizational Analysis*, edited by W. W. Powell and P. J. DiMaggio. Chicago, IL: University of Chicago Press.

Garfinkel, H. 1967. *Studies in Ethnomethodology*. Englewood Cliffs, NJ: Prentice-Hall.

Geertz, C. 1973. *The Interpretation of Cultures*. New York: Basic Books.

———. 1983. *Local Knowledge: Further Essays in Interpretive Anthropology*. New York: Basic Books.

Glaser, B. G. and A. Strauss. 1967. *The Discovery of Grounded Theory*. New York: Aldine.

Hammack, J. B. and M. L. Raines. 1981. *Space Shuttle Safety Assessment Report*. Johnson Space Center, Safety Division (5 March). Washington, DC: National Archives.

Jepperson, R. L. 1991. "Institutions, Institutional Effects, and Institutionalization." Pp. 143–63 in *The New Institutionalism in Organizational Analysis*, edited by W. W. Powell and P. J. DiMaggio. Chicago, IL: University of Chicago Press.

Nelson, R. R. and S. G. Winter. 1982. *An Evolutionary Theory of Economic Change*. Cambridge, MA: Belknap Press.

Pinch, T. and W. Bijker. 1984. "The Social Construction of Facts and Artifacts: A Unified Approach toward the Study of Science and Technology." *Social Studies of Science* 14:399–442.

Polanyi, M. 1958. *Personal Knowledge*. London: Routlege and Kegan Paul.

Porter, T. M. 1995. *Trust in Numbers: The Pursuit of Objectivity in Science and Public Life*. Princeton NJ: Princeton University Press.

Powell, W. W. and P. J. DiMaggio, eds. 1991. *The New Institutionalism in Organizational Analysis*. Chicago, IL: University of Chicago Press.

Scott, W. R. 1991. "Unpacking Institutional Arguments." Pp. 164–82 in *The New Institutionalism in Organizational Analysis*, edited by W. W. Powell and P. J. DiMaggio. Chicago, IL: University of Chicago Press.

Simmel, G. 1950. "Dyads and Triads," Pp. 122–69 in *The Sociology of Georg Simmel*. Translated by, Kurt Wolff. Glencoe, IL: The Free Press.

Spence, A. M. 1974. *Market Signaling*. Cambridge, MA: Harvard University Press.

Suchman, L. A. 1987. *Plans and Situated Actions*. Cambridge, England: Cambridge University Press.

Vaughan, D. 1986. *Uncoupling: Turning Points in Intimate Relationships*. New York: Oxford University Press.

———. 1992. "Theory Elaboration: The Heuristics of Case Analysis." Pp. 173–202 in *What Is a Case? Exploring the Foundations of Social Inquiry*, edited by C. Ragin and H. S. Becker. Cambridge, England: Cambridge University Press.

———. 1996. *The Challenger Launch Decision: Risky Technology, Culture, and Deviance at NASA*. Chicago, IL: University of Chicago Press.

———. 1998a. "How Theory Travels: Analogy, Models, and the Case of A. Michael Spence." Presented at the annual meeting of the American Sociological Association, San Francisco, CA.

———. 1998b. "Rational Choice, Situated Action, and the Social Control of Organizations." *Law & Society Review* 32:23–61.

———. 1999. "The Dark Side of Organizations: Mistake, Misconduct, and Disaster." *Annual Review of Sociology* 25:271–305.

———. 2001. *Theorizing: Analogy, Cases, and Comparative Social Organization*. Chicago, IL: University of Chicago Press. In preparation.

Wynne, B. 1988. "Unruly Technology: Practical Rules, Impractical Discourses, and Public Understanding." *Social Studies of Science* 18:147–67.

Zucker, L. G. 1977. "Institutionalization and Cultural Persistence." *American Sociological Review* 42 (5):726–43.

SECTION II

Discrimination and Classification

Discrimination and Classification: An Introduction

Apprehending and attending to stimuli represents the first phase of thought. But for thinking to progress, the human brain must sort through the data at hand. The brain must establish similarities and differences and ultimately cluster the information into meaningful categories. Cognitive scientists refer to this sorting process as *discrimination*; they refer to the categorization of data as *classification*.

According to cognitive scientists, human beings develop the ability to discriminate in early childhood (approximately two to seven years of age). The capacity to classify develops in middle to late childhood (approximately seven to eleven years of age). This timetable suggests certain critical differences in the cognitive life of the young. For example, suppose two children, one five years of age and the other ten years of age, are shown a grouping of objects—in this case, three apples and two oranges. Imagine next that the children are asked: Are there more apples or more oranges? Research indicates that both the five- and ten-year-old will answer the question correctly. Both possess the cognitive ability to discriminate between the two types of fruit. But suppose we ask a second question of the children: Are there more apples or more fruits? Research shows that the ten-year-old will answer the question correctly, while the five-year-old will likely be puzzled by the query. This is because the five-year-old lacks an advanced capability to which Jean Piaget referred as "the addition of classes" (Piaget 1952; 1954). According to Piaget, classification involves more than an awareness of difference; the process requires one to understand that subclasses (e.g., apples and oranges) can be combined and transformed into a broader, more general class (e.g., fruits). Further, the ability to classify requires one to recognize that the general class (e.g., fruits) can be broken down or reversed into the original two subclasses (e.g., apples and oranges).

Over the past several decades, cognitive scientists have worked to pinpoint the mechanisms by which the brain establishes similarities, differences, and general mental categories. Laboratory-based perceptual experiments have been especially helpful in this regard. The earliest projects explored the brain's recognition of "concrete" differences. Subjects participating in such studies typically compared stimuli with reference to some objectively measurable dimension—for example, brightness, length, or weight. Thus a subject might be asked to compare a pair of vertical lines and indicate whether the line on the right appears to be of greater, lesser, or equal length to the line on the left. Similarly, subjects might be asked to compare two shades of the color red and indicate if the first color block is brighter, duller, or of equal intensity to the second. As subjects discriminated and classified the characteristics of the stimuli before them, researchers documented the mental resources tapped in the decision-making process. They also recorded the speed with which subjects made their decisions and the degree of confidence they expressed in their choices.

Such experiments provide several insights on discrimination and classification. These studies elucidate the step-by-step mechanics involved in sorting and categorizing objectively different entities. We now know, for example, that individuals engaged in these mental tasks focus on new stimuli and continuously sample their characteristics. Such sampling generates an "information feed"—a stream of data that the brain processes and then matches to preexisting schemata. Experimental study shows that an information feed remains active until a critical threshold is reached: a level of evidence that favors one classification—same or different—over the other.[1]

As one might expect, discrimination and classification tasks vary in difficulty. As such, certain factors can complicate the execution of these procedures. Experimental studies show, for example, that the specific characteristics of the stimuli to which subjects are exposed can impact the evaluative process; the smaller the objective differences between stimuli, the more difficult the discrimination task. Under such conditions, subjects spend significantly more time reviewing stimuli. They often overlook objective differences, thus increasing classification errors. And when comparing stimuli with small objective differences, subjects express less confidence in their final classification decisions. Speed is also a factor in the discrimination and classification. Experimental work shows that subjects forced to discriminate under the pressure of time are more likely to neglect significant differences among stimuli. These misperceptions typically increase classification errors. Finally, discrimination and classification are sometimes influenced by subjects' response biases. When subjects begin an evaluation with certain expectations in mind, they often taint the information-gathering process. Under such conditions, subjects may abort the information stream when they have acquired sufficient data to confirm their predispositions. By failing to consider the full array of available data, subjects increase the likelihood of discrimination and classification errors.

Not all discrimination and classification tasks involve concrete differences. Often human beings must sort and categorize objects and experiences with reference to implied, subjective, or abstract criteria. In tracking such activities, cognitive scientists have identified several distinct discriminatory strategies, strategies that locate the act of comparison in specific sectors of the brain's vast data bank. Consider, for example, "analogical thinking." Analogical thinking enables the human brain to solve new problems by adapting specific experiences from the past. In recent years, Dedre Gentner (1989), Douglas Hofstadter (1995), and Keith Holyoak and Paul Thagard (1995) have developed sophisticated models of analogical thinking.[2] Such models suggest, for example, that analogical thinking occurs in four stages. Stage one involves an individual's encounter with a new problem. (New problems are typically called "target analogs.") In stage two, individuals search their memory for a "source analog"—that is, a past experience that resembles the new problem. During stage three, individuals compare the target and source analogs, taking mental inventory of their corresponding components. In the final stage of analogical thinking, individuals adapt the source analog, thus acquiring a solution for the new problem at hand.

While the stages of analogical thinking sound straightforward, the strategy involves a highly complex set of computations. When we consider the vast array of human experience, we realize that every individual stores thousands of source analogs each year. Thus each time a human being encounters a new problem, the brain must review a massive "data bank" of source analogs, retrieving the one that is most relevant to the problem at hand. In studying the computational tasks involved in analog retrieval, Holyoak and Thagard (1995) have successfully itemized three critical components of the process. According to the research team, the brain first compares target and source analogs in terms of "surface similarities." In this regard, the brain looks for visual or auditory parallels between the two analogs; it searches for source analogs that involve concepts similar to those tapped by the target analog. Second, the brain compares target and source analogs in terms of "structural similarities." In essence, the brain notes the relationships that connect the various dimensions of the target analog. It then searches source analogs, marking those that display similar structural connections. Finally, the brain compares target and source analogs in terms of present and past goals. The brain searches for source analogs that provide outcomes identical to those presently desired.

Data on past experience provides one benchmark by which human beings sort and assess new information. But discrimination and classification can be fueled by other types of data as well. For example, when human beings encounter abstract entities and ideas, they may come to understand them by equating them with familiar concrete phenomena. (Remember Forrest Gump's attempt at concretizing daily experience: "Life is like a box of chocolates.") Cognitive scientists refer to this strategy as "metaphoric thinking." George Lakoff, the leading expert on metaphoric thinking, has taught us much about the mechanics of this strategy.[3] Via Lakoff's research, we learn that the human brain houses multiple conceptual systems. Each of these systems in turn contains thousands of conceptual metaphors—a series of information links that match abstract and concrete phenomena (Lakoff 1995; 1987). When human beings encounter objects and ideas that seem complex or obscure, the brain invokes these metaphors; it forces new and unknown stimuli into familiar and tangible object categories. In so doing, conceptual metaphors enable human beings to interpret otherwise incomprehensible data; they allow the brain to locate new experience in navigable terrain.

The earliest work on metaphoric thinking depicted the strategy as more labor-intensive than either concrete comparison or analogical thinking. While the latter two processes typically involve literal interpretation, metaphoric thinking "invokes figurative devices to produce a broader aura of associations (Thagard 1998:87). Thus, to interpret metaphors such as "love is a battlefield," "all the world is a stage," or "time is money," cognitive scientists originally believed that the brain engaged in a multistaged exercise. The brain was thought to search first for a concept's literal meaning. If the brain failed to find this literal meaning, cognitive scientists believed the brain entered a second stage of assessment, a search for metaphoric meaning. The brain was thought to scan its data banks for symbolic equivalents that might link, for example, romance and war, daily life and drama, or personal effort and reward. Recent research suggests, however, that such multistaged models of metaphoric thinking were in error. Current experimental work indicates that the human brain is sufficiently sophisticated to search simultaneously for both literal and metaphoric levels of meaning. Thus metaphoric thinking occurs in conjunction with literal interpretation.[4] And despite the complexity involved in metaphoric thinking, research indicates that the process typically unfolds quickly and unconsciously.

Research on concrete comparison, analogical thinking, and metaphoric thinking has taught us much about discrimination and classification. Undoubtedly, human beings' abilities to sort and categorize information are fueled by the intricate functions of the brain. At the same time, we must remain mindful that brain functions are socioculturally situated. The data banks that allow human beings to draw similarities, recognize distinctions, and categorize such information emerge not only from the brain's physiological capacities, but also from the social circumstances and cultural contexts in which those capacities are exercised. Failing to include the broader sociocultural domain in the study of discrimination and classification can leave us with many unanswered questions.

Consider, for example, one of the previously stated findings on concrete comparison: the brain can easily detect gross objective differences, but can overlook and misclassify minor objective differences. While this finding sheds some light on the capacity of the human brain, the studies that document this trend cannot definitively specify that which constitutes a gross versus a minor objective difference. This is a critical omission, and yet one that is not wholly surprising. For socioculturally oriented research suggests that cultural norms rather than neural or cognitive criteria may define the "significance" of concrete differences. Witness, for example, reports of the Aleut Eskimos' unique ability to distinguish 33 different types of snow or the Solomon Islanders' uncommon capacity to recognize nine distinct stages of coconut growth.[5] The classification systems that allow for such detailed mental sorting are the products of cultural rather than cognitive sensitization. Knowing this, a thorough understanding of concrete comparison requires full specification of the ways in which cultural traditions, symbols, values, and beliefs can limit or enhance the perception of sameness and difference.

Similar issues arise in reviewing studies of analogical and metaphoric thinking. Unquestionably, these cognitive strategies involve intricate brain operations. But central to these "search and compute" missions are the benchmarks of comparison upon which they rely. The brain's selection of relevant analogies and metaphors may rest in part on the characteristics of new stimuli, the particulars of one's past experience, or the configuration of the brain's data banks. Yet the relevance of an analogy or a metaphor will also be defined by the values and beliefs that govern the sociocultural milieu in which reasoning occurs. Thus in one cultural context, life may be a bowl of cherries, in another, a valley of tears. At one historical moment, ignorance may be the root of misfortune; at another moment, it may be bliss. The beliefs, traditions, and values emphasized by a culture will steer the brain as it searches its data banks for appropriate analogies and metaphors.

It is these very issues—the sociocultural components of discrimination and classification—that engage the authors of this section. In the next three chapters, authors will highlight the ways in which sociocultural circumstance can direct comparative thinking. The authors will also explore the ways in which discriminative and classification strategies supercede the individual to become institutionalized social practices. In Chapter 4, for example, Wendy Espeland discusses "commensuration." Commensuration is a comparative strategy by which societies transform qualitative distinctions into quantitative ranks. (Cost-benefit analyses, survey responses, or standardized test scores represent common examples of commensuration.) While commensuration resembles the concrete comparisons executed in the human brain, commensurative judgments are jointly negotiated by agents in specific social spaces. Such negotiations establish a collectively accessible value matrix, one that objectifies and institutionalizes difference and ultimately shapes social thought and social action. In Espeland's words: "We use commensuration to enact revered principles and cultivate desired characteristics. . . . We perform commensuration to help to certify our objectivity and neutrality and to establish our authority" (p. 65). Thus in practicing commensuration, discrimination and classification become a sociocultural affair.

In Chapter 5, author Nicole Isaacson brings similar issues to bear as she situates metaphoric thinking in a sociocultural milieu. Specifically, Isaacson tracks the conceptual metaphors that drive the discourse surrounding the nature of the human fetus. In analyzing both medical and popular writings produced during the last two decades, she documents a growing tendency toward equating the fetus—a liminal, abstract entity—with the more concrete image of the premature infant Isaacson's research probes both the cultural conditions associated with this conceptual match and the social and political consequences that emerge from the match. In so doing, she illustrates the ways in which the institutionalization of a metaphor can change the perception of seemingly "natural" categories such as human nature and the essence of life.

Chapter 6 continues the focus on comparative strategies. But this entry represents a synthesis of sorts. Here, author Harrison White brings the processes of concrete comparison, signaling, and denial (processes discussed in Section I) to the economic marketplace. White contends that such cognitive processes form "the drive-train of any social vehicle" (see White, pp. 101), and he highlights signaling, denial, and comparison as institutionalized dimensions of production markets. In support of these claims, White charts the evolution of production markets as signaling mechanisms. He analyzes market action in terms of concrete comparisons and the rivalry profiles that such comparisons generate. Finally, he considers economic theorists' denial of markets in favor of optimal cost schedules, and he notes the ways in which this denial has impeded scholarly understanding of economic structures.

Endnotes

1. Douglas Vickers writes extensively on such discrimination and classification experiments. See Vickers (1979, 1980, 1985).
2. Evans (1968) is credited with the earliest models of analogical reasoning.

3. Raymond W. Gibbs (1994) also writes extensively on metaphoric thinking.
4. See, for example, Glucksberg and Keysar (1990); Keysar (1990).
5. To explore such studies, see Hiller (1933) and Lewis (1948).

References

Evans, T. 1968. "A Program for the Solution of a Class of Geometric Analogy Intelligence Test Questions." Pp. 271–353 in *Semantic Information Processing*, edited by M. Minsky. Cambridge, MA: MIT Press.

Gentner, D. 1989. "The Mechanics of Analogy Learning." Pp. 199–241 in *Similarity and Analogical Reasoning*, edited by S. Vosniadou and A. Ortony. Cambridge, England: Cambridge University Press.

Gibbs, R. W. Jr. 1994. *The Poetics of Mind: Figurative Thought, Language, and Understanding.* Cambridge, England: Cambridge University Press.

Glucksberg, S. and B. Keysar. 1990. "Understanding Metaphoric Comparisons: Beyond Similarity." *Psychological Review* 97(1):3–18.

Hiller, E. T. 1933. *Principles of Sociology.* New York: Harper and Row.

Hofstadter, D. 1995. *Fluid Concepts and Creative Analogies: Computer Models of the Fundamental Mechanisms of Thought.* New York: Basic Books.

Holyoak, K. J. and P. Thagard. 1995. *Mental Leaps: Analogy in Creative Thought.* Cambridge, MA: MIT Press.

Keysar, B. 1990. "On the Functional Equivalence of Literal and Metaphoric Interpretation in Discourse." *Journal of Memory and Language* 28:375–85.

Lakoff, G. 1995. "The Neurocognitive Self: Conceptual System Research in the Twenty-first Century and the Rethinking of What a Person Is." Pp. 221–43 in *The Science of the Mind: 2001 and Beyond*, edited by R. L. Solso and D. W. Massaro. New York: Oxford University Press.

———. 1987. *Women, Fire, and Other Dangerous Things.* Chicago, IL: University of Chicago Press.

Lewis, M. M. 1948. *Language in Society.* New York: Social Science Research Council.

Piaget, J. 1952. *The Origins of Intelligence in Children.* New York: International University Press.

———. 1954. *The Construction of Reality in the Child.* New York: Basic Books.

Thagard, P. 1998. *Mind: Introduction to Cognitive Science.* Cambridge, MA: MIT Press.

Vickers, D. 1979. *Decision Process in Visual Perception.* London: Academic Press.

———. 1980. "Discrimination." Pp. 25–72 in *Reaction Times*, edited by A. T. Welford. London: Academic Press.

———. 1985. "Antagonistic Influences on Performance Change in Detection and Discrimination Tasks." Pp. 79–115 in *Cognition, Information Processing and Motivation: Proceedings of the XXIII International Congress of Psychology*, vol. 3, edited by G. d'Ydewalle. Amsterdam: North-Holland.

CHAPTER 4

Commensuration and Cognition

Wendy Nelson Espeland

The sociology of culture appears poised to take a cognitive turn.[1] Witness the breadth of topics represented in this volume and the vitality of the exchange that was its impetus. Of course, understanding the social dimensions of classifications is nothing new in sociology. Our founding fathers, in their efforts to carve out a distinctive intellectual niche for sociology, were deeply concerned with the social dimensions of the categories we use to think, represent ourselves to one another, and express our desires. Emile Durkheim ([1912] 1995), Georg Simmel (1971; [1900] 1982), and George Herbert Mead (1934) were especially invested in understanding our dazzling capacity to create and order the social categories that we use to make our worlds and ourselves distinctive. While an abiding concern with understanding classification characterizes some of sociology's best cultural analyses, often our understanding of cultural boundaries has emphasized their normative dimensions at the expense of their cognitive ones.[2] But important advances in our efforts to theorize culture have rekindled interest in cognition on two fronts: a concern with agency and, paradoxically, its obverse, a concern with understanding power that is not directly linked to agents' intentional acts.

The discrediting of grand theory that makes sweeping assumptions about the homogenizing effects of culture has prompted us to rethink how we conceive of agency and the limits that culture imposes on it. How do we reconcile people's varied responses to culture that is embraced or resisted, restrictive or manipulated, a venue for innovation or mindless reproduction? No longer convinced by the vague, if potent, link that Talcott Parsons made between abstract values and concrete action, attention has shifted to accounting for variation and innovation in the effects of culture, in explaining how people on the ground adopt and manipulate culture, and in efforts to pin down the mechanisms by which people construct, inherit, or diffuse cultural categories. Ann Swidler (1986) has provided one influential approach for understanding our capacities as cultural agents by emphasizing how differently culture shapes not goals but strategies of actions in "settled" and "unsettled" times.

Efforts to understand power that is not the object of intentional calculations, what might be called the flip side of agency, has also prodded scholars to investigate cognition more closely. Antonio Gramsci (1971) and Michel Foucault (1980) offered two pivotal approaches for reconceptualizing power. In Gramsci's conception of hegemony, consciousness became crucial in distinguishing silent, tacit power from noisy, self-interested power. Foucault disrupts easy distinctions between power and knowledge; for him, the power that saturates discourse and disciplines bodies cannot be reduced to culpability or self-interest. Like Gramsci, Foucault's understanding of power requires us to account for what we do not notice, for the effect of discipline that is not experienced as such, for routines that seem natural. Both Gramsci and Foucault, in showing how power inserts and reproduces itself apart from intentional agents, force us to attend more precisely to the structure of attention, to how routines, discipline, and discourse can mute our imagination and encourage our submission.

So, despite the different theoretical dispositions of those investigating cultural agency and discursive power, classification and consciousness, core processes of cognition have become central to both projects. Both require knowledge of how classification becomes institutionalized and how this shapes attention in ways which, to use Paul DiMaggio's (1997) terms, make some actions and interpretations automatic, while others are deliberative. This distinction is crucial for understanding the effects of action. Things we do out of habit can have consequences different from actions that require conscious reflection. Habitual behavior requires no justification and can offer the stability and comforting reassurance of familiarity.

But both innovation and struggle can emerge from action that, once automatic, has become the object of scrutiny and speculation. To be challenged, power must first be noticed. To innovate, we must imagine possibilities that do not yet exist, and this is impossible when our actions no longer seem to flow directly from our intentions. A more nuanced appreciation of consciousness and classification is crucial for understanding the dynamics of power and innovation. It is especially important for sociologists to understand the cultural work that is involved in the movement between the automatic and the deliberative—with how the one becomes the other.

In this article, I investigate classification and its capacity to structure attention in a particular and somewhat peculiar realm: commensuration.[3] Commensuration involves using numbers to create relations between things. Commensuration transforms qualitative distinctions into quantitative distinctions, where difference is precisely expressed as magnitude according to some shared metric. Difference expressed in this way is a matter of less or more, not of kind. Common examples of commensuration include prices, survey responses, cost-benefit analyses, utility, gross national products (GNPs), and standardized test scores. Whether its target is commodities, attitudes, public policy, preferences, economies, or ability, commensuration is simultaneously a strategy of integration and distinction: it establishes a common relationship among objects. In doing so, it erases the distinctiveness of the things it encompasses. The quantitative relationships produced by commensuration make possible new forms of distinction as it obliterates old ones.

The capacity to make precise comparisons is so appealing to so many that commensuration and its products have acquired vast, powerful constituencies. The Scholastic Assessment Test (SAT), for example, establishes an exact relationship among the over two million high school students who took it this year. Students' "aptitude" is defined in relation to all other test-takers, as what percent of other test-takers scored higher or lower than they.[4] The test score that established their "aptitude" is the culmination of elaborate processes of commensuration that begin with standardized questions and answers that are quantified, weighted, and aggregated. No simple sum of correct answers, test scores incorporate the results of statistical analysis that assigns higher values to questions that fewer students answer correctly and lower values to questions that many students get right. Ability, established in this way, neglects all distinctiveness among students apart from whether and which questions they answer correctly in relation to everyone else. Differences in background, opportunities, and health are all subsumed into the composite scores that yield many new kinds of distinctions: how well this year's test-takers performed in comparison to previous years, how many people received perfect scores, which high schools produced the highest and lowest scores, what percentage of test-takers missed any given question, how much scores improved for those who took the test multiple times, how highly correlated scores were in different parts of the test. As any middle-class kid knows, the distinctions created by the SAT matter enormously.

Commensuration is important for understanding cognition because of its deep and pervasive influence in structuring so much of social life. It shapes what we notice and how we make things meaningful because it is a core strategy for creating new classifications. We use commensuration to enact revered principles and cultivate desired characteristics. We practice democracy through voting and polls. We administer standardized tests to establish merit, assure competence, and hold educators accountable to taxpayers and parents. We use share prices and price-earnings ratios to value firms and evaluate management. We create cost-benefit ratios to assess the efficiency of everything from air bags to laws. We make rankings to educate consumers about the cities in which they live, the colleges their children attend, the wines they drink, the movies they watch, the toasters they use, and the peanut butter they spread on their toast. We conduct risk assessments to reassure ourselves about uncertain futures. We perform commensuration to help to certify our objectivity and neutrality, establish our authority, express our values, simplify our decisions, and make us rational. Commensuration makes a complicated world seem easier to control. It bolsters our courage to act.

As a mode of classifying, commensuration is especially compelling for its cultural effects because of its relation with other modes of classifying. Commensuration is designed to transgress other social boundaries, other means of making and sustaining distinctions. As an expression of value, commensuration is fundamentally relative (Espeland and Stevens 1998:317). The meanings of commensurate objects depend on their comparisons with each other. When we use commensuration to help us decide things, value is based on the trade-offs we make between different elements of the decision. These trade-offs are structured as how much of one thing is needed to compensate for something else. For example, in deciding how much water to run down a river, we establish the value of the ecological benefits of the extra river water in relation to the value of cheap electricity or additional irrigated farmland that is foregone. Complicated decisions like this involve many layers of commensuration. Ecological benefits might involve the estimates of how much the eagle or fish population will increase, how many more acres of shrubs the new water will support, and the quality of the river water. Water quality alone has many dimensions that are made commensurate according to different scales: pH, water temperature, the concentration of saline or other particulates. These are just a few of the relevant dimensions. In order to trade off water quality against other ecological factors, all these different metrics have to be converted to a single scale. Weights that reflect someone's judgment about how important this impact is in relation to all others are then attached to each potential impact. All this work is required in order to attach a number to just one category of impacts in a decision that might involve hundreds of different kinds of impacts.

Commensuration entails the systematic organizing and discarding of information that in complicated decisions can be overwhelming. Commensuration constructs relevance: it is fundamentally a strategy for structuring attention that depends on systematic ways of collecting, organizing, and eliminating information. Because it reduces complexity, absorbs uncertainty, makes it easy to compare things or scenarios, and expresses differences as intervals, commensuration facilitates the creation and expression of hierarchy. Ranking is easy when one metric subsumes all value. Since commensuration eliminates so much information about its objects and because it represents them in such an abstract way, their link to practical experience and the people who value them is remote. The more people rely on commensuration to express the value of things, the less relevant will be local knowledge, practical experience, and empathy as legitimate bases for judgment. People who know the most about something, who understand its particularity and history, are often less able to make strong claims about it after their experience has been reduced to numbers. When commensurative practices for valuing are deeply institutionalized, as cost-benefit analyses are in most public policy arenas, they change the way people participate in politics. Discrediting or defending the numbers becomes crucial, and this changes who has the authority to speak. Creating commensurative routines is often work conducted by credentialed professionals. To appreciate the significance of commensuration, it is important to understand when we notice it, when we do not, how much work it requires, and by which processes we come to take it and its effects for granted.

Attention to Commensuration

As Eviatar Zerubavel teaches us, distinction is crucial for perception: "In order to discern any 'thing,' we must distinguish that we attend from that which we ignore" (1991:1). Commensuration directs attention in very specific ways. It can make the most incongruous objects alike. It can also make the most striking differences irrelevant. It creates new categories and new objects that become fundamental for the way we understand the world. Commensuration can also make whole classes of things irrelevant in ways that for practical purposes cause them to disappear. Since commensuration is so prevalent and so deeply institutionalized, we often barely notice it. When we glance at our watches, check the calendar, or compare prices, commensuration seems natural. It shapes our expectations, sometimes in ambiguous ways. Many assume that "every man has his price" and that "time is money"; we impatiently await the "bottom line" in presentations; we celebrate, as shoppers, the "bargains" we discover; we distinguish "normal" behavior from that which is atypical or pathological.[5]

We often make these judgments without thinking about the commensuration that they imply. The failure to commensurate is often more notable than its practice. When I was a consultant, a project manager requested a summary of the core social impacts associated with the plans we were evaluating. After I produced for him a cryptic paragraph, he asked me: "What are all these words doing here?" For this engineer, summarizing and comparing implied quantifying. Words could not accomplish the precision and clarity that he expected. One condition that influences how much we notice commensuration is how we classify the objects prior to our efforts to commensurate them.

HOW PRIOR CLASSIFICATION SHAPES ATTENTION TO COMMENSURATION

When commensuration is used to create relations between objects that already seem alike, we are less likely to notice it than when it creates relations among things that seem different (Espeland and Stevens 1998:316–17). Counting or measuring something seems distinct from commensuration when we take for granted the unity of the objects we are counting or the traits we are measuring. When the "alikeness" of the counted objects appears to us as a property of the object or trait we are measuring rather than something created by the numbers we impose, we do not recognize commensuration as such. The census as a scheme for counting people seems appropriate because our conception of "citizen" unifies the often very different people who comprise a nation's population. Without the coherence implied by citizenship, counting people with different racial or ethnic backgrounds, who speak different languages, practice different religions, or sustain different standards of living, seems more like artifice than enumeration (Porter 1986:41–42).

Intelligence offers another example of how prior conceptions shape our response to commensuration. Intelligence tests seem like a measure of intelligence rather than the commensuration of different characteristics because of how we conceive of intelligence: as a property of individuals, as a general characteristic that intelligent people share but one that gets expressed many ways, as something that can be broken down into discreet parts or indicators, as something that is stable over time and context. If we did not generally accept these characteristics of intelligence, if, for example, we believed that intelligence was an emergent property of groups, if it was highly contextual or compartmentalized, if it varied depending on someone's disposition that day, then intelligence tests would seem less like measurement and more like the commensuration of disparate indicators.

Conversely, if there is no prior category that makes the objects of commensuration seem alike, the common relationships that commensuration imposes on things seems arbitrary or artificial. In a decision about whether or not to tear down an old dam, the fate of the salmon that faced extinction and the economy of the community that bordered the lake the dam created were expressed in relation to one another as "costs" conveyed by prices. Commensurating salmon and a lakeside community seems jarring to us first because it transgresses the enduring boundary that we make between nature and society; but we also notice this commensuration because, aside from their significance to this particular decision, there is no overarching category that unifies the salmon and the residents. Their relationship to one another emerges only from their status as "decision factors" that are specific to this decision.

What gets defined as a decision factor may be influenced by organizational routines, by politics, by law, or by expertise that is unevenly distributed among potential participants. For the Army Corps of Engineers, the federal agency making this decision, the status of salmon as a legitimate decision factor is a relatively recent innovation. Although environmental impacts are now routine parts of policy analyses, their becoming so was a complex, conflictual process. But even when procedures such as cost-benefit analyses or other schemes that involve making trade-offs among decision factors become standard within the bureaucracies, since salmon and towns do not cohere except as decision factors for most people, routine procedures are not enough to make their commensuration seem natural. So when we attach prices to their fate, it seems that we are creating something new rather than simply measuring something.

Commensuration Creates New Things and New Relations among Things

The distinction between understanding quantification as counting or measuring and as creating relations among disparate things is important for appreciating the effects of commensuration. If we understand commensuration as measuring something "out there," we fail to grasp its constitutive power. The legitimacy of commensuration often hinges on the disavowal that something new is being created. I have just argued that we are more likely to notice commensuration when it creates new relations among things that are not already defined as somehow alike. But sometimes commensuration goes beyond creating new relations between existing things and instead creates new objects or new subjects. Such entities may seem remote and unreal at first, but if they acquire broad constituencies who use and defend them, if we insert them into our institutions and they become routine ways of interpreting the world, they become increasingly powerful, durable, and tangible.

Last year, a colleague and I paid $227 dollars for the right to pollute by releasing one ton of sulfur dioxide, one of the main components of acid rain, into our atmosphere (Levin and Espeland, 2000). Ours was one of 150,000 pollution permits that were auctioned off. We can now resell this futures option, exercise it sometime in the next seven years by emitting this amount of sulfur dioxide, or retire it. This new market-based approach to regulation represents a radical change in the way we regulate the environment. Whereas formerly, polluters were required to meet specific standards imposed on their plants, now they can decide that it is cheaper to buy pollution permits than to install scrubbers.

These new futures options are a triumph of commensuration that is both technical and cognitive. In order to create them, it was necessary to transform air pollution into a commodity, which in turn required that we conceive of it as discreet, standardized, fungible thing. That depended on imposing elaborate standardized techniques for continuously measuring emissions, devising bookkeeping procedures for certifying that the annual balance of emissions is offset by the equivalent balance of allowances, and creating a stable, trustworthy system for attaching and monitoring the prices of these new commodities. The liquidity of any commodity depends on convincing buyers, market makers, and sellers that equivalent commodities really are the same (Carruthers and Stinchcombe 1999). In this case, buyers (and regulators) must believe that a ton of pollutants emitted this year in Los Angeles is somehow equivalent to a ton of the same pollutants emitted seven years hence in New Jersey. This equivalency requires that we conceive of pollution as some proportion of an aggregate amount of pollution that is stable over time and distance. It depends on ignoring such distinguishing traits as the pollution producer, where and when it was emitted, how it interacts with other substances, and who will suffer from its effects.

Futures options are new objects that are created by a vast array of coordinated commensurative practices.[6] The constituencies for these objects include those who literally invest in them—the utilities that buy them, the brokerage firms that sell them, the environmentalists who retire them—and a broad array of regulators, policy entrepreneurs, and academic proponents. As the use of these options spreads to new substances and new arenas, as is quickly happening on a global scale, more people will find it natural to conceive of the future in terms of variations among discrete bundles of commensurate assets and to bet on the direction in which these variations move. In addition to such long-established futures options in wheat, pork bellies, soybeans, and butter it is now possible to buy futures options in virtually any currency, including the euro, weird hybrids that combine the currencies of one location with interest rates in another, the price of water, home mortgages, and even the weather (as measured by average monthly temperatures) of most major U.S. cities.

Although all commodities must be made commensurate, not all of the objects that commensuration facilitates are commodities. Our conceptions of some of our most fundamental social units are themselves the product of commensuration. Marc Ventresca (1995) argues that the modern census has played a crucial role in the development of the "nation-state" as meaningful entity: "modern states are statistical states," and the global spread of standardized methods for generating these statistics has helped turn traditional subjects into individual citizens and disparate peoples into comparable political entities (Ventresca and Yin, 1997).

Before the nineteenth century, people were counted differently from the way they are now. Those who did the counting mainly were interested in assessing taxes, extracting labor or resources, or conscription. Counts were partial rather than exhaustive, they focused on particular segments of a population—households, potential soldiers, or colonists—and they were conducted by agents without much specialized expertise in counting. Many counts were conducted by governing authorities for political reasons, but others were conducted for commercial or religious reasons. Those who conducted the census typically did so secretly and carefully guarded the information (Porter 1986:25). How these counts were conducted varied too; counts were often crude estimates at best or sheer fabrication at worst.

In stark contrast to these earlier "numberings of people," the modern census is systematically conducted at regular intervals by centralized governing authorities; they are full enumerations, including all those within carefully specified national territories; their scope is far broader than in earlier periods; they are conducted by experts; and above all, they are public.[7] During the 1860s, nations rushed to publish the statistical data that defined their populations, proudly displaying their data in graphs and charts at international exhibitions and in guidebooks for tourists. The concept of "population" as an exact number of people was itself largely a nineteenth-century idea, one that emerged from the "avalanche of printed numbers" generated after 1820 and the statistical regularities that could be derived from these. Prior to this period, the population of a country was "not yet a measurable quantity," for there were not yet the institutions necessary to make it one (Hacking 1990:18). For Ventresca, the modern census, in establishing the nation as a measurable quantity with distinctive collective characteristics, has transformed the way we conceive of political entities and their relations to one another. The census makes vivid and material populations as a meaningful characteristic and the nation-state as the object that these describe.

The nation-state is one example of how commensuration facilitates reification, the turning of relations and actions into things. Public opinion is another important example of this. It is well known among pollsters that their efforts to measure opinions might elicit, from respondents who wish to be helpful or look thoughtful, opinions they might not have previously held. Just as opinions can be generated by the act of measuring then, on a broader scale, "public opinion" as the aggregate will or beliefs of individual people is the product of opinion polling. How we have conceived of the public has changed historically (Herbst 1993:43–68). Modern conceptions of public opinion depend on a set of quantitative techniques for aggregating public sentiment. The first of these, general elections and straw polls, emerged in the late eighteenth and early nineteenth centuries. Beginning in the late 1920s, ratings for political radio programs and so-called "town hall meetings," despite their doubtful accuracy, were also taken as evidence of "public opinion."[8] Later, television ratings were used as evidence of public opinion. Now, of course, standardized sample surveys are widely used in opinion polling as the predominant mode of conveying and constituting public opinion, where ". . . through the magic of numbers and abstractions, poll responses seem a more authoritative reflection of what people are thinking . . . than an ordinary conversation with them would be" (Lohmann 1998:3). For Susan Herbst (1993:67) ". . . assumptions about the nature of public opinion evolved with the technology itself."

Another category of "objects" that commensuration helps to create is new types of subjects, a process that Ian Hacking (1990:6) calls "making up people." Enumeration requires categorization, he argues, and defining new categories of people can have powerful effects on how we "conceive of others and think of our own possibilities and potentialities." The average consumer, the average voter, the gifted child, the underachiever, the suboptimal worker, are all ways of understanding people that depend on relations that numbers create. Such classifications matter enormously for how we wield power, distribute resources, or understand ourselves in relation to others.

Commensuration and Invisibility

The capacity of commensuration to make some intangible things seem durable and real is a powerful effect that can change relations of authority. But so, too, is its capacity to obscure or erase existing objects or relations. In some cases, the link between what is "real" and what can be quantified is so close that failing to attach numbers to something amounts to a denial of that reality. For the people of Joslin, Illinois, a tiny town on the Rock River in western Illinois, the failure to commensurate stinks—literally. For over 30 years, residents have endured the terrible odors emanating from the giant meat-processing plant nearby. Although the specific source of odors is hard to pin down, the plant's open lagoons where wastewater is treated, its giant cattle pens, and the chemicals used in rendering are likely culprits. Depending on the weather, the volume of production, and just what part of an animal is being turned into what sort of commodity, the smell can be sickening and impossible to escape. Residents complain of burning eyes and noses, nausea, and sleeplessness they attribute to the odors. Jan Marsden says she "broke every window in her house closing windows in the middle of the night because the odors were so bad—it would wake you from a sound sleep" (Kendall and Cole 2000). Some have moved out of nice houses and away from neighbors they loved to escape the smell. They complain that the odor has made it hard to sell their property and that its value has declined.

The residents of Joslin and nearby communities have not suffered in silence. Soon after the plant was built in the 1960s, they began complaining about the smell. In the early 1970s they began filing lawsuits. Unlike some states, Illinois law defines odor as a form of air pollution. Residents' suits claimed that current owner of the plant, IBP, Inc., the world's largest producer of beef and pork and related products, was violating the state's anti–air pollution laws. Although the company has installed scrubbers and other technology designed to reduce the odor, it persists. Despite its remediation efforts, the suits it has quietly settled, and the fines it has already paid, IBP denies that it is breaking the law. Its lawyers argue that since the perception of smells is "subjective," so too are the charges being brought against them. Shelia Hagen, the company's general counsel, counters with: "Tell me what the standard is under Illinois state law and I will tell you if we are in violating them." Smells are hard to regulate because they are hard to measure. As James Gallaugher, the inspector for Illinois Environmental Protection Agency, puts it: "Our biggest problem in air pollution is odor. We don't have an odor meter. All we have is the nose on the end of the face." But that nose, so far, has not triumphed in court. Incommensurate odors, it turns out, are suspect odors. IBP continues to emit the smells that, while powerful enough to force residents to flee, lack the legal and ontological certitude that numbers confer.

Since odor *is* invisible to us, the link between commensuration and visibility may seem easier to establish with vapors than with other, more durable things. Yet the criteria of relevance that commensuration imposes can cause even the most tangible objects to disappear[9]—like the million people each summer who jump in an inner tube and float down the Salt River in central Arizona. When an economist, using techniques of contingent valuation, failed to derive a robust price for tubing down the Salt River, a popular form of recreation that a proposed dam would eliminate, the value of this recreation disappeared from the investigation of the dam's impact.

The economist in question was an experienced analyst with the Bureau of Reclamation, a dam-building agency in the Department of the Interior. As someone who was committed to an evenhanded analysis of both the costs and benefits associated with dam building, he devoted impressive energy and resources to trying to synthesize a demand curve for this popular, inexpensive, and largely unregulated recreation.

Graduate students surveyed tubers about their willingness to pay for this free recreation. They estimated how much people spent on the gas they used to reach the river, the inner tubes on which they floated and the sunscreen and beer they brought with them. But none of this panned out, since the attitudes tubers expressed in the surveys did not mesh with their behavior; the prices derived from this data flunked all sensitivity tests in what this frustrated economist described as a "failure of methodology." As a result, the "costs" associated with losing this type of recreation were neglected in the analysis of the dam. In effect, the millions of tubers affected by this decision disappeared without a trace.

There are clear patterns in failures to commensurate. Things like odor that are hard to measure often disappear in contexts where commensuration is taken for granted. When cost-benefit analyses are institutionalized as the most legitimate way of expressing value, as is true in many bureaucracies, things which are hard to assimilate to this form are often ignored. Things without market prices are more likely to disappear from analyses than are things with prices that are readily available or easy to derive. Part of the appeal of tubing was that it was a form of leisure that took place mainly outside of markets. We may value something precisely because it is not a commodity or because it is organized informally. Large-scale development plans often force people from subsistence economies into market economies. Attaching a price to something because it has no price strains the logic of cost-benefit analysis; it is a representation of value that contradicts the value it is designed to express.

Another common pattern in the failure to commensurate, and hence the "visibility" of things, is that commensurative routines often reflect the incentives of the organizations or people who do the commensurating. In many resource development agencies, standardized methods for establishing the often very "indirect" benefits of projects were devised long before such methods were established for deriving their costs.[10] This was the institutional bias that the economist who tackled tubing was trying to mitigate. Such institutional biases are typically prodevelopment, prompting some environmentalists to create techniques for commensurating things outside of markets. Establishing market values for nature remains controversial among environmentalists, because some believe that it reinforces an instrumental mode of valuing nature that they believe is fundamentally flawed.

We call things that are hard to measure "intangibles." How visible or tangible something is, especially in organizations, may be more a function of commensuration, and our ability to attach credible numbers to it, than of the properties of the object itself. Even though a company's "goodwill" is quite intangible in the sense that it is conveyed through indirect characteristics such as reputation or loyalty, there are well-established accounting techniques for assessing goodwill that make it "tangible" to shareholders. And even though the Salt River is packed with tubers every warm weekend, failing to establish a price for tubing made them organizationally and politically "intangible." Understanding how commensuration directs attention by understanding how it interacts with prior classifications, how it creates new objects and new categories of objects, and how it makes some things and some people invisible, is crucial for understanding its power and the varied ways it structures our lives. The significance of commensuration for structuring the way we apprehend the world is also revealed in how much and what kind of work is required in order to do it.

Commensurative Work

All commensuration takes work. How much work depends on just what is being commensurated, the scope of the commensurative task, people's investments in commensuration, and whether or not commensuration is resisted. As the tubing example illustrates, it often takes more work to commensurate things without market values. But as any accountant knows, when the stakes are high—when the products of commensuration are fateful to many and closely scrutinized—commensurating the value of things, even things with prices, can be an arduous task that requires enormous discipline, expertise, and often regulation. Making things commensurate often involves elaborate coordination, discipline, technical expertise, the capacity to invest in long-term projects, and money. That is one reason why commensuration flourishes in bureaucracies. Another reason is that since commensuration strips away particularizing characteristics, it is a powerful means for accomplishing the impersonality that characterizes bureaucracies.

How much work commensuration requires depends in a general sense on the state of the world. Since the meaning of commensuration hinges on prior classification, commensuration can fail when our commensurative ambitions outstrip our categories. Theodore Porter (1995:35–37) describes the "class of cultures" that resulted between French statisticians and local notables in their efforts to conduct a census in 1800. The men who ran the "Bureau de Statistique" believed that France could become more unified and its citizenry more knowledgeable if systematic information about each of its regions could be collected and disseminated widely. To this end, they sent out long questionnaires to prefects of each *département* requesting quantitative information about the population and the local economy; they requested data on occupations, property, wealth, patterns of land use, and volume of various products. The overwhelmed prefects, lacking the bureaucracy necessary to produce such numbers, turned to knowledgeable elite volunteers to help assemble this information. The bureau received from them not the completed questionnaires they requested, but a series of monographs that described in exquisite detail the local customs and people. The elaborate stratification and the complex regional differences that then characterized French society and the deep, particular knowledge of their informants overwhelmed the general categories that the statisticians wished to impose. Porter concludes: "France was not yet capable of being reduced to statistics." Uniform statistics had to wait for the state to become more centralized and the people less diverse. As Porter's work demonstrates, numbers often "remake the world." But for some uses, the world must be "remade" before the numbers can be attached.

SYMBOLIC COMMENSURATION

The motives behind commensuration will also determine how much work it requires. While commensuration is often justified in terms of its technical accomplishments, sometimes it is most desired for its symbolic effects. Consider the long history of double-entry bookkeeping.[11] Max Weber, Werner Sombart, and Joseph Schumpeter all make strong claims about the relationship between double-entry bookkeeping accounting, rationality, and the emergence of capitalism. Sombart (1953:38) goes so far as to suggest that: "The very concept of capital is derived from this way of looking at things; one can say that capital, as a category, did not exist before double-entry book-keeping." Developed by northern Italian merchants sometime during the late thirteenth or early fourteenth century, double-entry bookkeeping is distinguished from earlier forms of accounting because all transactions were entered twice, once as a debit, once as a credit. All three theorists claim that the technical superiority of double-entry bookkeeping explains its close relationship with capitalist development.

Yet for centuries, Italian and English merchants who used the double-entry system did so in such a sloppy and unsystematic way that the clear technical advantages made possible by this technique were not realized. Why did these merchants go to the considerable trouble of learning and using this commensurative technique if they failed to use it in a way that allowed them to exploit its technical advantages? For these merchants, it appears, the symbolic significance of double-entry bookkeeping was for a long time more important than its technical advantages. This accounting technique signaled, in a precise and easily interpretable rhetorical style, to themselves, their partners, and to God, that they were trustworthy and of good character; hence it was more valuable to them for its capacity to legitimate their business transactions than to track them precisely.

When the symbolic significance of commensuration overrides its technical salience, the strict discipline that it can impose may sometimes be avoided. When commensuration is desired for its "ritualistic assurance" (Feldman and March 1981:177–78) or for symbolic value that can be achieved even when it is "decoupled" from practice (Meyer and Rowan 1977), commensuration may be a superficial symbolic exercise. This takes far less work than is required when commensuration and the categories and objects it produces penetrate to the core of an enterprise. But as Porter (1995) has shown, for vulnerable elites, conflict, intense scrutiny, or the introduction of new and powerful audiences such as courts or regulators can force commensurative practice to conform more closely to its symbolic claims. The evolution of the sloppy but devout bookkeeper of the fifteenth century to the meticulous bean counter of the nineteenth century was spurred by developments in capital that enrolled new and broadening constituencies for precise accounting: capital's increasingly far-flung investors, their hired agents, and the emerging nation-states that might be called in to enforce contracts or settle disputes, all became vested in imposing more rigorous, standardized commensurative techniques.

COMMENSURATING INCOMMENSURABLES

How much work and what kind of work required to make things commensurable also depends on whether commensuration is resisted or not. This in turn depends heavily on the classificatory schemes that are in place prior to commensuration and on the nature of our investments in these categories. Although commensuration is pervasive and a powerful device for organizing social worlds, it is sometimes resisted as inappropriate or immoral. Whether it is used to integrate information or aggregate values, commensuration deconstructs preexisting forms and boundaries and creates new ones. As a strategy of integrating different things, it destroys the integrity of the forms it usurps. When the value or meaning of something is intimately connected with its form, commensuration transforms the meaning of that which it is trying to convey.

Things that we believe have intrinsic or absolute value, things about which we refuse to make trade-offs, are antithetical to commensuration. Defining something as incommensurable can be one way that we express some of our most cherished values, so commensuration is often deeply threatening to sacred things. Whether incommensurable things are conceived of as sacred, priceless, unique, or inalienable, whether they encompass land, blood, kin, identity, or rights, defending them can be a potent political strategy. How much effort is required to commensurate what has been defined as incommensurable will vary: the depth of attachment people feel about what is incommensurable, if it is closely tied to people's identities or interests, if commensuration seems threatening, if people mobilize to resist it, and whether the incommensurableness of a category is well established, widely shared, or firmly institutionalized will all affect how arduous the task of commensurating incommensurables will be.

Orme Dam, the same dam that would have eliminated tubing on the Salt River, would have had far graver consequences for the Yavapai, a small Native American tribe.[12] Their Fort McDowell Reservation was situated just below the proposed dam site at the confluence of Arizona's Salt and Verde rivers. The reservoir created by the dam would have inundated most of the reservation, which had been their home since its founding. Before white conquest, the Yavapai had lived for centuries in large sections of central Arizona. During the nineteenth century, they endured repeated massacres, starvation, brutal forced resettlements, and diseases spread by close contact and poor sanitation at the hands of the military and white settlers who wanted their land. Despite untold deaths, they continued to press for their own reservation. Finally, in 1903, Teddy Roosevelt established their reservation on a miniscule portion of what had once been their ancestral land. Within a few years of its creation, the Yavapai were already fending off efforts to remove them from their land. Orme Dam was the latest and most serious threat.

The Yavapai's ties to their land were forged from their long and painful struggle to retain it. The sacrifices of their ancestors made this land sacred to them. They believed that their intimate relationship to this particular land was what made them Yavapai. Appreciating what made it unique was crucial for understanding what made them distinctive. The Orme Dam decision was so threatening because they believed that their survival as a people was at stake: without this land, they could not be Yavapai. In the official investigation of Orme Dam and its alternatives, one group of bureaucrats was committed to including the devastating impact of the dam for the Yavapai. Their strategy for doing so involved using rational decision-making models to integrate and evaluate all the impacts, good and bad, associated with the proposed dam. These models required that the impacts of the various plans be made commensurate with one another, so that the advantages of flood control and water storage associated with the dam would be traded off against its ecological damage and the hardship it would cause the Yavapai community.

But for the Yavapai, the procedures that were being used to assess and represent their hardships were inappropriate. Most believed that it was wrong to value their land as a commodity or in relation to other things. Their identity as Yavapai hinged on their appreciation of the incommensurability of their land. The bureaucrats, in attaching a "fair market price" to their land, in quantifying their suffering in relation to the harm done to others, in "measuring" the degradation of their culture, were imposing techniques that were themselves a repudiation of Yavapai values. These techniques were not simply misrepresenting the effects of the decision for the Yavapai, but the Yavapai themselves.

And so the Yavapai resisted not only the implications of this decision but the terms in which their interests were being expressed. Their political protests reinserted into the public debate those parts of the decision that the bureaucrats' techniques for commensuration excluded or minimized: their long history of conflict over their land, its symbolic significance, the moral implications of this decision. The Yavapai's deeply held belief in the incommensurability of their land and culture, its implication for their identity, and the stakes of this decision were conditions that fostered strong resistance to the commensuration that the bureaucrats imposed. While the Yavapai were unable to control the framework of the decision and could not prevent this commensuration, their resistance was fateful for the outcome. Orme Dam was never built, and the Yavapai are even more articulate and effective defenders of the incommensurability of their culture.

Even if resistance is not overt or directly tied to group identities, the transgressing of what Fiske and Tetlock (1997) have called "taboo categories"—categories that "impose moral limits on fungibility"—requires cultural work. This work often takes the form of blurring the boundaries between the commensurable and incommensurable or trying to legitimate commensuration by linking what seems suspect to something that is culturally secure. Plasma centers offer an illuminating example of how these types of cultural strategies are enlisted to legitimate dubious commensurative practices.

Unlike other blood donation centers, plasma centers are for-profit businesses that pay people for donating their plasma. Plasma is the straw-colored liquid part of blood that transports blood cells throughout the body. Plasma is mostly water but it also contains essential proteins, nutrients, and hormones that are crucial in maintaining the proper balance of fluid in the bloodstream. Most plasma centers are owned by large drug companies that use the plasma they collect to manufacture pharmaceuticals such as the clotting factor that hemophiliacs need and the antibodies used in therapy for rhesus incompatibility. Donating plasma involves removing a unit of someone's blood, using a centrifuge to separate the red blood cells from the plasma, and reinfusing the blood cells back into the donor's arm.[13] Since plasma is replenished quickly compared to blood cells, healthy people can donate it twice a week and can earn between $150 and $200 per month for their plasma if they donate regularly. To make a profit, plasma centers must cultivate a steady stream of healthy donors who can spare a few hours each week. This requires convincing some people who need extra money that it is morally appropriate to sell their blood.

The stigma associated with selling plasma has several sources. We feel ambivalent about selling blood because of its deep symbolic weight. The sacredness of blood, its capacity to sanctify that which is profane, its use to symbolize life, death, or primordial ties and to express sacrifice are enduring and powerful themes. The commodification of blood violates our sense of its sacredness. Selling blood is symbolically tantamount to selling life, which conflicts with our moral sense of life as priceless. The phrase "blood money" conveys the tainted quality of money paid for something that should not have been sold. Selling blood also seems shameful since the Red Cross and other nonprofit blood collection agencies have helped to reinforce the normative standard of donating blood as an exemplary altruistic service, one that reflects a concern for humanity and strengthens social ties among community members (Titmuss 1971). The stigma associated with selling blood is linked, too, with our shame at violating the integrity of our bodies and the desperation that this implies.

Turning blood into a commodity has proven to be a tricky cultural project for this industry. Plasma centers have had to devise strategies for defusing or managing the stigma that is associated with selling one's blood. While this stigma is not shameful to all plasma donors, the most desirable donors—the young, healthy, and stable—often feel it most keenly. Some plasma centers, especially those catering to college populations, go to great lengths to mitigate this stigma. They know that if they downplay the economic incentives too much, they will not reach their target population of people seeking quick cash. If altruism were people's main motive, they would simply give blood in the literal sense. Also, since most people are not even aware that you can make money by selling your plasma, potential donors need to have the economic advantages of plasma donation explained to them.

One general strategy that plasma centers use to manage the stigma associated with selling blood is to try to conflate the economic and altruistic motives for selling one's plasma. They attempt to portray selling plasma as a charitable act, blurring the boundaries between gift and commodity. Advertising campaigns often use phrases like "Earn money while you help others." They consciously mimic the ad campaigns of the Red Cross and other organizations that cater exclusively to those who give blood. A radio ad campaign announced the worldwide shortage of plasma and the desperate need for donors, and only at the end mentioning that donors are compensated for their "time" spent donating. Since paying for "time" is less symbolically loaded than paying for blood, the payments that donors receive are often framed in these terms.

Because college students are especially appealing donors, many plasma centers locate near large universities, advertise in student newspapers, and design elaborate Web sites to attract student donors. These Web sites typically offer testimonials from the recipients of plasma products explaining how these products helped save lives. One provides emotional guidance to would-be donors, explaining: "Donors feel good about themselves knowing they are making a priceless contribution to people in need."[14] They also offer testimonials from plasma donors carefully selected to contradict the negative stereotypes of people who sell their blood. One donor explains that having once needed plasma products himself, he feels morally obliged to reciprocate. Plus, he adds, almost as an afterthought, the extra money is nice. College students, young mothers, people saving for special occasions all tell their stories in ways that help to normalize the process.

While the incommensurability of blood is unlikely to implicate the identities of potential donors as the commensuration of their land threatened Yavapai identity, many donors find the experience unsettling in ways they are not always able to articulate. Some sense they are violating some cultural taboo, and their ambivalence about selling blood is pronounced enough to prompt industries to create careful strategies for easing the transgression of this vague but evocative cultural boundary.[15] The relationship between commodification and commensuration is a complex one. For anxious plasma donors, their disquiet is probably linked more to the selling of blood rather than to the generic act of commensuration that this requires. But there is a close link between commodification and commensuration. All commodities require prices and so must be made commensurate with one another, but not all forms of commensuration take the form of prices. However, as commodification spreads and prices become the increasingly hegemonic symbol of value, other modes of expressing value may be deemed inferior.[16]

Asserting the incommensurability of something, whether it is land, culture, or blood, can itself be a powerful cultural statement about its value and how we ought to treat it.[17] In a provocative essay, Friedland and Alford (1991:232, 248) describe how institutions, as patterns of activity and symbolic systems that transcend particular organizations (e.g., capitalism, democracy, bureaucratic states, families, religion) construct distinctive patterns of action (commodification, popular participation, rationalization, community, obligation) and modes of valuing (prices, votes, rules, emotions, moral principles). Since people and organizations participate in multiple institutions, they have at their disposal multiple, inconsistent, and sometimes contradictory "institutional logics"; the space or tensions that may arise between incompatible institutional logics can be exploited in ways that give rise to struggle, elaboration, or innovation in the way we act, think, represent, and value, which can sometimes "transform the institutional relations of society. . . ."

Friedland's and Alford's analysis of institutional logic helps us understand both when claims about incommensurables are made and why these claims may generate the elaboration of both culture and conflict. For plasma centers, the trouble begins when commodification as a pattern of action and prices as a mode of valuing are imposed on blood, something that has traditionally valued according to a competing institutional logic where blood is a gift and its donation is an altruistic act. This has prompted corporate efforts to try culturally to reconstruct, or at least blur, the distinction between gifts and commodities, between value that is grounded in moral obligation and value that is expressed by money, between what is priceless and what is priced precisely. The Yavapai's reactions were, of course, more pronounced; they explicitly rejected the mode of valuing that the state was trying to impose on them, and incorporated this rejection into their resistance. Claims about incommensurables are more likely to emerge when commensuration threatens a valued identity or when institutional logics about how to value conflict are unclear (Espeland and Stevens 1998:332).

Commensuration and Institutionalization

How we come to appreciate and defend incommensurable categories is useful, both for how it helps illuminate the role that institutional logic plays in defining institutional boundaries, and for how it illustrates how confrontations between institutional logics create possibilities for institutional change or contestation. Yet one of the most impressive features of commensuration is the way it often seems to transverse institutional domains readily, the way it can be easily adapted and exploited by differing institutional logics.

In our initial foray into real estate markets, my husband and I were somewhat taken aback when, before we looked at our first house, our realtor handed us the summary test scores of all the schools in the neighborhoods in which we would be looking at houses. We first thought this was her effort to appease academics' well-known obsession with their children's education, but we later realized that knowing and disseminating test results was a routine part of her job. It's not surprising that potential home owners care about the quality of the schools in the neighborhoods they might be joining. But the direct relationship between test scores and real estate markets is an interesting example of how commensuration can directly shape action across a broad range of institutional spheres. A cursory history of the SAT helps illustrate how commensuration becomes institutionalized, why it is a technology that is so easily exported across so many kinds of boundaries, and why its capacity to transform existing institutions is so great.

THE SAT AND SUCCESS IN AMERICA[18]

James Bryant Conant was a man with big ideas and the clout to enact them. A brilliant chemist of humble origins, he became deeply involved in both the development of the atom bomb and the reconstruction of Europe after World War II. But one of his most enduring contributions was his pivotal but lesser-known role as a prime architect in the reconstruction of the American education system. Conant became convinced that America in the early twentieth century was undergoing a deep and destructive transformation from an open, democratic society to one controlled by a hereditary aristocracy. As president of Harvard at a time when it was filled with the mainly unintellectual sons of wealthy families who, like their fathers, had graduated from New England's boarding schools, Conant witnessed firsthand how social background affected opportunity. He was determined to change Harvard by enrolling more boys like him, talented students for whom college was not a finishing school but a path for mobility, and to select them from across the nation. One of his first acts as president in 1933 was to establish a small national scholarship program for promising scholars of modest means. The question was how to pick these exceptional boys?

Conant charged George Chauncey, assistant dean at Harvard, with finding a way to distribute these new scholarships. Chauncey was a passionate devotee and promoter of the relatively new technology of standardized testing. He was convinced that uniform tests could be developed to create a rational, fair, and affordable means of sorting people—lots of people. While others might argue about the various roles that testing should play in education—as a tool for identifying the intellectual elites who should run things, for rationalizing education, imposing tough standards, or curbing the capricious power of teachers—George Chauncey kept his eye on the instrument. He was content to let others debate its implications. Not wishing to limit the scope of this technology to a few scholarships at Harvard, Chauncey imagined testing as providing objective guidance for Americans seeking their rightful places in society.

The evolution of testing from an unfamiliar technology developed by a few zealous psychologists to a vast regime anchored by the mammoth Educational Testing Service with its nearly-monopolistic powers to determine American's access to higher education is surely one of the more dramatic examples of successful and rapid institutionalization in recent memory. In Nicholas Lemann's (1999a) intriguing account, standardized testing went from a device for doling out a few scholarships at Harvard to a deeply entrenched system for calibrating precisely one's place in a national system of rewards and opportunities. In so doing, it became the object of our "national obsession." In the process of its own institutionalization, testing facilitated sweeping changes in American education. In the first half of the twentieth century, few went to college, and college was thought to be largely unrelated to economic success. Admissions in elite schools depended on social background and one's ability to pay tuition. Once admitted, academics mattered less than polish, and people generally attended college near their homes. Within fifty years, higher education had expanded enormously (60 percent of high school graduates now go to college) and it became a primary vehicle for screening elites and assuring economic success; admissions were now characterized by intensively and uniformly scrutinizing a national pool of applicants for "merit."

While the speed and scale of testing's entrenchment is remarkable, its development follows some familiar institutional patterns. The first of these involves institutional innovation that entails exploiting a newly available technology. As James March (1994:34) has argued, young technologies provide rich environments for innovation, where searches stimulated by past success foster further success. Change accumulates as technology designed in one field for one purpose is imported to other fields (often in fragmented, bumpy ways) by different groups of actors who use it for different purposes. This process of innovation and change is similar to that analyzed by Clemens (1997) and Westney (1987) in late nineteenth-century America and Japan, respectively, to explain how organizational models and practices that developed in one context can lead to broad institutional changes when they are selectively appropriated in other contexts. The role that Conant and Chauncey played is also consistent with other arenas in which entrepreneurial brokers fluent in different institutional fields helped diffuse new practices (DiMaggio 1982).

When George Chauncey began investigating how best to measure the merit of potential scholars, he had several strategies from which to choose. The already existing College Boards were long essay exams administered by a consortium of leading northeastern universities. The exams were not widely available, lasted several days, and were tediously graded by professional readers. Furthermore, since they were devised less to screen applicants than to force prep schools to standardize their curriculum, anyone who had not gone to prep school would flunk them. What Chauncey needed was a uniform test that would measure individual achievement across a wide variety of local schools. His prototype came from the army, the only institution to have administered mental tests on a large scale. During World War I, the army used standardized intelligence tests to determine quickly who should be selected to be officers. These tests, although developed for completely different reasons and poorly administered under extreme conditions, were variations on earlier intelligence tests and could be given cheaply and quickly to huge numbers of dispersed people.[19] To select the first lucky scholarship recipients who would help diversify Harvard, Chauncey chose one variation of the army's test. Created by Carl Brigham, a young psychometrician who had worked closely on the army test, it was called the Scholastic Aptitude Test.

Chauncey first administered the SAT in 1934 to Harvard's potential "National Scholars" from public high schools in the Midwest. By 1937 he managed to convince Harvard and the other Ivy League schools to administer these "Scholarship Exams" to all potential scholarship students. This worked so well that Chauncey proposed creating a new national testing agency that would be charged with brokering all standardized education tests and with developing new ones. The creation of a centralized testing agency, a contested enterprise among testing advocates, was given a big boost during World War II. During the war, elite colleges quietly replaced the old College Board exams they used for their paying applicants with the SAT. More importantly, it once again became imperative for the military to sort recruits quickly according to their abilities. Before the war's end, millions of inductees would have taken some version of an intelligence test that would help determine their role. Chauncey masterfully exploited his many contacts to secure a contract from the navy to administer a new test, a modified version of the SAT, for a new program to determine who should be trained for advanced technical jobs and who should be immediately deployed. In a matter of two months, Chauncey's tests established the wartime fates of over 300,000 high school boys. Shortly after the war, Chauncey's success in managing this testing feat helped him to consolidate the centralized testing agency that he longed for: the Educational Testing Service. He remained its leader for decades.

The diffusion of the SAT suggests other general patterns of institutional change. One is that the status of early adopters matters for how readily others converge on a practice (e.g., Zucker 1988). If a land-grant college, rather than Harvard, had been promoting standardized tests, and if Conant and Chauncey had not been able to enlist their broad networks of contacts in their efforts to expand and standardize testing, others would have felt less compelled to follow their example. The demands of war, an "exogenous shock" that helped normalize testing and propel its centralization, created new opportunities for exploiting and propelling standardized testing, and in the process helped to consolidate a powerful new constituency for standardized tests: the military. Whether the problem was who should become officers, or matching jobs with ability, or, later, deciding whom to select for service and whom to defer, standardized testing offered a cheap, defensible procedure.

For colleges, the problem that testing solved shifted from to whom to award scholarships, to whom to admit; as both opportunities for higher education and applicant pools expanded (geographically and in sheer volume), this became an increasingly big job with increasingly fateful consequences. With more people going to college, where you went mattered more, and admissions became more complex and more competitive. This prompted the creation of other mediating institutions that produced newer and even broader constituencies with distinctive interests in standardized tests. Companies such as Stanley Kaplan and Princeton Review, which help test-takers improve their scores, have a direct economic stake in the significance of standardized tests. The organizations that emerged to rank, evaluate, and accred colleges use test scores as criteria in their assessments. Such commitments to testing further increased its prominence and importance and encouraged the development of additional routine practices for attending to tests.

Beginning in 1990, for example, *U.S. News and World Report*, a mainstream weekly newsmagazine, began publishing its own rankings of colleges, professional schools, and graduate programs. These widely publicized rankings have become increasingly influential in shaping the reputations of schools and people's decisions about where to attend. One heavily weighted criterion in these rankings of schools and programs is the test scores of the students who are admitted to them. For administrators with aspirations of upward mobility, either for themselves or their schools, the test scores of their students are now even more tightly linked to their reputations, and they monitor them closely. Practically, this means that low-scoring students are a direct threat to rankings. However stellar students might appear in other ways, whatever other advantages they might bring to a program, these students become an increasingly risky luxury. This is just one way that the legitimacy and hegemony of testing gets reproduced.

If, as Arthur Stinchcombe claims (1978:40), an institution has authority to the extent that it is regarded as inevitable, the emergence of broad, powerful constituencies with distinct sets of investments in an institutional practice such as testing certainly enhance its authority. Constituencies foster inevitability in several ways: by enrolling broad networks of people and organizations with new investments in the legitimacy of the practice (which can lead to what Lynn Zucker (1988) calls "legitimacy by contagion"); and by excluding people and practices who might threaten the inevitability of institutional practices with alternatives or dissent. The "unconventional" students who disappear from graduate or professional programs because of their low test scores are unavailable either as examples that repudiate institutional biases or as potential dissenters.

A perhaps even more powerful way of creating inevitability involves the ways in which constituencies help produce behavior that conforms to the categories that institutional practices produce. Consider the behavior and opportunities available to high-scoring test-takers. The child with perfect SAT scores is admired (and envied) by peers and his or her parents, lauded by teachers and counselors, courted by colleges, bestowed with scholarships and honors, all of which can further enhance one's abilities. Or consider the "gifted" child, a label that is typically the result of scoring in the top percentiles of standardized tests (Margolin 1994); once imposed, it opens up whole networks of opportunities that are unavailable to other test-takers: special enrichment classes, summer programs, talented teachers, engaged, smart classmates, scholarships, and so on. These opportunities create smarter, better-prepared, more sophisticated students, whose advantages accumulate. "Gifted" students may internalize the label by thinking about themselves and their education differently; they may work harder, take more difficult classes, become more confident, feel freer to take risks, and so on. This behavior fulfills the label's promise in ways that make it "self-validating" (Porter 1986; 1995). When tests are used to evaluate schools, "teaching to tests" can produce similar patterns of self-validating behavior. As many analyses have shown, the taken-for-granted quality of institutional practices depends heavily on how and where they are embedded. Their relative embeddedness and the sense of order that they convey may explain their durability and influence better than their performance (Brint and Karavel 1991). For a test that explains only 16 percent of the variance of someone's grades in his or her first year of college, the SAT is a remarkably secure institution.

DISTINCTIVE CHARACTERISTICS OF COMMENSURATION THAT MAY PROPEL DIFFUSION

Having looked at some of the general institutional processes of diffusion as they apply to standardized testing, it may be helpful to consider the distinctive attributes of commensuration as a general practice that help explain its broad diffusion across institutions. An obvious place to begin is that commensurative strategies are *designed* to integrate things. They do so by breaking down heterogeneous, lumpy, preexisting distinctions and converting these into sleek, new, quantitative ones. As strategies of integration, commensurative practices are a simplifying device par excellence. They simplify in two basic ways: by reducing the volume of what we have to pay attention to, and by imposing a uniform form on it; the latter makes information easier to assimilate than when it is presented in multiple forms.[20] If you want to know whether Harmon Killebrew or Kirby Puckett was the better hitter, it is easier and quicker to compare their batting averages than to ponder their different hitting styles, the pitches they liked, the pitchers they faced, and so on. (But as any baseball fan knows, statistics never really resolve any such arguments, since part of their pleasure derives from deconstructing statistics and reinserting heterogeneous attributes.) As the demand for linking disparate things together increases, so will the demand for strategies of commensuration. The global project of integrating economies and nations has been a boon for commensuration.

Commensuration is abstract and flexible. This makes it easier to transport to new contexts, first in the literal sense, in that the average test scores of a city's schools can fit into a realtor's purse or a page of GNPs can summarize world economies; but abstractness and flexibility also enhance its portability in a more figurative sense by making it easy to apply to many different contexts. Commensuration makes the particularity that characterizes the content of choices largely irrelevant; the universal character of numbers makes them accessible to multiple audiences, overcoming the social distance that is created by differing languages, cultures, geography, history (Porter 1986; 1995). The abstractness of commensuration also makes its logic easy to reproduce, making it appear transparent.[21] This is especially appealing in situations when decisions must be publicly defended to various audiences. But the transparency of commensuration is, of course, only apparent because hiding behind its abstractness are all the uncertainty and ambiguity of what it has absorbed. Like graduate student coders housed in back offices, those who most directly confront the arbitrariness involved in decontextualizing complex practices or views by imposing on them abstract logics or standardized forms are often hidden from view.

Commensuration's associations have also eased its travels. A practice that guarantees formal inclusion is politically useful, especially in making democratic claims. If it can be demonstrated that a particular concern or effect has been incorporated into the relevant trade-offs, then claims about exclusion are harder to sustain. The long pairing of commensuration with rationality enhances its ideological potency, since the value of looking or being rational is hard to resist.[22] Its close links with commodification mean that it triumphs as markets do. For all these reasons, commensurative practice and its products have penetrated so deeply into so many fields that we hardly notice it or the transformations it facilitates.

Conclusion

We divide reality into "islands of meaning," according to Eviatar Zerubavel (1991), by doing two things—lumping and splitting. From out of the continuous flow of time and experience or the contiguous reach of space we partition our social worlds into chunks, deploying strategies for constructing similarities that we group together and strategies for creating differences that we keep apart with mental voids. However various are our compartments or their contents, the urge to compartmentalize is deep, probably universal, since meaning and perception require categories. One reason why commensuration is such an interesting and restless cognitive process is because it inverts this core way of creating meaning. Commensuration bridges the mental voids that we create to keep differences at bay, and it transgresses the boundaries we erect to contain sameness. But in this process, new forms of sameness and difference are invented, since, as Zerubavel also explains, transgressions are often creative.

Commensuration is a creative, even radical, transgressive process, and its practice is spreading quickly. Commensuration creates new things, new relations among things, and new patterns of noticing and ignoring the nuts and bolts of cognition. It presents itself as a unifying force, yet it is embodied in disparate forms that produce different effects: from the dazzling algorithms that drive mechanical stock trading, to the standardized answers we tick off on census forms, commensuration can elicit many responses. We need to appreciate the significance of the sameness and difference created by its various forms. Commensuration shapes how individuals think and what institutions do. One of its appealing features is that it offers a site, or a mechanism, for analyzing how cognitive processes move across levels of organizations, something that Paul DiMaggio (1997) and others have urged us to do.

At the risk of sounding grandiose, commensuration can help us better understand the distinctiveness of the divide we have erected between ourselves as modern, and those who precede us, who are not. For Anthony Giddens (1990), the period in which we live is not so discontinuous with the past so as to require a new label; it is less post modern than the fruition of the consequences of modernity. The chief characteristics of being modern, for him, involve the creation of distinctive social institutions that accelerate the pace and scope of change, that "disembed" social relations by extracting them from local contexts and reorganize them across vast and compressed dimensions of time and space, that produce systematic forms of knowledge that are distinctively "reflexive" in their continual referring and adjusting to one another. Commensuration is intimately involved in each of these processes. And if this connection between commensuration and modernity seems far-fetched, I hope, at least, I have convinced you that commensuration is worth investigating.

Endnotes

1. Thanks to Karen Cerulo, Bruce Carruthers, Peter Levin, Mitchell Stevens, and Marc Ventresca for their helpful suggestions, intellectual inspiration, and congenial support.
2. Barry Schwartz (1981) and Eviatar Zerubavel (1985, 1991) exemplify the former. Stephen Turner (2000) and Charles Camic (1988) make the latter point, emphasizing the role that imitation and habit, respectively, play in the processes of our becoming social, sentient beings.
3. This essay relies on work done collaboratively with Mitchell Stevens (Espeland and Stevens 1998).
4. The original name for the test, the Scholastic Aptitude Test, was changed in 1994. According to Nicholas Lemann (1999b), those who administer the test prefer to refer to it by its acronym in order to avoid discussing "exactly what the test is meant to measure."

5. Our conception of "normal" as typical, as the opposite of deviant or pathological, emerges from the statistical regularities discovered in the nineteenth century. For Hacking (1990:163), the "magic" of the word is the way we use it to elide ancient distinctions—fact and value, is and ought—to say two things at once: that something is typical, and thus desirable. This double meaning of norm and normal suffused Durkheim's work and is often implied in much social analysis.

6. For a superb account of the development of the first futures option in grain, see William Cronon (1991:97–147).

7. As Ian Hacking (1990:20) describes this shift, "If there is a contrast in point of official statistics between the eighteenth and nineteenth centuries, it is that the former feared to reveal while the latter loved to publish."

8. Later, in presenting the results of a national survey of radio audiences commissioned by the radio industry, Paul Lazarsfeld describes the findings as illuminating the characteristics of the "average American" and the "average consumer" (Lazarsfeld and Kendall 1948).

9. See Espeland (1998).

10. See, for example, Hammond (1960, 1966). The Bureau of Reclamation included as "indirect" benefits of a dam they wanted to build the value of the wheat that would grow on the irrigated land as well as the value of the bread that would be baked from that wheat (cited in Lohmann 1998).

11. See Carruthers and Espeland (1991).

12. See Espeland (1998:183–222).

13. Plasmapheresis was first developed during World War II to alleviate critical blood shortages. For shock, which causes many casualties, it is more important to replace blood volume than blood cells. Unlike whole blood, plasma can be dried and stored for long periods; it is also universally acceptable and eliminates the problems associated with blood typing. For more, see Espeland (1984).

14. Retrieved March 13, 2000 (http://www.stough-plasma.com). Notice that the donor's payment does not detract from his or her "priceless contribution."

15. The social significance of incommensurable categories varies, depending on how central they are for defining our roles and identities and the passion we attach to them. Joseph Raz distinguishes between trivial forms of incommensurable categories and those that are vital expressions of some core value. For some relationships, believing in their incommensurable qualities might be a qualification for having them. Raz (1986:345–57) terms these "constitutive incommensurables." For the Yavapai, land was a "constitutive incommensurable." See also Tetlock (forthcoming). In DiMaggio's terms (1997), identities are "hot schemata" that make them more extensive and central mechanisms for simplifying cognition.

16. Critics of cost-benefit analysis and ethical commensuration have argued that we deceive and diminish ourselves when we reduce the complex and plural ways we value nature and each other to a single form. See, for example, Anderson (1993), Lohmann (1998), Nussbaum (1986), O'Neil (1993), Radin (1996), Sunstein (1994), Tribe (1972), and Wiggens (1987).

17. Establishing the incommensurability of something need not always hinge on some deep cultural value, however. We have more mundane reasons for and ways of marking the specialness of things. As Viviana Zelizer (1994) has shown, people use both simple and ingenious ways of subverting the commensurability of money: they may store it in a special jar, hide it in a drawer, wrap it in gift paper, or simply earmark its use for distinct purposes. But each of these practices impedes its fungibility.

18. My heading comes from Lemann's (1995) article, "The Structure of Success in America." This section is based on his book (1999a) and two related articles. These are deeply informed by Robert Merton's (1938) analysis of the structure of opportunity in "Social Structure and Anomie."

19. Alfred Binet, a French psychologist, designed the first intelligence test in 1905. Lewis Terman, a professor at Stanford, championed the test as a way to measure inherent intellectual ability, which he labeled "I.Q." Terman helped convince the army that assessing "I.Q." was a good way to select officers, and thus launched the first mass use of mental tests (Lemann 1999b).
20. This process is similar to those described by DiMaggio (1997) in that we are more apt to notice information and absorb it more quickly if it is embedded in existing schemata.
21. People's "commitment to the transparency of numbers" spurred the flourishing of public statistics in the early nineteenth century. To the extent that numbers could speak for themselves, they would remain uncontaminated by politics and opinion. This was, of course, a rhetorically useful position (Porter 1995:78).
22. Nussbaum (1986) describes how closely Plato linked the two.

References

Anderson, E. 1993. *Value in Ethics and Economics.* Cambridge, MA: Harvard University Press.

Brint, S. and J. Karavel. 1991. "Institutional Origins and Transformations: The Case of American Community Colleges," Pp. 337–60 in *The New Institutionalism in Organizational Analysis,* edited by W. W. Powell and P. J. DiMaggio. Chicago, IL: University of Chicago Press.

Camic, C. 1988. "The Matter of Habit." *American Journal of Sociology* 94(5):1039–87.

Carruthers, B. and W. Espeland. 1991. "Accounting for Rationality: Double-Entry Bookkeeping and the Rhetoric of Economic Rationality." *American Journal of Sociology* 97(1):31–69.

Carruthers, B. G. and A. L. Stinchcombe. 1999. Social Structure of Liquidity: Flexibility, Markets, and States," *Theory and Society* 23(3):353–82.

Clemens, E. S. 1997. *The People's Lobby: Organizational Innovation and the Rise of Interest Group Politics in the United States, 1890–1925.* Chicago, IL: University of Chicago Press.

Cronon, W. 1991. *Nature's Metropolis: Chicago and the Great West.* New York: Norton.

DiMaggio, P. 1982. "Cultural Entrepreneurship in Nineteenth-Century Boston, Part I: The Creation of an Organizational Base for High Culture in America." *Media, Culture and Society* 4:33–50.

———. 1997. "Culture and Cognition." *Annual Review of Sociology* 23:263–87.

Durkheim, E. [1912] 1995. *The Elementary Forms of Religious Life.* Translated by Karen E. Fields. New York: The Free Press.

Espeland, W. N. 1984. "Blood and Money: Exploiting the Embodied Self." Pp. 131–55 in *The Existential Self in Society,* edited by J. Kotarba and A. Fontana. Chicago, IL: University of Chicago Press.

———. 1998. *The Struggle for Water: Politics, Rationality, and Identity in the American Southwest.* Chicago, IL: University of Chicago Press.

Espeland, W. N. and M. L. Stevens. 1998. "Commensuration as a Social Process." *Annual Review of Sociology* 24:313–43.

Feldman, M. and J. G. March. 1981. "Information in Organizations as Sign and Symbol." *Administrative Science Quarterly* 26:171–86.

Fiske, A. P. and P. Tetlock. 1997. "Taboo Trade-offs: Reactions to Transactions that Transgress the Spheres of Justice." *Political Psychology* 18(2):255–97.

Foucault, M. 1980. *Power and Knowledge,* edited by C. Gordon. Brighton, England: Harvester Press.

Friedland, R. and R. R. Alford. 1991. "Bringing Society Back In." Pp. 232–63 in *The New Institutionalism in Organizational Analysis,* edited by W. W. Powell and P. J. DiMaggio. Chicago, IL: University of Chicago Press.

Giddens, A. 1990. *The Consequences of Modernity.* Stanford, CA: Stanford University Press.

Gramsci, A. 1971. *Selections from the Prison Notebooks.* Edited and Translated by Q. N. Hoare and G. Nowell Smith. London: Lawrence & Wishart.

Hacking, I. 1990. *The Taming of Chance*. Cambridge, England: Cambridge University Press.

Hammond, R. J. 1960. *Benefit-Cost Analysis and Water-Pollution Control*. Stanford, CA: Food Research Institute of Stanford University.

———. 1966. "Convention and Limitation in Benefit-Cost Analysis." *Natural Resources Journal* 6:195–222.

Herbst, S. 1993. *Numbered Voices: How Opinion Polling Has Shaped American Politics*. Chicago, IL: University of Chicago Press.

Kendall, P. and P. Cole. 2000. "Meat Plant Brings Odor to the Court." *Chicago Tribune*, April 11, section 1, pp.1, 14.

Lazarsfeld, P. F. and P. F. Kendall. 1948. *Radio Listening in America: The People Look at Radio—Again*. New York: Prentice-Hall, Inc.

Lemann, N. 1995. "The Structure of Success in America." *Atlantic Monthly*, August, pp. 41–60.

———. 1999a. *The Big Test*. New York: Farrar, Straus and Giroux.

———. 1999b. "Behind the SAT." *Newsweek*, September 6, pp. 52–7.

Levin, P. and W. Espeland. 2000. "Pollution Futures: Commensuration, Commodification, and the Market for Air." Presented at the conference on Organizations, Policy, and the Natural Environment: Institutional and Strategic Perspectives, April 28–30, Evanston, IL.

Lohmann, L. 1998. "Whose Voice Is Speaking? How Opinion Polling and Cost-Benefit Analysis Synthesize New 'Publics.'" *The CornerHouse Briefing* 7: May.

March, J. G. 1994. *A Primer on Decision Making*. New York: The Free Press.

Margolin, L. 1994. *Goodness Personified: The Emergence of Gifted Children*. New York: Aldine.

Mead, G. H. 1934. *Mind, Self and Society*. Chicago, IL: University of Chicago Press.

Merton, R. 1938. "Social Structure and Anomie." *American Sociological Review* 3:672–82.

Meyer, J. W. and B. Rowan. 1977. "Institutionalized Organizations: Formal Structure as Myth and Ceremony." *American Journal of Sociology* 83:340–63.

Nussbaum, M. 1986. *The Fragility of Goodness*. Cambridge, England: Cambridge University Press.

O'Neil, J. 1993. *Ecology, Policy and Politics*. London: Routledge.

Porter, T. M. 1986. *The Rise of Statistical Thinking, 1820–1900*. Princeton, NJ: Princeton University Press.

———. 1995. *Trust in Numbers*. Princeton, NJ: Princeton University Press.

Radin, M. 1996. *Contested Commodities*. Cambridge, MA: Harvard University Press.

Raz, J. 1986. *The Morality of Freedom*. Oxford, England: Oxford University Press.

Schwartz, B. 1981. *Vertical Classification: A Study in Structuralism and the Sociology of Knowledge*. Chicago, IL: University of Chicago Press.

Simmel, G. [1900] 1982. *The Philosophy of Money*. Translated by T. Bottomore and D. Frisby. London: Routledge & Kegan Paul.

———. 1971. *On Individuality and Social Forms*, edited by Donald N. Levine. Chicago, IL: University of Chicago Press.

Sombart, W. 1953. "Medieval and Modern Commercial Enterprise." Pp. 25–40 in *Enterprise and Secular Change*, edited by F. C. Lane and J. Riemersma. Homewood, IL: Irwin.

Stinchcombe, A. L. 1978. *Theoretical Methods in Social History*. New York: Academic Press.

Sunstein, C. 1994. "Incommensurability and Valuation in Law." *Michigan Law Review* 92:779–861.

Swidler, A. 1986. "Culture in Action: Symbols and Strategies." *American Sociological Review* 51:273–86.

Tetlock, P. E. Forthcoming. "Coping with Trade-Offs: Psychological Constraints and Political Implications," in *Political Reasoning and Choice*, edited by A. Lupia, M. McCubbins, and S. Popkin. Berkeley, CA: University of California Press.

Titmuss, R. M. 1971. *The Gift Relationship*. New York: Pantheon.

Tribe, L. 1972. "Policy Science: Analysis or Ideology?" *Philosophy and Public Affairs*. 2:66–110.

Turner, S. 2000. "Imitation or the Internalization of Norms: Is Twentieth Century Social Theory Based on the Wrong Choice?" Pp. 83–118 in *Empathy and Agency: The Problem of Understanding in the Human Sciences*, edited by H. H. Koegler and K. R. Stueber. Boulder, CO: Westview Press.

Ventresca, M. J. 1995. "When States Count: Institutional and Political Dynamics in Modern Census Establishment, 1800–1993." Unpublished Ph.D. dissertation, Department of Sociology, Stanford University, Stanford, CA.

Ventresca, M. and X. Yin. 1997. "Representing Economy and Society: Comparative Trends in What States Count, 1800–1970." Presented at the American Sociological Association Annual Meeting, New York.

Westney, D. E. 1987. *Imitation and Innovation: The Transfer of Western Organizational Patterns to Mejia Japan.* Cambridge, MA: Harvard University Press.

Wiggens, D. 1987. *Needs, Values, Truth.* Oxford, England: Oxford University Press.

Zelizer, V. A. 1994. *The Social Meaning of Money.* New York: Basic Books.

Zerubavel, E. 1985. *The Seven Day Circle: The History and Meaning of the Week.* Chicago, IL: University of Chicago Press.

———. 1991. *The Fine Line: Making Distinctions in Everyday Life.* Chicago, IL: University of Chicago Press.

Zucker, L. 1988. "Where Do Institutional Patterns Come From? Organizations as Actors in Social Systems," Pp. 23–52 in *Institutional Patterns and Organizations: Culture and Environment*, edited by L. G. Zucker. Cambridge, MA: Ballinger.

CHAPTER 5

Preterm Babies in the "Mother Machine"

METAPHORIC REASONING AND BUREAUCRATIC RITUALS THAT FINISH THE "UNFINISHED INFANT"

Nicole Isaacson

In the last three decades, American society has been increasingly "fetally fascinated." This preoccupation with the fetus takes many forms, including ongoing debates about "fetal rights," fetal consciousness, fetal tissue research, fetal surgery, visualizing the fetus, and commodifying the fetus (Casper 1998; Daniels 1993; Duden 1993; Franklin 1991; Petchesky 1987; Stabile 1992). The cultural obsession with the fetus *in utero* is understandable, given the implications for women's reproductive rights and the powerful emotions that fetal representations evoke. At the same time, this fetal focus has obscured another important cultural phenomenon, the ever-increasing presence of what could be called the "*ex utero*" fetus or premature infant.

The American understanding and classification of premature infants has changed dramatically from the late nineteenth century to the present. What were categorized previously as miscarriages, abortuses, "weaklings," or unsalvageable fetuses are now called "premature infants," subject to a variety of medical and social interventions designed to finish what nature has failed to complete.

Nonetheless, the premature baby remains an "unfinished infant," not yet constituting a consistently uniform or clearly bounded subject. I suggest that the premature infant, commonly assumed to be a natural subject, is in fact a product of specific social and cultural forces. For these reasons, the contemporary phenomenon of the premature infant provides an opportunity to examine the social process of boundary renegotiations accomplished through the cognitive practices of metaphoric reasoning and bureaucratic ritual.

In this chapter, I examine a selection of cultural artifacts that communicate socially shared meanings about prematurity. Specifically, I sample newspaper, popular magazine, and science journalism articles from 1988 to 1997. In addition, I draw upon selected medical journals and "neonatal narratives" (parental accounts of premature babies). I focus upon public discourse because it is an integral part of how we culturally conceptualize the premature infant. In so doing, I illustrate the ways in which discursive and institutional practices such as metaphoric reasoning and bureaucratic ritual negotiate the tensions and contradictions inherent in prematurity.

The Unfinished Infant

I call the premature baby the "unfinished infant"—unfinished in both physical and conceptual terms. The premature baby at birth is physically unfinished. The lungs are not fully developed, limiting efficient oxygen exchange and possibly leading to permanent lung damage. The skin may be porous and permeable, allowing a pathway for infections. The baby's genitalia may not be fully formed, the eyes may be fused shut, a heart valve may not seal as it should at birth, and the infant may have little or no body fat, leading to problems in thermoregulation. Premature babies may suffer from apnea (forgetting to breathe). In addition, the delicacy of the immature veins and arteries in the brain may lead to intraventricular hemorrhage or "brain-bleeds" that may cause substantial neurological damage for the baby.[1] The very profound physical immaturity of the premature infant means that it is "unfinished" at birth and must be technologically and medically supported in numerous ways in order to sustain life.

The births that we classify as premature have been in a state of flux for many years. For example, 20 years ago, a 24-week-old birth would have been classified as a miscarriage, stillbirth, or unsalvageable fetus. Today, a 24-week-old birth is classified as a premature infant, known more specifically as a "micropreemie" or a very, very low-birthweight baby. In this way, the premature baby is not simply physically incomplete but is also conceptually unfinished. As a not-yet-finalized entity, the premature infant's meaning is neither stable nor singular. Prematurity is socially and culturally constructed rather than inherently given by nature.

As the premature infant is unfinished both physically and conceptually, there are tensions and contradictions embodied in its image and in the discourse that surrounds it. The premature infant is both fetus and baby at once—a hybrid. As such, the premature infant is fascinating because it exists on the borderlines of humanity; it is a conceptually hybrid creature, socially assigned the status of baby while retaining its biotemporally[2] fetal character. The compositional heterogeneity of the premature infant, to be both fetus and baby concurrently, presents undeniable problems for classification and creates anxiety for those concerned with corporeal integrity. The hybrid fetus-infant[3] is in a liminal state.

Liminality poses not only a challenge but also a potential threat to an established social order. Entities that are liminal trouble previously established categories. Mary

Douglas (1966) has noted that objects that fall outside cultural classification systems are often perceived as dangerous (see also Butler 1990). Liminal entities, with "their . . . indeterminate attributes" (Turner 1969:95) disturb our normal patterns of classification: "Their condition is one of ambiguity and paradox, a confusion of all the customary categories. . . . This coincidence of opposite processes and notions in a single representation characterizes the peculiar unity of the liminal: that which is neither this nor that, and yet is both" (Turner 1969:97–99). As liminal entities, hybrids are boundary figures that repeatedly deny our attempts to assign them clear and stable meanings. I suggest that prematurity, because of its unfinished and hybrid nature, disrupts our mental horizons as to who is fully or completely human. However, we do not call a premature infant an "extrauterine fetus"; we have made a commitment to conceptualizing a 25-week-old birth, for example, as a premature infant.

Interestingly, even full-term infants are potentially "unfinished." For example, according to an Orthodox rabbi, Jewish law states that a baby who dies before 31 days of life is not mourned, there is no funeral, and the family does not sit shiva, the Jewish mourning ritual (Pitock 1996). Because the newborn baby is excluded from the traditional Jewish rituals and practices surrounding death, the infant is symbolically located outside the circle of humanity; one does not mourn an infant who was not fully acknowledged as part of the community. Philosopher Peter Singer suggests that a newborn infant is "clearly not a person in the ethically relevant sense" (1995:217) and proposes a period of 28 days after birth "before an infant is accepted as having the same right to life as others" (p. 217). Although acknowledging the 28 days as a somewhat arbitrary boundary, Singer's point is that the newborn baby is itself unfinished in terms of its capacities (awareness of self) as well as in terms of parental attachment and acceptance of the baby into the family and larger moral community. This point is echoed cross-culturally amongst groups that practice infanticide or which do not recognize the baby as a member of the community until after a naming or other welcoming ceremony.

As our mental horizon[4] has expanded to include the previously previable fetus in the category of legitimate baby, we are faced with a variety of challenges to our cognitive perspective of who is truly human. Thus cultural and political concerns, rather than viability and technological prowess, determine the point at which an infant is culturally "finished."

Data and Methods

Since the premature infant is a product of specific cultural and social forces, I examine a selection of cultural artifacts that communicate socially shared meanings about prematurity. Specifically, I sample newspaper, popular magazine, and science journalism articles from 1988 to 1997. In addition, I draw upon selected medical journals and "neonatal narratives" (parental accounts of premature babies). All selected articles were coded and analyzed using NUDIST, a qualitative research program.

I selected the 1988 to 1997 time period for several reasons. It was in 1989 that the trial use of surfactant therapy, a new treatment for respiratory problems in premature infants, began to be used widely in hospitals caring for acutely preterm newborns (Jobe 1993).[5] The introduction of surfactant therapy in the late 1980s and early 1990s was a dramatic advance in neonatal care, helping to lower premature infants' threshold of viability to 24 weeks of gestation, a little more than half the length of a normal pregnancy.[6] The extreme prematurity of these babies helps highlight the boundary problems that occur in distinguishing between fetus and baby. As antichoice groups frequently note, fetuses that could be legally aborted now also could be hooked up to respirators and medically treated as newborn premature infants.

This increased boundary-blurring between fetus and premature infant has created difficulties for medical personnel as well as women seeking second-trimester abortions. For example, several hospitals in the San Francisco Bay area now limit second-trimester abortions because of the difficulty in persuading nurses to participate in the procedure: "The nurses said the aborted fetuses looked too much like the 'preemies' they were tending elsewhere" (Tumulty 1990:10).

During this same time period, there also have been increasing attempts to constrain women's reproductive choices as well as a tremendous growth in the reproductive technologies available to some groups of women and men. The ongoing public struggle over these cognitive boundaries shows no signs of abating despite continuing technological advancements. In this context of increased institutional control over who has access to specific reproductive choices and technologies, the ways premature infants are represented in public discourse have implications for women's future reproductive choices.

I selected newspaper articles by searching Dow Jones Interactive, an online database of over 6,000 leading newspapers and magazines. Each year, from 1988 to 1997, was searched individually using the words "premature infant," "premature infants," "premature baby," "premature babies," "preterm infant," "preterm infants," "preterm baby," and "preterm babies" as search terms. Articles that did not deal directly with premature infants or that focused specifically on multiple births were eliminated. When versions of the same article appeared in different newspapers (taken off the Associated Press wire service), I selected the longest of the articles. This process yielded 653 articles, from which I then drew a proportional random sample of 30 percent, resulting in a sample of 201 newspaper articles.

Magazine articles were identified in several ways. I first searched the Reader's Guide to Periodical Literature (RGPL) from 1988 to 1997. I used the following terms in conducting all searches in the RGPL: Babies, Incubators, Infants, Children, Multiple Births, Premature, Quadruplets, Quintuplets, Respiratory Diseases, Twins, Triplets. Frequently, articles are listed under more than one heading, which provided me with an additional check to ensure that I was not missing relevant articles. In addition to the RGPL, I employed the search engines Lexis-Nexis, Ethnic News Watch, and Dow Jones Interactive to increase both geographic and racial/ethnic coverage of the topic of prematurity. All 49 magazine articles from 1988 to 1997 were included in the analysis.[7]

Selected texts were examined in two ways. First, I interrogated the construction of the texts themselves, asking, for example, what metaphors are employed, what the tone of the article or narrative is, and how the author describes the site, participants, and technology encountered. My analysis of the texts revealed that there are specific discursive strategies that cognitively finish the premature infant. Second, I examined accounts of institutional practices that "finish" the premature infant, thus constructing a human subject. The fact that such practices exist underscores the liminality of the premature infant, highlighting the active cultural processes involved in marking the premature baby as human.

Metaphoric Reasoning and Finishing the Unfinished Infant

I have identified three discursive and visual strategies employed in public discourse that act to stabilize the position of the premature infant on our mental horizon. These discursive strategies revolve around metaphoric reasoning and constitute specific cultural practices that cognitively establish the premature infant as a human baby worthy of care.

THE MIRACLE METAPHOR

The first discursive strategy involves the social power of specific metaphors that dominate descriptions of premature infants. Reading popular articles and science journalism written over the past decade, one can see the creation of specific representations of prematurity. Certain metaphors in these narratives present organizing images for the reader: "Metaphor, through its familiar literal referent, appears to offer self-evident, socially shared meaning to the unfamiliar" (Brown 1992:13). Metaphor and analogy help to define and naturalize the unknown (Stepan 1986). Discourse analyst Michael Shapiro (as quoted in Mentor 1998) stresses examining what he calls the "social depths" of certain forms of representation. In other words, why are certain images and metaphors emphasized at the expense of others?

In the case of the premature infant, the "miracle" metaphor is frequently used. This metaphor helps to present a cohesive narrative, ignoring contradictions or alternative perspectives. This is not to claim that all popular media articles were uniformly positive. However, out of a random sample of 250 newspaper and magazine articles from 1988 to 1997, 59 percent of all article headlines were coded as positive, meaning that the general tenor of the article presents a happy or positive perspective regarding the premature baby or the subject of prematurity in general. Of these headlines, 23 percent specifically used the word "miracle" in describing a premature baby's survival. A text search for the word "miracle" in the sample indicated that 22 percent of all articles used the word in referring to premature infants.

Article titles like "The Littlest Miracle" (Phillips 1988), "A Medical Miracle" (Fischer 1988), "Smallest of Miracles" (Cummings 1997), "A Premature Miracle" (Belgin 1990), and "The Miracle of Caleb" (Ansorge 1996) present a narrative where miraculous events occur and babies survive despite poor or even hopeless prognoses: "Her mother was told she was stillborn, by a doctor who was sure she would die. But then the tiny preemie, already cold and stiff, unaccountably started to breathe. That was just the beginning of the miracle" (Raymond 1992:107). Commonly, the baby is portrayed as a "fighter" who overcomes all odds to survive despite a bleak prognosis: "When he [Trent] reached one kilogram (2.2 pounds), Debbie and the staff celebrated with a 'kilo party.' Everyone began calling Trent 'Little Rambo'" (Phillips 1988:78). By utilizing the discourse of the miracle, the premature infant's presence is scripted as a wondrous occurrence, almost a gift, whose existence, however hard-won, is an extraordinary event recognized even by medical professionals: "Trent is living proof that miracles can happen, [Dr. Shoemaker] said" (p. 78). Or as another doctor commented: "When you consider his start in life, and you look at him now, you really do begin to believe in miracles" (Fischer 1988:174).

The framing of Trent's survival as a "miracle" by parents, medical staff, and the media ignores the difficult physical challenges he will face throughout his life. Trent is blind, underweight for his age, more susceptible to illness than full-term babies, and at risk for significant learning disabilities (Phillips 1988; Manginello and DiGeronimo 1998). As one researcher wryly notes, "babies have been referred to by media and parents as 'miracles' even though it is generally considered an unfortunate event when a baby is born . . . too early" (Harris 1998:14). Yet, while an author may describe how the infant is attached to a breathing apparatus and undergoes surgery or other painful procedures, these interventions typically are superceded in the narrative by the miracle of survival and the fighting spirit of the premature baby.

The metaphor of the miracle, by obscuring or overshadowing the many techno-logical and medical interventions that enable most premature babies to survive, helps naturalize or perhaps supernaturalize the premature infant. It is the will of the baby, the "fighter," and the unspoken but implied will of a higher power that miraculously finish the premature infant.

THE "MOTHER MACHINE" METAPHOR

Technological interventions are often discursively resituated as maternal. The tech-nology in a neonatal intensive care unit (NICU) often can be overwhelming, especially for parents who may have a critically ill baby lying motionless in an incubator, barely visible beneath tubes and monitors. To deal with the artificial, alien realm of the NICU, which is so antithetical to the idealized vision of mother and newborn at home amid flannel blankets and teddy bears, machinery is reconcep-tualized as nurturing and maternal. Often for example, incubators are described as "mother machines," "artificial wombs," or "a window into the womb." One typical account of premature-infant care clearly establishes this maternal connection: "Jasmine's incubator has a quilted cover with a dark lining. The shaded enclosure and quiet environment of the neonatal units are meant to simulate a mother's womb" (Huber 1996:S9). Another account describes a baby's Isolette as "a sort of artificial womb—which kept him cozy, warm and relatively germ free" (Helgason 1993:1A). One father wrote of his first vision of his premature infant:

> The spectacle of my daughter overwhelmed me—a wrinkled, wizened body, covered with fine hair so thick it seemed like fur. And her size! A baby shorter than my shoe! Patches and electrodes attached to her body, wires running to equipment I knew nothing about. Tubes running to her mouth, down her throat. Beeps and clicks and pulsating lights. But they were all necessary. They were the machines that would mother her and care for her. . . . The nurse knew that I too was a stranger in a strange land. She briefly explained what each alien machine was, the mothers that were to replace Faye. (Pfister and Griesemer 1983:28–29)

In this passage, the father is grappling to make sense of this "brave new world" (p. 29). By perceiving the machine as the "mother" of the premature baby, we reinvent the familial world, albeit in a cyborgian sense. The machine as mother is a kinder, gentler technology, one which is more accessible, understandable, familiar, and ultimately taken for natural.

The inversion of mother and machine is taken to its logical, if ludicrous, extreme in another article on "kangaroo care." Kangaroo care is the practice of holding a premature infant, dressed only in a cap and diaper, against a parent's chest, skin to skin. Kangaroo care began as a practice in hospitals in poorer countries that could not afford incubators and was adopted in the United States after studies found it effective in helping stabilize a premature infant's vital signs. In describing kangaroo care, the author writes: "The mother, in a sense, becomes a human incubator" (Anonymous 1992:24). Now the mother imitates the machine. The incubator becomes naturalized; ignored is the fact that the machine is the simulacrum of the woman—it is the mother, not the machine, who is the original incubator.

PICTURING PREMATURITY: NORMALIZING THE REPRESENTATION
OF PRETERM INFANTS

Iconographic appeals to babyhood typically downplay technological interventions and normalize the premature infant. Specific strategic visual representations thus mediate messages about prematurity: "Like narratives, visual images provide concrete enactments of abstract values" (Condit 1990:81). A variety of images reappears in texts guiding perceptions of the premature infant as a finished baby.

For example, one magazine article provided a detailed description of a NICU, carefully outlining all the myriad kinds of equipment that a premature baby might encounter there. However, the article closed with the following statement:

> More than technology has been brought to bear on neonatal problems. Neonatal care is extraordinarily intensive, requiring constant monitoring and attention. After visiting with David, a now healthy 13 day old about to be released from the neonatal ward, Mass General's Dr. Kushner pointed to a large rocking chair he had been sitting in, one of several in the room used by doctors and nurses to observe and rock the babies. "That," said Kushner, "is the best piece of technology in the room." (Lunzer 1985:125)

In addition, the photograph accompanying this article, "Wired for Life," prominently features the aforesaid rocking chair occupied by a woman (perhaps a mom) holding a baby in a blanket. A doctor kneeling by the side of the chair is examining the infant. Consigned to the background of the photograph are some distant incubators and other unidentifiable machinery. The subtitle to the photograph is "And don't underestimate the rocking chair itself" (p. 124).

In this example one of the classic practices of parenthood, and specifically motherhood—rocking the baby in the rocking chair—is used to reconceptualize the artificial world of the NICU into a nursery, albeit one with some very high-tech machinery. The claim by Dr. Kushner that the rocking chair is the "best piece of technology" in the NICU belies the fact that many premature babies would never make it into the rocking chair without the incubator, IVs, sensor technology, respirators, ultrasounds, drug therapies, and surgeries that are used to keep babies alive long enough for their parents to rock them to sleep. As an organizing image, the rocking chair helps stabilize our perception of the premature infant by drawing on classic icons or referents of infancy. The reader can then draw on this familiar, reassuring image, the rocking chair, to read the premature infant as a regular baby, despite all the high-tech equipment which surrounds it.

Another frequently used image is that of the tiny premature baby's footprints. The footprint is an evocative visual trope because it draws upon a commonly viewed document: the birth certificate. Most people have viewed either their own, their child's, or a family member's birth certificate and have seen their tiny footprints. The birth certificate, with its footprint, officially marks an infant's legal acceptance into the human community. Therefore, to view this premature baby's impossibly tiny but indelibly human footprint causes the viewer to perceive and conceptualize the premature infant as a fully finished baby. The 24-week-old premature infant's footprint looks identical to a full-term baby's footprint. We then synechdochically extend the unseen image to cognitively construct a perfect, small baby in our minds without having to confront the many differences between the two (Condit 1990).

Another common image is that of the premature baby wearing a parent's wedding ring around her or his arm or leg. The wedding ring, typically the father's, serves most obviously to emphasize dramatically and visually the premature infant's unbelievably tiny size: "How small? Her parents have a picture of Tahnie in the incubator wearing a gold band. It's her father's wedding ring" (Haynes 1993:1). Yet on a more subtle level, the infant's wearing of the ring serves another purpose. Wedding rings symbolize the marriage contract between a man and woman; slipping the ring around the infant's arm suggests to the viewer that the baby is part of the family, a legitimate offspring worthy of the care and protection society affords to valued children.

Boundaries and Borderline Babies: Bureaucratic Rituals of Prematurity

People recognize each other as human beings, part of a collective group, through a variety of cultural practices and rituals. Greeting others, handshakes, making eye contact—all these acts recognize the other's membership in the human community. Newborn babies, however, present a challenge to these standard ritual practices of human interaction. Infants are initially, largely unresponsive recipients of cultural practices recognizing their humanity: "To any but a mother a new-born child hardly seems human. It appears rather to be a strange little animal . . . exquisitely finished, even to the fingernails, . . . but not friendly, not lovable" (Cooley 1983:81–82). The infant's first smile is thus a source of joy and delight for the baby's caregivers. It is one of the baby's first social recognition of another individual. Premature infants, because of their extremely small size and their more "fetal" attributes (e.g., fused eyelids, lanugo, and lack of body fat) do not even have the advantage of being "exquisitely finished." Their unfinished state makes the cultural practices that recognize their human status even more important.[8]

LIFE RITUALS: THE APGAR SCORE

The bureaucratic rituals of medical organizations are part of the cultural practices that help impose clear categories on the ambiguous form of the premature infant. One of the most important of these rituals is the APGAR score. Before the institutionalization of the APGAR score to evaluate a newborn's physical condition, many premature infants weighing less than 1 kilogram at birth were classified by medical staff as previable.[9] This classification meant that any births less than 1 kilogram were not bureaucratically recognized as ever having been living babies:

> "Previable" and severely malformed newborns were placed in a cold corner of the delivery room and allowed to die. . . . Everyone tried to ignore the gasping respirations—death never came quickly enough to relieve their acute, but silent, discomfort. The outcome of the delivery was reported as stillborn. (Silverman 1992:972)

The APGAR score "did away with the fiction of labeling marginal neonates as 'stillborn'" (p. 973); the subsequent systematic classification of newborns provided a ritualized medical practice that insisted upon identifying even low-scoring neonates as living babies. The APGAR score, while an important and useful source of information about the newborn, also created a clear, unambiguous set of parameters for defining live births.

DEATH RITUALS

Hospitals have developed institutionalized ways for officially recognizing a premature baby's death. In the United States, some NICUs will give parents a small box with pictures of the baby, footprints, a birth certificate, and lock of hair "to help parents grieve, to acknowledge that they did have a baby, however briefly" (Frey 1995:47). By developing memory boxes, or "grief baskets," for both premature and even stillborn babies, hospital staff engage in a practice that acknowledges that the premature infant was a person whose death constitutes a loss for parents. Most states in America facilitate this practice by requiring burial or cremation if a premature birth is at least 20 to 21 weeks gestation or has a heartbeat even though these births are not medically viable (Robinson et al. 1999:267).

By contrast, in the province of Quebec in Canada, premature infants born weighing less than 500 grams are legally defined as "surgical waste—like an excised appendix or a cyst—rather than a complete human being" (Anonymous 1994) and after death are incinerated with other hospital refuse. Upon hearing one woman's objections to the disposal of her premature son's body in this manner, a hospital spokesperson replied that according to the province regulations, "one could say that the woman did not deliver a baby" (Anonymous 1994). Here, the institutional practices of the state and hospital unequivocally draw the boundary between unfinished and finished humans on the basis of weight; 500 grams is the cutoff point for completeness, according to the law. In this case, no baby was born. For the would-be mother, the law denies institutional validation of the existence of her premature infant:

> Her eyes wet with tears, Nicole Vaillancourt steadies her voice and says her infant son was more than "surgical waste" and deserved a proper burial. "I didn't have a chance to say goodbye to my child. . . . My father died 15 years ago, and I can go see him at the cemetery. My son should be buried with him. A mother has a right to bury her child." (Anonymous 1994)

Without tangible evidence of the *ex utero* birth (e.g., picture, footprints, lock of hair) or a grave to visit, all Vaillancourt has to support her claim to motherhood is ultrasound pictures of her unborn fetus: "Like any proud parent showing off a child's photograph,

Vaillancourt holds up copies of ultrasound pictures, pointing to the blur that was her un-born baby" (Anonymous 1994). But Vaillancourt is not like any other parent, a blur is not a baby, and without the "right to bury her child," Vaillancourt's unnamed baby remains officially classified as "surgical waste," too unfinished to qualify for human status.

Conclusion

The various discursive strategies and bureaucratic rituals outlined in this paper illu-minate some of the processes by which we cognitively "finish" the public idea of the premature infant. These strategies represent various attempts to restore classificatory stability to the disruption that the premature infant creates in our mental horizons. The premature infant is neither a naturally nor technologically defined subject. Rather, this protohuman requires "finishing" through a variety of discursive and rit-ual processes before admission to the human community. By establishing a cognitive framework for perceiving and relating to the premature infant, we clarify the bound-aries between who counts as finished and who remains incomplete.

Endnotes

1. See Manginello and DiGernomino (1998) for an extensive discussion of the many long- and short-term physical problems premature infants may face.
2. See Zerubavel (1981).
3. See Isaacson (1996).
4. See Zerubavel (1991).
5. Surfactant is a fatty substance in the lungs naturally produced by the fetus *in utero* at around 34 weeks of gestation. Sufactant coats the alveoli (small air sacs) of the lungs, keeping them ex-panded and facilitating the exchange of oxygen and carbon dioxide (Sammons and Lewis 1985).
6. Mortality rates for premature infants weighing between 601 and 1300 grams at birth (known as "micropreemies" and "very, very premature infants") declined significantly after the wide-spread introduction of surfactant for this group of neonates. See Horbar et al. (1993).
7. Some of these search terms did not list articles but instead cross-listed a different term(s). For example, the search term "Babies" always referred the reader to "Infants." However, I continued to check my original terms in each volume in order to ensure that there was no change over time.
8. Heimer and Stevens note the organizational need for NICU social workers to attend to "symbolic propriety" in order "to affirm the humanness of infants hovering on the fault line between life and death." (1997:159).
9. Named after Dr. Virginia Apgar, who developed the scoring system in 1953, the APGAR score evaluates an infant's physical condition one minute and five minutes after birth. Infants are given a score between 0 and 2 for five different physical indicators: heart rate, respiration, muscle tone, response to stimuli, and color (Apgar 1953).

References

Anonymous. 1992. "Skin-to-Skin Care: Preemies Benefit from a Marsupial Habit." *Prevention* (September) 44:22–23.

Anonymous. 1994. "Baby-Burial Mom Says Premature Baby More than 'Surgical Waste'" *Winnipeg Free Press*, October 3.

Ansorge, R. 1996. "The Miracle of Caleb: Year-Old Boy Is Living, Squealing Proof of Newborn Hope's Success." *Colorado Springs Gazette*, November 19, p. El.

Apgar, V. 1953. "A Proposal for a New Method of Evaluation of the Newborn Infant" *Current Research in Anesthesia and Analgesia* 32:260–67.

Belgin, J. 1990. "A 'Premature' Miracle: Perth Amboy Officers Deliver Healthy Baby Girl Despite 'Early Arrival' and Complications." *Star Ledger*, March 29.

Brown, J. 1992. *The Definition of a Profession: The Authority of Metaphor in the History of Intelligence Testing, 1890–1930*. Princeton, NJ: Princeton University Press.

Butler, J. 1990. *Gender Trouble: Feminism and the Subversion of Identity*. New York: Routledge.

Casper, M. 1998. *The Making of the Unborn Patient: A Social Anatomy of Fetal Surgery*. New Brunswick, NJ: Rutgers University Press.

Condit, C. 1990. *Decoding Abortion Rhetoric*. Urbana, IL: University of Illinois Press.

Cooley, C. 1983. *Human Nature and the Social Order*. New Brunswick, NJ: Transaction Publishers.

Cummings, E. 1997. "Smallest of Miracles." *Lancaster New Era*, December 6.

Daniels, C. 1993. *At Women's Expense: State Power and the Politics of Fetal Rights*. Cambridge, MA: Harvard University Press.

Douglas, M. 1966. *Purity and Danger*. London: Routledge & Kegan Paul.

Duden, B. 1993. *Disembodying Women: Perspectives on Pregnancy and the Unborn*. Cambridge, MA: Harvard University Press.

Fischer, A. 1988. "A Medical Miracle." *Redbook*, November, pp. 127, 172, 174.

Franklin, S. 1991. "Fetal Fascinations: New Dimensions to the Medical-Scientific Construction of Fetal Personhood." Pp. 190–205 in *Off-Centre: Feminism and Cultural Studies*, edited by S. Franklin, C. Lury, and J. Stacey. London: Harper Collins Academic.

Frey, D. 1995. "'Does Anyone Here Think This Baby Can Live?'" *New York Times Magazine*, July 9, pp. A22–31, 36.

Harris, M. 1998. "The Social Construction of Prematurity: Negotiations in an Intensive Care Unit." Unpublished Ph.D. dissertation, University of Washington, Seattle, WA.

Haynes, D. 1993. "Mother's Day Gift." *Portland Oregonian* May 6, p. 1.

Heimer, C. and M. Stevens. 1997. "Caring for the Organization: Social Workers as Frontline Risk Managers in Neonatal Intensive Care Units." *Work and Occupations* 24(2):133–63.

Helgason, J. 1993. "A Tiny Baby Grows into a Major Miracle," *Dayton Daily News*, December 25, p. 1A.

Horbar, J., E. Wright, and L. Onstad. 1993. "Decreasing Mortality Associated with the Introduction of Surfactant Therapy: An Observational Study of Neonates Weighing 601 to 1300 Grams at Birth." *Pediatrics* 92(2):191–96.

Huber, M. M. 1996. "Quiet Reigns in MCV High-Tech Preterm Units: Baby's Surroundings Altered to Limit Environmental Stress." *Richmond Times Dispatch*, May 5, p. S9.

Isaacson, N. 1996. "The 'Fetus-Infant': Changing Classifications of *In-Utero* Development in Medical Texts." *Sociological Forum*, September, 11(3):457–95.

Jobe, A. 1993. "Pulmonary Surfactant Therapy." *New England Journal of Medicine* 328(12):861–67.

Lunzer, F. 1985. "Wired for Life." *Forbes*, August 26, pp. 124–25.

Manginello, F. and T. DiGeronimo. 1998. *Your Premature Baby: Everything You Need to Know about Childbirth, Treatment, and Parenting*. New York: John Wiley and Sons.

Mentor, S. 1998. "Witches, Nurses, Midwives and Cyborgs: IVF, ART, and Complex Agency in the World of Technobirth." Pp. 67–89 in *Cyborg Babies: From Techno-Sex to Techno-Tots*, edited by R. Davis-Floyd and J. Dumit. New York: Routledge.

Petchesky, R. 1987. "Fetal Images: The Power of Visual Culture in the Politics of Reproduction." *Feminist Studies* 13(2):263–92.

Pfister, F. and B. Griesemer 1983. *The Littlest Baby: A Handbook for Parents of Premature Children*. Englewood, NJ: Prentice-Hall.

Phillips, C. 1988. "The Littlest Miracle." *Reader's Digest*, July, pp. 75–79.

Pitock, T. 1996. "Dreaming of Michaela." *Tikkun*, November, 11(6):54.

Raymond, B. 1992. "Kristen's Story." *Good Housekeeping*, August, 215(2):107, 187–89.

Robinson, M., L. Baker, and L. Nackerud. 1999. "The Relationship of Attachment Theory and Perinatal Loss." *Death Studies* 23:257–70.

Sammons, W. and J. Lewis. 1985. *Premature Babies: A Different Beginning*. St. Louis, MO: C.V. Mosby Company.

Silverman, W. 1992. "Overtreament of Neonates? A Personal Retrospective." *Pediatrics* 90(6): 971–76.

Singer, P. 1995. *Rethinking Life and Death: The Collapse of Our Traditional Ethics*. New York: St. Martin's Press.

Stabile, C. 1992. "Shooting the Mother: Fetal Photography and the Politics of Disappearance." *Camera Obscura* 28:179–205.

Stepan, N. 1986. "Race and Gender: The Role of Analogy in Science." *Isis* 77:261–77.

Tumulty, K. 1990. "The Abortions of Last Resort." *Los Angeles Times Magazine*, January 7, p. 10.

Turner, V. 1969. *The Ritual Process: Structure and Anti-Structure*. Ithaca, NY: Cornell University Press.

Zerubavel, E. 1981. *Hidden Rhythms: Schedules and Calendars in Social Life*. Chicago, IL: Chicago University Press.

———. 1991. *The Fine Line: Making Distinctions in Everyday Life*. Chicago, IL: Chicago University Press.

Cognition in Social Constructions

MARKET RIVALRY PROFILE VERSUS
COST SCHEDULE

Harrison C. White

Cognitive habits are the drive-train of any social vehicle. They leave traces in socio-cultural patterns that come out of social constructions, which shape those very habits, which have become visible only through social enactment. Let us take production markets as the social constructions. We begin with *signaling*, move on to sketch the whole market mechanism, and end with economic theorists' *denial* of markets in favor of optimal cost schedules contrived in their own minds. We look to *participants'* minds.

Production Markets as Signaling Mechanisms

Production markets evolve as signaling mechanisms. Each market spreads the risks and uncertainties in successive commitments made by its producers, even as these producers continue to eye one another.[1] Each producer is seeking a footing, looking to and at a market profile across his or her set of commitments; call it a *rivalry profile*. Repeated enactment of this profile of choices makes it into a signaling mechanism that is jointly constructed as well as recognized in those very choices—a market as social construction.

Any rivalry requires a basis in and indeed generates *comparability*. Rivalry in a production market depends on the emergence of an observable ordering by quality among its particular set of competing producers, an ordering that indexes even as it establishes comparability. This is an ordering both of producers and of their product flows by quality as that is perceived in common by the purchasers as well as by the producers themselves.

The market profile thus translates present indefiniteness from across the market downstream into a definite menu based on the most recent commitments from a well-known set of like peers, commitments that have been fulfilled and accepted down-stream. It proves possible to index which particular profile emerges along a particu-lar path of development, and thus to index a particular history with a single number, a "historical constant." This constant (designate it as k,) picks one from among the ar-ray of profiles of each which could sustain itself in subsequent sets of commitments for the given context of other markets and firms.

But as yet this mechanism, this social vehicle, does not have rear wheels mounted. These producers and their whole market are typically serving as an intermediary which continuously *procures* a variety of input flows from the producers in markets upstream, markets for yet other goods and services—just as the given market typi-cally is contributing also through its flows variously to yet other markets downstream from it. Somehow the rivalry profile and its signaling mechanism must be building in responsiveness to that upstream procurement context. Otherwise this social con-struction would not reproduce itself and so would not be recognized.

Because the upstream context shapes how and how much its constituent producers make, and thus shapes their *costs*, there are not two but rather a succession of three distinct roles interacting for the shaping of each rivalry profile of choices: down-stream purchasers, producers, and upstream suppliers—front wheels plus driver plus back wheels of this social vehicle.

Is there, then, a "cost profile" too, a sort of dual to the rivalry profile? No, because of asymmetry in the uncertainties to which the rivalry profile is the constructive reaction. There are lots of uncertainties around producers, as around all actors. But many of these can be converted to risk, which is to say they can be handled on an actuarial basis, even if not literally through taking out insurance. Producers orient toward the primary uncertainty they perceive in making commitments in their mar-ket. Call this the *Knightian uncertainty*, in honor of Frank Knight (1921), who early and lucidly emphasized how central to business-action was this incomputable uncer-tainty. Markets oriented upstream can also be observed in one period or another, but here let us stick with the market oriented downstream toward sales, with its market profile as joint screening of Knightian uncertainty, which then activates cost estima-tions by each firm.

Observability governs the framing of rivalry. Each competing producer, in order to estimate the rivalry profile in which it is caught up, scans the market positions of its peers. Concretely, it scans the volume and price of other producers in order to find apt footing for itself by suitable commitment to volume of its own. This commitment in turn signals the others its own location on this very profile of rivalry which they are thereby together constituting in continuing reenactment of last month's or quarter's pattern of commitments.

The producers thus sidestep having to calibrate directly the quality and thence the potential valuation assignable by purchasers to each producer's flow of product or service. The trade-off, of course, is that they have to toe the line of equal valuation insisted upon by purchasers. This line is marked by the ratio of valuation by the said purchasers to money they pay a producer. This ratio is kept the same for each producer, though said purchasers cannot select which particular ratio above breakeven obtains. This ratio is the same because a producer who offers too much product at said price or, to put it the other way, asks too much price for said volume of its particular distinctive product, could see all sales vanishing into the hands of peer producers. Some of such sales loss would no doubt go to quite different markets, as when hotshot motorists shift to motorcycles in protest of escalating sports car prices.

That is the first third of the argument. The description has been kept qualitative but it has been successfully translated into a mathematical model. This is a model of market mechanism as a socially constructed set of cognitive habits by which choices of producer commitment level guide and confirm each other in optimizing their own situation within that frame. Details can be suppressed, but just glance at Figures 6–1 and 6–2. These are a stylized illustration of a market profile together with the general parameter map produced from the model. On this map, distinct varieties of market correspond to different areas; a particular point in each of four areas is indicated.[2]

These results can be shown to account for half a dozen and more phenomena concerning production markets for which existing theory cannot account. For example, in many lines of business, accolades for higher quality in a firm's product accompany a cost structure that is *lower* than that of any peer judged of lesser quality. In the map of Figure 6–2 this is the area marked PARADOX as variety of market. Second, since the historical constant k can take any of the ranges of value shown in Figure 6–2, the model denies that there is a determinate outcome for a market even for given context.

FIGURE 6–1

Market profile and cost schedules yielding terms-of-trade for seven producers: stylized.

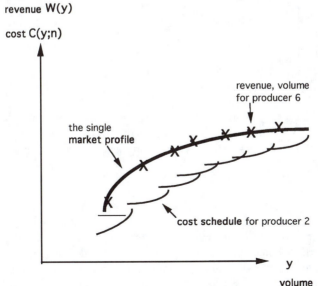

revenue W(y)

cost C(y;n)

revenue, volume for producer 6

the single market profile

cost schedule for producer 2

y

volume

FIGURE 6–2

Map of market varieties in parameter space for production market downstream.

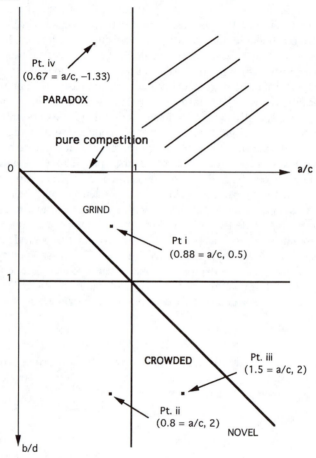

The model denies the mantra of "supply equals demand." Perhaps most basic, the model explains why production markets typically have distinct identities and but a dozen or fewer members—each of whom continues to make nonzero profits.

Cost

Second come details on cost and also on the mechanics of modeling. A market profile guides each producer to its optimizing choice; the producer then continues, subject to the earlier choices having been accepted by the downstream side of the market. Optimizing is getting the most net return, the greatest gap between revenue and cost. The rub is that cost still lies, at the time of commitment, in the future of that firm's subsequent organization of actual production out of its procurements. But the saving grace is that the producers have come to see, back on this upstream side of theirs, the uncertainties as actuarial, as accountable, so that they are comfortable with relying on estimates of likely costs according to the scales of production to which they consider committing. This can be portrayed in a simple graph showing how cost is thought to rise with volume produced in a period. Examples of such cost curves are contained in Figure 6–1.

It proves feasible to set all this up mathematically using elegantly simple approximations to the contextual facts of valuations. These are known as Cobb-Douglas functions (Nerlove 1965). Explicit solutions are obtained, although most often, extensive numerical computations are required to establish predictions from substituting into the equations a given set of facts about reaction tendencies of the various producers and their suppliers and customers. Such is not our concern here.[3]

Already we have established some sense for the standing of the market profile as a cognitive construct, a construct that is at the same time a joint social construction. Now shift the focus to what these producers are seeing as their own individual cost situations. Memberships in the production markets are, after all, historical outcomes of an evolutionary sifting process. The given market would not have established and maintained itself unless there were some degree of coherence among this particular set of producers as to their costs, such that cost expectations line up with their acknowledged order by quality. So the equations in the market model index the cost situation each firm perceives for itself by its position in quality order.

On the other hand, remember, these firms do *not* pierce the veil of uncertainty over buyers. Instead, they substitute observation of a market profile strung out of their own choices, made from watching each other's actions. Each sees these as the set of viable choices available. Given that, the best choice for a given firm will depend on the costs it expects to shoulder, depending on the production volume to which it commits. The firm will decide on that volume which maximizes the gap between the market profile (common to all of them) and its own individual cost assessment curve— among curves which do nest next to each other in line with quality order. And if buyers validate the market profile with the anticipated volumes of purchases from each, then the executives need not question their cost assessment.

The specific cost function, the cost schedule chosen for a firm in my market model, is simple. This is as it should be in order to capture the real-world, nonmathematical basis of assessments by executives. The analyst cannot second-guess firms' expectations and still come up with an account of what transpires in markets. Let others— economists—play pied pipers who insist on their superior ability to chart the firm's optimal course. The excuse that evolutionary pressure will force the firm to just that course, that single course identified by economistic wisdom, is meretricious.

So much for discriminating between the phenomenology of cost schedules and that of rivalry profiles—while yet articulating how they mutually support one another as cognitive habits within a socially constructed mechanism. Cost schedules can indeed be more individual and private in operation as compared to rivalry profiles, but all the more do they require and derive from cultural forms engrained in the discourse registers of that line of business and across many lines of business (Halliday 1976; Gumperz 1982; White forthcoming). They are cultural routines or artifacts into which are poured particularities of their own situation (Duranti and Goodwin 1992).

Market Competition

Now to the third part of my model, which features the economists' drama of pure competition.

Economic theory has paid a heavy price for not understanding how the production market forms as a social construction, one in which cognitions of various parties guide each other and thereby interlock in a mechanism for market decisions. Economic theorists have not been able to agree (cf. Schmalensee and Willig 1989) on any realistic account of their own for the production market, even half a century after Chamberlin (1933) sketched its key features. Their individualistic presuppositions continue to mire economic theorists in speculations about the speculations which they impute to businesspeople considering their own market situations.

But theorists must produce theory. So economists resort to a fiction of pure competition to explain away actual markets. This supplies them with some local outcomes that they can cumulate into macroeconomic prognostications, in principle at least (Carlton 1989), and with which they can assert completeness and consistency in their general theory of an economy into which production markets must be fit (Hicks 1946, chap. 10).

Even as an approximation, however, pure competition fails for important, common sorts of markets. In particular it fails for markets whose member firms experience increasing returns to scale from their production process, corresponding to the CROWDED region in the market map of Figure 6–2. In that sort of context, pure competition pushes toward monopoly. Thus economic theorists would be bereft of any market model for this context of increasing returns to scale except for their expedient of fudging the issue by supposing, without any appreciable evidence, that a curve for unit cost that is decreasing must eventually rise again—the infamous "U-shaped curve" (Panzar 1989).[4]

Even so, limitation of cost context is *not* the main problem with pure competition theorizing. Except for these increasing returns to scale contexts, the pure competition mechanism that economists propound works well as to its mathematical machinery. Its *substance*, however, is largely based on *presumed free entry and exit of whole firms to and from a market with little identity*, to a veritable shadow. So we must move toward unraveling the mystery of how and why economic theory engages in this mystification of markets.

Economic theory has, without much self-awareness, in fact turned away from the market, the market it apotheosizes as an abstraction, to theorize the cost structure of the firm, which has been found to be the easier target. An elaborate structure has been built up resting on this foundation of suppression of actual market mechanism. The putative cost schedule is thereby slid in as the focus of theory of production markets!

But first note that this supposed "cost schedule" is the subject of much skepticism within the discipline of economics. There are countercurrents from economists who are actually versed in live business and wish to offer it effective counsel—and who scoff at these "cost schedules" of the theorist. So let us pause to examine this considerable debate among economists about the validity of *any* cost schedules.

Some economists thus go beyond being uneasy about these cost schedules and press their discipline to be more coherent as regards these constructs. Bela Gold is one of the few economists not only to recognize the problematics of cost but also to go on to do explicit field studies and model construction. In concluding his magisterial review of both theory and observation in economics of cost, Gold (1981:20) first points to the necessity of going beyond a comparative statics framework in order to deal with how innovation, strategy, and disequilibrium are rooted in evolving cognitions—of the managers, not of the economists:

> The current state of technology represents a system of ideas, theories and explorations, which reaches far beyond actual applications at any given time. This makes it difficult indeed to determine which innovations should be barred from evaluations of scale effects.

Much the same argument is made by Nelson and Winter (1982). But Gold also points to avoidance practices by economic theorists even within the equilibrium framework of comparative statics, such as around the U-shape curve cited earlier.

In each of their two approaches to cost (Gold 1981), economists are wrong. Sometimes they conceive cost schedules as an engineer would steam tables for engines, and occasionally they even turn to engineers for estimates of cost across different sizes of some type of production facility. By direct investigation an engineer could uncover that certain ranges of conversion ratios of heat for work were or were not obtainable. But the proper analogue for a social scientist is to see that whether returns to scale are increasing is, in large part, a question of what managers in those firms have come to believe and thus practice.

There will be some reality checks on a given manager, but they will be limited not only by the scope of variability in contexts actually being experienced by those production operations, but also by the continuing parallel choices and responses by other managers. If managers work a rivalry profile with routine success in market reproduction, they need not come to doubt their understandings of the form of their cost schedules, understandings no doubt partially shared across actors in their discourse register. This is why even increasing returns to scale can be integrated with market mechanism when both are seen to be matters of sociocultural construction by managers, not just technical facts of a sort of engineering.

The trap that ensnares economic theory is implicit reliance on pure competition theory in the very formulation of the construct, here cost schedule, in terms of which the market is to be analyzed. For evidence turn to the beginning, avowedly foundational, chapter of the most recent definitive handbook of economic analysis of industrial organization (Schmalensee and Willig 1989). There is some pretense of using engineering knowledge of technology to establish cost curves. The first chapter's author (Panzar 1989) entitles it "Technological Determinants . . ." Although this chapter speaks much of empirical studies, one has to wait until near the end for examples.

These are, in a narrow technical sense, well done as statistical estimations—but estimations of what? In these examples, technology is losing importance, and so are accounting studies and rough field studies such as those by pioneer economist Bain (1950). Instead one turns away from the actual market interface under ostensible study. One says that the producers will be price takers with respect to their back side, their inputs—and so, thank heaven, there is no market problematic. Then comes the big step. One simply equates cost with the revenue received by the producer! Surely a madcap procedure?

Not if one insists on pure competition as applying to this market interface one has just turned away from in awe of reality. For under pure competition each producer faces a fixed price whatever volume it projects offering, and in conclusion, neither it nor any of its peers—whether or not they have parallel cost structures—will do better than break even. Hence cost *is* revenue in this fairy-tale world. Voila! One need not measure cost at all!

Now examine how a distinguished econometrician, Marc Nerlove (later followed by Christensen and others), enacts the theorists' prescriptions in tangible models, the basis of the examples in the handbook. Even here there is madness. These businesses are so smart (despite slaving on for zero profits, according to economic theory) that one has them unerringly choosing that combination of inputs that optimize, that is, minimize, costs. Thus one regresses the observed market revenues, of firms at various times, over the sets of inputs at prices assumed (variously for labor, raw materials, etc., to some degree of disaggregation). Little causal insight has been offered, little probing of reality, but considerable effort is given to measuring accurately this misspecified model. One improves on logarithmic regression by moving to loglog regression. It all looks very scientific and advanced but it is in fact nonsense in substantive terms.[5]

Perhaps this is too abstract. Consider another of the econometric case studies surveyed by Panzar (1989), that of airlines by Cave and associates. The regression (now without the loglog wrinkle) is of revenue versus air passenger miles (and number of cities and so on)! But are not air passenger miles the *output*?? Why is the cost schedule a regression on output, as seen *ex post*. What does that have to do with the putative cost framing within which managers decided on operations for the next period?

This debate among economists also reveals that they are all overlooking that a cost schedule, in order to have effect on managerial decision for the firm in a market, must be a construct, a set of ways of organizing and interpreting perceptions that is in use by managers. The plural here is crucial: cost schedules are real because something like them is current in discourse among many managers; it is part of their business register of discourse.

Conclusion

Finally, the payoff. This argument has underlined that social constructions are necessarily also cultural constructions at two levels. One is the level of transmissible beliefs and general algorithms of practices such as accounting. Then there is the operative level of discourse, in which the cost schedule, like other aspects of market mechanism, comes into effect. "The" market mechanism is in fact a compound of somewhat distinct submechanisms such as the cost schedule, some of which are more explicitly inscribed culturally than others.

Many claims and assertions have been made. But as yet there are no results from or even proposals for investigation of the cognitive practices and habits argued to underlie the claims and assertions. Several factors conspire to confuse the observer, and intricate indeed is the slippage between observer and participant viewpoints and between observer and participant cognitions. There is much to be done.

Endnotes

1. To save circumlocutions, I refer only to cognizing habits of individuals. Sometimes, indeed, the perception, cognition, or choice which is at issue will be that of an individual executive; but more commonly, there will be arrays and coalitions which get recognized and variously named within that market context as actors in their own right, be they firms or parts thereof, trade associations, industries, or production markets proper.
2. Each point corresponds to a whole package of profiles such as that in Figure 6–1, one for each value of k. One profile for each point is portrayed in White (1999, Figures 7–9). Consult the manuscript for a full account of the model.
3. White (1999) provides a full account.
4. Long ago, the Committee on Price Determination of the elite National Bureau of Economic Research commented that, *ceteris paribus*, long-run cost curve would seldom be relevant to the problems confronting an enterprise: see discussion of Bela Gold review below.
5. For a fuller argument, with modeling details and graphs offered by Nerlove (1965), see White (1999, Chap. 8).

References

Bain, J. S. 1950. *Cost Structures*. New York: Macmillan.

Carlton, D. W. 1989. "The Theory and the Facts of How Markets Clear: Is Industrial Organization Valuable for Understanding Macroeconomics?" Pp. 909–46 in *Handbook of Industrial Organization*: *I, II*, edited by R. Schmalensee and R. D. Willig. Amsterdam, Netherlands: North-Holland.

Chamberlin, E. H. 1933. *The Theory of Monopolistic Competition*. 1st ed. [8th ed. 1962] Cambridge, MA: Harvard University Press.

Duranti, A. and C. Goodwin, eds. 1992. *Rethinking Context: Language as an Interactive Phenomenon*. New York: Cambridge University Press.

Gold, B. 1981. "Changing Perspectives on Size, Scale, and Returns: An Interpretive Survey." *Journal of Economic Literature* 19:5–33.

Gumperz, J. 1982. *Discourse Strategies*. New York: Cambridge University Press.

Halliday, M. A. K. 1976. *System and Function in Language: Selected Papers*, edited by G.R. Kress. London: Oxford University Press.

Hicks, J. 1946. *Value and Capital*. London: Macmillan.

Knight, F. 1921. *Risk, Uncertainty and Profit*. Cambridge, MA: Houghton Mifflin.

Nelson, R. and S. Winter. 1982. *An Evolutionary Theory of Economic Change*. Cambridge, MA: Harvard University Press.

Nerlove, M. 1965. *Estimation and Identification of Cobb-Douglas Production Functions*. Chicago, IL: Rand McNally.

Panzar, J. C. 1989. "Technological Determinants of Firm and Industry Structure." Pp. 3–60 in *Handbook of Industrial Organization*: *I, II*, edited by R. Schmalensee and R. D. Willig. Amsterdam, Netherlands: North-Holland.

Schmalensee, R. and R. D. Willig, eds. 1989. *Handbook of Industrial Organization*: *I, II*. Amsterdam, Netherlands: North-Holland.

White, H. C. 1999. "Markets in Networks." November, Columbia University, Department of Sociology. New York, NY. Unpublished Manuscript.

———. Forthcoming. "Modeling Discourse In and Around Markets." *Poetics*.

SECTION III

Representation and Integration

Representation
and Integration:
An Introduction

Section II focused on the techniques and strategies by which we sort and organize information. But according to cognitive scientists, these processes are inexorably tied to two distinct characteristics of the brain: the brain's warehouse of representational constructs (including concepts, frames, formats, and schemata), and its capacity to integrate new information with such constructs. For cognitive scientists, representational constructs constitute the very fuel of thought; they are critical data banks within the brain's elaborate processing apparatus.

For decades, cognitive scientists have probed the nature of representational constructs. They have also explored the ways in which the structure of such constructs directs cognitive activity. The earliest inquiries focused on "concepts," the most basic of the brain's representational tools. One can define concepts as mental categories that partition and cluster information in the brain according to certain essential attributes or characteristic properties. According to cognitive scientists, all concepts display three specific qualities: each possesses certain critical features; each possesses a set of rules that relates its features; and each possesses a set of rules that distinguishes its features from those that define other concepts.

Cognitive scientists tell us that concepts serve multiple functions in the complex process of thought. First, concepts become a benchmark by which to measure and assess new information. Thus, armed with the concept "dog," the healthy functioning brain can correctly classify an encounter with a neighbor's German shepherd, a colleague's mutt, or a passerby's Chihuahua. Similarly, the concept "automobile" directs the healthy functioning brain to the shared attributes of Volkswagen Beetles, Honda Accords, and Chevrolet Corvettes. Second, concepts enable interpretation. For example, if one recognizes a neighbor's pet as a wolf rather than a dog, one can interpret the situation as dangerous and tailor one's actions accordingly. Similarly,

recognizing the differences between a child and an adult allows one to interpret behaviors in terms of an actor's true capacities. Third, concepts enable generalization
and prediction. When a new object or event is interpreted with reference to a particular concept's defining features, it becomes possible to anticipate outcomes and like-
lihoods. For example, if one knows that dogs respond positively to affection and de-
fensively to aggression, one can predict any dog's likely response to a menu of
possible overtures. Similarly, if one knows the defining features of the concept "wedding," one can anticipate the outcome of any particular marriage ceremony. Finally,
the use of concepts allows the brain to produce specific instances of a class. In this
way, concepts allow the brain to convert general properties to particular cases. Thus
when a friend expresses the desire for a "warm and cuddly pet," one might accurately
respond with a puppy, a kitten, or a rabbit. Similarly, a call for a "rich and decadent
dessert" might reasonably result in a hot fudge sundae, a creamy cheesecake, a pecan
pie, or a deep chocolate mousse.

In addition to defining the nature and function of concepts, cognitive scientists
have studied extensively the issue of concept formation.[1] For example, inspired by
philosophers such as Plato, Leibniz, and Descartes, scholars such as Noam Chomsky
(1972; 1980) and Jerry Fodor (1975) argued that concepts are innate constructs,[2] the
essences of a complex mental "hardware" that is common to all human brains. But
among cognitive scientists, the more dominant view of concept formation suggests
that concepts are learned through experience. Studies conducted by Jerome Bruner
(Bruner et al. 1956) and Dianne Berry and Donald Broadbent (1984)[3] link concept
formation to basic principles of learning such as stimulus-response associations and
elaborate hypotheses-testing sequences—mental exercises that allow human beings
methodically to establish the order of things.[4]

Beyond concept formation, the issue of concept structure—that is, the specifics of
that which constitutes a concept—proves most central to the concept research. In
particular, the nature of a concept's "critical features" and whether or not such features truly exist proves a hotly debated issue. A perspective called "the classical
view"[5] represents the earliest statement on this subject. The classical view defines a
concept's critical features as characteristics that are singly necessary and jointly sufficient to define a class. For example, the concept "prime number" is uniquely
defined by referring to two and only two critical features: "divisible by ± 1" and
"divisible by itself." Similarly, the concept "bird" is properly defined by referring to
the critical features "warm-blooded vertebrate," "produced from eggs," "possessing
feathers," "possessing two wings," "possessing a beak," and possessing two legs."
According to the classical view, defining features strictly itemize the parameters of a
concept; they also provide fixed criteria for evaluating new information and deciding
whether or not new instances represent members of a concept.

Many cognitive scientists take issue with the classical view's treatment of defining
features. Eleanor Rosch,[6] for example, calls for a more flexible approach. According
to Rosch (who relied heavily on Ludwig Wittgenstein's work), the classical view
fails to acknowledge several key points. First, many concepts have no fixed defining
features. For example, consider the concept "game." What is a game? Is it an activity
enjoyed by all participants? (But then, what about the "sore loser"?) Is it an activity
enjoyed by those of all ages? (When was the last time you saw a four-year-old playing bridge or a forty-year-old playing London Bridge?) Is it strictly employed for

fun . . . played during leisure time? (But what about professional sports?) Does it involve multiple players? Is it competitive? (How about solitaire?) According to Rosch, the problematic nature of defining the "game" suggests that for many concepts, defining features may exist as resemblances or general qualities rather than precisely stated criteria.

Second, the classical view fails to recognize that in certain cases, specific examples are better than others in illustrating a concept's defining features. For example, a bluefish is typically considered a better example of the concept "fish" than a sea horse; an apple is considered a better example of a "fruit" than a tomato; a colonial home is considered a better example of a "house" than a teepee.[7] The "best example" phenomenon suggests, according to Rosch, that concepts exist as averages or ideals rather than exact representations. Finally, in many cases, it is simply unclear as to whether an object is a member of a concept. For example, is a television part of the concept "furniture"? Is a scooter part of the concept "vehicle"? According to Rosch, the fuzziness of conceptual boundaries suggests that defining criteria can never be completely exhaustive.

Rosch's objections gave rise to another view on concept structure: the "prototype view." The prototype view of concepts promotes a "best example" premise. Rather than defining the concept according to strict defining features, this approach suggests that concepts are organized around an ideal, one that embodies the most typical features of a concept's instances. From this perspective, it is the similarity between newly encountered objects/events and the concept's prototype that determines if or how well any particular instance belongs to the concept. Thus the prototype for musical instruments may allow one readily to include a violin or a clarinet as part of the concept while rejecting the inclusion of a kazoo or a set of spoons. Similarly, a timpani drum or a cymbal may be highly compatible with the prototype of a "percussive instrument," while a piano, technically percussive in nature, may prove too atypical of the concept. By freeing defining features from the precision of the classical view, proponents of the prototype view claim to bring flexibility to the nature of concept structure and realism to our understanding of concept application.

While many of those researching concept structure agree with Rosch's criticisms of the classical view, some fail to embrace the prototype view as a viable alternative. Scholars such as L. R. Brooks (1978) believe that the notion of a prototype may be *too* abstract and flexible. Brooks argues that general rules or ideal types cannot always define a concept. Rather, a concept is often defined by the individual instances that constitute it. To understand better the heart of Brook's critique, consider the following example. I place a large, red object before you and ask: Is this a tomato? Rather than calling up a prototype in your mind, you reason: this object looks just like the tomatoes my mother used to grow in her garden; therefore, this object is a tomato. In this example, the defining features of the tomato were not derived from general information. Rather the defining features were retrieved from the experience of a specific object. Such an approach to concept structure is referred to as the "exemplar view." Unlike either the classical or prototype view, the exemplar view offers a taxonomic approach to concept structure. It locates a concept's critical or defining feature squarely within direct observation and personal experience rather than abstract rules. As such, the exemplar view suggests that concepts may not be complete and prestored categories. Rather, they are constructs that are created and enhanced as individuals move from context to context.

Both the prototype and empirical views of concepts are actively applied in current research agendas. Yet many believe that these models provide only partial knowledge of concept structure. Thus scholars such as Susan Carey (1985) and Frank Keil (1987) have proposed one final perspective on concept structure—an approach that they define as more holistic in nature than the classical, prototype, or empirical views. This model, referred to as the "theory-dependent view," does not consider the concept as an isolated construct. Indeed, proponents of this view argue that concepts cannot be considered one by one, as units independent from one another. Rather, adherents of the theory-dependent view define concept structure with reference to the wider network of beliefs in which a concept is embedded; they argue that one's beliefs or implicit theories about relevant subject matters direct both the construction of concepts and the interconnections one recognizes between multiple concepts.

To illustrate this premise, consider the following example. A man is legally separated from his wife and is dating other women. If you believe that a legal separation frees one from the restrictions of marriage, then you may conceptualize this man as a "bachelor" and evaluate his dating behavior as normal. If, however, you feel marriage is a union sanctioned in heaven, indissoluble by earthly law, then you will conceptualize this man as "a married man" and evaluate his behavior as immoral (Fillmore 1982). With these examples, proponents of the theory-dependent view argue that concepts such as "bachelor" and "married man" are the product of both experience and broader beliefs—that is, experience contributes to the development of one's beliefs, and in turn, one's beliefs create intricate mental networks that buffer the structure of the concept. In this way, the theory-dependent view differs from other existing models. This approach requires that concept structure be considered relative to a broader mental system.

Cognitive scientists' extensive inquiries into concepts and concept structure have spurred an equally vigorous focus on more elaborate or higher-level representational constructs—that is, intricate combinations of concepts that form semantic networks. "Frames" exemplify one such entity. According to Marvin Minsky (1975), frames are static constructs that allow human beings to represent stereotyped interactions or situations. These situations can include ordered expectations about objects or settings—for instance, the typical layout of a kitchen or the typical content and configuration of a floral centerpiece. Frames may also include event sequences—for instance, what happens first, second, third, and so on, when one dines at a restaurant or goes to a birthday party.[8] In all such circumstances, Minsky argues that two sets of features constitute a frame: features that are *always* true of a given interaction or situation, and features that can take on a variety of different values as the interaction or situation demands. (The latter are called "terminal slots."[9]) For example, consider the frame for a traditional classroom experience. Such a frame will contain features that are always true—the room will have four walls and a ceiling, the class will contain an instructor and students, the class will involve communication in the form of reading, writing, and speaking, and so on. But the classroom frame will also contain terminal slots that change from experience to experience. These slots might address the size of the class, the configuration of seats, the form of communication (lecture versus discussion), the subject matter, and so on.

Cognitive scientists contend that human beings develop a repertoire of situational and interactional frames—configuration frames for home or office, play frames, work frames, danger frames, intimacy frames, and so on. Via these constructs, the brain forms a structured set of expectations within which new situations can be evaluated. Some researchers, Charles Fillmore (1975) among them, suggest that human beings also develop special linguistic frames called "formats." Formats are systems of linguistic choices associated with prototypical instances of a frame. While frames help human beings to process actual experience, formats help human beings to process reports and descriptions of experience. Thus formats allow human beings to distinguish public discourse from private or intimate discussion; they allow human beings to discriminate between factual and fictional accounts, between drama and comedy, and so on. Utilizing formats, the brain can successfully interpret incoming text, language, and "secondhand" experience.

One final type of representational construct proves important to cognitive scientists. Sir Frederick Bartlett (1932) introduced "schemata" in conjunction with his research on memory. According to Bartlett, schemata are the most abstract of the brain's representational apparatus. As such, these constructs differ significantly from other representational tools. While concepts, frames, and formats consist of specified sets of expectations, schemata consist of an organized framework of relations that must be completed with concrete details. Thus schemata constitute highly generalized knowledge structures, abstract guidelines and rules that help human beings infer meaning.

How does the brain incorporate details into existing schemata? The following example helps to illustrate the process. Suppose that over the past week, you learn that several of your colleagues have fallen victim to the flu. Then today, you discover that your colleague Mary came to work feeling nauseous and ill. How would you make sense of Mary's condition? According to cognitive scientists, the healthy functioning brain would review stored knowledge for an explanatory framework that *best* fits the details of Mary's situation. In this instance, a schema for contagious disease would provide a plausible option. Such a schema would embody a general principle—that exposure to a specific illness increases the likelihood of contracting that illness. Since the details of Mary's particular experience fit this general mental model, cognitive scientists argue that the brain would likely invoke the contagious disease schema to interpret Mary's condition. Mary's specific details would "fill in" the general outline held in the brain's data banks. And together, the previously held model and the newly acquired particulars would create a plausible and meaningful scenario.

Note that the application of plausible schemata may produce meaningful interpretations. However, such interpretations may not always prove accurate. In reviewing the case of Mary, for example, it is also possible that her nausea resulted from food poisoning, overindulgence in alcohol, or the early stages of pregnancy. But because the schema for contagious disease encompasses Mary's total experience (Mary was exposed; Mary is now sick), the brain will likely select it as the most appropriate interpretive tool. In essence, the brain tends to match incoming particulars to the most likely scenario—even if this "best fit" is ultimately not the true fit.[10]

When one reviews cognitive scientific research on representation and integration, it becomes clear that the field's central focus is on the brain's "primary operating system." Most lines of inquiry strive to identify the internal structures of the brain, plot their configuration, and explore the ways in which those structures interface, both with one another and with incoming data. To be sure, each of these tasks is critical to understanding the process of thought. Yet these tasks alone do not comprise a sufficient intellectual agenda. A full understanding of cognition demands that we explore the representation and integration of information as it is situated within sociocultural context. For while sociocultural factors may not determine how mental constructs are initially acquired, such factors may help us to understand why certain constructs become so widely shared among social actors while others do not. Similarly, while sociocultural factors may not pinpoint the structure of mental constructs, such factors may help us to understand when and why certain constructs are invoked and applied over others. And while sociocultural factors may not elucidate the ways in which mental constructs interface with one another, such factors may help us to better understand the ways in which mental constructs interface with the external world, thus steering, shaping, and limiting shared definitions of reality and patterns of social action.

It is the sociocultural aspects of representation and integration that occupy the authors of this section. Each author explores the ways in which contexts can beckon and favor certain concepts, frames, and formats. Further, each explores the ways in which such representations, once institutionalized, can narrow or misdirect definitions of reality. In Chapter 7, for example, Robert Wuthnow considers the sociological study of morality. Wuthnow contends that such moral inquiry has been unduly restrictive. This is because sociologists' conceptions of moral inquiry are largely shaped by specific "exemplars" —that is, works frequently cited as prime instances of such inquiry. (For Wuthnow, the works of Mills or Bellah provide illustrative examples.) Without in any way disparaging the importance of these writers, Wuthnow argues that exemplars of moral inquiry may have misdirected scholarly attentions. By embracing these exemplars of moral inquiry, the field has come to overlook the moral components contained within the majority of social scientific works. In so doing, the field has fallen subject to the influence of a false dichotomy. The false dichotomy is between value-laden and value-free inquiry, between the normative and the empirical, between the prescriptive and the positivist, or between the moral and the amoral. In Chapter 7, Wuthnow problematizes the exemplars of moral inquiry. He argues that such an exercise can help sociologists to abandon false dichotomies and embrace instead a true conceptual dichotomy, one that sets aside the normative and the empirical in favor of considerations for autonomous and embedded selves. According to Wuthnow, reconceptualizing moral inquiry in terms of this true dichotomy will both broaden and crystallize sociological treatments of morality.

In Chapter 8, I too focus on the ways in which concepts can restrict or misdirect both scholarly and popular thinking. The study of social relations provides the site for my inquiry. My work begins with a simple observation. In any review of the literature on social relations, one inevitably notes a long-standing reliance on certain "theory-dependent" conceptions of social relations—concepts such as *Gemeinschaft* versus *Gesellschaft, mechanical* versus *organic solidarity, primary* versus *secondary relations, direct* versus *indirect relations*, and so on. These concepts and the analytic models from which they emerged have established a rigid, singular view of relational development. Such models suggest that relations in societies such as the United States evolve in a linear fashion. As such societies grow and develop, they experience a "natural" shift from the "we-ness" of national community to the "me-ness" of individualism—a shift that is the unfortunate yet inevitable price of an increasingly complex, modern society. Over the past several years, I have been studying relational development relative to historical data on social behaviors, attitudes, cultural products, and images (in the United States from around 1850 to 1995). These data fail to support notions of a one-way path leading from "we" to "me" relations. Indeed, these data suggest that the concepts typically applied to the study of social relations may be blinding us to certain realities of social and cultural life. Spurred by this finding, my work pursues two critical research questions: What sustains analytic concepts that often contradict empirical reality? And can concepts so well entrenched in both scholarly and popular thought be successfully redefined? In the hope of answering these questions, Chapter 8 examines the role of both cultural scripts and specific social events in the creation and sustenance of "fixed conceptualizations."

The next two chapters move beyond concepts, focusing readers on higher-level representational constructs. In Chapter 9, David Altheide demonstrates the distinctive contributions that a sociocultural approach can bring to the study of cognitive frames and formats. Like most social scientists, Altheide rejects the notion of frames as static entities—innate constructs that lie in the ready, waiting to be tapped. Rather, Altheide treats frames as dynamic sociocultural constructs, entities of the mind rather than the brain. His work examines the ways in which frames are formed and fashioned in the service of interaction. Further, he examines the ways in which interpretive frameworks give rise to communication formats, structures that guide the meaning-making activities of those once removed from face-to-face interaction. To explicate fully the role of frames and formats in perception and decision making, Altheide takes readers to the world of media news. Analyzing news coverage, he illustrates the ways in which media narrators use certain frames and formats to construct actively a "discourse of fear." Altheide tracks this discourse over time and, in so doing, demonstrates that the public's fears are not necessarily tied to actual incidence or probable risk. Rather, he shows that news frames and formats shape audience understandings and expectations of what to fear and how to avoid it.

In Chapter 10, William Gamson focuses readers on formats as well. His work examines the institutionalization of formats—the systematic pairing of certain themes with particular information arrangements. Gamson takes readers to the world of policy discourse, where he identifies the institutionalized formats that guide public dialogues. Like Altheide, he chooses media news as his entree to this venue, and within that context, he examines the formatting of stories on abortion. Gamson analyzes discourse on both sides of the abortion debate and, in so doing, shows that a "personalization format" has come to dominate all abortion policy discourse. Referencing broader research on discourse, the author notes that his findings represent a general trend in the formatting of the news. Indeed, he suggests that personalization, a format formerly reserved for private exchange, has become a regular feature of media policy coverage. Having established this pattern, Gamson explores the reasons behind this unexpected format transfer. More important, he explores the ways in which the media's application of the personalization format can alter audience perspective and thus empower readers and viewers.

Endnotes

1. See Nelson and Gruendel (1981) or Hirschfeld (1994) for a general review of this literature.
2. In later work, Fodor (1998) reconstitutes innateness as "mind dependence."

3. Years earlier, of course, Lev Vygotsky ([1934] 1962; [1934] 1978) promoted this position.
4. See, e.g., Bower and Trabasso (1964) or Levine (1966).
5. Note that the classical view is sometimes referred to as "the definitional view."
6. See, e.g., Rosch (1977); Rosch and Mervis (1975).
7. Malt and Smith (1984) empirically document this phenomenon.
8. This definition is similar to Roger Shank's and Robert Abelson's (1977) notion of "scripts."
9. According to Minsky, terminal slots carry default values that can be reset as new data presents itself.
10. Because schemata are so closely linked to the study of memory, research on schematic development and application will be discussed in Section IV as well.

References

Bartlett, Sir F. 1932. *Remembering*. Cambridge, England: Cambridge University Press.
Berry, D. C. and D. E. Broadbent. 1984. "On the Relationship between Task Performance and Associated Verbalizable Knowledge." *Quarterly Journal of Experimental Psychology. A Human Experimental Psychology*. 36(2):209–31.
Bower, G.H. and T. R. Trabasso. 1964. "Concept Identification." Pp. 32–94 in *Studies in Mathematical Psychology*, edited by R. C. Atkinson. Stanford, CA: Stanford University Press.
Brooks, L. R. 1978. "Nonanalytic Concept Formation and Memory for Instances." Pp. 160–215 in *Cognition and Categorization*, edited by E. Rosch and B. B. Lloyd. Hillsdale, NJ: Erlbaum Associates.
Bruner, J. S., J. J. Goodnow, and G. A. Austin. 1956. *A Study of Thinking*. New York: Wiley.
Carey, S. 1985. *Conceptual Change in Childhood*. Cambridge, MA: MIT Press.
Chomsky, N. 1972. *Language and Mind*. 2d ed. New York: Harcourt Brace Jovanovich.
———. 1980. *Rules and Representations*. New York: Columbia University Press.
Fillmore, C. J. 1975. "An Alternative to Checklist Theories of Meaning." Pp. 123–31 in *Proceedings of the First Annual Meeting of the Berkeley Linguistics Society*. Institute of Human Learning, University of California at Berkeley, CA.
———. 1982. "Toward a Descriptive Framework for Spatial Deixis." In *Speech, Place, and Action: Studies in Deixis and Related Topics*, edited by R. J. Jarvella and W. Klein. Chichester, England: Wiley.
Fodor, J. 1975. *The Language of Thought*. New York: Crowell.
———. 1998. *Concepts: Where Cognitive Science Went Wrong*. Oxford, England, and New York: Oxford University Press.
Hirschfeld, L. A. 1994. "The Child's Representation of Human Groups." *Psychological Learning and Motivation* 31:133–85.
Keil, F. C. 1987. "Conceptual Development and Category Structure." Pp. 301–34 in *Language Development: Language, Cognition, and Culture*, edited by U. Neisser. Hillsdale, NJ: Erlbaum Associates.
Levine, M. 1966. "Hypothesis Behavior by Humans during Discrimination Learning." *Journal of Experimental Psychology* 71:331–38.
Malt, B. C. and E. E. Smith. 1984. "Correlated Properties in Natural Categories." *Journal of Verbal Learning and Verbal Behavior* 23:250–69.
Minsky, M. 1975. "A Framework for Representing Knowledge." Pp. 211–77 in *The Psychology of Computer Vision*, edited by P. H. Winston. New York: McGraw-Hill.
Nelson, K. and J. Gruendel. 1981. "Generalized Event Representation: Basic Building Blocks of Cognitive Development." Pp. 131–58 in *Advances in Developmental Psychology*, edited by M. E. Lamb and A. L. Brown. Hillsdale, NJ: Lawrence Erlbaum.

Rosch, E. 1977. "Human Categorization." In *Advances in Cross-Cultural Psychology,* vol. 1, edited by N. Warren. London: Academic Press.

Rosch, E. and C. G. Mervis. 1975. "Family Resemblances: Studies in the Internal Structure of Categories." *Cognitive Psychology* 7:573–605.

Shank, R. C. and R. P. Abelson. 1977. *Scripts, Plans, Goals, and Understanding: An Inquiry into Human Knowledge Structures.* Hillsdale, NJ: Lawrence Erlbaum Associates.

Vygotsky, L. S. [1934] 1962. *Thought in Language.* Cambridge, MA: MIT Press.

———. [1934] 1978. *Mind in Society,* edited by M. Cole, V. John-Steiner, S. Scribner, and E. Souberman. Cambridge, MA: Harvard University Press.

CHAPTER 7

Moral Inquiry in Cultural Sociology

Robert Wuthnow

Cultural sociology, perhaps more than any other specialty area within the discipline, is positioned to play an important role in the study of values, beliefs, moral constructs, and other normative issues. These topics are central to the theoretical traditions on which cultural sociology is founded, and many cultural sociologists continue to be interested in them. However they are defined, moral constructs are generally framed discursively; they depend on the symbolic creation and maintenance of cognitive maps and they are embedded in larger narrative traditions of values and beliefs. Yet cultural sociologists also have reason to distance themselves from moral inquiry. The study of moral topics may be confused with taking normative positions on these topics. The effort to establish itself as a respected field within sociology may be pursued by sharply distinguishing the approach and subject matter of cultural sociology from related fields in which normative arguments are more common, such as cultural studies and moral philosophy.

I argue that the distinction between empirical and normative approaches in cultural sociology is largely exaggerated. For various reasons that can themselves be subjected to examination, a few works receive attention as exemplars of moral inquiry. But closer consideration shows that nearly all research in cultural sociology includes a normative component as well as an empirical one. In contrast, there is a more useful distinction that helps to locate the distinctive contributions of cultural sociology. This is the distinction between autonomous moral selves and socially embedded moral actors. Popular understandings of morality, as well as traditional philosophical and theological approaches, generally emphasize autonomous moral selves. Morality is thus distinguished from social or political concerns insofar as emphasis is placed on personal virtues and vices, willpower, character, and discretion. Cultural sociology differs in emphasizing the social contexts and the socially constructed meanings and understandings that guide individuals and groups.

When Morality Becomes Fashionable

The importance of moral inquiry was driven home to me unexpectedly one evening as a result of reflecting on a jarring statement uttered by a talk-show host. During a commercial break in the evening news, Larry King came on to announce that his guest that night would be "America's Moral Leader: William Bennett." How fashionable it has become, I mused, to talk about morality: first Jerry Falwell, then William Bennett, and now virtually every academic gathering is replete with discussions of normative issues.

An essay by Alan Wolfe (1998), entitled "Social Science and the Moral Revival: Dilemmas and Difficulties," presents a rich exploration of the ways in which recent public events have resulted in greater attention being paid to moral concerns by social scientists. It carefully examines the various arguments that have previously been advanced to inhibit moral inquiry in the social sciences and, in my view, effectively refutes most of these arguments. These include arguments in the liberal tradition that oppose moral inquiry on grounds that it deflects attention from class issues, power, and the role of public policy; arguments rooted in a positivist perspective on the social sciences that object to any kind of normative inquiry; and arguments emerging from contemporary pluralist or multiculturalist emphases that deny the possibility of finding anything more than relativistic answers to moral questions.

Wolfe provides scant evidence that there has actually been a revival of interest in moral inquiry in sociology, although he cites a few works that have sold well or received awards from the discipline. He also points out that sociologists can study moral issues without adopting the stance that moral convictions are always good. Indeed, he asserts that morality sometimes needs to be investigated because it becomes rigid and exclusionary. Wolfe obviously approves of the revival he sees among social scientists in studying moral issues. And, together with the series on "moral sociology" that he edits for University of Chicago Press and his own books on moral obligation in sociology, the moral opinions of middle-class Americans, and Americans' understandings of virtue and vice, Wolfe's essay clearly extends an invitation to cultural sociologists to engage in moral inquiry.

However, to the casual reader, Wolfe's essay may evoke a response similar to mine upon learning that William Bennett had become America's moral authority: Why is it that certain writers and not others are singled out as the moral voices of the social sciences? Or, framed differently: If there is indeed a "moral revival" in the social sciences, why does it appear that so few are engaged in this revival?

The reason this may be a question worth considering is that our impressions of what it may mean to be engaged in moral inquiry within the social sciences are largely shaped by the exemplars whose work is most frequently cited as instances of such inquiry. Just as William Bennett's writing on virtue, outrage, and crime, as well as his frequent television appearances, create an image of what it means to be moral, so too do the allusions in scholarly writing to the work of certain academics. To its credit, Wolfe's essay surveys a relatively wide swathe of such work; yet even here, there appear to be certain affinities among the handful of writers whose work receives greatest attention, whereas the contributions of many other scholars is neglected.

A consideration of what may be involved in being fashionably moral (or, more accurately, becoming a social scientist whose writing on moral inquiry is fashionable) is thus a way to understand the place of moral inquiry within the social sciences generally and in cultural sociology more specifically. More than just a plea for recognizing wider contributions, a consideration of this sort can reveal some of the assumptions that may prevail in the social sciences about moral inquiry.

As a starting point, I want to consider the fact that a handful of writers are mentioned over and over in discussions of moral inquiry. A generation ago, C. Wright Mills was one of the most frequently mentioned, perhaps because of his trenchant criticisms of the norms of the middle class but also because of his critical attitude toward the power structure of his own discipline.[1] In the past decade or two, Robert Bellah has been one of the more frequently mentioned social scientists in such discussions, particularly since the publication of his coauthored work *Habits of the Heart* (1985). Mills would certainly have been regarded as a contributor to cultural sociology had the subfield been so identified in the 1950s, and Bellah (along with his coauthors) has been the focal point of much discussion in cultural sociology since at least the early 1980s. For the wider scholarly audience, Mills and Bellah are the William Bennetts in discussions of moral inquiry; other writers are seldom mentioned. Hence the question: What is the fine art of being fashionably moral? And what does it tell us about the symbolic distinctions that govern moral inquiry in cultural sociology?

There are several, perhaps only partially facetious answers that might be given to this question—answers that can be given without in any way disparaging the importance of writers such as Mills and Bellah. From observing their work, it seems clear that moral inquiry—in sociology, at least—comes at a price. To claim a moral voice requires gaining some distance from one's profession, and this act of distancing reinforces the impression that the discipline as a whole is either amoral or antagonistic to moral inquiry. Some of this distancing is methodological, it appears, for Mills and Bellah relied more heavily on qualitative information than on statistics. In addition, a moral inquirer apparently has to be persuaded that evil is abroad in the land. A writer must call people to repent, although not necessarily in religious terms. Such scholars are often accused of wearing their sentiments on their sleeves. And rightly so. As a moral critic, one does not separate oneself from one's intellectual role; they are one and the same. Above all, the key to being fashionably moral is to say things that are slightly out of fashion. Not too far out of fashion, but a bit out of vogue. If one is C. Wright Mills, one does not openly embrace Stalinism but criticizes the power elite. Robert Bellah eschews Horatio Alger but harks back to Tocqueville.

Close readings of *White Collar* and *Habits of the Heart* suggest another possibility about the fashionableness of moral inquiry. This has to do with the results that these books' popularity has, after the fact, on readers' reactions and on further scholarly reflection. Had it not been for the fact that these books sold well in the popular market, they might well be viewed quite differently. Let us suppose that academic circles are not free of jealousy. When books sell so well that their authors receive exceptional publicity (not to mention unusual royalty checks), fellow colleagues may be prompted to examine these works more closely than they otherwise would. Close examination may indeed mean critical examination. Questions are raised about why the book is drawing such a large audience and whether that audience is being misled. The empirical foundations of the book may be found wanting, leading critics to regard the book more as moral advocacy than as solid scholarship.

James Davison Hunter's *Culture Wars: The Struggle to Define America* (1991) provides another example of how popularity may result in a kind of tension between perceptions of scholarly work and perceptions of moral advocacy. Written as a scholarly work, this book attracted considerable attention among reviewers in a number of fields and went through more than a dozen printings. Although it was written in an even-handed style intended to provide an accurate description of the normative arguments of special interest groups on the extreme right and extreme left, it was more favorably received by proponents of conservative policies. Conservatives seemed to resonate with the idea that they were engaged in a fundamental philosophical struggle. Increasingly, this response came to frame the normative debates surrounding the book rather than Hunter's own policy recommendations, which, among other things, emphasized the need for American democracy to entertain frank discussions of public issues and to provide avenues for different views to be expressed rather than shutting off public debate to the point that violence emerged. The book's popularity, together with its largely qualitative evidence, encouraged other scholars to take issue with its central thesis. Perhaps propelled by concern that the book seemed to be playing into the hands of right-wing extremists, many subsequent scholarly investigations presented evidence that came to be interpreted as a refutation of the cultural war's reality.

If moral inquiry is tainted with the reactions that may come from the sheer popularity of books, then there may be negative repercussions within an entire subfield. It is not unreasonable to suggest that such repercussions have been evident in cultural sociology. Serious scholars may be inclined to argue that they would not want to engage in moral inquiry if it means writing a book that does not pass scholarly muster (and point to some best-selling works as examples). Moral inquiry then becomes associated with writing for a popular audience, with placing passions ahead of evidence, or in other ways with compromising scholarly standards.

To come to my point, then, we see in such figures as Mills and Bellah, first, that there is a false dichotomy that often clouds discussion of moral inquiry in the social sciences, and second, that there is a true dichotomy that deserves greater emphasis. Both dichotomies are cultural constructions that depend on the exemplars that become fashionably moral.

The Dichotomy between Facts and Values

The false dichotomy (and of course calling it "false" is hyperbole) is between value-laden and value-free inquiry, between normative and empirical, between prescriptive and positivist, or between moral and amoral. These are categories that unfortunately still frame the debate about moral inquiry in the social sciences, probably in part for some of the reasons I have just suggested. They are evident in Wolfe's essay and in philosophical distinctions between facts and values. They correspond to casual observations of the social sciences. If observers single out Mills and Bellah as moral protagonists, they just as quickly assert that the pages of most sociology journals are devoid of moral judgment. William Bennett would probably find Mills and Bellah worthy of his attention, but not the work of most other social scientists.

If Wolfe is right, there has been considerable recognition in recent years that social science cannot be as value-free as it was once regarded. The reason for this awareness may be, as Wolfe contends, that scholars have been shaken by recent political events. He has in mind the political changes that have overtaken Eastern Europe in the past decade and the calls that have been voiced in the United States for social scientists to pay closer attention to questions of citizenship, civil engagement, and democracy. These developments have, in his view, created greater interest in moral inquiry than was true three or four decades ago.

This line of argument could well be broadened and even recast. If recent political developments have challenged the idea of value-free social science, certainly it is possible to see that similar challenges grew out of the Civil Rights movement and the Vietnam War protests that engulfed American campuses during the late 1960s and the 1970s. It may also be that the 1950s were an exceptional decade in the social sciences, one characterized by cold war faith in science and technology and in the application of scientific models to human problems to a greater extent than was true either in earlier or in more recent decades. What many social scientists who write about moral inquiry may be reacting to is in fact the sense that too much emphasis was placed on empirical research within a positivist framework during that era, and that it has become necessary to bring moral inquiry back into the social sciences.

But distinguishing the moral and the empirical seldom gets us much beyond decrying certain imbalances. Closer consideration shows that Mills and Bellah assembled empirical data to support their moral arguments. Mills' concern about middle-class conformity was grounded in observations; Bellah's study was based on more than a hundred qualitative interviews. In fact, consider for a moment the possibility that all (or nearly all) social research is rooted in or related to normative judgments. As an example, first of someone outside of cultural sociology, consider the work of William Julius Wilson (1996). This work is usually not included in the roster of moral criticism. Wilson says African Americans in inner cities have trouble because there are no jobs. Is there not a moral implication in this argument? Provide jobs. Wilson is usually regarded as a public policy analyst because his interest is in policies that would alleviate the lack of jobs in inner-city neighborhoods. He emphasizes the role of government more than that of individuals, families, churches, or other community organizations. If moral inquiry involves values or normative judgments, however, these are certainly present in Wilson's arguments. The plight of minorities in urban areas is, in his view, clearly a problem to be overcome, and policy makers as well as the average citizen have a moral responsibility to initiate change. Or, as another example, consider the survey research conducted by Berkeley sociologist Charles Y. Glock in the 1960s and 1970s.[2] Although Glock's work was generally regarded as more empirically oriented than normatively focused, one of his surveys demonstrated that anti-Semitism is reinforced by certain kinds of religious beliefs. That finding, as it happened, played a large role in the Second Vatican Council's renunciation of anti-Semitism.

I would venture that almost any social science study has some link to a moral implication or value. Often it is about equality or justice. Are minority groups being treated fairly? The basic value is not in question, but the evidence may be, and so there appear to be endless empirical debates in the literature and fine-grained studies that seem to have little to do with normative claims. Yet the aim of these studies is to contribute to the realization of a value.

Of course there is inevitably a division of labor among practitioners. Some social scientists focus more on getting the data right. Others do better at advocating solutions. But the idea that only a few are worth considering in moral debates is, as I say, misleading.

Let me clarify an important point. Academic politics is not above people trying to claim the high ground. Those with strong moral commitments sometimes believe their colleagues have none. One prominent sociologist was fond of calling his colleagues dust-bowl empiricists. Another complained that one of his more distinguished colleagues had no soul. And some of these complaints may have merit. As Thomas Kuhn (1970) pointed out some years ago in his work on scientific paradigms, scientists are easily caught up in puzzle solving. Their work becomes a kind of game. Many, of course, are committed to the pursuit of knowledge for its own sake. I am suggesting only that it is harder to separate values from empirical work than many theorists of the social sciences once thought.

In cultural sociology, drawing a sharp distinction between empirical social science and moral inquiry is just as misleading as in other areas. Consider another example. Wendy Griswold, whose work in cultural sociology has significantly advanced our understanding of the social aspects of the arts and literature, has for some years been conducting research about Nigerian romance novels.[3] The work involves meticulous data collection and analysis and, to some, probably seems remotely connected (if connected at all) to moral concerns. Indeed, it might be admired especially by sociologists who think moral inquiry should be bracketed from consideration in the interest of performing rigorous and dispassionate empirical investigations. Yet Griswold's interest is ultimately driven by concerns about colonization and how it has transformed the very thought processes of indigenous peoples. Her methods and concepts have been helpful in many others' work on moral and religious topics. Her own writing may stop shorter than, say, Bill Wilson's does in advocating specific social policies. But the thought patterns she identifies in these novels help both in relativizing our own and in showing the sweeping consequences of colonial domination.

When cultural sociologists specifically address morality and moral codes, then it is even harder to draw a clear line between the empirical and the normative. As an example, we might consider *Imperiled Innocents: Anthony Comstock and Family Reproduction in Victorian America*, by Nicola Beisel (1997). Because this book is a careful application of cultural sociology to empirical data, and because it deals with a period well in the past, the casual reader might consider it largely devoid of normative implications. But Elisabeth Clemens, in a review of the book published in the *American Journal of Sociology*, recognizes that the book has merit both as a contribution to the purely scholarly development of the field and to moral inquiry. She writes:

> *Imperiled Innocents* persuasively demonstrates the empirical power of cultural analysis and its significance for at least one core theoretical question in the discipline, the production and reproduction of class. . . . Beisel has constructed both an elegant work of cultural analysis and a powerful theoretical lens through which to reconsider the moral controversies of our own time. (1998:1484)

Clemens is pointing to the fact that studies even of episodes a century old can have implications for how we think about contemporary moral debates. Extended to the present, Beisel's study suggests that part of what may be driving adherents of the Moral Majority or Christian Coalition, what may account for the appeal that William Bennett and Pat Buchanan have in certain segments of society, is the concern of lower-middle-class and working-class parents that their children will not maintain or improve the social position that these parents have struggled to attain.

A similar conclusion may be drawn about Michele Lamont's *Money, Morals, and Manners: The Culture of the French and the American Upper-Middle Class* (1992). Here again is a book based on extensive empirical information (collected from in-depth interviews with American and French men in professional and managerial occupations). Its scholarly orientation is drawn from the literature on cultural capital, and the study aims to show that there are several standards of normative evaluation that upper-middle-class men use to define themselves and to establish that they are people of worth: not only being "cultured" (in the sense of having good artistic or literary taste and fine manners), but also wealth or socioeconomic achievements, and such "moral" considerations as honesty and integrity, discipline, and altruism. In subsequent work, Lamont has shown that working-class men in France and the United States employ these same normative criteria, especially those involving moral standards, to legitimate their sense of personal worth. Several larger normative implications emerge from this work: first, that the working class is not devoid of morality or limited in their powers of moral reasoning (as some developmental models have suggested); second, that blacks and whites misuse their own moral preferences to apply negative racial stereotypes to the other group; and third, that universalistic moral standards can result in particularistic or exclusionary group boundaries.

To be sure, I may be accused of selecting examples that merely prove the general rule that social scientific research is devoid of moral meaning by providing exceptions. Nevertheless, the larger argument is that what appears on casual inspection to be without moral significance often turns out to have such significance when examined more closely. Nor is this connection accidental. Most theoretical and epistemological perspectives in the social sciences bracket moral inquiry from empirical research only for strategic reasons, rather than on grounds of deeper principles. Thus a perspective such as behaviorism has deep moral implications, as many of B. F. Skinner's writings made clear. The problem was not that it lacked a moral dimension, as many critics claimed, but that its moral implications were ones with which they disagreed. Similarly, rational-choice theory is currently accused of lacking a moral dimension; yet, as some rational-choice theorists have shown, the perspective can be brought to bear on difficult moral questions.[4]

Before moving to my other point, I also want to qualify my argument about the distinction between normative and empirical approaches. Although the two must not be separated, they also should not be conflated. I have been interested in discussions involving public opinion polls, especially those that drew frequent attention in the media during the investigation of the scandal involving Bill Clinton and Monica Lewinsky. For instance, one night I was watching a call-in program on C-SPAN. A woman called to say she did not believe polls showing that approximately 70 percent of Americans separated the president's private morality from his job performance.

(I do not recall the exact question.) She said she had asked many of her friends and gotten quite different results. The talk-show host, to his credit, then gave a quick summary of how polls are done, discussed sampling, and talked about their accuracy in predicting elections. He said the discrepancy could be explained by the fact that people tend to have friends who think the same way they do. In a huff, the caller declared, "Well, I still don't believe it," and hung up. There was a great deal going on in that exchange. But at one level it was evidence of our penchant to believe that social science research should confirm our moral convictions. Other callers, in fact, suggested that we *should* excuse the president—the reason being that the polls said so.

This is the point at which I have trouble with social science. I want research to be connected to moral reasoning and have argued that it often is. But I do not want morality to be entirely dependent on it. If a poll shows that 70 percent think it is acceptable to discriminate on the basis of race, I want to have a prior basis for saying that this is still wrong.

The sense in which a sharp dichotomy between empirical cultural sociology and moral inquiry in cultural sociology is false, then, is in the first instance a result of recognizing that virtually all social scientific studies have a moral or normative component. I emphasize this because it forces us to reconsider the idea that only a few sociologists (like Bellah or Wolfe) do moral inquiry, while the majority are engaged in hard-nosed (soulless) empirical investigations. In my view, moral inquiry is a pervasive aspect of nearly all work in cultural sociology. Having said this, I want to acknowledge that many particular publications may not emphasize normative applications. These publications range from close analyses of factual evidence to discussions of conceptual and theoretical debates within the subfield.

Another sense in which the distinction between facts and values is misleading has to do with the inevitability of bringing a particular perspective or cultural bias to one's work. Although social scientists aim for universality, they bring the biases of their social position to their studies, and these biases often reflect the particular values of the white American middle class and the more specific academic subculture of American higher education. Beyond these general considerations, cultural sociologists are especially likely to face difficulties in drawing a firm line between empirical and normative inquiry. As the examples I have given suggest, studies that deal with moral issues from an analytic perspective usually imply something about how we evaluate those moral claims. Indeed, good cultural sociology is often judged by its ability to provide a perspective or interpretation that the proponents of moral standards may not have previously considered.

Two Kinds of Moral Selves

This brings me to my other point: What, then, is the role of social science? Does it have anything distinctive to offer in moral debates? Here I want to defend a different dichotomy. Much of what we mean when we talk about moral behavior focuses on individual action—on the individual as a moral actor—and thus on the role of will, volition, conviction, resolve, behaving according to certain deeply held principles, and accepting responsibility for one's behavior. We might call this the autonomous self. I do not mean that autonomous selves bear no moral responsibility to other people. I mean, rather, that they are conceived to be people who are wholly responsible for their own actions. The autonomous moral self is generally thought to have emerged most clearly in Kantian philosophy, especially in the idea of the individual as a kind of demigod, capable of and responsible for making wise moral decisions. The same conception of the individual is evident in Nietzsche but also in some interpretations of Lockean and other classical liberal notions of the free citizen bound to social obligations only by contractual preferences. The main expression of an autonomous moral self, however, has been at the level of popular culture, where the preachments of Protestant pietism have prevailed, and where these preachments have been supplemented by Horatio Alger images of the strong-willed rugged individualist who triumphs over evil through heroic acts of personal moral resolve.

The social sciences generally take a different view. They emphasize the influences that impinge on the individual—the contexts and relationships forming the matrix in which individuals behave. We might call this the embedded self. For cultural sociologists, the embedded self is a social construction. It depends on the scripts available to individuals for interpreting themselves. Moral positions, according to this interpretation, are generally not invented by individuals but reflect the moral rhetoric to which they have been exposed in families, neighborhoods, schools, and religious communities. The embedded self still has freedom to make his or her moral choices, but the social sciences insist that this freedom is constrained by available ideas, economic resources, and social obligations. This, too, can be a false dichotomy if we assume we have to make a choice between a purely autonomous self and an embedded self. It is useful, however, in pointing to the source of some of the most contested aspects of contemporary moral debates. Again, consider some examples.

First, a rather naive one: the proverbial welfare chiseler. The welfare chiseler is an autonomous self—a person who basically chooses to live in poverty and to cheat the system. In popular parlance, we say the welfare chiseler has a moral problem—needs to shape up, take responsibility. If we talk about welfare as a "social problem," rather than as a moral failing of the welfare chiseler, we usually mean something different. People are on welfare because there are no jobs in the inner city, we might say, which is why William Julius Wilson's work is sometimes described as social policy analysis rather than moral inquiry. But the idea that welfare is a social problem and not simply an individual problem does not remove it from the arena of moral discussion. It only suggests a different solution. It suggests that voters or taxpayers (or employers) must share some of the responsibility.

Another simple example that comes closer to cultural sociology is the labeling theory of deviance. It suggests that juvenile delinquents are not just bad people but that they behave in bad ways because they have been labeled as bad people. Social scientists waver between views such as this and perspectives that attach greater responsibility to the individual delinquent, but on balance they are often inclined to emphasize environmental factors as well as those over which an individual may exercise control.

In both these examples, the result of social science perspectives is to shift blame—often from the accused to the accuser. And this is one reason why social science is often regarded as a form of ideology. But I want to suggest that the story is more complicated. Take recent work on single parenting as an example. It shows fairly decisively that children in single parent families suffer: they often do not do as well in school, have higher dropout rates, experience emotional trauma, have more trouble rearing their own children, and so on. But the studies also show that these effects are much worse in low-income families than in more affluent families. The moral implication has been mixed. Researchers argue that parents should take their marriage vows more seriously—a moral obligation in the traditional sense that emphasizes the responsibility of the autonomous self. They also argue that more should be done to help low-income families, such as income maintenance or day-care plans. Of course observers disagree about where the emphasis should be placed. But this is an example of how research broadens the debate. It does so like this: Do we agree that children's well-being is one of our cherished values (along with personal happiness, freedom, and so on)? If so, then staying married is a way to attain it. And staying married involves both resolve on the part of spouses and some commitment to shape institutions in a way that supports marriage.[5]

The idea of an embedded self, though, runs deeper than any of these examples suggest. It is reflected in Max Weber's insistence that social arrangements are composed of *moral* action as opposed to merely instrumental transactions. Morality here means a bond or a set of commitments that is part of the woodwork, so to speak, because it is institutionalized in patterns of behavior and in the logics of thought and discourse. An embedded self is equally reminiscent of Emile Durkheim's lifelong interest in the bases of moral community. For Durkheim, commitments are reinforced by participation in the community. For instance, rituals empower the individual participants, strengthening their resolve but also shaping their will in ways beneficial to the solidarity of the group.

An embedded self is rather different from the rugged individualist who heroically makes moral decisions solely on the counsel of his or her own heart. An embedded self tries to do what is right but recognizes that personal failures may be overcome by social conditions (by good institutions). In the final analysis, it takes good people to write good laws and to construct good institutions. Yet good laws and good institutions are likely to be stronger even than good individuals.

As Durkheim recognized, embedded selves nevertheless change as social conditions change. The self that takes its cues from a tight-knit tribal group may be of little use in a complex industrial society. And this observation brings us full circle to C. Wright Mills and Robert Bellah. What sets them apart, it seems to me, is not just their concern for moral questions but their interest in the kinds of selves we must have to sustain a good society. Mills was troubled by the social conformity of the 1950s, Bellah, by the expressive individualism of the 1980s. Both recognized that social conditions made it impossible simply to be the people we had been in the past.

What are the challenges today? As I have suggested elsewhere (Wuthnow 1998), we live increasingly in a world of *porous institutions*—institutions that encourage the flow of goods and information and even of people; a world of open markets, electronic information transfer, of weakened national boundaries. Evidence across a number of social spheres indicates that porousness has increased significantly in the past half-century. These indications include the cumulative effects of divorce and remarriage in creating what have come to be termed "blended families"; the declining percentage of grandparents who live with or near their children and grandchildren (and thus the diminishing likelihood of strong intergenerational bonds being forged); the rapid growth of the temporary labor force; corporate outsourcing and downsizing which make for more tenuous relationships between employers and employees; the growing number of mergers and new businesses; the rapid increase in daily stock market volume that suggest porousness in the economic sphere; and the fact that immigration has risen to near-record highs since the middle 1960s, while residents communicate less often with neighbors and are less likely to join long-term community organizations but are more likely to interact sporadically with soul mates via long-distance phone calls or e-mail and do short-term volunteer work through complex networks of nonprofit organizations. Porous institutions involve high levels of uncertainty and require high degrees of individual adaptability. Short-term, strategic commitments frequently replace enduring obligations.

The idea of porous institutions is meant to emphasize the fact that the institutional fabric is not simply coming unraveled, as some observers have argued, but is changing dramatically in character, partly in response to new information technologies and a more closely integrated global market, and partly as a result of the end of the cold war and a more dynamic economy. More frequent short-term transactions involving people, goods, and information are facilitated by a large variety of brokers, including stock brokers, divorce lawyers, travel agents, and computer technicians. But these mechanisms, worrisome as they may be to scholars who fear that meaningful relationships and social solidarity require more enduring commitments, are evidence that institutions are adapting rather than simply eroding.

Porous institutions nevertheless demand changes in the ways individuals think about themselves and their moral obligations. Individualism is not the problem. That is, the growing fluidity of contemporary life is not primarily a result of individuals elevating their selfish interests over long-term commitments to neighborhoods, employers, and kin. Nor is this fluidity an indication that individuals have become too strong-willed or too focused on their own resources. To the contrary, we need strong selves, people with internal resources that help them make decisions in the face of uncertainty. Put simply, people can no longer rely on long-term membership in groups or communities to provide them with morals and norms; instead, individuals must choose their groups and communities, reflect on competing norms inscribed in the different communities to which one may belong, and have sufficient ego strength to choose options that run against the grain. Strong selves are nevertheless ones who know how to ferret out the information they need. They piece together information from the loose networks—the support groups, the chat rooms, the professional affiliations, the referral systems, and the friends—on whom they rely. They are not without morality, although their commitments may suffer because of the instabilities of social institutions. Their moral cues come less from uniform traditions or from logically compelling arguments than from the accretions of experiences in divergent contexts. Understanding the changing ways in which selves are constructed and how new institutional realities are transforming the nature of moral deliberation is one of the most serious challenges that scholarly work in cultural sociology can address.

And in this respect, William Bennett may be our moral leader after all. Not because of his political conservatism or his Catholic orthodoxy or his public condemnations of wrongdoing, but because of knowing that virtue is grounded in stories—stories drawn from many traditions, stories that provide templates for our own experiences, stories that connect us loosely with the changing circumstances in which we live.[6] Cultural sociology has paid increasing attention to the social role of such narratives. It has shown their importance in political discourse, in religious rhetoric, and in personal accounts of family experiences, work, and social upheaval. Narratives provide the cultural tools for individuals to construct coherent explanations of why they make decisions and how these decisions are linked to deeper values or to social relationships. In this sense, the social sciences, too, are stories. They remind us that the world is populated not solely by heroes and villains, not just by Bennett's narrative exemplars of virtue or vice; it is also a world of inequality and organizations, a world of laws and opportunities. Our morality must take account of these social realities as well, refining them if we can, and letting them refine us.

Endnotes

1. See especially Mills (1960, 1983).
2. Glock and Stark (1966).
3. Forthcoming book from Princeton University Press.
4. Hardin (1990).
5. See especially McLanahan and Sandefur (1996).
6. Bennett (1996).

References

Beisel, N. 1997. *Imperiled Innocents: Anthony Comstock and Family Reproduction in Victorian America*. Princeton, NJ: Princeton University Press.
Bellah, R. N., R. Madson, W. Sullivan, A. Swidler, and S. Tipton. 1985. *Habits of the Heart: Individualism and Commitment in American Life*. Berkeley, CA: University of California Press.
Bennett, W. J. 1996. *The Book of Virtues*. New York: Simon & Schuster.
Clemens, E. S. 1998. "Review of *Imperiled Innocents: Anthony Comstock and Family Reproduction in Victorian America*." *American Journal of Sociology* 103(5):1483–85.
Glock, C. Y. and R. M. Stark. 1966. *Christian Beliefs and Anti-Semitism*. New York: Harper & Row.
Hardin, R. 1990. *Morality within the Limits of Reason*. Chicago, IL: University of Chicago Press.
Hunter, J. D. 1991. *Culture Wars: The Struggle to Define America*. New York: Basic Books.
Kuhn, T. S. 1970. *The Structure of Scientific Revolutions*. Chicago, IL: University of Chicago Press.
Lamont, M. 1992. *Money, Morals, and Manners: The Culture of the French and the American Upper-Middle Class*. Chicago, IL: University of Chicago Press.
McLanahan, S. S. and G. Sandefur. 1996. *Growing Up with a Single Parent: What Hurts, What Helps*. Cambridge, MA: Harvard University Press.
Mills, C. W. 1960. *The Power Elite*. New York: Oxford University Press.
———. 1983. *White Collar: The American Middle Class*. New York: Oxford University Press.
Wilson, W. J. 1996. *When Work Disappears*. New York: Knopf.
Wolfe, A. 1998. "Social Science and the Moral Revival: Dilemmas and Difficulties." Pp. 227–50 in *In Face of the Facts: Moral Inquiry in American Scholarship*, edited by R. W. Fox and R. B. Westbrook. Washington, DC: Woodrow Wilson Center Press.
Wuthnow, R. 1998. *Loose Connections: Joining Together in America's Fragmented Communities*. Cambridge, MA: Harvard University Press.

CHAPTER 8

Individualism . . . *Pro Tem*

RECONSIDERING U.S. SOCIAL RELATIONS

Karen A. Cerulo

Financial analysts are quite busy these days forecasting the economic terrain of the new millenium. Advice on "best buys" and market hot spots abound. Economic pundits are everywhere. But within this tidal wave of financial prescriptions, one investment strategy outweighs the rest. Simply stated: invest in the individual!

Contemporary analysts contend that the market is deconstructing and "the idea of 'the mass' is about to meet its end."[1] Consumers are being urged to prepare themselves for a different economic experience. Within the next five years, so the analysts say, everything from your blue jeans to your morning coffee blend to your child's Barbie doll will be customized—tailor-made to your personal specifications. Your PC will be custom-built; your daily planner will be personalized with your important dates and events. Each day, you will access the news via specialized online newscasts, transmissions restricted to the features, stock quotes, and sports scores of particular interest to you. When you shop, Internet vendors will greet you with individualized shopping suggestions, ideas fashioned to your unique preferences and tastes. In the new millennium, customization represents the order of the day, and according to the experts, today's consumer "can rightfully expect to be served as an audience of one."[2]

An audience of one . . . it is a self-centered society that market analysts describe. Yet the dawn of such a world comes as no surprise to many. Since the 1970s, a bevy of intellectuals have warned of a growing individualism[3] in America. In 1976, author Tom Wolfe anointed the "me generation"—a cohort of "zealous individualists" devoted only to the project of themselves.[4] Three years later Christopher Lasch proclaimed that a "culture of narcissism," had "carried the logic of individualism to the extreme of a war of all against all, the pursuit of happiness to the dead end of a narcissistic preoccupation with the self."[5] Through the 1980s and 1990s, scholars wrote of rising selfishness, declining civility, suburban isolation, and the loss of community. By the millennium's end, many saw Americans as hopelessly disengaged— from everything but themselves. Indeed, political scientist Robert Putnam declared the "death of Civic America,"[6] while sociologist Amitai Etzioni described the United States as a nation "heavily burdened with the antisocial consequences of excessive individual liberty."[7,8]

Are these analysts and intellectuals correct in their depictions of American society? In reviewing social life in the United States during the past three decades, do we indeed find that social relations have slowly moved from something approximating civic community to an anomic world of self-centered strangers? And if so, is such me-centered individualism a terminal condition or simply *pro tem*?

In an effort to answer these questions, this chapter sets as its goal four specific tasks. First, I present a wide variety of data on American attitudes and behaviors circa 1965 to 1995. In so doing, I challenge claims of a growing American individualism. Data reporting what Americans of this era actually thought and did reveal that the growth of individualism was and is limited in scope and, in many cases, a temporary phenomenon. After demonstrating that historical data do not confirm fears of a growing individualism, I begin to explore the reasons why such claims emerge and persist. Specifically, Section II of this chapter examines two critical practices: social scientists' fixed conceptualization of social relations, and cultural producers' periodic projection of unithematic scripts of social relations. The section fully defines these practices and outlines the ways in which these activities can misdirect both popular and scholarly perceptions of individualism's presence. If fixed conceptualization and unithematic scripting lead to misperception, one must necessarily inquire as to why these practices are adopted or maintained. In search of an answer, Section III of this chapter probes the structural conditions that encourage cultural producers to forward unithematic cultural scripts (in this case, scripts of individualism). Section III also explores the ways in which such scripts can strengthen the often immutable power of a scholarly theoretical tradition. The chapter concludes on a note of broader sociological debate. Based on the present research, I question the very models by which social relations[9] are typically conceptualized and mapped, and I suggest a new, more flexible conceptual framework by which to analyze social relations.

The Era of Me?

In reading the work of many journalists, analysts, and prominent social scientists, one gets the sense that a die has been cast. Many argue that since the 1970s, alienation and anomie, loneliness, disconnectedness, and selfishness have come to characterize the American experience. By now, the details of the argument are familiar. It is said that relations based on cohesive community or strong common interests began to erode in the postwar era. The country reconfigured as it moved through periods of sprawling suburbs, organizational men, and generation clashes. By the 1970s, a growing individualism began to dominate the American social scene; social relations came to be forged on the basis of personal pleasure and gain. This trend grew through the final decades of the century, with greed and new high-tech capabilities creating a milieu in which social connections and interactions are mediated solely by those people and objects which contribute to the personal project of the self.

What triggered the transition from a community-oriented society to a world of self-occupied actors? Many social theorists describe this change as the product of a long-term linear development pattern. Proponents of this "linear model," as I call it, suggest that the relational life of the United States began in a cohesive, homogeneous, cooperative community—a *Gemeinschaft* or small-town experience. But as American society modernized and expanded, it evolved toward a more instrumental, perhaps even an anomic condition. With modernization came a shift from "we-centered" to "me-centered" relations. Each new technology, each leap forward delivered expansion at the cost of connection. Each developmental stride overpowered or slowly eradicated the important interaction rituals that comprised the very notion of local community.[10] Thus modernization and technological advancement may have delivered the "global village" foretold by Marshall McLuhan (1964), but in the view of many social scientists, that village is a place in which inhabitants remain strangers in their own neighborhoods.

Is this picture of contemporary American society accurate? When we examine the attitudes and behaviors of Americans over the past three decades, do we find a set of patterns and practices that confirm the march toward individualism? Over the past two years, I have reviewed a number of social scientific works that argue for a growing individualism (including works by Andrew Cherlin, Amatai Etzioni, Robert Lane, Robert Putnam, Richard Sennett and commentators such as William Bennett). I have also reviewed a wide variety of data that address the cues of individualism identified by such authors. In comparing attitudinal and behavioral data with the rhetoric of the period, I find that the data fail unequivocally to confirm a dramatic shift toward individualism. Rather, data on American attitudes and behaviors from 1965 to 1995 provide a very complex and multifaceted picture of U.S. social relations.

AMERICAN ATTITUDES AND BEHAVIORS, 1965–1995

To be sure, there are several areas in which national level data support a growing individualism. Figure 8–1 illustrates some of these attitudinal and behavioral trends.[11]

For example, many point to the changing configuration of American families and households as a cue of a growing individualism. And indeed from 1965 to 1995, national data reveal an increase in the percent of single people in the U.S. population, the percent of divorced people in the U.S. population, and the percent of U.S. one-person households. Each of these trends suggests a greater propensity on the part of Americans to "go it alone."

Several other indicators confirm the increased "me-centeredness" of this period. For example, Figure 8–1 shows that when it comes to sociability, Americans generally decreased the time they spent socializing with their immediate neighbors. In turn, Americans increased the time they devoted toward the very individualistic project of personal grooming. The data also show increases in certain attitudes that champion personal freedom. For example, public approval for suicide increased during this period.

FIGURE 8–1
Indicators of increased individualism.

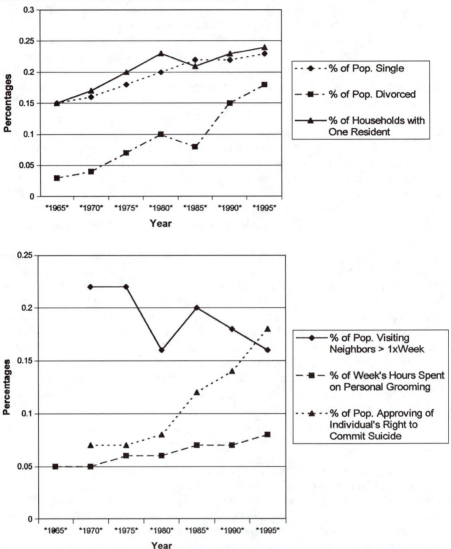

But while the indicators just reviewed suggest a definitive shift toward individualism, it is important to note that other national level data question that trend. Indeed, many attitudes and behaviors of the period suggest only a "temporary flirtation" with individualism. Consider abortion, an act often cited as a hallmark of individual freedom. Figure 8–2 reveals that both abortion rates and Americans' approval ratings for abortion increased from 1970 to 1980. But in 1981, such increases subsided. From 1981 to 1995, abortion rates actually decreased; and after 1980 Americans' approval

FIGURE 8–2

Indicators of temporary individualism.

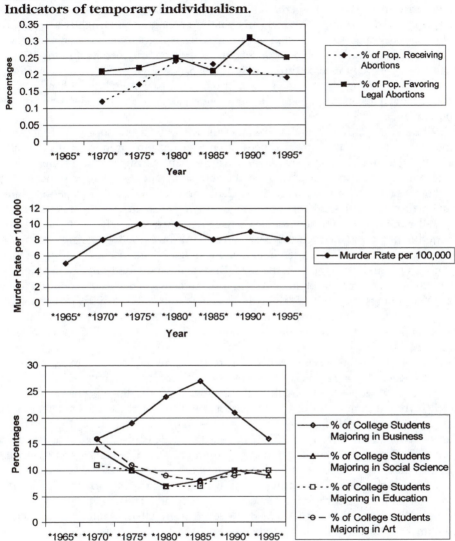

ratings for abortion proved rather erratic. Violent crime rates—murder rates in particular—are often cited as a cue of excessive personal liberty. However, the murder rates recorded for the period in question fail to display the linear increase that would confirm a growing individualism (see Figure 8–2). While U.S. murder rates increased from 1965 to 1975, rates leveled off between 1976 and 1980. From 1981 to 1995, murder rates generally decreased.

Similarly, consider the popularity of various college majors during the period in question. Business—a field many feel is a trademark of the "me generation"—increased in popularity from 1970 to 1985; however, the major saw a precipitous decrease in its popularity after 1985. Art—perhaps the extreme expression of individualism—actually declined during the 1970s and early 1980s, rebounding only slightly after 1985. Now consider majors in education and social science—prototypically nonindividualistic in thrust. While the number of such majors temporarily declined in the 1970s, that trend generally reversed from 1981 to 1995 (see Figure 8–2). Taken together, these indicators suggest that the growth of individualistic attitudes and behaviors is not linear and absolute. Often the growth of individualism is a short-lived, reversible phenomenon.

While some attitudes and behaviors suggest only a temporary shift toward individualism, note that others suggest no movement toward individualism at all. For example, in an increasingly individualistic society, we might expect community-oriented activities such as church membership and church attendance to decrease. Yet these behaviors remained relatively stable from 1965 to 1995. In a period of individualism, we also might expect more and more people to seek the independence of self-employment. Yet here too, such rates remained relatively stable during the period in question (see Figure 8–3). In an era of growing individualism, we might expect to find cues of decreased interaction with family and friends. Yet Figure 8–3 suggests remarkable stability in this area. Despite the purported surge of individualism, indicators of parent-child contact and social contacts between adults and their parents, siblings, and friends display little change from 1965 to 1995. In a period of individualism, we might expect to see increases in prototypically individualistic acts such as suicide. Yet suicide rates remained stable from 1965 to 1995 (see Figure 8–4).

Note too that in an era of growing individualism, we might expect to see changes in Americans' reported levels of satisfaction with their community. Similarly, we might expect people to lose faith in the communal spirit, judging others to be increasingly selfish or dishonest. Yet Americans' attitudes on these matters remain relatively stable from 1965 to 1990 (see Figure 8–4, p. 142). Only from 1991 to 1995 do we see some minimal increase in dissatisfaction and distrust. In total, the data presented in Figures 8–3 and 8–4 fail to support a growing individualism in America. Rather, these data suggest little change in many relevant attitudes and behaviors.

In reviewing Americans' attitudes and behaviors from 1965 to 1995, one final trend bears noting. Several indicators clearly challenge any growth in individualism. Rather, much data suggests the sustenance or growth of communally oriented sentiments. For example, if individualism were truly surging, we might expect to see an increase in self-gratifying behaviors such as smoking or alcohol and drug use. Yet Figure 8–5 (p. 143) shows that such behaviors generally decreased from 1965 to 1995. During an era of individualism, we might expect to see individuals withdrawing their support from community-oriented causes such as higher education, fraternal clubs, and organizations. Yet Figure 8–5 shows that voluntary contributions to such organizations increased steadily from 1965 to 1995. In concert with this trend, government expenditures on social welfare programs, social security, Medicare, and veterans' benefits consistently increased during this period as well (see Figure 8–6, p. 144). So too did public support for such spending, albeit in a jagged fashion (see Figure 8–6). And if individualism were truly surging, we might expect individuals to report a sense of detachment or a decreased trust in others.

FIGURE 8–3

Indicators showing no movement toward individualism.

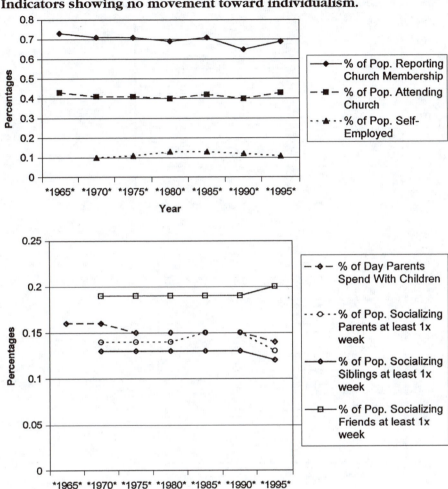

However, Figure 8–6 suggests just the opposite. Americans' trust in others increased from 1965 to 1995. Taken together, these data indicate that many of Americans' attitudes and behaviors from 1965 to 1995 were actually more "other-oriented" than they were "me-oriented."

To be sure, the 31 indicators presented here constitute only a portion of the many measures of social relations. Yet I would argue that increasing our review of such indicators would lead to a similar end. While some of these additional measures would support a growing individualism, others would refute it; still others would suggest only a temporary shift or no movement toward individualism at all. Contemporary studies of American individualism confirm my argument. For example, in a recent *New York Times* poll,[12] researchers asked Americans how much importance they

FIGURE 8-4
Indicators showing no movement toward individualism.

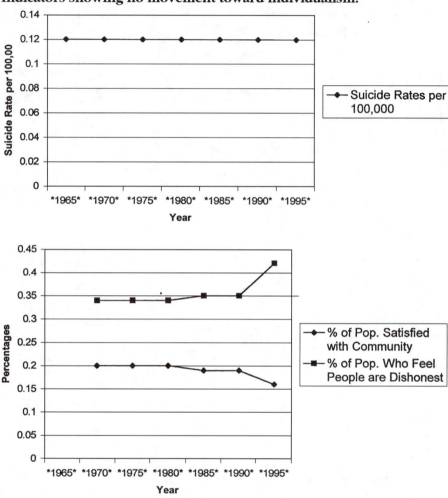

attached to 15 specific values. Some seemingly individualistic dimensions such as "being responsible for your own actions" and "being able to stand up for yourself" ranked among the most important values for those sampled. However, very close behind were more communally oriented sentiments such as "being able to communicate your feelings (to others)," "having faith in God," and "having children." In support of increased individualism, Americans ranked "having enough time for one's self" as more important than "being involved in the community." Yet, in support of other directedness, Americans ranked "being a good neighbor" as more important than "being financially secure" or "being physically attractive." Thus in this "bowling alone" world of which Robert Putnam and others lament, it seems clear that

FIGURE 8–5
Indicators challenging growth of individualism.

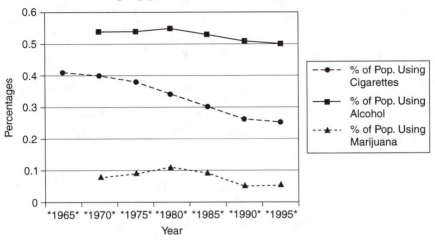

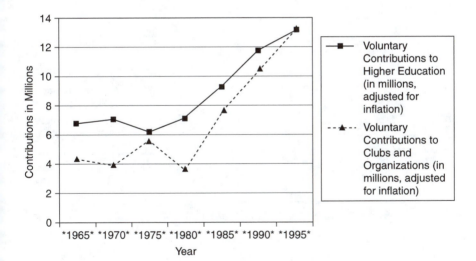

Americans live a multifaceted existence. While Americans have indeed grown more individualistic in some regards, they have grown more communal in others or simply exhibited no change in either direction. Indeed, a careful study of American attitudes and practices firmly suggests that American social relations are a highly complex phenomenon.

In light of such complexity, what gives rise to generalizations that bemoan a one-way road to detachment and anomie . . . and why do these claims of a growing individualism persist?

FIGURE 8–6

Indicators challenging growth of individualism.

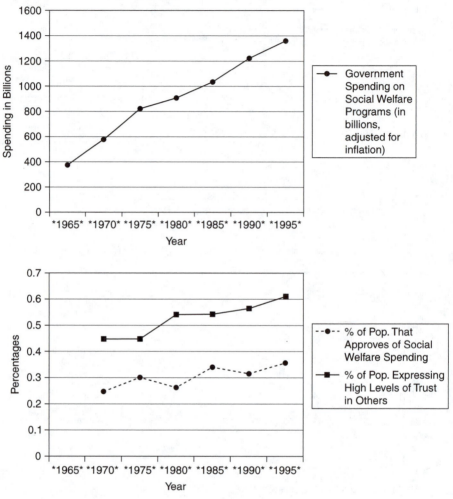

Explaining the Rhetoric of Individualism

I argue that two factors help perpetuate claims of a growing individualism. The first involves a predisposition in sociological analysis—a predilection for what I call a "linear model" of social relations. The linear model represents a *fixed conceptualization*— an institutionalized mode of thought that frames relational development in unidirectional terms. As this section will show, sociologists' loyalty to the linear model is firmly entrenched, guided by strong and long-standing theoretical traditions. But sociologists' invocation of the linear model is further advanced by certain cultural trends. This section will demonstrate that at certain historical moments, cultural scripts of individualism come to dominate the social scene. As these *unithematic scripts* saturate specific historical periods, they become intermittent reinforcements of established theoretical premises. In so doing, cultural scripts of individualism divert scholarly attention away from empirical contradictions of institutionalized "explanations."

FIXED CONCEPTUALIZATION: THE REIGNING LINEAR MODEL

The linear model of relational development represents a cornerstone of sociological thinking. The model invokes a set of bipolar categories to capture changing relational structures. Further, it describes movement from one relational pole to the other as a unidirectional process, a transition triggered by the modernization of society. According to the linear model, modernization represents a spark that drives societies down a one-way path of development; it triggers a steady progression from a "we-centered" to a "me-centered" experience.

Ferdinand Tonnies's ([1887] 1957) introduction of *Gemeinschaft* and *Gesellschaft* initiated the tradition to which I refer. In describing what he believed to be two opposing types of social relations, Tonnies wrote:

> All intimate, private, and exclusive living together, so we discover, is understood as life in *Gemeinschaft. Gesellschaft* is public life—it is the world itself. . . . *Gemeinschaft* is the lasting and genuine form of living together. In contrast to *Gemeinschaft, Gesellschaft* is transitory and superficial. Accordingly, *Gemeinschaft* should be understood as a living organism, *Gesellschaft* as a mechanical aggregate and artifact. ([1887] 1957:32, 34)

Tonnies's concepts set an important tone for the study of social relations. *Gemeinschaft* and *Gesellschaft* established for social theorists an "either-or" vantage point from which to examine and differentiate social relations. Further, the categories attached a value to the different relational forms. *Gemeinschaft* encompassed the face-to-face and the familiar, the intimate and the enduring—indeed the vital paste of a "good society." *Gesellschaft*, in contrast, suggested a modern, anonymous world. The category connoted impersonal, transitory, and segmented relations, the "mere coexistence of people independent of each other" ([1887] 1957:32).

Emile Durkheim ([1893] 1933) promoted a vision similar to Tonnies's in specifying "mechanical solidarity" and "organic solidarity." In describing social relations, Durkheim argued:

> We shall recognize only two kinds of positive solidarity. The first (mechanical) binds the individual directly to society without any intermediary. In the second (organic), he depends upon society because he depends upon the parts of which it is composed. . . . the society in which we are solidarity in the second instance is a system of different, special functions which definite relations unite. ([1893] 1933:129)

Durkheim's model reinforced the either-or dichotomy established by Tonnies. His categories suggested two distinctly different moments in a society's relational development. And while Durkheim characterized both mechanical and organic solidarity as positive relational forms, the latter condition clearly embodied a more precarious existence. Durkheim spoke of organic solidarity as integral to modern existence. Yet the mediated relations that defined organic solidarity carried with them the potential for social severance; relations based on mediated exchange presented the greater likelihood of individualism and, perhaps, a risk of anomie.

Georg Simmel, too, analyzed relational development as a linear march from one relational pole to another. Simmel differentiated rural or "small-town relations" from those of the "metropolis," and he consistently assigned primacy and richness to the former. For Simmel, modernized metropolitans reacted with head rather than heart, making them "insensitive and quite remote from the depth of personality" ([1908] 1950:411). The author viewed citizens of the metropolis as the victims of multifacity, their relations mediated only by the means of exchange:

> The metropolitan man reckons with his merchants and customers, his domestic servants and often even with persons with whom he is obliged to have social intercourse. These features of intellectuality contrast with the nature of the small circle in which the inevitable knowledge of individuality as inevitably produces a warmer tone of behavior, a behavior which is beyond a mere objective balancing of service and return. ([1908] 1950:411)

For Simmel, metropolitans were individuals in the extreme, lacking expressive contact and a strong sense of we-ness.[13]

The linear model established by Tonnies, Durkheim, and Simmel became a controlling force in modern sociologists' approach to relational development. For example, Louis Wirth's[14] influential work on the "mass society" reiterated the vision of relational development as a passage from cohesive community to anomic individualism. Kingsley Davis,[15] too, deferred to this perspective in conceptualizing instrumental "secondary groups" relative to Cooley's intimate "primary groups."[16] The linear model of relational development drove the works of Merton and Gouldner as well, as it guided the distinctions and groundings attributed to local versus cosmopolitan thinking.[17] And such thinking clearly encouraged Edward Boldt's differentiation of "structural tightness" and "structural looseness."[18] Indeed, even recent works by theorists such as Norbert Elias, Anthony Giddens, Mark Granovetter, Jurgen Habermas, Richard Sennett, and Edward Shils[19] exhibit a similar loyalty to the linear model; the model's tenets explain these authors' emphases on themes such as the blurred distinctions between the public and private sphere, the growing influence of weak ties, the dissipation of civic-mindedness, and increased intrusions into intimacy.

Undeniably, the linear model of relational development has dominated the study of social relations for over a century. But in recent years, several scholars have begun to question the model's core premises. In a recent presentation to the American Sociological Association, for example, Claude Fischer asked: Just how individualistic are present day Americans? When do they favor the individual over the collective? Analyzing data from the World Values Study, 1990–1993, and the International Social Survey Programme, 1985–1995, Fischer suggests that current visions of a growing American individualism are in error. He writes:

> Americans are not more but usually *less* favorable to the individual than other western peoples. . . . Moreover, the ultimate ends Americans endorsed in these surveys are more often supra-individual than individualistic—e.g., "God's laws" over personal conscience. (Fischer 2000:8, 9)

Studies by James Hunter and Carl Bowman (1996) and Everett Ladd (1999) draw similar conclusions. These projects provide extensive data showing that Americans often place the collective good and the civic community above personal interests.

Indeed, Robert Wuthnow (1998) argues that Americans may be as connected and communally oriented as ever. What has changed, argues Wuthnow, is the way in which Americans create their communal ties:

> As Americans sense the fragmentation of their communities, many are now talking seriously about making connections with other people. . . . But these connections are often looser than was true in the past. Instead of lifelong ties with their neighbors, or joining organizations that reward faithful lifelong service, people come together around specific needs and to work on projects that have definite objectives. (1998:7–8)

These studies and others like them urge us to rethink the reigning linear model. The surge to me-ness so long promoted by the model may be more of an erratic sputter—a movement felt in some social sectors and not others, a movement much less targeted and uniform than the model purports.

But rethinking an established tradition will, no doubt, prove difficult. For even those who acknowledge the weaknesses of the model continue to work within its boundaries.[20] Indeed, many critics of the linear model (including those cited in the previous paragraphs) often cling to the very concepts that they claim to problematize. In questioning the model's utility, these critics will nevertheless perpetuate bipolar categories such as communalism versus individualism. Rather than dismantling the model's very foundations, such scholars will redefine relational development by adjusting projected ratios of communalism to individualism, leaving intact the model's overall parameters.

Nearly two decades ago, Charles Tilly argued that social change and resulting relations can no longer be studied as a "coherent general phenomemon, explicable *en bloc.*"[21] Indeed, Tilly is now among a small chorus of voices encouraging students of relational development to leave the linear model behind and embark on a fresh, detailed consideration of social practices, social connections, and the cultural contexts in which those elements are embedded (see, e.g., Cerulo 1997; Cerulo and Ruane 1997, 1998; Cerulo, Ruane, and Chayko 1992; Collins 1981, 1988; Emirbayer 1997; Emirbayer and Mische 1998; Fischer 1992, 1997, 2000; Granovetter 1985; Meyrowitz 1985, 1996; Tilly 1998, 2000; Wuthnow 1998). This call for progress, while undeniably compelling, has met with a quiet response. What explains sociologists' lack of action in this regard?

Sociologists' resistance to conceptual change may rest, in part, in the nature of scientific inquiry. When it comes to relational development, most sociologists are practicing what Kuhn called "normal science."[22] Students of relational development have come to revere early statements on the topic (i.e., Tonnies, Durkheim, and Simmel), treating them as the foundation for future study. This foundation has powerfully steered the field, such that subsequent works have never moved beyond the further articulation and specification of the original model's elements. In order for sociologists to abandon the linear model, certain anomalies must appear—findings that systematically contradict the model's premises or significantly deviate from its predictions. These anomalies must accumulate, thus presenting a challenge to a firmly entrenched theoretical tradition.

Of course, one could argue that sufficient anomalies to the linear model currently exist. Indeed, throughout this work, I have cited both data and studies that clearly contradict the model's claims. Thus something beyond the process of normal science is contributing to the intellectual inertia that characterizes the study of relational development. In the next section, I suggest that anomalies to the linear model have been effectively overshadowed not just by scholars working to sustain a long-held tradition of thought, but by thematic surges emanating from the cultural arena—surges that function as intermittent reinforcements of the linear models' tenets. The pages that follow will illustrate one such surge. I will demonstrate that the years 1970 to 1984 represent one of several American historical periods marked by the production of unithematic cultural scripts—in this case, scripts of individualism. In the 1970s and 1980s, scripts of individualism saturated the cultural arena. Products and images of the era presented individualism as America's controlling force. In so doing, cultural scripts promoted the notion that a single relational form constituted American society. Because this cultural message was so forceful and targeted, I argue, it breathed new life into the linear model. Saturating the field with cultural scripts of individualism functioned to strengthen the theoretical status quo. This period of saturation was one of many that occurred between 1850 and 1995 (see Cerulo in preparation), with each serving to reinforce and legitimate institutionalized modes of thought.

UNITHEMATIC CULTURAL SCRIPTS:THE INDIVIDUALISM SURGE OF 1970 TO 1984

In American culture, images of the individual have always occupied a central role. Consider the explorer who single-handedly forges a new path, the entrepreneur whose unique vision leads to immense success, the innovator, withdrawn and independent, marching to her/his own drummer, the hero whose solo efforts inevitably win the day. But these cultural characters, while omnipresent, have generally shared the cultural stage. The individual has typically coexisted with several other images and themes: portraits of the "everyman/everywoman" that constitute small-town, cohesive community; the images of newcomers and enclaves that form America's pluralistic melting pot; and the stories of conflict that remind us of our nation's internal oppositions and struggles.

While multithematic offerings represent the norm for American culture, I have discovered that certain historical moments present "interruptions" to that pattern. In reviewing U.S. cultural images and objects produced during the last 150 years, I have identified particular eras that exhibit what we might call cultural surges of individualism—periods in which individualistic images overpower the projection of other cultural themes. During these times, unithematic scripts of individualism come to dominate the cultural discourse.

This phenomenon is aptly illustrated in the American cultural scripts forwarded from 1965 to 1995. My research shows that the cultural images of 1965 to 1969 conformed to multithematic cultural norms. But in 1970, scripts of individualism began to dominate the cultural menu. From approximately 1970 to 1984, these unithematic scripts completely overpowered other cultural messages. Only in the mid-1980s did the theme of individualism recede, taking its place among several other popular American motifs.

Products from any number of cultural sectors confirm the individualistic surge I am describing. Consider first the popular music field. In the 1960s, the popular music industry promoted both musical groups and solo acts. Groups, however, clearly dominated the musical charts. But in the 1970s, record companies shifted their focus. The solo project began to monopolize the charts, as musical groups gave way to stand alone performers. It all began in 1971, when The Beatles disbanded to form four solo acts. Soon after, Simon left Garfunkel, Cher left Sonny, Diana Ross left her Supremes, Eric Clapton left Cream, and eventually Michael Jackson left his four brothers. As groups disbanded, the industry aggressively recruited a new type of musical persona—solo stars who could write, play, and perform their own music. Hot figures of the era included Joan Armatrading, David Bowie, Harry Chapin, Alice Cooper, John Denver, Roberta Flack, Andy Gibb, Billy Joel, Elton John, Carole King, Gordon Lightfoot, Barry Manilow, Don McLean, Olivia Newton-John, Helen Reddy, Linda Ronstadt, Carly Simon, Bruce Springsteen, Rod Stewart, Donna Summer, and James Taylor.

Figure 8–7 gauges the rise and fall of the individual in popular music.[23] The graph provides data on the proportion of top-ten hits (1965–1995) recorded by groups versus solo acts. From 1965 to 1970, note that group acts outnumber the solo acts of the era nearly three-to-one. However in 1970, solo acts begin to dominate the charts. The stand alone star retains control of the charts through 1984. Only in the late 1980s and early 1990s do solo acts return to a subordinate status.

Like popular music, the themes of the era's best-selling books thrust the individual temporarily to the foreground.[24] My research shows that from 1965 to 1970, the topic of individualism co-existed with other thematic emphases. For example, in 1965, the introspection of Saul Bellow's *Herzog* accompanied the community tales provided by Bel Kaufman's *Up the Down Staircase* and James Michener's *The Source*. Similarly, in 1967, Eric Berne's self-help manual *Games People Play* stood side by side with William Manchester's compelling account of a nation's grief in *Death of a President*. Indeed, from 1965 to 1969, only 27 percent of the best-sellers in my sample forwarded individualism as the primary theme. But in 1970, the literary emphasis of best-sellers changed dramatically. From 1971 through 1984, the individualistic themes of fiction books such as *Jonathan Livingston Seagull, Once Is Not Enough, Centennial, The Thorn Birds*, and *Overload* dominated the best-seller list. In nonfiction, self-oriented titles such as *The Sensuous Man, I'm OK, You're OK, Open Marriage, Winning through Intimidation, Your Erroneous Zones*, and *Looking Out for No. 1* ruled the day. Indeed from 1970 to 1984, nearly 60 percent of the best-sellers in my sample forwarded individualism as the central theme. But by 1985, the emphasis on individualism had waned considerably. From 1985 to 1989, only 30 percent of best-sellers stressed the topic. And while the best-sellers of the 1990s saw some renewed interest in individualism, such themes constituted less than half of the topics promoted during this period (see Figure 8–7).

Hollywood exhibited a surge of individualism from 1970 to 1984 as well. While a multiplicity of themes—race relations (*In the Heat of the Night, Guess Who's Coming to Dinner*), class relations (*Che, Dr. Zhivago, Oliver*), family and nation (*The Sound of Music*)—characterized the films of 1965 to 1969, individualism saturated the products of 1970 to 1984. During this period, the freestanding hero became Hollywood's favorite icon. Initially, such heroes took on the guise of a lone vigilante: *Billy Jack* (1971), *Dirty Harry* (1971), *Shaft* (1971), Popeye Doyle (*The French*

FIGURE 8–7
Indicators of individualism surge in pop music, bestsellers, and television.

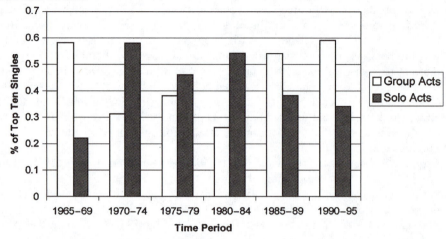

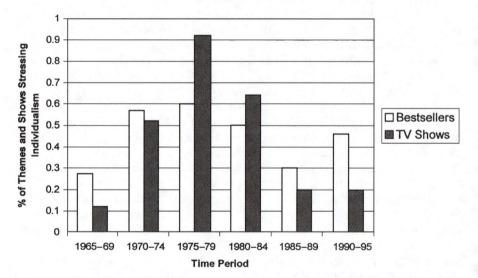

Connection, 1971), *Serpico*, (1973), Charles Bronson (*Death Wish*, 1974), Chris McCormick (*Lipstick*, 1976), or Travis Bickle (*Taxi Driver*, 1976). Later, the icons of individualism became more generalizable—common men and women bucking the tide and often winning, as did Rocky Balboa (*Rocky*, 1976) Tony Manero (*Saturday Night Fever*, 1977), Luke Skywalker (*Star Wars*, 1977), Kimberly Wells (*China Syndrome* (1978), Norma Rae (*Norma Rae*, 1979), and Harold Abrahams and Eric Liddell (*Chariots of Fire*, 1981). Accompanying the icons of individualism were themes that encouraged personal exploration, introspection, and self-gratification. Recall films such as *Diary of a Mad Housewife* (1970), *Carnal Knowledge* (1971),

Klute (1971), *Up the Sandbox* (1972), *Last Tango in Paris* (1973), *Summer Wishes, Winter Dreams* (1973), *Alice Doesn't Live Here Anymore* (1974), *Shampoo* (1975), *Network* (1976), *Looking for Mr. Goodbar* (1977), *An Unmarried Woman* (1978), or *Manhattan* (1979). Indeed, from 1970 to 1984, stories of individual struggle and the search for personal identity dwarfed the themes of family, community, and nation.

Figure 8–8 more precisely delineates Hollywood's promotion of individualism. The figure contains data on both Oscar award winning films and box office hits, from 1965 to 1995.[25] From 1965 to 1969 only one Oscar winner promoted an individualistic theme. *A Man for All Seasons* (1966) revolved around the strong will of Thomas More and his relentless fight for his beliefs. But from 1970 to 1984, the emphasis on individualism grew dramatically; 10 of the period's 15 winners

FIGURE 8–8
Indicators of individualism surge in films and theatre.

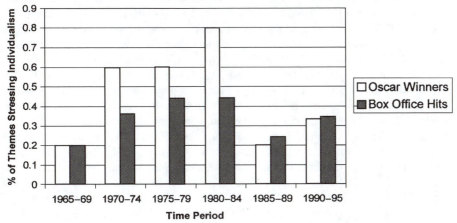

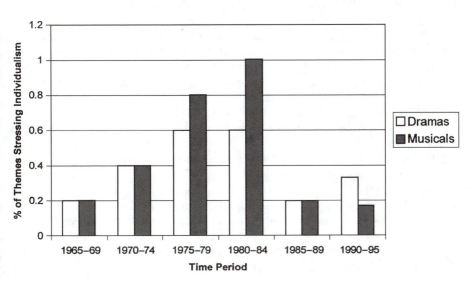

(67 percent) promoted individualistic themes. These included stories of extraordinary figures such as *Patton* and *Rocky*, and tales of personal introspection such as *Terms of Endearment*. But emphasis on the individual waned from 1985 to 1995. Only three of the era's eleven Oscar winners (27 percent) stressed individualism as a major focus (*Out of Africa*, *Dances With Wolves*, both stories of "pioneers," and *Forrest Gump*, an indictment of a self-absorbed generation). The same trend characterized box office winners of 1965 to 1995. Figure 8–8 summarizes the themes of the top five grossing films for each year of the period.[26]

Theater productions, too, displayed a sudden surge of individualism in the 1970s and 1980s. Stories of family, neighborhood, and nation, so popular in the 1960s (for example, *The Subject Was Roses*, *Fiddler on the Roof*, *The Fantastiks*, *Generation*, *Half A Sixpence*, *I Do, I Do*, *Mame*, *1776*, *The Price*, and *You're a Good Man Charlie Brown*) gave way to sagas of iconic heroes (*Amadeus*, *Barnum*, *The Bell of Amherst*, *Big River*, *Evita*, *Godspell*, *Jesus Christ Superstar*, and *Pippin*), intense explorations of the self, and thoughtful reflections on the very role of the individual in society (*A Chorus Line*, *Chapter Two*, *Da*, *Equus*, *Find Your Way Home*, *The Elephant Man*, *The Heidi Chronicles*, or *Same Time, Next Year*). Data on the Tony award winners of 1965 to 1995 illustrate the *pro tem* surge of individualistic themes. Figure 8–8 shows that from 1965 to 1970 only three Tony-winning plays and musicals (20 percent) stressed individualism. But from 1970 to 1984, that figure changed dramatically. During this era, 63 percent of Tony award winning plays and musicals foregrounded individualistic themes. The stress on individualism finally receded between 1985 and 1995, with only 27 percent of Tony award winners emphasizing such topics.[27]

The surge of individualism I am describing is evident in the television offerings of 1965 to 1995 as well. I examined the top-rated TV shows of 1965 to 1995, coding each show's overall emphasis; these data provided a picture that mirrored the trends in other cultural arenas (see Figure 8–7). A mere 10 percent of the shows broadcast from 1965 to 1969 emphasized themes of individualism. Hit shows of this era (e.g., *Andy Griffith*, *Bewitched*, *Bonanza*, *Dick van Dyke*, *Family Affair*, *Gomer Pyle U.S.M.C.*, *Gunsmoke*, *Hogan's Heroes*, *The Lucy Show*, *Mayberry R.F.D.*, and so on) were much more likely to focus on family, camaraderie, and neighborhood. In contrast, 71 percent of the shows broadcast from 1970 to 1984 promoted individualistic themes such as autonomy, independence and self-exploration (e.g., *All in the Family*, *Charlie's Angels*, *Dallas*, *Dukes of Hazzard*, *Maude*, *Dynasty*, *Private Benjamin*, *Three's Company*). But as the 1980s progressed, themes of individualism receded to the background, with only 20 percent of shows broadcast from 1985 to 1995 emphasizing this issue. Indeed, shows of 1985 to 1995 often returned to familial and community themes (e.g., *Cheers*, *Cosby*, *Family Ties*, *Grace Under Fire*, *Growing Pains*, *Roseanne*).[28]

My research shows that scripts of individualism invaded the sports arena as well. One example of this trend can be found in sports anthologies of the era. Most such histories describe the 1970s and early 1980s as a period that sacrificed the "team" in favor of "star" players. Within this thematic frame, such anthologies emphasize individual-oriented events over more community-directed action. For example, coverage of free agency, a movement that empowered individual baseball players in contract negotiations, dominates many historical discussions of the era. The emergence of a "star system" in basketball garners much attention as well. Indeed, these topics completely overpower discussions of more team-oriented activities. But consider that the 1970s saw two strong, group-based strikes, one in the NFL (1970) and one in Major League Baseball (1972), both of which delayed season openings as players joined together to protest team owners' contributions to the pension funds. However, anthologies devote little space to these incidents, favoring instead episodes that edify the individual.

In describing the world of sport during the 1970s and early 1980s, anthologies also stress the rise of nonteam sports: boxing, golf, swimming, tennis, track and field. Note that participation and attendance in these individual-oriented sports increased no faster than participation and attendance in team sports such as baseball, basketball, football, or softball.[29] Yet the cultural scripts projected in sports anthologies suggest that individualistic sports were dominating the period.

To further illustrate the highly biased nature of the era's sports scripts, I considered the sport images projected in popular magazines of the day. I analyzed the covers of two general-interest magazines: *Time* magazine (1965 to 1995) and *Life* magazine (1965 to its demise in 1985). These magazine data confirm the surge of individualism that I have noted in other cultural arenas. For example, from 1965 to 1969, 75 percent of sport-related covers featured full teams (e.g., the New York Mets) or members of team sports (e.g., baseball player Mickey Mantle, quarterback Joe Namath, or hockey player Bobby Hull). But in 1970, this imagery began to change. During the period 1970 to 1984, 61 percent of sport-related covers featured "stars" of single-player sports—Muhammad Ali (boxing), Jimmy Connors (tennis), Bobby Fischer (chess), Dorothy Hamill (figure skating), Carl Lewis (track and field), Cathy Rigby (gymnastics), Secretariat (horse racing), and Mark Spitz (swimming). Only after 1984 did this surge of individualism reverse itself. From 1985 to 1995, only 30 percent of covers featured individualistic sports; team sports regained the center stage.

The surge of individualism I have been describing reached beyond the popular culture arena. Scripts of individualism are similarly found in cultural sectors such as education, law, and science. Consider, for example, some of the important themes of the educational arena from 1965 to 1995. To be sure, equal opportunity was a constant dimension of the era's educational philosophy. But from 1971 to approximately 1982, many would argue that scripts of individualism temporarily overpowered those of equal opportunity. In the 1971, for example, the "Open Classroom" took the American educational system by storm.[30] The open classroom was driven by an educational philosophy that rejected a structured or standardized curriculum. The program's proponents argued that each student's activities should be governed by her or his specific interests and needs. In the open classroom, students were free to move about as they wished; they were encouraged to pursue their own interests and seek answers in their own special way. Indeed, classrooms were physically restructured to encourage this kind of inquisitiveness.[31] By the decade's end, every state's primary educational curriculum reflected the open-classroom philosophy. Further, the philosophy began to infiltrate secondary school systems as well. The 1970s introduced the "nongraded high school," a place in which students were encouraged to work at their own pace until they felt a command of the materials.

The college curriculum, too, shifted toward individualistic ideals. During the 1970s, colleges gradually diminished or dropped standard core requirements for degrees. Instead, students were encouraged to develop personalized majors and curricula, ones that emphasized each student's special interests. A large percentage of students chose courses in yoga, Zen, or transcendental meditation, turning inward and seeking to exercise some personal control over their self-development. Psychology, the science of the individual became the single most popular major of the decade. Nationally, enrollments in psychology graduate programs increased 114 percent from 1970 to 1974, and the demand for psychology professors nearly tripled during the same period, rising from 2,500 positions in 1970 to 7,000 in 1975 (Bondi 1995; Van Sotter 1991).

In the late 1970s, certain federal educational policies also promoted individualistic themes. For example, Individual Educational Plans (IEPs) developed as a result of two public movements, the Vocational Rehabilitation Act of 1973 and the Education for All Handicapped Children Act (1975). Via the IEP program, individualized agendas were written for each handicapped child in a school district. These plans customized an educational regime in keeping with each child's abilities and special needs (Van Scotter 1991).

But while individualism dominated the educational scripts of the 1970s and early 1980s, it is important to note that this surge subsided later in the decade. At this time the open classroom came under severe attack, triggering a return to rigorous educational structure. Core requirements were reinstated at the college level, and courses on self-reflection and meditation slowly disappeared. Even psychology's popularity came to an end as a glut of psychology majors flooded the job market in 1980. Thus individualism's dominance of educational scripts was a strong but temporary phenomenon.

Consider now the surge of individualism that penetrated the legal sphere from 1965 to 1995. A review of the era's Supreme Court decisions illustrates my point. In choosing the cases it wishes to hear in any given year, the Supreme Court signals a cultural focus and sets the parameters of a cultural agenda. With every legal decision, the court fine-tunes that agenda; each decision details a script that favors, enhances, stabilizes, or curtails the rights of various social sectors.

I studied landmark decisions rendered from 1965 to 1995.[32] These cases can be classified according to one of five types: (1) decisions that favored the rights of the individual;[33] (2) decisions that favored the community or the state over the individual;[34] (3) decisions that established equality between two or more social groups;[35] (4) decisions that elevated the rights of one group over another;[36] and (5) a default category most frequently including decisions involving government checks and balances.[37] Based on these classifications, Figure 8–9 presents data that summarize the cultural scripts embodied in the Supreme Court's decisions.

Figure 8–9 shows a surge of proindividualism decisions, one that roughly coincides with surges of individualism occurring in other cultural domains. During the late 1960s and throughout the 1970s, proindividual rulings constituted the largest proportion of all Supreme Court decisions. Only at the onset of the 1980s did the court reverse this emphasis. At that time, anti-individual decisions began to dominate the Supreme Court agenda, a trend that continued through the early part of the 1990s. It is worth noting that none of the remaining case categories displayed concentrated thematic surges. The proportion of Supreme Court decisions involving equality and antiequality issues remained rather stable from 1965 to 1995. Also, in reviewing

FIGURE 8–9

Indicators of individualism surge in Supreme Court decisions and Nobel prize winners in science and medicine.

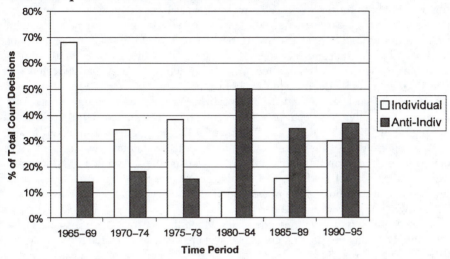

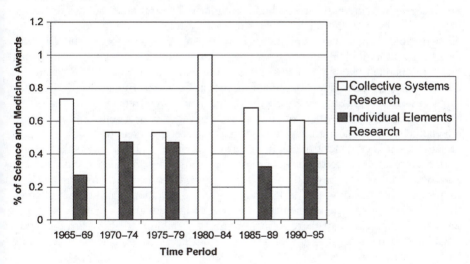

decisions belonging to the default category, I found no discernible pattern; the proportion of cases addressing such issues increased and decreased independent of other court themes.

Finally, I turn to science and medicine. As one reviews the scientific accomplishments honored between 1965 to 1995—those cited as the most important discoveries of their era—an interesting pattern emerges. The period's Nobel prize–winners represent two distinct types of research. Some awards went to projects addressing broad systems and the interrelationship between system parts—that is, the total or collective system. For example, in 1965, Richard P. Feynman, Julian Schinger, and Sin-Itiro Tomonaga were honored for their work on theories relating to the interaction between radiation, electrons, and positrons. Similarly, in 1969, chemist Omar Lars was honored for his work on the reciprocal relations that enable the thermodynamics of irreversible processes. And likewise, in 1969, the physiology and medicine award went to Max Delbruck, Alfred Hershey, and Salvador Luria for their work on the replication mechanisms of viruses. In contrast, other of the era's awards went to projects that focused on isolated features of a system—projects that dissected systems into highly individualistic pieces. For example, in 1973, the physics prize went to Leo Esaki, Ivar Giaever, and Brian Josephson for their work on tunneling. (Tunneling studies individual electrons able to penetrate a potential barrier through a narrow region of solid.) Similarly, in 1977 chemist Ilya Prigogine was honored for his work on outgrowths of dissipative systems—organisms that can sustain themselves and grow in opposition to the drift toward universal chaos. And in 1978, biologists Werner Arber, Daniel Nathans, and Hamilton Othanel Smith were recognized for their work on a specific enzyme in the simian virus, one capable of breaking the molecule down into 11 well-defined parts.

Figure 8–9 illustrates the frequency with which these two styles of research were rewarded. Note that research on collective systems is clearly favored throughout this 30-year period. From 1965 to 1969, for example, 73 percent of all awards went to projects emphasizing collective systems. Similarly, 72 percent of the awards named between 1980 and 1995 went to research on total systems. But during the 1970s there was a notable change in this emphasis. From 1970 to 1979, a period in which we witness surges of individualism across various cultural sectors, nearly half of the Nobel prizes (47 percent) went to projects emphasizing individual elements of a system. To be sure, such projects never dominate the scientific arena. But in the 1970s, such projects were recognized and awarded with unusually high frequency.

In visiting this wide variety of cultural sectors—music, best-sellers, film, theater, television, sports, education, law, and science—it becomes clear that scripts of individualism saturated American culture from approximately 1970 to 1984. Yet it is important to recall that the same was not true for Americans' behaviors and attitudes. Americans did not display a dramatic increase in individualistic practices. Behavioral and attitudinal moves toward individualism were temporary or limited in scope. Thus, in many ways, the unithematic scripting of individualism created a false impression. The intensity of these scripts promoted a singular focus, a vision of individualism on the rise. In reality, however, actual practices reflected a much more varied social experience.

If the scripts of individualism, so prominent from 1970 to 1984, did not reflect social behaviors and attitudes, what explains their intense presence? Why did culture promote a reality so at odds with the world of experience?

Scripts of Individualism and Periods of Diffuse Instability

I argue that the scripts of individualism reviewed heretofore did not reflect actual changes in societal relations. Rather, these scripts were *reactive* in nature. The social events of the 1970s and 1980s presented Americans with a prolonged and broad-based period of social change and uncertainty—a condition I refer to as *diffuse instability*. During this period, I argue that scripts of individualism were employed as a powerful cultural tool, one that suggested the potential for control in an unstable, unpredictable environment.

DIFFUSE INSTABILITY, 1970–1984

Two important characteristics are critical to the definition of diffuse instability. First, such periods combine *both* social change and social uncertainty, two qualities that do not necessarily travel in unison.[38] Second, diffuse instability is not concentrated in a single social sector. Rather, the change and uncertainty associated with this condition represents a broad-based phenomenon—change and uncertainty are distributed *across* the social system. This distinction is important, for when instability is concentrated in a single social sector, it can take on catastrophic proportions. In contrast, instability distributed across various social sectors disperses disruption, thus moderating the disturbance in any given sector.[39]

Reviewing several economic, political, scientific, technological, and family-related events of the 1970s and early 1980s aptly illustrates the diffuse instability of the period. Change and uncertainty can be simultaneously charted across these social sectors. Yet such instability was not catastrophic; it did not devastate any single sector of American society. Rather, instability created a broad-based impact—one that transformed but did not destroy. Consider first the economic realities of the period. During the 1970s, the United States witnessed the unprecedented combination of two economic conditions: inflation and stagnating economic growth. The experience proved so novel to both politicians and economists that they coined a special term to describe it—*stagflation*. Stagflation presented a serious challenge to Americans; the condition often proved unpredictable. Inflation's cures tended to increase the stagnation of business, and all efforts to jump-start the business sector sent inflation out of control. To make matters worse, stagflation was accompanied by a variety of other unsettling economic events. For example, the United States experienced two significant oil crises: the OPEC oil embargo of 1973 to 1974 and the fuel shortages associated with the 1979 Iranian revolution. Further, the government entered into a new and controversial alliance with American big business. Amidst much public objection, the government initiated the practice of "corporate bailout," rescuing first Lockheed, in 1970, and then Chrysler, in 1979. On the international front, the United States continued to suffer significant trade imbalances. Indeed, the plight of American businesses grew increasingly uncertain as Europe and Japan threatened U.S. dominance of world markets. Finally, the U.S. government "broke frame" with familiar economic policies, suspending the free exchange of U.S. gold for foreign-held dollars, an action that many believe devalued the dollar. Each of these events kept the economic realm in a steady stream of flux and unpredictability. Things were clearly changing, and the results of such change could not be easily predicted.

During the period in question, change and uncertainty plagued other social spheres as well. In the political arena, the Watergate scandal of 1972 to 1973 marked the first modern instance of a presidential indictment—a sitting president publicly charged with the intentional obstruction of justice. Watergate also led to the first presidential impeachment trial in over 90 years, bringing dishonor and suspicion to a previously strong American presidency. By the trial's end, the nation had experienced the un-precedented resignation of its two highest governing officials; Vice President Spiro Agnew resigned in 1973, and President Richard Nixon resigned in 1974. Politics proved equally unsettling in the international arena. Recall the U.S. experience in Vietnam. After the longest war in American history, the United States was unable to declare victory in Vietnam. Thus, for the first time in decades, the United States was forced to recognize clear limits in its power abroad. In 1973, the United States settled for a much-criticized peace treaty, withdrew its troops from Vietnam, and declared victory. But within two years, America's defeat was made explicit. The world watched as the United States evacuated its Saigon embassy, leaving the South Vietnamese government to surrender to the North. In the face of U.S. vulnerability in Vietnam, challenges to American dominance became more and more frequent. The 1970s saw numerous anti-U.S. terrorist threats and attacks. At the decade's end, such animosity culminated in an act of global humiliation. On October 23, 1979, a group of Iranian militants seized 53 members of the American consulate in Tehran and held them hostage for 444 days. The incident undermined American authority, leaving the United States in a new and strange position—politically challenged, internationally degraded, and unsure of its future political leverage.

Beyond economics and politics, several other events kept change and uncertainty at the forefront of the American agenda. Science and technology, for example, took the nation to new, uncharted territory. While such developments promised rapid and valuable progress, they also forced Americans to grapple with the very nature of humanity, vulnerability, and control. Consider, for example, the area of genetic engi-neering. During the 1970s and early 1980s, the discovery of "recombinant DNA"[40] garnered widespread public attention and intense public scrutiny. This new science promised staggering medical advances, including new treatment strategies and new advances in drug synthesis. At the same time, the procedure raised deep concerns among both scientists and the general public. Many worried about the potential for scientists to create new, unpredictable, and potentially harmful organisms. Spurred by the ambivalence surrounding genetic engineering innovations, the U.S. govern-ment imposed strict guidelines on recombinant DNA research.[41] But despite these safeguards, environmental groups, scientific groups, and the press continued to ques-tion this scientific "advancement." While enthralled with the changes promised by genetic engineering, Americans remained uncertain with regard to the technology's ultimate results.[42]

In the 1970s, nuclear power raised America's uncertainty quotient as well. A decade earlier, atomic energy plants had enjoyed immense popularity. However, en-thusiasm all but disappeared with a meltdown of a nuclear reactor at the Three Mile Island atomic energy plant in Harrisburg, Pennsylvania. The disaster raised serious questions regarding atomic energy's viability, and such doubts sent the nuclear power industry into deep decline.[43] Industrial wastes, another by-product of scientific and technological advancement, became a cause for concern as well. Recall Love Canal, a suburban community in upstate New York. In 1977, it became clear that the com-munity was being destroyed by the long-term dumping of toxic industrial wastes. Be-cause of the Love Canal, Americans were forced to rethink the often high price of progress, and the secrecy and deception that surrounded the Love Canal affair left many Americans feeling doubtful about the safety of their land and water.[44]

In the early 1980s, a medical issue rocked Americans' sense of security. AIDS, an incurable disease, began to monopolize the discourse on national health. The number of reported AIDS cases in the United States rose from 225 in 1981 to 40,000 in 1987. By the decade's end, hundreds of thousands of Americans would be infected with the disease. In the early 1980s, AIDS was perceived as a new epidemic, presenting a period of change and crisis in public health. And with so much about the disease still undiscovered (i.e., causes, cure, effective treatments), public uncertainty increased dramatically: "Fears grew among many in the population that the disease could be contracted through the air; through touching, kissing, or being sneezed on; through using a toilet seat previously used by someone with HIV; or even through mosquitoes. Although researchers tried to dismiss such misconceptions about the disease, myths and fears persisted for many . . . a sense of fatalism set in for many people."[45]

The growth of information technologies brought change and uncertainty to Americans as well. As the microchip, fibre optics, satellite transmission, and desktop personal computers began to surface in the 1970s and early 1980s, it became clear that communication and information exchange was about to be completely overhauled. New information technologies took control of telephone systems, automated banking machines, and assembly lines; they made possible the organization and analysis of massive data banks, thus increasing the potential for discovery and surveillance. Such technologies allowed for ultrasound and magnetic resonance images of the body; they influenced even the mundane activities of day-to-day living: the watches people wore, the cars they drove, the mail they received, and the games they played were all revolutionized by computer-related technologies. New information technologies brought tangible change to Americans' lives. But would such change make certain human skills and functions obsolete? In the 1970s and early 1980s, many felt uncertain about the outcome of America's high-tech "revolution."[46]

Finally, consider the change and uncertainty that plagued the American family. In the 1970s, the structure of the family was dramatically altered. For example, in 1960, married couples with children represented the dominant household form (44.2 percent). But by 1980, this family form constituted only 30.9 percent of all households. The numbers of men and women living alone nearly doubled during the same twenty-year period, and the percentage of the population that never married increased by nearly 30 percent. Increases could also be found in the median age at first marriage, the divorce rate, the cohabitation rate, and the number of unwed mothers. Clearly, the very concept of family was undergoing significant change. And as new family forms and household arrangements began to replace the familiar nuclear unit (e.g., blended families, single-parent households, same-sex partnerships), Americans grew increasingly uncertain about the future of the nation's most central institution.[47]

Space constraints make it impossible for me fully to detail the diffuse instability of the 1970s and early 1980s. Yet even this short discussion suggests that change in the United States was sufficiently widespread as to keep Americans temporarily "off balance." To be sure, the instability of the period was not paralyzing or devastating. Yet disruption of the era was significant enough to challenge Americans' sense of security. In essence, the events of the 1970s and early 1980s projected a sense of looming vulnerability. Such events made Americans question both their sense of personal control and the ability (or the desire) of government to protect them from new and changing conditions. These sentiments were reflected in public opinion polls of the era. For example, Gallup polls taken throughout the 1970s and early 1980s repeatedly showed that the majority of Americans expressed feelings of uncertainty regarding their future economic well-being, their personal well-being, the future of the environment, the trustworthiness of government, and the position of the nation in the international arena.[48]

LINKING THE CULTURAL AND THE SOCIAL

What links scripts of individualism to a period of diffuse instability? Why would such a self-oriented message saturate an era of widespread change and uncertainty? The scripts of individualism reviewed in this chapter and the historical events they accompanied provide us with an opportunity to speculate on these questions.

Certainly, the scripts of individualism that dominated the 1970s and early 1980s in no way *reflected* the instability of the period; they did not explicate or illustrate the conditions from which they emerged. Consequently, I argue that these scripts represented a powerful *reaction* to difficult and confusing social circumstances; they promoted a message of personal control—a message of survival. Scripts of individualism suggested to social actors that in the face of adversity, the individual can fight back and prevail. When social life appears to be slowly eroding, individual initiative can turn the tide. As such, scripts of individualism offered a coping mechanism of sorts, a prescription for personal action at a time when instability derailed predictability and threatened established social patterns.

In defining scripts of individualism as reactive cultural projects, I necessarily define cultural producers as active social agents. I suggest that the cultural producers of the 1970s and early 1980s made conscious decisions to project individualism over other available messages. Such a scenario is in keeping with Ann Swidler's contention that "culture is not a unified system that pushes action in consistent direction. Rather, it is more like a 'toolkit' or repertoire. . . . [From it] actors select differing pieces for constructing lines of action" (1986:277). I argue that in any given era, cultural producers have an array of institutionalized scripts at their disposal: scripts of civic community (e.g., "we're all one people"), scripts of pluralism (e.g., "America is a melting pot"), scripts of bilateral conflict (e.g., "it's them versus us"), and so on. They may choose to project several of these messages simultaneously, or, as was true from 1970 to 1984, they may emphasize one script over all other available "tools."

The period 1970 to 1984 is not the only example of a time in which scripts of individualism saturate the cultural arena. In ongoing research, I am reviewing the American cultural scripts projected during the last several decades. I have found, for example, that scripts of individualism proved dominant from roughly 1918 to 1929. And like the historical era reviewed in this chapter, the years 1918 to 1929 were characterized by diffuse instability. In addition, I have found that scripts of individualism recede to the cultural background in the absence of diffuse instability. My preliminary research shows, for example, that scripts of individualism were rather scarce during periods of concentrated, catastrophic change such as the Great Depression. Such scripts played only a minor role during the world wars—eras in which external forces seriously threaten the nation's security. Note too that scripts of individualism failed to dominate periods of stability and prosperity. For example, during the 1950s or the 1990s, the theme of individualism was accompanied by a variety of other messages—scripts of communalism, pluralism, and bilateralism.

Can we explain the patterns behind cultural script selection? Why do producers opt for unithematic scripts in certain eras while forwarding a heterogeneous menu during other eras? And when unithematic scripts are chosen, what explains the specific theme that is paired with a particular social condition? Here I present two research hypotheses. First, I suggest that periods of change and uncertainty encourage cultural producers to converge on a single strategy of action, what Swidler describes as an "explicit, articulated, highly organized meaning system . . . a unifed answer to problems of social action" (1986:278–79). During periods of change and uncertainty, unithematic scripts may offer a targeted remedy to a complex set of problems. Such scripts may help bring focus to a confusing, erratic environment.[49] Second, I suggest that the particular theme cultural producers promote during periods of change and uncertainty may be directly related to the specific source of the disruptive condition. Here again, I rely on Swidler's argument that "it is the concrete situations in which cultural models are enacted that determine which take root and thrive and which wither and die" (1986:280; see also Cerulo 1995, 1998).

Based on ongoing analysis, I argue, for example, that individualized innovation represents the most common message in conditions of diffuse instability. In the face of broad-based yet manageable change and uncertainty, cultural producers seem inclined to issue a "hands-on" appeal that encourages "everyman/woman" to "break frame," take personal control, and create new solutions and new strategies of organizing activity. My preliminary research also suggests that times of catastrophic, concentrated change meet with a very different cultural response. During such eras, cultural producers seem to favor a communally oriented message. Periods of catastrophic change may appear so threatening that the strength of numbers is required. Under such conditions, cultural scripts may represent an attempt to reinvigorate collective cohesion.

Again, these findings are preliminary. Only more extensive study will fully illustrate the complex relationship between the social and cultural domains. Toward that end, I am exploring the American cultural scripts projected from 1850 to 1995, and I am noting the social milieus from which these scripts emerged. Using these data, I am recording those periods in which unithematic scripts saturated the American scene. I am attempting to document that such scripts were consciously projected— that is, imposed from the top down rather than being the product of simultaneous frame switches by many interdependent actors. I also am working toward determining the extent of these scripts' impact. For example, are those in various social locations similarly impacted by these products and images? What behaviors and attitudes are most dramatically influenced by cultural scripts? Which are not at all affected? In so doing, I hope to chart the varying strength of culture's impact on the social environment.

Revisiting the Fixed Conceptualization of Social Relations

In addition to exploring the complex interaction between the social and cultural domains, the present project encourages us to revisit linear models of social relations. Fixed conceptualizations of social relations, so prominent in the social sciences,

continue to reinforce concerns for a growing individualism. Yet actual data on behavior and attitudes (both from my own study and from others cited throughout this
chapter) suggest that trends toward individualism are neither linear nor absolute.
Rather, individualism, as a form of social relations, is both limited in scope and
coexistent with other relational forms.

Taking data on Americans' behaviors and attitudes to heart, one must conclude that
the currently dominant linear models of relational development have diverted our
attention from the reality of American social relations. These linear models have
directed us to "see" a growing individualism that may be largely a cultural construction. Must our analyses of social relations be confined by reigning linear models? Is
there a viable analytic alternative—one that will provide a better "fit" between actual
occurrences and our perception of them?

RELATIONAL POLYPHONY

In concluding this chapter, I urge social scientists to step back from long-standing
linear models of relational development. Here I present an alternative—an approach
to social relations that relies on a more fluid analytic frame. Specifically, I suggest
that we think of American society as an entity that resides in a state of *relational
polyphony*. Relational polyphony describes a condition in which *different forms of
social relations simultaneously coexist*. In a polyphonic society, relational forms
blend in intricate ways to form a complex social composition.

My historical research suggests that since 1850 four particular relational forms
provide the "counterpoint" of the composition we call American society. I list these
forms here along with a brief definition of each:

- *Individualism*: Individualistic relations revolve round the project of the self.
  Under such conditions, a society's concerns for the individual take precedence over those directed toward the greater collective or any subsectors of
  that collective. Individuals' self-gratification and self-actualization become
  the dominant goal of social interaction. Social connections tend to be particularistic and built on self-specific needs.
- *Pluralism*: Pluralistic relations emerge when social interactions are directed
  toward the peaceful coexistence of multiple groups. Various sectors of a society work to maintain mutual understanding; they work toward a system in
  which resources can be shared. Under pluralistic conditions, compromise and
  collaboration represent the dominant modes of social interaction. And while
  *intra*group ties remain the strongest form of connection, weak yet flexible *inter*group ties are encouraged and exercised.
- *Bilateralism*: Bilateral relations suggest a condition in which a "them-versus-us"
  mentality guides social interaction. Behavior is not directed toward a single,
  unifying end. Rather, dominance over the "other" represents social interaction's central goal. When bilateralism is in force, conflict and organized competition present the most frequent modes of interaction. Strong bonds are built
  with in-group members, while connections to out-group members are discouraged. As a result, bilateral relations create a collective divided in two—a
  former whole now dissolved into distinct, bipolar sectors.

- *Communalism*: Communalism emerges from a targeted collective focus.[50] Social actors become connected via a specific task, event, or characteristic. Thus, during such periods, a sense of familiarity, "like-mindedness" or "we-ness" moves to the foreground of collective attention. Similarities are stressed over differences; common knowledge is stressed over specialized knowledge. The good of the citizenry takes precedence over any subgroup or individual.

These ideal types suggest very different social experiences. Thus one might reasonably inquire as to whether these four relational forms could indeed coexist at a single historical moment or in a single society. What would relational polyphony look like "in practice"?

One need search no further than contemporary America to see relational polyphony at work. Several current trends and practices help to illustrate the point. In today's society, for example, new communication technologies can greatly facilitate individualism. One can indeed customize rather than consolidate, demand rather than compromise, insulate rather than commune, creating the audience of one to which so many analysts refer. Thus individuals can shirk their local community vendors, choosing instead to name their own price for goods online. They can forego the media's general menu and, with services such as Direct TV, customize each day's news and entertainment to personal tastes and interests. Via the Internet, one can create Web sites and homepages that celebrate and parade the self. And one can downscale the scope of interaction, taking advantage of the capacity to bank and invest, receive personalized medical evaluations, obtain psychological counseling, even meet a romantic interest—all without entering the physical community. In this way, contemporary American society can, under certain circumstances, be reduced to its most basic constituent parts, with those parts remaining only loosely or instrumentally connected—and sometimes disconnected.

At the same time, contemporary America can be and is mapped according to pluralistic relations. Present-day society can be rightfully defined as a set of overlapping, interlocking "circles" (i.e., baby boomers, Catholics, gun control supporters, new democrats, etc.), with social action directed by the ways in which these circles configure and coalesce. Such pluralistic relations become quite visible, for example, when we attend to the political realm. For in building a constituency, today's successful candidate can no longer rely on person-to-person connections or blind party loyalty. Rather, constituencies represent a coalition of compatible interest groups—collections of voters with overlapping values who work toward a common goal. (In the 2000 elections, for example, the Bush constituency was built in part on an alliance of fiscal conservatives, pro-lifers, gun freedom advocates, etc., while the Gore constituency favored an alliance of fiscal moderates, pro-choice advocates, and gun control supporters, etc.) These same pluralistic relations mark the current economic environment as well. In this regard, many argue that the era of the stand-alone corporation is over. Profit is increasingly contingent on successful "business-to-business" alliances. Production must be linked to service, brick-and-mortar operations must be linked to e-commerce industries, companies from diverse sectors must form partnerships, and so on. Indeed, the most successful businesses of the past decade are those that either facilitated the linking of previously disconnected corporate circles (e.g., Ariba, Commerce One, etc.) or those that initiated such alliances on their own (e.g.,

Barnes and Noble, Home Depot, Intel, etc.). In yet another area, note that pluralistic relations are becoming increasingly common in the entertainment sphere. More and more, producers are adopting "character crossovers" as a means of uniting otherwise disconnected television audiences. Producer David E. Kelly, for example, used character crossovers to build a coalition between fans of *Ally McBeal* and *The Practice*. Similarly, the ABC network is using the technique to forge an alliance between the fans of its three daily soap operas *All My Children*, *One Life to Live*, and *General Hospital*. Via character crossovers, previously disjointed groups forge together; certain characters facilitate shared viewer commitment to a set of crosscutting interests. These examples and others like them remind us that pluralistic relations are alive and well, an intricate element of contemporary America. Such relations reside in concert with the audience of one.

Of course, contemporary American society can and does periodically divide according to dualistic conflict. Certain events and issues pit white against black, male against female, pro-life against pro-choice, big business against government, and so on. Such controversies force either/or choices and forge relations on the basis of social actors' bilateral affiliations. When conflict is prolonged, it can ultimately institutionalize the tracks and tiers that divide a society. In contemporary America one can identify several events that have temporarily transfixed social actors to the proverbial "line in the sand." For example, the Rodney King trial, the O. J. Simpson case, and the Amadou Diallo proceedings crystallized and fed America's racial divide. The events surrounding the brutal murder of Matthew Shepard emphasized the schism surrounding gay rights issues. The "Million Mom March" on Washington directed us to the growing divide between antigun activists and NRA supporters. And the Microsoft antitrust case underscored the boundaries that separate government and big business. These issues and many similar controversies emphasize bilateralism's continued presence in American society. During such periods we see that social relations often develop in opposition rather than in conjunction with the "other."

And yet, faced with certain social events, Americans will temporarily ignore all social partitions. They will attend to collective concerns over all other issues. During such periods, communalistic relations move to the foreground of action. Actors band together (albeit for short spans of time) in what I have previously termed moments of "high collective focus"—periods in which members of a society join in a single, targeted point of attention (Cerulo 1995). Via collective focus, social actors come to form a national or civic community—a public able to express shared perspectives and support a common agenda. We witness such communalistic relations in widespread efforts aimed at solving national problems. Consider campaigns designed to eliminate school shootings and the large-scale efforts employed to avoid the Y2K problem at the millennium's end. Similarly, we witness communalistic relations in the face of American human interest stories. Recall, for example, the intense focus that surrounded the untimely deaths of Princess Diana and JFK Jr. That same singular gaze transfixed the American collective to the Oklahoma City bombing and its aftermath. And finally, we witness communalistic relations in what Nina Eliasoph (1998) calls the "community of talk"; these are topics about which the large majority of social members can fluently and affably converse—for example, Mark McGuire's 70th home run and the latest winner of *Who Wants to be a Millionaire* or *Survivor*. Far from the anomic existence attributed to contemporary American society, communalistic relations infuse society with a sense of group-mindedness. And while communalism does not constitute the sole substance of social relations, it nevertheless makes its presence felt as it coexists with other relational forms.

I offer these examples of American social relations in service of a broader conceptual point. Specifically, I am arguing that in any complex society such as the United States, individualism, pluralism, bilateralism, and communalism simultaneously contribute to the society's relational map.[51] To be sure, the relative concentration or dominance of each relational form sometimes shifts from location to location and from time to time—just as the primary melody of a polyphonic composition often shifts from voice to voice as the piece progresses. But in contradiction of the long-standing tenets of the linear model of relational development, I argue that multiple relational forms have long coexisted and continue to coexist in American society. Our society has not abandoned civic community; it has not been overrun by individualism. Rather, it exists as a rich kaleidoscope of relational forms—forms that configure and reconfigure in various ways to create new and different realities through time.

Conclusion

If growing individualism is a cultural construction rather than a social fact, then for sociologists an important paradigm shift is in order. We must step away from models that assume the gradual unraveling of communalism—models that argue for an inevitable flow toward a me-centered world. Instead, we must explore the reasons why cultural images of individualism come to dominate certain historical moments and certain social contexts.

A more extensive study of individualism in America provides one means toward that end. Broadening this chapter's base of inquiry will help to delineate further the social conditions that both facilitate and impede the production of scripts of individualism. Such work will allow us to explore more extensively the intentions behind such cultural production. And it will help us to determine the specific impact of individualistic scripts on social attitudes and behaviors.

But the "noise" that exists between cultural depictions of individualism and the social action they accompany also raises broader questions about the relationship between the cultural and social domains. The findings presented in this chapter remind us that the cultural and the social are not bound by a simple causal relationship; culture does not simply reflect social structure, or vice versa. Rather, each sphere develops in response to the progression of the other, suggesting both the unique integrity of the cultural and the social, as well as the powerful symbiosis between the two. The study of individualism represents one avenue by which to study this symbiotic relationship. But only patient and extensive empirical inquiry will provide us with the full scope of this intricate interaction.

Endnotes

1. Quoted from an interview with Ira Matathia, CEO of the trend-watching *Brand Futures Group: The Wall Street Journal Report*: WCBS, show no. 869, May 23, 1999.

2. Ibid.
3. I define individualism as a relational form that prioritizes the individual over any group, community, or institution.
4. Wolfe (1976:143).
5. Lasch (1979:xv).
6. Putnam (1998:1; also see 2000).
7. Etzioni (1996:xvii, xv).
8. In the 1970s, the work of Wolfe and Lasch signaled an increasingly vocal intellectual emphasis. Many central and well-respected thinkers—e.g., Marin (1975), Schur (1976), and Sennett (1977)—lamented a growing individualism as well. Throughout the 1980s and 1990s, concerns of this nature grew (e.g., Bellah et al. 1985:142–63). Some, for example, wrote of the suburban isolation spawned by individualism (e.g., Baldassare 1986; Baumgartner 1988). Others noted an increase in Americans' selfishness and a parallel decline in Americans' civility, trust, and happiness (e.g., Cherlin 1999; Collier 1991; Lane 2000; Nock 1993). Still others mourned the loss of a coherent "public" and sought ways to reestablish a clear moral consensus (e.g., Cherlin 1999; Calhoun 1998; Etzioni 1993; Ferrarotti 1988, 1998; Sandel 1996; Waltzer 1997). Amidst this field, the growing centrality of "the self" and "agency" in the social science literature speaks to the rise of the individual actor as a unit of social analysis.
9. When I use the term "social relations," I refer to the types of connections and the patterns of interaction that structure the broader society.
10. Specific proponents of the linear model will be discussed later in this paper.
11. Data for these figures were obtained from *The Gallup Poll* (1972–1996), the *General Social Survey* (1972–1999), Littman (1996), PBS Broadcasting (2000), Robinson and Godbey (1997), and U.S. Bureau of the Census (1965–1997).
12. Staff editor Marjorie Connelly designed the survey, conducted between July 17 and 19, 1999. A total of 1,178 adult Americans were interviewed by phone. See Cherlin (1999) for details.
13. In comparing Durkheim's concepts to those of Toennies and Simmel, it is important to note a critical difference. Toennies framed *Gemeinschaft* and *Gesellschaft* as strictly "either-or" concepts. Similarly, Simmel viewed the metropolis as an eventual replacement of small-town life. In contrast, Durkheim believed that mechanical and organic solidarity could be coexisting forms. "These two societies really make up one," wrote Durkheim. "They are two aspects of one and the same reality, but none the less they must be distinguished" (1933:129). True to the linear model, however, Durkheim clearly implied that, as modernity progressed, organic solidarity would become a more common experience than mechanical solidarity.
14. See Wirth (1938).
15. See Davis (1949).
16. Lewis Coser (1956) makes a similar distinction in writing of loose versus close groups.
17. See Gouldner (1957) and Merton (1968). Merton (1968:447) specifically notes the links between his categories and Tonnies's work.
18. See Boldt (1978).
19. See, e.g., Elias (1978), Giddens (1991), Granovetter (1973), Habermas (1991), Sennett (1977), and Shils (1966).
20. Robert Wuthnow (1998) represents a notable exception to this rule. His concepts of "loose connections" and "porous institutions" provide us with the basis for new thinking on social relations.
21. Tilly (1984:11–12).
22. See Kuhn [1962] 1996:10)
23. Data derived from Murrells (1984) and Whitburn (1996).
24. Using summaries found on the Cader Books Web site (http://www.caderbooks.com), I coded the themes of the three best-selling fiction books and the three best-selling nonfiction books

for each year during 1965 to 1995. A second coder, blind to the hypothesis, recoded 10% of the sample. Inter-coder reliability was 86%.

25. I determined the theme of Oscar-winning films by coding summaries of each movie. The summaries were derived from http://www.imdb.com, accessed June 2000. Data on box office sales was derived from http://www.worldwideboxoffice.com, retrieved June 2000. A second coder, blind to the hypothesis, recoded 10% of the sample. Inter-coder reliability was 87%.

26. It is interesting to note that the ethos of individualism also governed the ways in which the period's films were made. During the 1970s, the American film industry welcomed the era of "auteurs." American filmmakers moved away from studio-marked productions, preferring to make their films personal projects of the individual. Films came to be identified by a director's unique "signature."

27. Data derived from G. Brown (1997) and Green (1996).

28. Famighetti (1999), McNeil (1991), and O'Neil (1998) provide data on television ratings.

29. See the U.S. Bureau of the Census (1982–1983, tables 400–401; 1989, tables 386–387).

30. Many educational specialists, especially those involved in early-childhood education, became intrigued with such programs as they existed in the British schools. Some contend that Charles Silberman's influential book, *Crisis in the Classroom* (1970), helped to bring the open classroom to American schools.

31. In the 1970s, the most popular building design for new elementary schools was one that contained few or portable walls.

32. To collect this data, I read and classified every decision listed in *The Oxford Guide to United States Supreme Court Decisions* (Hall 1999). This source rendered 222 cases for review. In a larger project, I am supplementing these data with a systematic sample of *all* cases reviewed by the court during the period 1850–1995.

33. *Eisenstadt v. Baird*, decided on March 22, 1972, offers a prototypical example. This judgment deemed it unconstitutional for the state to ban the distribution of contraceptives to unmarried individuals. Justice William Brennan wrote: "It is the right of the *individual*, married or single, to be free from unwanted government intrusion into matters so fundamentally affecting a person as the decision whether to bear or beget a child" (Hall 1999:83).

34. *Hudson v. Palmer*, decided on December 7, 1983, provides a prototypical example. The Supreme Court ruled that the right to privacy does not extend to prisoners.

35. *Georgia v. McCollum*, decided on June 18, 1992, offers a prototypical example. The case states that states cannot eliminate prospective jurors on the basis of their race.

36. *Washington v. Davis*, decided March 1, 1976, provides a prototypical case. The Supreme Court ruled that entry tests (in this case, written qualifying exams for acceptance to the police force) which appeared to favor the skills of whites over African Americans were not necessarily unconstitutional.

37. *Goldwater v. Carter*, decided on December 13, 1979, offers a prototypical case. Here the Supreme Court reversed a court of appeals ruling which granted the president authority to overturn a treaty without the approval of Congress.

38. For example, the Allied victory in World War II brought change to the United States and the world. But that change ended the uncertainty inflicted by the very condition of war. Thus the conclusion of World War II embodied a time in which change reestablished predictability. Similarly, the U.S. presidential election of 2000 spurred the nation into weeks of uncertainty. A national vote too close to call left the identity of the next president in doubt. Yet this unexpected turn of events occurred in the context of a well-entrenched political process. Thus the election's uncertainty was resolved with little change to the nation's political structure.

39. In light of this criterion, one would exclude the Great Depression of the 1930s, for example, as illustrative of diffuse instability. To be sure, the Great Depression involved both change (great prosperity to severe hardship) and uncertainty (a slow, labored recovery that was

difficult to gauge). However, change and uncertainty were heavily concentrated in the economic realm. While economic disruption was catastrophic, other social sectors such as the family and politics fought to maintain the status quo. These arenas provided havens (sometimes real, sometimes figurative) from severe economic disruption.

40. Recombinant DNA is not found in nature. To create it, one must combine parts of a DNA string from one organism with parts of a DNA string from another organism.

41. These guidelines were not relaxed until the mid-1980s.

42. See Bains (1987); Watson and Tooze (1981).

43. See Gallup (1979).

44. See Brown (1981).

45. See Bondi (1996:381, 383); also see Nelkin, Willis, and Parris (1991).

46. See, e.g., Yourdon (1986).

47. See Coontz (1992); U.S. Bureau of the Census (1965–1997).

48. See, e.g., Gallup (1974, 1975, 1976, 1998a, 1998b, 2000).

49. Unlike Swidler, I am not assuming that unithematic scripts (i.e., cultural tools) necessarily alter all social attitudes and behaviors. Based on my study of American life during 1965 to 1995, I would argue that the impact of these cultural tools is particularized in certain social domains.

50. Elsewhere, I have discussed extensively the concept of collective focus. The term refers to "the points of reference to which a collective body is directed—the range of issues considered by the collective body as well as the depth of that concern. . . . [Collective focus] provides a gauge of a national population's macrocognitive solidarity" (Cerulo 1995:92).

51. This proves true when we view society at the macrolevel, considering social relations across "horizontal space." It also proves true when we view society "vertically," examining relations at the national versus the local versus the interpersonal level. For more on relational polyphony across various levels of analysis, see Cerulo and Ruane (1998).

References

Bains, W. 1987. *Genetic Engineering for Almost Everybody.* New York: Pelican.

Baldassare, M. 1986. *Trouble in Paradise: The Suburban Transformation in America.* New York: Columbia University Press.

Baumgartner, M. P. 1988. *The Moral Order of a Suburb.* New York: Oxford University Press.

Bellah, R. N., R. Madsen, W. M. Sullivan, A. Swidler, and S. M. Tipton. 1985. *Habits of the Heart: Individualism and Commitment in American Life.* Berkeley, CA: University of California Press.

Boldt, E. D. 1978. "Structural Tightness, Autonomy, and Observability: An Analysis of Hutterite Conformity and Orderliness." *Canadian Journal of Sociology* 3:349–363.

Bondi, V. 1995. *American Decades, 1970–1979.* Detroit, MI: Gale Research Inc.

———. 1996. *American Decades, 1980–1989.* Detroit, MI: Gale Research Inc.

Brown, G. 1997. *Show Time.* New York: Macmillan.

Brown, M. 1981. *Laying Waste: The Poisoning of America by Toxic Chemicals.* New York: Pocket Books.

Calhoun, C. 1998. "Community without Propinquity Revisited: Communications Technology and the Transformation of the Urban Public Sphere." *Sociological Inquiry* 68(3):373–97.

Cerulo, K. A. 1995. *Identity Designs: The Sights and Sounds of a Nation.* The Rose Book Series of the American Sociological Association. New Brunswick, NJ: Rutgers University Press.

———. 1997. "Re-framing Sociological Concepts for a Brave New (Virtual?) World." *Sociological Inquiry* 67(1):48–58.

———. 1998. *Deciphering Violence: The Cognitive Structure of Right and Wrong.* New York: Routledge.

————. In preparation. *Individualism Pro Tem: Rethinking Social Relations in America.* Book manuscript in preparation.

Cerulo, K. A. and J. M. Ruane. 1997. "Death Comes Alive: Technology and the Reconception of Death." *Science As Culture* 6(28,3):444–66.

————. 1998. "Coming Together: New Taxonomies for the Analysis of Social Relations." *Sociological Inquiry* 68(3):398–425.

Cerulo, K. A. J. M. Ruane, and M. Chayko. 1992. "Technological Ties That Bind: Media Generated Primary Groups." *Communication Research* 19(1):109–29.

Cherlin, A. J. 1999. "I'm O.K., You're Selfish." *New York Times*, October 17, pp. A44–45.

Collier, J. L. 1991. *The Rise of Selfishness in America.* New York: Oxford University Press.

Collins, R. 1981. "On the Micro-Foundations of Macro-Sociology." *American Journal of Sociology* 86:984–1014.

————. 1988. "Toward a Neo-Meadian Sociology of the Mind." *Symbolic Interaction* 12: 1–32.

Coontz, S. 1992. *The Way We Never Were.* New York: Basic Books.

Coser, L. 1956. *The Functions of Social Conflict.* Glencoe, IL: The Free Press.

Davis, K. 1949. *Human Society.* New York: Macmillan.

Durkheim, E. [1893] 1933. *The Division of Labor in Society.* New York: Free Press.

Elias, N. 1978. *The Civilising Process.* Translated by Edmund Jephcott. New York: Urizon Books.

Eliasoph, N. 1998. *Avoiding Politics: How Americans Produce Apathy in Everyday Life.* Cambridge, England: Cambridge University Press.

Emirbayer, M. 1997. "Manifesto of a Relational Sociology." *American Journal of Sociology* 103:281–317.

Emirbayer, M. and A. Mische. 1998. "What Is Agency?" *American Journal of Sociology* 104:962–1023.

Etzioni, A. 1993. *The Spirit of Community: Rights, Responsibility, and the Community.* New York: Crown Publishers.

————. 1996. *The New Golden Rule.* New York: Basic Books.

Famighetti, R., ed. 1999. *The World Almanac and Book of Facts 2000.* Mahwah, NJ: World Almanac Books.

Ferrarotti, F. 1988. *The End of Conversation: The Impact of Mass Media on Modern Society.* New York: Greenwood.

————. 1998. "The Reality of the Virtual." *La Critica Sociologica* 125:136–40.

Fischer, C. S. 1992. *America Calling: A Social History of the Telephone to 1940.* Berkeley, CA: University of California Press.

————. 1997. "Technology and Community: Historical Complexities." *Sociological Inquiry* 67(1):113–18.

————. 2000. "Just How Is It That Americans Are Individualistic?" Presented at the annual meetings of the American Sociological Association, August, Washington DC.

Gallup, G. Jr. 1972–1996. *The Gallup Poll*, vols. 101–146. Princeton, NJ: Gallup.

————. 1974. *The Gallup Poll*, vol. 103 (January). Princeton, NJ: Gallup.

————. 1975. *The Gallup Poll*, vol. 115 (January). Princeton, NJ: Gallup.

————. 1976. *The Gallup Poll*, vol. 126 (January). Princeton, NJ: Gallup.

————. 1979. *The Gallup Poll*, vol. 165 (April). Princeton, NJ: Gallup.

————. 1998a. "Record Number of Americans Optimistic About the Economy." Poll Release, March 1998. Retrieved September 2000. (http://www.gallup.com/poll/releases/pr980328.asp).

————. 1998b. "Americans' Satisfaction and Well-Being at All-Time High." Poll Release, October 1998. Retrieved September 2000. (http://www.gallup.com/poll/releases/pr981023.asp).

————. 2000. "Gallup Social and Economic Indicators: Satisfaction With Personal Life, 1979–1998." Retrieved September 2000. (http://www.gallup.com/poll/indicators/indpersonallife.asp).

General Social Survey. 1972–1999. Cumulative Codebook 1999. Retrieved September 1999. (http://www.icpsr.umich.edu/GSS99/codebook).

Giddens, A. 1991. *Modernity and Self-Identity.* Stanford, CA: Stanford University Press.

Gouldner, A. W. 1957. "Cosmopolitans and Locals: Toward an Analysis of Latent Social Roles." *Administrative Science Quarterly* 2:281–306.

Granovetter, M. 1973. "The Strength of Weak Ties." *American Journal of Sociology* 78: 1362–80.

———. 1985. "Economic Action and Social Structure: The Problem of Embeddedness." *American Journal of Sociology* 91:481–510.

Green, S. 1996. *Broadway Musicals: Show by Show.* 5th ed. Milwaukee, WI: Hal Leonard Corporation.

Habermas, J. 1991. *Structural Change in the Public Sphere.* Stanford, CA: Stanford University Press.

Hall, K. L. 1999. *The Oxford Guide to United States Supreme Court Decisions.* New York: Oxford University Press.

Hunter, J. D. and C. Bowman. 1996. *The State of Disunion,* vol. 2. Ivy, VA: In Media Research Educational Foundation.

Kuhn, T. S. [1962] 1996. *The Structure of Scientific Revolutions.* Chicago, IL: University of Chicago Press.

Ladd, E. C. 1999. *The Ladd Report.* New York: Free Press.

Lane, R. E. 2000. *The Loss of Happiness in Market Democracies.* New Haven, CT: Yale University Press.

Lasch, C. 1979. *The Culture of Narcissism: American Life in an Age of Diminishing Expectations.* New York: W. W. Norton.

Littman, M. 1996. *A Statistical Portrait of the U.S.* Lanham, MD: Bernam Press.

Marin, P. 1975. "The New Narcissism." *Harper's,* October, pp. 46–54.

McLuhan, M. 1964. *Understanding Media: The Extensions of Man.* New York: McGraw Hill.

McNeil, A. 1991. *Total Television: A Comprehensive Guide to Programming from 1948 to the Present.* New York: Penguin Books.

Merton, R. K. 1968. "Continuities in the Theory of Reference Group Behavior." Pp. 422–40 in *Social Theory and Social Structure.* New York: Free Press.

Meyrowitz, J. 1985. *No Sense of Place.* New York: Oxford University Press.

———. 1996. "Shifting Worlds of Strangers: Medium Theory and Changes in 'Them' versus 'Us.' *Sociological Inquiry* 67(1):59–71.

Nelkin, D., D. P. Willis, and S. V. Parris, eds. 1991. *A Disease of Society: Cultural and Institutional Responses to AIDS.* Cambridge, England, and New York: Cambridge University Press.

Nock, S. L. 1993. *The Costs of Privacy: Surveillance and Reputation in America.* New York: Aldine De Gruyter.

O'Neil, T. 1998. *The Emmys.* New York: Perigee.

PBS Broadcasting. 2000. "Family." *The First Century Measured.* Retrieved December 21, 2000. (wysiwyg://27/http://www.pbs.org/fmc/book/4family11.htm).

Putnam, R. D. 1998. "The Strange Disappearance of Civic America." *New Prospect Inc.* (http://epn.org/prospect/24/24putn.html).

———. 2000. *Bowling Alone: The Collapse and Revival of American Community.* New York: Simon and Schuster.

Robinson, J. P. and G. Godbey. 1997. *Time for Life.* University Park, PA: Pennsylvania State University Press.

Sandel, M. J. 1996. *Democracy's Discontent: America in Search of a Public Philosophy.* Cambridge, MA: Belknap Press.

Schur, E. 1976. *The Awareness Trap: Self-Absorption Instead of Social Change.* New York: Quadrangle-New York Times.

Sennett, R. 1977. *The Fall of Public Man.* New York: Knopf.

Shils, E. 1966. "Privacy: Its Constitution and Vicissitudes. *Law and Contemporary Problems* 31:281–306.

Silberman, C. E. 1970. *Crisis in the Classroom.* New York: Random House.

Simmel, G. [1908] 1950. *The Sociology of Georg Simmel.* Translated and edited by K. H. Wolff. New York: Free Press.

Swidler, A. 1986. "Culture in Action: Symbols in Strategies." *American Sociological Review* 51(2):273–86.

Tilly, C. 1984. *Big Structures, Large Processes, Huge Comparisons.* New York: Russell Sage Foundation.

———. 1998. *Durable Inequality.* Berkeley, CA: University of California Press.

———. 2000. "How Do Relations Store Histories?" *Annual Review of Sociology* 26:721–23.

Tonnies, F. [1887] 1957. *Community and Society.* Translated and edited by Charles A. Loomis. East Lansing, MI: Michigan State University Press.

U.S. Bureau of the Census. 1965–1997. *Statistical Abstracts of the United States*, 85th–118th editions. Washington, DC: U.S. Government Printing Office.

Van Sotter, R. 1991. *Public Schooling in America.* Santa Barbara, CA: ABC-CLIO.

The Wall Street Journal Report: Show no. 869, May 23, 1999.

Waltzer, M. 1997. *On Toleration.* New Haven, CT: Yale University Press.

Watson, J. and J. Tooze. 1981. *The DNA Story: A Documentary History of Gene Cloning.* San Francisco, CA: W. H. Freeman.

Whitburn, J. 1996. *The Billboard Book of Top Forty Hits.* New York: Billboard Publications, Inc.

Wirth, L. 1938. "Urbanism as a Way of Life." *American Journal of Sociology* 44:1–24.

Wolfe, T. 1976. "The Me Decade and the Third Great Awakening." Pp. 126–67 in *Mauve Gloves & Madmen Clutter and Vine.* New York: Farrar, Straus and Giroux.

Wuthnow, R. 1998. *Loose Connections: Joining Together in America's Fragmented Communities.* New York: Oxford University Press.

Yourdon, E. 1986. *Nations at Risk: The Impact of the Computer Revolution.* New York: Yourdon.

CHAPTER 9

Tracking Discourse

David L. Altheide

This chapter addresses communication and experience. The following pages are a modest attempt to set forth the relevance of mass communication formats and content for analysis of the intersection between culture and cognition. My work also attempts to bridge some conceptual and methodological divides in mass communication research. The paper prioritizes a conceptual and methodological approach to the study of mass media—tracking discourse. This approach looks for key words and follows them across time and various topics in order to see how these elements emerge as powerful symbols that in turn guide individuals-as-audience-members to extend these symbols across arenas of experience in the quest for meaning. Ongoing news media research involving "fear" will be used as an example of the process.

How we think and how we act are connected in several paradoxical ways. One social science perspective on this process, set forth in the work of George Herbert Mead (Mead and Morris 1962) and a legion of symbolic interactionists (Blumer 1969; Hall 1997), is that mind, self, and society are intricately connected. The general emphasis is on the communication and interpretation processes that play out in social interaction between two or more individuals. For Mead, brains and minds are not synonymous, and indeed, mind is not something that is entirely owned and operated by the individual; it is something posited and affirmed as a kind of beacon of meaning and orientation. While Mead was not overly concerned with physiology or the electronics of constructs such as synapses and the like, he was aware that all are social constructions (Brissett and Edgley 1990), that our actions provide a context of meaning for audiences to affirm whether we are thinking at all, whether there is a mind behind the face, and above all, whether things make sense. Several generations of sociologists and psychologists have studied how social reality is presented, affirmed, discussed, and negated in hundreds of social arenas and social institutions (Goffman 1959). This work, then, with the help of many others, is the essential foundation for the notion that reality is socially constructed (Berger and Luckmann 1967; Burke 1966, 1969; Schutz 1967). Indeed, Schutz's (1967) notion about the significance of the "natural attitude" in everyday life hinged on his thoughtful elucidation of a process through which societal members engage in intersubjective understanding. Schutz's analysis of interpretive procedures contributed to ethnomethodology's agenda of investigating commonsense understanding as features of situated language use (Cicourel 1974; Douglas 1970), and provided an early approach to a "cognitive sociology." This general perspective, and particularly the notion that cultural actors acquire and use communication logics in interpreting reality in social situations, informs this chapter.

The thinking process is connected at some point to the world of experience and the taken-for-granted. Both take place in contexts of meaning. And both are connected to audiences with whom we communicate. As Zerubavel (1997) argues, how we perceive, attend, classify, assign meaning, and reckon with time is subject to cultural variation. Culture gives us the broad as well as specific contexts of meaning and "scripts," or plausible statements and courses of action that will be accepted by others familiar with situations we share (Carey 1989). Complex rules of communication involve the interaction between minds, seldom seen but always presumed, and selves, and social situations. The critical point is that what we think about and talk about are reflexively joined to how we communicate.

One social science concept that draws together these parts is known by various terms as the "definition of the situation," or the sense of "what we have here," "what we're doing," and "we know what it means." Questions involving the nature, process, and consequences for defining the situation cut across most social science theory and research. I argue that the process involving the definition of the situation is a significant act of power.

My main interest concerns the role of the mass media and popular culture in shaping such definitions, including what we think about and discuss, the language we use in doing this, and the interpretive frameworks we bring to bear on events. In recent years, more researchers are focusing on the role of the mass media and popular culture in influencing members' definitions and perspectives about social reality, including the shaping of culture, communication formats, the formulation of the mundane, and policy issues and practical matters in both high places and everyday life (e.g., Altheide 1985, 1994; Best 1995; Cerulo 1998; Couch 1984; Crane 1992; Ericson, Baranek, and Chan 1991; Ferraro 1995; Ferrell and Sanders 1995; Gerbner and Gross 1976; Glassner 1999; Meyrowitz 1985; Snow 1983). Zerubavel's (1997) provocative discussion of collective memory seems pertinent for a broader understanding of the contributions of a culturally informed approach to an emerging cognitive sociology:

> A *mnemonic tradition* includes not only what we come to remember as members of a particular thought community but also *how* we remember it. . . . Needless to say, the schematic mental structures on which mnemonic traditions typically rest are neither "logical" nor natural. Most of them are either culture-specific or subculture-specific, and therefore something we acquire as part of our mnemonic socialization. (pp. 87, 89)

My argument is that the mass media provide a lot of material about our "mnemonic socialization." The media socialize us via content as well as in a logic of perception and expectation about the appearance, shape, form, and rhythm of credible information about experience. Tracking discourse is one way to investigate the prevalence and impact on public communication about social issues. A few general comments about content pertaining to crime and fear will be followed by an overview of mass media formats and the logics they carry.

Crime, Fear, and the Media

The mass media provide a lot of cultural experiences for citizens about crime and fear. Numerous news reports about fear pertain to children. The news media's emphasis of fear with children is consistent with work by Warr (1992) and others on the significance of "third-person" or "altruistic fear"—the concern for those whom you love or are responsible. Specifically, Warr found that children are the most common object of fear in households. Much of this concern is generated around crime and drugs. For example, in the mid-1990s, crime and violence were regarded by 27 percent of the public as the most important problem facing the country today.[1] Except for a brief appearance by "immorality, crime, and juvenile delinquency" in 1965, crime did not reappear among the top public concerns until around 1990, when drug abuse was cited by 18 percent as the second most significant problem.

    Kenneth F. Ferraro's important work on the fear of crime suggested the concept "perceptual criminology," or the notion that "many of the problems associated with crime, including fear, are independent of actual victimization . . . because it may lead to decreased social integration, out-migration, restriction of activities, added security costs, and avoidance behaviors" (Ferraro 1995). Figure 9–1 is an adaptation of Ferraro's insights.

FIGURE 9–1
Fear reactions (partly adapted from Ferraro 1995).

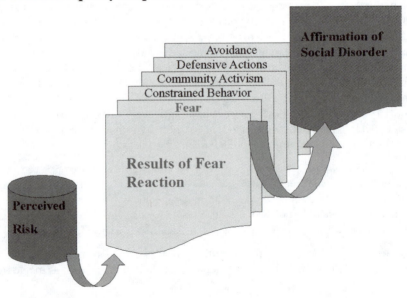

Similarly, two journalists (Westfeldt and Wicker 1998) very critical of the news coverage of crime, observed:

> In 1997, even as the prison population was going up and the crime rate was falling the public rated "crime/gangs/justice system" as "the most important problem facing the country today"—and by a large margin.

As they chronicled the preoccupation with crime by local newspapers and TV broadcasters in promoting a fear of crime agenda, the authors observed the culpability of national and prestigious news outlets in pushing the same views, including TV network news:

> The Center for Media and Public Affairs reported in April 1998 that the national murder rate has fallen by 20% since 1990—but the number of murder stories on network newscasts rose in the same years by about 600% . . . not including the many broadcasts of or about the O. J. Simpson trial. (1998:46)

These views are consistent with other research on the impact of news (Chiricos, Eschholz, and Gertz 1997) and other programming on public perceptions of crime and its causes (Sasson 1995).

It is clear, then, that numerous studies document Americans' increasing concern for their safety, notwithstanding a plethora of evidence that social life is much safer and healthier for the majority of citizens. And while some researchers have examined the place of fear in some cultural venues of American life (Glassner 1999), most accounts do not significantly expand our understandings beyond those set forth by Hadley Cantril and his colleagues over 60 years ago (Cantril et al. 1940). I contend that the mass media are central players in socializing audiences on what and how to experience culture, and that the language and imagery associated with popular culture are integrated into everyday life routines; they inform perceptions beyond the specific programming parameters. The study of fear exemplifies my point.

While fear is commonly associated with crime, I suggest that fear provides a discursive framework of expectation and meaning within which crime and related "problems" are expressed. Media practices and major news sources (e.g., law enforcement agencies) have cooperatively produced an organizational "machine," fueled by entertainment and selective use of news sources, which simultaneously connects people to their effective environments even as it generates entertainment-oriented profits (Altheide 1997). As one law enforcement official stated about Arizona's televised "crime-stoppers" dramatizations: "If you can have a little entertainment and get your man, too, that's great." This discourse resonates through public information and is becoming a part of what a mass society holds in common: We increasingly share understandings about what to fear and how to avoid it.

Fear is a key element of creating "the risk society," organized around communication oriented to policing, control, and prevention of risks (Ericson and Haggerty 1997; Staples 1997). A constitutive feature of this emerging order is a blanket reminder of fear: "Fear ends up proving itself, as new risk communication and management systems proliferate" (Ericson and Haggerty 1997:6). More is involved in media socialization than content and images of certain characters and story scenarios. It is the way popular culture is organized and presented, including its underlying logic and formats, which shapes audience expectations, preference, and ability to recognize one type of program rather than another, one type of action as "credible" rather than another. Because popular culture is so pervasive and the entertainment orientation infuses virtually all forms of public communication, it is important to be aware of underlying organizational principles.

News agencies have creatively adjusted "newswork" and news production to fit with entertainment formats (Altheide 1997:28). The packaging of information is done in organizational contexts that are dedicated to generating profits through entertaining programs and content. The news business does this with formats, themes, and frames and by promoting evocative discourses that are recognized and routinely used by audiences.

Formats pertain to the underlying organization and assumptions of time (temporal flow, rhythm), space (place and visual editing), and manner (style) of experience (Snow 1983). Formats are basically what make our "familiar experiences" "familiar" and recognizable as one thing rather than another; that is, we can quickly tell the difference between, say, a TV newscast, a sitcom, and a talk show. The entertainment emphasis contains elements of action noted by Goffman and others but clarified by Snow (Snow 1983) in his work on the rise of "media culture." First, there is an absence of the ordinary; second, there is the openness of an adventure, outside the boundaries of routine behavior; third, the audience member is willing to suspend disbelief. In addition, while the exact outcome may be in doubt, there is a clear and unambiguous point at which it will be resolved (Berg 1989; Zhondang and Kosicki 1993).

Frames are like the border around a picture that separates it from the wall and from other possibilities. An example is treating illegal drug use as a "public health issue" as opposed to a "criminal justice issue." These are two different frames that entail a way of discussing the problem and the kind of discourse that will follow. Frames focus on what will be discussed, how it will be discussed, and above all, how it will not be discussed (Altheide 1976; Epstein 1973; Fishman 1980). Themes are more basically tied to the format used by journalists, who have a short time to "tell a story" that the audience can "recognize," "that they have probably heard before," and moreover, to get specific information from sources that can be tied to this (Iyengar 1991).

The "problem frame" emerged with the entertainment dimension of news and has "refined" the way in which fear has been deployed across American culture (Altheide 1997). The mass media and especially the news business contributed to the emergence of a highly rationalized "problem frame," which in turn generates reports about "fear" rather than danger. A secular alternative to the morality play, problem frame characteristics include narrative structure, universal moral meanings, specific time and place, no ambiguity, a focus on disorder, and cultural resonance. The problem frame combines the universal logic and moral meanings of a morality play (Unsworth 1995) with the temporal and spatial parameters of a situated news report—something happened involving an actual person in an actual location. However, unlike a morality play, in which the characters are abstractions facing death and damnation, news reports focus on "actual" people and events, packaging the entire narrative as "realistic" and "teaching" the audience about the nature and causes of "disorder" (Ericson, Baranek, and Chan 1989). Complex and often ambiguous events and concerns are symbolically mined for moral truths and understandings presumed to be held by the audience.

The focus on media forms and logic of communication underlies an expanding agenda for understanding how the mass media can influence culture in terms of content, messages, and agenda, as well as the prevailing media logic(s) that pervades the popular culture shared by many segments of society, albeit unevenly. I draw on this general perspective to offer an approach that is helpful in following continuity and change over time in public documents.

FROM CONTENT TO DISCOURSE

There have been numerous creative studies of the content of popular culture in general and news media in particular. However, students of culture are aware that what also matters is not only the repetition of, say, certain words and action (e.g., violence; Gerbner and Gross 1976), but whether and to what extent a view of the social world is actually adopted and applied to everyday life situations. While research clearly suggests that public opinion is closely in line with news media accounts on issues ranging from politics (Zhondang and Kosicki 1993) to crime as a problem (Fishman 1980; Surette 1998; Taschler-Pollacek and Lukesch 1990; Warr 1983), how such issues change over time in terms of media language and application is less apparent. I refer not only to crime beats, using institutionalized "crime" news sources (e.g., the police), but also to extending the coverage as a matter of discourse. When something becomes a matter of discourse, it is not mere words that matter but, rather, more of an orientation and perspective on the world. This perspective may be more directive and adapted by audience members with repetition.

One way to approach these questions is by "tracking discourse," or following certain issues, words, themes, and frames over a period of time across different issues and across different news media. Tracking discourse is also a qualitative document analysis technique that applies an ethnographic approach to the content analysis of new information bases accessible through computer technology, for example, NEXIS (Altheide 1996; Dijk 1988; Grimshaw and Burke 1994; Wuthnow 1992). Involving twelve steps, tracking discourse entails initial familiarity with a sample of relevant documents before drafting a protocol, which is then checked for reliability and validity with additional documents. For example, in the study of "fear" to be discussed below, a protocol was constructed to obtain data about date, location, author, format, topic, sources, theme, emphasis, and grammatical use of the word "fear" (as noun, verb, or adverb). However, materials may also be enumerated and charted. Once collected, the materials were placed in an information base and analyzed qualitatively using Microsoft Word 7 and NUD*IST, a qualitative data analysis program, as well as quantitatively with a Microsoft Excel spreadsheet.

The approach blends interpretive, ethnographic, and ethnomethodological approaches with media logic, particularly studies of news organizational culture, information technology, and communication formats. Several elements are involved:

1. A comprehensive information base that is readily accessible;
2. A rationale for comparative searching over time;
3. Enumerating shifts and trends;
4. Examining denotative and connotative shifts;
5. Combining words into meaningful patterns and themes;
6. Expanding patterns into other mass media and popular culture.

Informed by conceptual and theoretical insights about the organization of newswork, and especially the role of entertainment formats and the use of themes, tracking discourse moves from specific words (or groups of words) to themes and linkages of specific issues and topics over time. Through the use of Boolean searches (e.g., "fear" within ten words of "crime") documents can be found and analyzed, search terms adjusted, and additional searches performed of either random or "theoretical samples" (e.g., "fear" within ten words of "schools" before the shootings at Columbine High School in 1998). The capacity to examine numerous documents with specific conceptually informed search terms and logics provides a way of "exploring" documents, applying "natural experimental" research designs to the materials, as well as retrieving and analyzing individual documents qualitatively. Moreover, because the technology permits immediate access to an enormous amount of material, comparative exploration, conceptual refinement, data collection, and analysis can cover a longer time period than other technologies afforded.

This approach can be illustrated with a substantive example tracing the discourse of fear, a project with which I have been involved for about a decade. With the help of several research assistants, I examined news reports for a ten-year period (1987 to 1996) from the *Arizona Republic*, *Los Angeles Times*, and *New York Times*, and ABC newscasts primarily through LEXIS-NEXIS, but also through the Vanderbilt Television News Index and Archive when appropriate. Initial manifest coding of fear and related topics then incorporated emergent coding and theoretical sampling in order to monitor changes in coverage and emphasis over time and across topics. On the one hand, this approach makes it possible to answer such questions as: Is fear associated with different topics over time? On the other hand, the latent and emergent approach is very conducive to "problem frame" analysis (Altheide 1997) as well as systematic comparison of thematic emphases. The general point to keep in mind in following some of the steps is that over time, an orientation to fear develops such that it becomes part of a broader framework.

DISCOURSE OF FEAR

A discourse of fear may be defined as the pervasive communication, symbolic awareness, and expectation that danger and risk are a central feature of the "effective environment," or the physical and symbolic environment as people define and experience it in everyday life (Pfuhl and Henry 1993:53) (see Figure 9–2). The general model is rather straightforward: when a word is repeated frequently and becomes associated routinely with certain other terms and images, a symbolic linkage is formed (see Figure 9–3). For example, fear is a pervasive meaning and symbol in American culture. Frequently associated with "crime," fear is more expansive, and our research shows that it covers a much wider symbolic territory than crime. Tracking discourse permits gauging how "closely" together similar words appear as part of thematic emphasis and discursive practices. Indeed, after repeated usage together, the initial meaning of a word, for example, "gang," can incorporate "fear" as a connotation (see Figure 9–4).

Examining how the discourse of fear applies to children can be illustrated with some data. The overall aim was to query thousands of newspaper articles about how

FIGURE 9–2
Processing topics as fear.

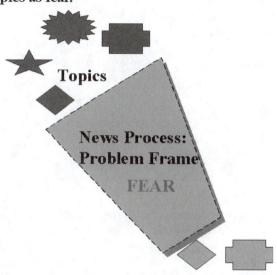

children were positioned with respect to fear over a several-year period in order to observe significant changes in symbolic linkages. Figure 9–5 indicates how use of the word "fear" increased in association with children, particularly in headlines. Moreover, the places where children go also increased, including schools, neighborhoods, and community.

FIGURE 9–3
Transforming fear and topics.

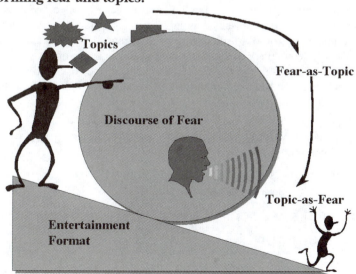

FIGURE 9–4
The newsworthiness of fear.

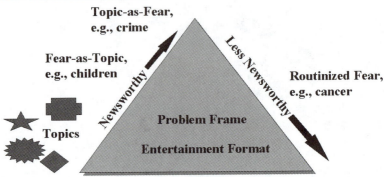

Fear becomes a matter of discourse when it "expands" beyond a specific referent to use as a more general orientation (Dijk 1988; Ericson, Baranek, and Chan 1989). As suggested in previous work (Altheide and Michalowski 1999), entertainment formats contribute to the emphasis on "fear" rather than, say, "danger," which is more specific and more easily incorporated within an everyday life perspective. When fear is repeatedly used with children and the spaces they occupy (e.g., schools), a meaningful association emerges. Over time, with repeated usage, nuances blend, connotations become denotations, fringes mix with kernels, and we have a different perspective on the world. This is why the distinctions between meaningful borders such as children, school, and community are so important. When they are joined with fear, more than a visit is in the works; there is an incursion.

One analytical distinction is between parallel and nonparallel or insidious use of fear in news reports. Referring back to Figure 9–3, parallel fear refers to the alignment of the coverage with the event and the emotions or concern of the individuals involved. It tends to be localized, momentary, and individually or case-oriented. Stated differently, a news topic or event will be presented as an occasion or instance of fear (topic-as-fear, or TAF). Nonparallel insidious use of fear refers to general, pervasive, and unfocused use of the word, often in place of another more parallel adjective or adverb. Nonparallel use of fear operates as a perspective, as an evocative framework within which a discourse of fear may be attached connotatively to the topic at hand. In this instance, fear

FIGURE 9–5
Fear in headlines and children in text, as percent of all headlines with fear, AR, LAT, NYT, 1987, 1994, 1995, 1996.

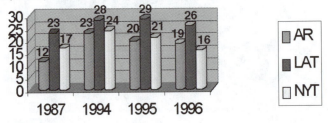

FIGURE 9–6
An emerging discourse of fear.

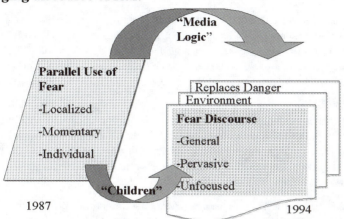

1987   1994

becomes the topic but can be associated with a specific event or activity (fear-as-topic, or FAT). Often the topic is not even an event or a specific act but holds forth an orientation and a context of meaning for symbolically linking the topic to fear.

As Figure 9–6 suggests, parallel use of fear is more common in 1987 than in 1996. In the 1980s, fear was used in a more parallel way, referring to specific events and circumstances. In the 1990s, fear was used in a less parallel way; it was more generalized, and pervasive, with an unfocused standpoint. It is when the nonparallel use of fear prevails that we may recognize the emergence of a discourse of fear.

Analysis of themes and topics provides some illustrations of the subtle but consistent differences in overall reporting between the 1980s and the 1990s. The following example relates a specific fear about children's safety in 1987:

> Officials said they fear that foreign drug dealers now are using unescorted children to carry their goods. ("'Ideal for the Job': Customs Agents Find Child Carrying Heroin," *Arizona Republic*, April 23, 1987)

But note how the fear frame directed the coverage in a 1994 article about school safety. In 1994, fear was the frame surrounding the association of children and schools, and illustrates the lengths to which school officials must go to abate these fears:

> The academic challenges are being made more difficult by the disturbing presence and growing fear of crime and violence in our schools. To fight back, police forces are beefing up patrols of schools, and nearly 20 percent of surveyed communities now regularly use metal detectors to detect weapons. ("Bullets Rival Books as School Concern; Violence Plague Not Just City Ill, New Report Says," *Arizona Republic*, November 2, 1994)

As fear is acknowledged to spread beyond the big cities to suburbs, it is the domain of comfort and serene everyday life of children that is reportedly damaged. Fear moves from the news sections about specific events to other sections of the newspaper. Even the suburbs are infected, as suggested in the following *Arizona Republic* article in the Life Section, especially when "stay-at-home" moms are less often at hand to ward off the hostile encroaching environment. The excerpt illustrates how fear as a condition of life coexists with "latchkey" children who must contend with pervasive gang influences:

> The pervasive fear of crime in city and suburb has made it impossible for a child to play independently, even on its own block, without an adult hovering nearby. With fewer stay-at-home moms, there are fewer children around to play with during the day. There are also fewer children per household, so homes have no built-in gang." ("Lazy Summer? Not for Modern Kids," *Arizona Republic*, July 6, 1995)

By the mid-1990s, fear as a taken-for-granted descriptor of the environment was well established. Fear had moved from specific associations with crime to defining the environment and it had become part of the discourse for accounting for experiences. The following excerpt from an article in the *Arizona Republic* cast a specific event, the shooting of a woman, as another example of the deteriorating "small-town life" to a world of fear:

> Hers was the name that shattered the innocence and security of small-town life and *glued it back together with fear.* Nickie Fater. Loving wife. Dedicated mother. Gunned down while loading groceries into her car. ("Red Ribbon Event Honors Victims of Violence," *Arizona Republic*, October 21, 1996; my emphasis)

Tracking the emergence of fear as part of suburban reality and such family-oriented activities as buying groceries and attending schools offers opportunities for family spaces to be marketed for their safety potential. Fear, business, planning, and design can coexist, as suggested by an article in the *Arizona Republic* Business Section:

> "Crime may not be up, but fear is definitely up," said Salvatore, a partner with Architekton, an architectural firm in Tempe. "If there are design principles that we should follow to assist in getting rid of the fear or making that fear less, it's our task to take those principles and put them into effect." ("Tempe Has Designs on Buildings That Protect People," *Arizona Republic*, July 9, 1995)

In the later years of the study, other fear-related accounts can likewise be characterized as moving to a more *generalized, pervasive, unfocused standpoint.* With this emphasis emerges a discourse of fear as a more general symbolic category and guideline. We may refer to this as an insidious parallel use of the word fear in replacing adjectives such as "concern," "worry," and so on. For example:

> The rezoning case has angered Arrowhead residents who *fear* that a shopping center in their midst would bring crime and congestion; but most neighbors to the east of the site support the rezoning as the best possible solution, given the existing zoning, which is general commercial and multifamily ("Arrowhead Referendum Effort Alive Despite Signature Flap," *Arizona Republic*, Glendale Community Section, July 24, 1995; my emphasis)

And another:

> Counterfeit designer goods are illegal if they have a counterfeit registered trademark. And with the Super Bowl planned for the Valley next year, Arizona authorities *fear* fans' appetites for licensed sports merchandise will fuel the crime. ("Designer Knockoffs Providing Genuine Headaches for Officials," *Arizona Republic*, Valley and State Section, February 21, 1995; my emphasis)[2]

Most "participants" in morality plays about crime and fear were reported to fear crime, including children who were cast in an article about how adults fear them! The association of fear with children and issues relevant to children's problems—children as victims—was indicated in a 1994 article, "Study Confirms Some Fears of U.S. Children." The story explored the ways in which childhood home environments have changed (e.g., divorce) from 1960 to 1990. Several pieces examined how people continue to fear crime even though the crime rates have dropped. Two articles in 1995 and 1996 stressed how citizens still fear crime, as well as how politicians push crime as the major problem. Several articles examined how fear of crime in the suburbs continues to rise.

One *New York Times* article, "Fear Itself; Finding New Reasons to Dread the Unknown" (Weiner 1995), used the subway gassings in Tokyo the previous week to launch into a discussion of fear in popular culture but particularly in everyday life. In keeping with a shift in later years to an unparalleled use of fear more as a condition and feature of social life, this article drew on various sources, including psychologists and sociologists, in constructing a report about pervasive fear. Accepting as valid the notion that more fearful events are creating increases in fear, the author implicitly asks if society is moving forward or backward. With a somewhat reflective thrust on whether we are really more threatened, the dominant message is that there is really so much fearful stuff surrounding us that the world is really fearful, although perhaps not as bad as some would believe:

> We are living in toxic times. The boundaries of the body feel as vulnerable as the borders of the country. Invisible, unknowable threats have replaced nuclear bombs as the source of collective fear. . . . The fear is airborne, a toxic cloud—a fear of dying that is fast becoming a fear of living. There's a heart attack hidden in your tuna with mayo, a coronary in that carton of Szechuan chicken. Live smoke-free or die. . . . "A sense of fear is increasing," said Kenneth Manges, a Cincinnati psychologist who specializes in treating people with post-traumatic stress syndrome. "People are afraid of viruses, they are afraid of getting AIDS, they are afraid of the more-resistant strains of tuberculosis, they are afraid of gonorrhea and syphilis. And people are not calmed by health officials' assertions that the threat of harm from infectious diseases is an unlikely event. They no longer have the level of trust." (Weiner 1995)

Conclusion

Tracking discourse is one modest attempt to investigate the organization, structure, denotations, and connotations of mass media reports over time. It is a perspective as much as a method, inspired by questions posed by cultural sociologists about changing social definitions. As such, it can be helpful for systematically observing changes in public language and monitoring how social control terminology and perspectives (e.g., fear) are ordered and integrated across various social issues.

Not only is our past newsworthy, but our futures can also be shaped by images of the past that are reified and acted upon. As more of our social reality is informed by mass-mediated images shaped by entertainment formats, we must understand the processes through which multiple realities are set forth, a few supported, and others put aside as irrelevant. A discourse of fear is one key area that has been cultivated for decades by the entertainment media and formal agents of social control alike. The latter are often the "sources" or "experts" for the former, but the routine display of numerous statements, images, and anticipations of fear provides a cultural and cognitive baseline of experience for more and more societal members. A discourse of fear offers a conceptual elaboration for a process through which numerous messages resonating with themes of fear can be circulated, recast, and institutionally promoted through public policies, media reports, popular culture, and cognitive frameworks. What happens to other discourses—of trust, community, and fellowship, for example—in the face of the discourse of fear is not my topic but it is surely worthy of investigation. Ultimately, social worlds may resemble news worlds, steeped in fear with a hopeful glance for the heroic. Let us study them.

Endnotes

1. Gallup 1995 poll, as quoted in the *Sunday Oregonian* August 8, 1999, p. F1.
2. *New York Times* articles in the mid-1990s reflected a similar focus on fear as discourse. Particularly noteworthy were such themes as fear of one another, fear of what we cannot see or control, fear creating a domino effect in society.

References

Altheide, D. L. 1976. *Creating Reality: How TV News Distorts Events*. Beverly Hills, CA: Sage.
———. 1985. *Media Power*. Beverly Hills, CA: Sage.
———. 1994. "An Ecology of Communication: Toward a Mapping of the Effective Environment." *The Sociological Quarterly* 35:645–83.
———. 1996. *Qualitative Media Analysis*. Newbury Park, CA: Sage.
———. 1997. "The News Media, The Problem Frame, and the Production of Fear." *The Sociological Quarterly* 38:646–68.
Altheide, D. L. and R. S. Michalowski. 1999. "Fear in the News: A Discourse of Control." *The Sociological Quarterly* 40:475–503.
Berg, B. L. 1989. *Qualitative Research Methods for the Social Sciences*. Boston, MA: Allyn and Bacon.
Berger, P. L. and T. Luckmann. 1967. *The Social Construction of Reality: a Treatise in the Sociology of Knowledge*. New York: Doubleday.
Best, J., ed. 1995. *Images of Issues*. Hawthorne, NY: Aldine de Gruyter.
Blumer, H. 1969. *Symbolic Interactionism: Perspective and Method*. Englewood Cliffs, NJ: Prentice-Hall.
Brissett, D. and C. Edgley. 1990. *Life as Theater: A Dramaturgical Sourcebook*. New York: Aldine de Gruyter.
Burke, K. 1966. *Language as Symbolic Action; Essays on Life, Literature, and Method*. Berkeley, CA: University of California Press.
———. 1969. *A Rhetoric of Motives*. Berkeley, CA: University of California Press.
Cantril, H., H. G. Wells, H. Koch, H. Gaudet, and H. Herzog. 1940. *The Invasion from Mars: A Study in the Psychology of Panic*. Princeton, NJ: Princeton University Press.
Carey, J. 1989. *Communication as Culture: Essays on the Media and Society*. Boston, MA: Unwin Hyman.

Cerulo, K. A. 1998. *Deciphering Violence: The Cognitive Structure of Right and Wrong*. New York: Routledge.

Chiricos, T., H. Eschholz, and M. Gertz. 1997. "Crime, News and Fear of Crime: Toward an Identification of Audience Effects." *Social Problems* 44:342–57.

Cicourel, A. V. 1974. *Cognitive Sociology: Language and Meaning in Social Interaction*. New York: Free Press.

Couch, C. J. 1984. *Constructing Civilizations*. Greenwich, CT, and London: JAI Press.

Crane, D. 1992. *The Production of Culture*. Newbury Park, CA: Sage.

Dijk, T. A. 1988. *News as Discourse*. Hillsdale, NJ: L. Erlbaum Associates.

Douglas, J. D. 1970. *Understanding Everyday Life: Toward the Reconstruction of Sociological Knowledge*. Chicago, IL: Aldine Publishing Company.

Epstein, E. J. 1973. *News from Nowhere*. New York: Random House.

Ericson, R. V., P. M. Baranek, and J. B. L. Chan. 1989. *Negotiating Control: A Study of News Sources*. Toronto, Canada: University of Toronto Press.

———. 1991. *Representing Order: Crime, Law and Justice in the News Media*. Toronto, Canada: University of Toronto Press.

Ericson, R. V. and K. D. Haggerty. 1997. *Policing the Risk Society*. Toronto, Canada: University of Toronto Press.

Ferraro, K. F. 1995. *Fear of Crime: Interpreting Victimization Risk*. Albany, NY: State University of New York Press.

Ferrell, J. and C. R. Sanders. 1995. *Cultural Criminology*. Boston, MA: Northeastern University Press.

Fishman, M. 1980. *Manufacturing the News*. Austin, TX: University of Texas Press.

Gerbner, G and L. Gross. 1976. "The Scary World of TV's Heavy Viewer." *Psychology Today*. 10:89–91.

Glassner, B. 1999. *The Culture of Fear: Why Americans Are Afraid of the Wrong Things*. New York: Basic Books

Goffman, E. 1959. *The Presentation of Self in Everyday Life*. Garden City, NY: Doubleday.

Grimshaw, A. D. and P. J. Burke. 1994. *What's Going on Here?: Complementary Studies of Professional Talk*. Norwood, NJ: Ablex.

Hall, P. M. 1997. "Meta-Power, Social Organization, and the Shaping of Social Action." *Symbolic Interaction* 20:397–418.

Iyengar, S. 1991. *Is Anyone Responsible?: How Television Frames Political Issues*. Chicago, IL: University of Chicago Press.

Mead, G. H. and C. M. Morris. 1962. *Mind, Self, and Society from the Standpoint of a Social Behaviorist*. Chicago, IL. University of Chicago Press.

Meyrowitz, J. 1985. *No Sense of Place*. New York: Oxford University Press.

Pfuhl, E. H. and S. Henry. 1993. *The Deviance Process*. New York: Aldine de Gruyter.

Sasson, T. 1995. *Crime Talk: How Citizens Construct a Social Problem*. New York: Aldine de Gruyter.

Schutz, A. 1967. *The Phenomenology of the Social World*. Evanston, IL: Northwestern University Press.

Snow, R. P. 1983. *Creating Media Culture*. Beverly Hills, CA: Sage.

Staples, W. G. 1997. *The Culture of Surveillance: Discipline and Social Control in the United States*. New York: St. Martin's Press.

Surette, R. 1998. *Media, Crime and Criminal Justice: Images and Realities*. Belmont, CA: West/Wadsworth.

Taschler-Pollacek, H. and H. Lukesch. 1990. "Viktimisierungsangst als Folge des Fernsehkonsums? Eine Studie an alteren Frauen." (Fear of Victimization as a Consequence of Television Viewing? A Study of Older Women). *Publizistik*. 35:443–53.

Unsworth, B. 1995. *Morality Play*. London: Hamish Hamilton.

Warr, M. 1983. "Fear of Victimization: A Look at the Proximate Causes." *Social Forces* 61:1033–43.

———. 1992. "Altruistic Fear of Victimization in Households." *Social Science Quarterly* 73:723–36.

Weiner, T. 1995. "Fear Itself; Finding New Reasons to Dread the Unknown." *New York Times*, March 26, section 4, p. 1.

Westfeldt, W. and T. Wicker. 1998. *Indictment: The News Media and the Criminal Justice System.* Nashville, TN: First Amendment Center.

Wuthnow, R. 1992. *Vocabularies of Public Life: Empirical Essays in Symbolic Structure.* New York: Routledge.

Zerubavel, E. 1997. *Social Mindscapes: An Invitation to Cognitive Sociology.* Cambridge, MA: Harvard University Press.

Zhondang, P. and G. Kosicki. 1993. "Framing Analysis: An Approach to News Discourse." *Political Communication* 10:55–69.

CHAPTER 10

How Storytelling Can Be Empowering[1]

William A. Gamson

Critics of American media often focus on the strong tendency to personalize broader social issues. As Bennett (1996:39) articulates the criticism:

> If there is a single most important flaw in the American news style, it is the overwhelming tendency to downplay the big social, economic, or political picture in favor of the human trials and triumphs that sit at the surface of events. In place of power and process, the media concentrate on the people engaged in political combat over the issues. . . . When people are invited to "take the news personally," they can find a wide range of private, emotional meanings in it. However, the meanings inspired by personalized news are not the shared critical and analytical meanings on which a healthy democracy thrives. Personalized news encourages people to take an egocentric rather than a socially concerned view of political problems.

Furthermore, this media practice of personalization is strongly reinforced by a broader set of sociocultural forces that discourage thinking about issues in collective terms. Gans (1979:51) describes individualism as an enduring value in the news. Individuals, acting on their own terms rather than collectively, are continually presented as "a source of economic, social, and cultural productivity" and "a means of achieving cultural variety."

Not just news but also entertainment and advertising are heavily implicated in the process. Merelman (1984:1) tells us that a "loosely bounded culture prevents Americans from controlling their political and social destinies, for the world which loose boundedness portrays is not the world of political and social structures that actually exists. It is, instead, a shadowland, which gives Americans little real purchase on the

massive, hierarchical political and economic structures that dominate their lives."
Merelman analyzes the role of television in particular in promoting a loosely
bounded culture that backs people away from politics and directs them toward a private vision of the self in the world.

By this account, U.S. media discourse actively discourages grassroots constituencies in their attempts to articulate and develop a sense of themselves as a community
of action. I do not dispute the criticism but I am wary that it ignores the potential
agency of social movements in a contingent process. Bennett (1996:40) recognizes
but does not develop the contingent nature of personalization when he writes: "The
tendency to personalize the news might be less worrisome if human interest angles
were used to 'hook' audiences into more serious analysis of issues and problems.
However, the focus on personal concerns is seldom linked to more in-depth analysis."
How frequently this actually happens is an empirical matter and is likely to vary from
issue to issue. That it can and sometimes does happen should lead us to ask what conditions need to be present for it to occur. It is not inevitable that personalization un-
dermines the capacity for collective action and, under certain conditions, it can be a
tool for promoting it.

The Benefits of Personal Narrative

The defense of narrative rests on a countercritique that focuses on the shortcomings
of a discourse that privileges disembodied, abstract, emotionally detached argumentation as the normative standard for discussion of public issues. Fraser (1995; 1997)
points to the tendency to forget the socially constructed nature of such categories as
public and *private*. To treat them as natural categories describing the world blinds us
to their potential for exclusion.

Public and private have a gendered subtext in which the public realm is a male
sphere, and its norms and practices reflect this in subtle (and often not-so-subtle)
ways to exclude "feminine" modes of participation. One of the tasks of critical theory, Fraser argues, should be to "expose ways in which the labeling of some issues
and interests as 'private' limits the range of problems, and of approaches to problems,
that can be widely contested in contemporary societies" (1995:28). "The point is that
there are no naturally given, *a priori* boundaries here. What will count as a matter
of common concern will be decided precisely through discursive contestation"
(1997:86).

The norms and practices governing policy discourse privilege certain forms of
presentation over others. In particular, the normative standards regarding policy discourse derive from specific institutional contexts in western society—in particular
parliaments and courts. As Young (1996:123) observes, "Their institutional forms,
rules, and rhetorical styles have defined the meaning of reason itself in the modern
world." Claims of universality are made, but "the norms of deliberation are culturally
specific and often operate as forms of power that silence or devalue the speech of
some people." Further:

> The norms of deliberation privilege speech that is dispassionate and disembodied. They
> tend to presuppose an opposition between mind and body, reason and emotion. They tend
> falsely to identify objectivity with calm and absence of emotional expression. . . . These

differences of speech privilege correlate with other differences of social privilege. The speech culture of white, middle class men tends to be more controlled, without significant gesture and expression of emotion. The speech culture of women and racial minorities . . . tends to be more excited and embodied, more valuing the expression of emotion, the use of figurative language, modulation in tone of voice, and wide gesture. (Young 1996:124)

Warner (1992:383) also calls our attention to the disembodied voice of the bourgeois public sphere and its implications for exclusion. "Self-abstraction from male bodies," he observes, "confirms masculinity. Self-abstraction from female bodies denies femininity. . . . The bourgeois public sphere has been structured from the outset by a logic of abstraction that provides a privilege for unmarked identities: the male, the white, the middle class, the normal."

Young makes an especially strong case for the importance of storytelling as an appropriate and desirable form of policy discourse. "Narrative," she writes, "fosters understanding across . . . difference without making those who are different symmetrical." It reveals experiences based on social locations that cannot be shared fully by those who are differently situated. She uses the example of wheelchair-bound people making claims on university resources: "A primary way they make their case will be through telling stories of their physical, temporal, social, and emotional obstacles" (Young 1996:131). Storytelling promotes empathy across different social locations. Similarly, Sanders (1992) points out that narrative complements arguments, tending to be more egalitarian, since everyone is an expert on their own experiential knowledge.

Narratives in Abortion Discourse[2]

The exclusionary effect of delegitimizing personal narrative is especially evident on an issue such as abortion. Consider the implications of discounting experiential knowledge and storytelling. The existential experience of the dilemma of an unwanted pregnancy is gender-specific. If one rules out talking about such experiences in policy discourse, the silencing falls unequally on men and women.

Personalization, in this argument, only opens discursive opportunities. Whether and how much these personal narratives actually increase grassroots constituencies' sense of themselves as a community of action depends on how such stories are utilized as hooks. Telling one's personal story in the media *can* be part of a process of articulating a collective identity and developing a clearer sense of a group's symbolic interests. It has often functioned this way on the abortion issue.

In 1962, when abortion was not yet a topic for general public discourse, Sherri Finkbine told her personal human-interest story to a friend who worked for the local newspaper where she lived.[3] Finkbine, married with four young children and pregnant with a fifth, had been taking a sleeping pill that her husband had brought back from a European trip several months earlier. The drug, it turned out, was thalidomide—the side effects of which were only then becoming known. She had taken the strongest possible dosage. Her physician advised her that the odds for serious fetal deformity were very high and suggested a therapeutic abortion, for which she applied.

A newspaper story by her friend appeared the next day, without identifying her by name, but under the black-bordered headline: "Baby-Deforming Drug May Cost

Woman Her Child Here." Within hours of the paper's appearance, the hospital cancelled her scheduled abortion, which under existing state law was legal only if the life of the mother was in danger. A few days later, her physician asked for a court order to perform the abortion, identifying the Finkbines by name in the legal request.

Wire services picked up the story, and the Finkbines were soon deluged with reporters as well as letters and phone calls from total strangers, expressing their views. Some of the callers made death threats against her and her children, and the FBI was brought in to protect her. Wanting to escape the pressure and publicity, she and her husband fled to Sweden, where she applied for permission for a therapeutic abortion under a law that allowed fetal deformity as one ground for approving it. Returning home after obtaining the abortion, she lost her job, and the calls and letters continued for some time.

For Sherri Finkbine personally, having her story told in the media was hardly an empowering experience. In retrospect, though, we can see it as playing a central role in a process in which a "private" matter that one did not talk about in public became an issue of "public concern" and hence a legitimate arena for public policy debate. The personalization furthered this transformation and helped an emerging abortion reform movement articulate a collective identity. The Finkbine case was clearly a story with a hook. It provided a critical discourse moment in which mediators for relevant constituencies were stimulated to reflect and comment on how the issue of abortion should be understood best. Media personalization in this case served to encourage rather than discourage grassroots citizen action.

In the 1970s and later, not only in the United States but in Germany and other countries as well, the "speak-out" became part of the repertoire of both the abortion rights movement and the antiabortion movement. Telling one's personal story in public, and having it carried in media discourse in this context, is what one might call a form of *collective personalization*—one is adding one's story to a growing array of such stories, representing a collective witness more than merely an individual one.

Because of the existence of movements on this issue, the lesson is unlikely to be divorced from the story. There are, of course, different arrays of stories with different lessons. Antiabortion groups encourage personal stories about abortions that are later deeply regretted, while abortion rights groups encourage personal stories about how horrible it was to face an unwanted pregnancy in the days when abortion was illegal and unsafe. Each array carries its own lessons built into the narrative. Personalizing, in this movement context, encourages the articulation of collective identities and symbolic interests.

Let's Get Real

Media discourse in the United States contains many complaints about the excessive abstraction of abortion discourse and the lack of rootedness in the concrete reality of women with unwanted pregnancies. Syndicated columnist Ellen Goodman expresses this theme most clearly in a 1983 opinion column.[4] Goodman calls for "a new vocabulary" to replace "the verbal war of attrition" in which "we've been stuck for a decade." The two groups have "lobbed names and accusations at each other across the public terrain." The problem, in Goodman's view, is that: "the complex moral dilemmas of abortion end up straight-jacketed by Constitution-speak. In the end, we can talk only about individual rights, the right to life and rights to privacy."

Goodman emphasizes the dangers of excessive abstraction. The problem is that the abstract argument about principles that goes on in the legal system is: "so removed from the argument that goes on in the mind of a woman faced with an unwanted pregnancy. The private struggle is less over rights than over responsibilities. It is less about conflicts with others than connections to them. It has less to do with the ability to carry a pregnancy for nine months than to care for a child for 18 years."

Goodman cites Gilligan's (1982) research on women with an unwanted pregnancy facing a decision on whether or not to have an abortion. The questions in their minds were not about rights but about caretaking responsibilities: "Am I prepared to take care of this life? Is it responsible to have a child I cannot take care of?" These women, Goodman argues, "did not engage in metaphysical arguments about 'life.' " She suspects that most of us understand this and "know instinctively that unless we're willing to take care of every unwanted child from birth to adulthood, we have to leave the decision . . . to one who carries the responsibilities. But it is unsettling that there is no way to come into the legal system discussing this complex moral view. The language of law has few words in common with the language of personal discourse."

Elizabeth Janeway, reviewing two books on abortion in the *Los Angeles Times* (October 1983), makes a similar point. "For women," she writes, "responsible parenthood isn't something to talk about, it's something to do—day and night; over and over; in sickness and health, poverty, plenty, and confusion. . . ."

Apparently, even constitutional lawyers such as Lawrence Tribe agree about the curse of excessive abstraction. In a section of his book, *Abortion: The Clash of Absolutes* (Tribe 1990), excerpted by the *Los Angeles Times*, Tribe makes the point that the conflict is, for most people, internal within most of us rather than between opposing camps. He takes up *Roe v. Wade* not as a legal case but as the story of "Jane Roe." Jane Roe is a pseudonym for a real person, Norma McCorvey, with "an entirely human story, one that has become by now familiar to many, a story similar to other stories repeated all over the United States every day." McCorvey lived in Texas, where abortion was permitted only if the mother's life was in danger, and she was poor, with little education, or the money to travel to some place where abortion was legal. When she learned from her lawyer that the Supreme Court would hear her case, she exclaimed: "My God, all those people are so important. They don't have time to listen to some little old Texas girl who got in trouble."

Fifteen years after Roe, Norma McCorvey admitted that she made up a story about how she got pregnant to hide the fact that, as Tribe puts it, "she had gotten 'in trouble' in the usual way." Tribe asks, why she felt the *need* to make up a story, deftly making the question one about the conditions in society that contribute to making pregnancies that are unwanted: "Better education, the provision of contraception, indeed the creation of a society where the burden of raising a child is lighter, are all achievable goals lost in the shouting about abortion."

The debate about principles creates invisible abstractions in which either the real woman or the real fetus disappears, reduced to ghostly anonymity. Many who can readily envision the concrete humanity of a fetus, who hold its picture high and weep, barely see the woman who carries it and her human plight. To them, she becomes an all-but-invisible abstraction. Many others, who can "readily envision the woman and her body, who cry out for her right to control her destiny, barely envision the fetus within that woman and do not imagine as real the life it might have been allowed to lead. For them, the life of the fetus becomes an equally invisible abstraction."

Personal Narratives

Advocates on both sides often introduce their own personal stories into media discourse. They see it as a way of reaching their audience in a way that abstract argument fails to do. Robin Toner, in a 1989 *New York Times* article, quotes Faye Wattleton, president of Planned Parenthood, describing how she tries to speak to the person "who has that sense of compassion, who says, 'Yes, I know somebody who was in a tough bind once, and it's not so easy to make these decisions.' " Kate Michelman, director of NARAL, often describes her own personal decision to have an abortion, indicating that she decided to discuss it publicly because "the more of us who speak out, the more understanding people will have of the complicated nature of this decision, and the more real we'll become. We're real people, with real lives and real families who faced some complicated decisions in our lives." Similarly, Wattleton talks about her experiences as a young nurse before abortion was legal: "It's not theoretical to me. I remember those women who came in with botched abortions."

The journalistic practice of profiling activists as persons, considering them outside of their public roles, contributes to this effort. The *Los Angeles Times* featured a long profile of Wattleton (by *Washington Post* reporter Paula Span), emphasizing her religious background as the daughter and granddaughter of fundamentalist ministers, and seeing that influence in the "rhythmic rise and fall of her voice" as she preaches the "gospel" of reproductive rights. The narrative emphasizes her experience as a graduate student in nursing, witnessing a 17-year-old young woman dying after a botched abortion, noting her comment that "It was not an isolated incident." Her personal life is treated as a relevant, important part of the profile, particularly her time bind in raising her 11-year-old daughter alone after a divorce: "She tries to compensate for her wearying schedule by not being away from home more than two nights in a row and by almost never working weekends."

Michelman is also the subject of a profile in a 1989 *Los Angeles Times* article by Karen Tumulty. Again her personal life is treated as a central part of the narrative—her Catholic background (including nine years of Catholic school), her desertion by her husband, leaving her with three young children. Most importantly, the story includes her own difficult decision (in 1969) to have an abortion when she realized that she was pregnant with a fourth child and at a loss as to how she would support the three children she already had.

The political point of the story comes in her discovery that the difficult decision was not her decision to make. She had to convince a panel of doctors she had never met before, "relating the most intimate, humiliating details of her private life. And, in one final indignity, she had to get written permission from the man who had walked out on her." "One of the most important decisions of my life was out of my hands," Michelman recalls. "I finally understood how little control women really had over their own lives."

Personal narratives are often used to buttress antiabortion policies as well. In a 1994 *Los Angeles Times* article, Susan Carpenter McMillan, a television commentator and spokesperson for the Pro-Family Media Coalition of Southern California, describes her dismay at current publicity about an abortion that she had 21 years earlier. As a media-savvy professional, she recognized that the story could not be contained. She writes: "It was just too juicy; the voice of Right to Life having undergone an abortion herself." Describing herself at the time of the abortion as a pro-choice college student, she recalls her agony and doubts, lying alone on the gurney, "in those last seconds of consciousness before the anesthesia set in."

McMillan uses her personal narrative to make the case against abortion: "I know millions of women across this country feel as I do about abortion. We all somehow know deep down inside that we alone made a horrible decision and no coined phrase about choice and rights or the denial of biological and fetal facts can ever erase the truth. For we as mothers instinctively know during those moments of aloneness, that we ended the lives of separate human beings growing inside us."

The use of personal narratives is a continuing feature of media coverage of the abortion issue, even in such elite newspapers as the *New York Times* and the *Los Angeles Times*. Of 46 articles sampled in 1994, including news accounts as well as commentary, we found that 13 percent of them contained such stories, providing details of private experience and using them to draw political conclusions.

Prime-Time Television

There is a surprisingly large amount of newspaper commentary about a different medium—prime-time television dramatizations. The attention by other media transforms these media texts into events, newsworthy in their own right.

The stimulus event for several 1962 articles was an episode in a popular CBS courtroom drama, *The Defenders*. The particular episode, titled "The Benefactor," features the trial of a physician who has been arrested for performing an illegal abortion on a teenage rape victim. The protagonist, "Dr. Montgomery," has had his own daughter die at the hands of a quack abortionist and is determined to use his medical expertise to prevent other desperate young women from suffering a similar fate. As Condit (1990:124) notes, a crusading and idealistic doctor performing an abortion to end the pregnancy of a desperate rape victim presents "one of the most rhetorically compelling cases possible."

One commentator, the *New York Times* television critic Jack Gould, suggests that the play has "penetrated the national curtain of embarrassed silence" about the estimated 1.2 million illegal abortions that occur annually in the United States. Gould approves the breaking of the silence on a matter of legitimate *public* concern. He complains about simplifications and weaknesses in the play but notes that it is "sensational only to the extent that the subject matter was unusual for the home screen." Gould's comments indicate the breakdown of a taboo on abortion as a topic of public discourse—that is, the breakdown of the boundary between a "private" matter and a topic "appropriate" for the public sphere.

Gould's view of appropriateness was not universally shared as he recognizes. "Certainly the subject matter would not rank among the most palatable of . . . themes," he conceded. "Naturally, there are objections to any form of discussion of abortion." Many CBS affiliates refused to clear the episode or shifted the time slot to later in the evening, when children would, presumably, no longer be watching. The Boston CBS affiliate, which refused to show it at all, commented that treatment of abortion "would be shocking to many viewers." Condit (1990) notes that all three of the original sponsors pulled out, and a Catholic magazine urged its readers to send their presumably critical comments to the replacement sponsor.

The centrality of television prime-time drama in the metadiscourse on abortion is underlined by a *Los Angeles Times* article on the *anniversary*, in 1992, of "Maude's Dilemma," a two-part episode in a popular television entertainment drama shown 20 years earlier. The program "Maude," starring Bea Arthur as the ascerbic 47-year-old grandmother, was in its opening season. CBS estimates that between the two episodes and reruns, an estimated 65 million people watched Maude face the dilemma of an unwanted pregnancy. Maude eventually resolves the dilemma by electing to have an abortion, a decision which Lewis Beale, writing in the *Los Angeles Times* two decades later, calls a "watershed in TV history, an event that brought the battle over choice into the prime-time arena."

As the drama unfolds, both Maude and her husband are privately appalled at the prospect of raising a second family at their age, but each thinks the other really wants the baby. Legality is not an issue, since Maude and her family live in New York, where the 1970 reform law had already made abortion a legal option. Maude's daughter, a committed feminist, is the first to bring up and advocate an abortion, but Maude is torn. The script includes arguments by sympathetic characters for and against Maude's having an abortion, but the producers rejected a resolution through a false pregnancy or a miscarriage as a "cop-out."

In the spring of 1989, while the Supreme Court was pondering its decision in the *Webster* case, a television dramatization again made the news—in this case, an NBC made-for-TV movie, *Roe v. Wade*. The movie tells the story of Norma McCorvey, the real-life woman behind the pseudonym "Jane Roe," whom we met earlier in Lawrence Tribe's account. A *New York Times* article by Bill Carter describes NBC as "tiptoeing on a tightrope" as it steered the movie out in front of the public.

Carter describes the laborious three-year-long development process for the film, with a "staggering 19 drafts" of the script. The movie's executive producer, Michael Mannheim, emphasized NBC's concern with balance: "They wanted to make certain that the various points of view were represented." NBC followed the program with an hour-long news special, anchored by Tom Brokaw, on the abortion issue. Alison Cross, the film's scriptwriter, called the extended rewrite process "brutal," but in the end felt very happy with the result: "I actually wonder if all that battling didn't make it better, if it didn't refine it in some way." The film's director, Gregory Hoblit, expressed his intent to take "a hugely important abstract argument and make it tangible, understandable, and human. . . . I'd like to think thoughtful people will find it a considered, thoughtful film."

Thorburn (1987) argues that television is the primary medium of "consensus narrative," the primary source of "shared stories" that explain "life as an American." Condit (1990), building on his argument, adds that: "Prime time television . . . [is] essential to understanding the ways in which public, explicitly political, discourse makes the crucial transition into the cultural vocabularies of everyday life." She was able to identify some 15 episodes of prime-time television entertainment series in which the issue of abortion was the primary dramatic fodder, and to obtain video-tapes of most of these episodes, viewing them directly (although a few were available only as scripts).

Condit does an especially extended analysis of an episode of the police show, *Cagney and Lacey*, which she describes in some eight pages including detailed quo-tations from the transcript. This very same show, excerpted to a half-hour with com-mercials and subplots deleted, was also used by Press (1991) and Press and Cole (1999) as a stimulus for focus-group discussions with working-class and middle-class women. Press and Cole asked the women about their reactions to the positions expressed by the characters, and devote several pages to describing its plot.

Cagney and Lacey is a well-crafted show, and the abortion episode displays com-plexity and subtlety in its treatment. The protagonists are two female police sergeants, Christine Cagney and Mary Beth Lacey. Cagney is Catholic, single, and extremely uncomfortable with the idea of abortion. Lacey is married, visibly preg-nant in this episode, and happy with the prospect of having a child, but is strongly pro-choice on abortion policy. They are brought into contact with the abortion issue through their job. First they are called upon to protect and assist a poor Hispanic woman who is seeking a legal abortion at a clinic that is being blockaded by antiabortion demonstrators; later, they are called upon to track down and arrest a clinic bomber.

Various characters voice the views of the participants in the contemporary abortion discourse pretty much as advocates would like them presented. Arlene Crenshaw, the leader of a local antiabortion group, confronts the ambivalent Cagney as she and Lacey are trying to restrain a picket line so that women can pass through to the clinic: "Sergeant, human beings are being murdered here every day. . . . If you were in Nazi Germany and you saw lives being taken by the thousands, wouldn't you do every-thing in your power to stop that?" Arlene is portrayed as sincere and committed, if a bit "straight-laced or severe" in Condit's characterization.

Various elements of pro-choice frames are presented through different characters, but especially through one of the central protagonists, Mary Beth Lacey. The dramatic tension is heightened by the viewer's knowledge, through Lacey's conver-sation with her supportive husband, that as a 19-year-old she had an abortion. It was in the days before abortion was legal, and she had experienced the terrors of seek-ing an illegal abortion, finally using her savings for college tuition to go abroad, where she could complete the procedure under safe and sanitary conditions. The dramatic resolution of the differing views on abortion occurs through the confronta-tion of the two protagonists in a complex dialogue, which Condit quotes at length (1990:131–32).

In Condit's interpretation of this show, it translates the public discourse on abor-tion: "into the cultural realm in two ways. First, characters enacted the life conditions alleged by the public dialogue to be lived by real people in 'real life.' . . . Second, these characters spoke the discourse of the social movement activists, but they did so in a carefully narrowed and re-personalized fashion. Through these two mechanisms, the program gave meaning to 'abortion' and the surrounding vocabularies in private conditions rather than as general social abstractions." While this episode has a pre-dominantly pro-choice subtext, it nevertheless treats the abortion choice as morally undesirable—"neither an 'easy choice' nor a replacement for birth control and positively inappropriate for happily married women."

This same resolution is, in fact, typical of television dramatizations of abortion. "Legal permission was not translated into cultural sanction," Condit observes. Taking these programs as a whole, she concludes that abortion in the world of network prime-time television was a woman's choice but morally undesirable under many circumstances. Most of the episodes highlighted family values of childbearing and mothering. If there are policy implications, they suggest that abortion should be permitted but discouraged, that abortions should be "safe, legal, and rare."

Television translated political-legal discourse into the concrete reality of everyday life in ways that showed the influence of both pro-life and pro-choice frames and promoted cultural compromise. "The various components of the compromise," Condit argues (1990:142), "were not arrived at through 'argumentation,' and therefore, it would be difficult to justify its particular elements argumentatively. The compromise was, however, both discursively and rationally generated. The discursive form was narrative and the rationale was that of a response to the material realities of the audience's lives. It was a working compromise, a pragmatic resolution rather than a philosophical one. Perhaps that suggests more clearly than anything the limits of philosophy for governing or understanding public life."

In sum, the meanings inspired by personalization in this instance are, *pace* Bennett, shared and critical and support a socially concerned view of political problems. Indeed, they can be seen as a way of bridging personal and collective identities and fostering the development of constituencies as communities of action.

Conclusion

American media discourse permits but discourages grassroots constituencies in their attempts to articulate and develop a sense of themselves as a community of action. The media practice of personalization does not in itself encourage it, but it provides a discursive opportunity for a mobilizing field of actors to transform a personal sorrow or triumph into a public cause. Movements and media have a common interest in personalization.

For an active-citizen model of democracy, journalistic norms should demand that personalization be hooked to a more serious analysis of issues and problems. This analysis should illuminate Merelman's shadowland and lift the veil on the broader political and economic forces that affect individual lives—using the personal narrative for illustration. In this way, media discourse becomes a useful tool for bridging the language of everyday life and policy discourse. When there is more than one plausible narrative, as there usually is, let the media be a site for competing narratives.

In fact, there is strong evidence that U.S. media discourse on abortion does an excellent job of integrating the language of everyday life. Personal narratives often appear in our newspaper sample, thereby legitimating the appropriateness of experiential knowledge. But really to appreciate the bridging process, we must broaden our conception of policy discourse to include prime-time television and movie dramatizations of social policy issues. These media forums are crucial to understanding how policy discourse "makes the crucial transition into the cultural vocabularies of every-day life" (Condit 1990).

I find myself in the unaccustomed position of having only kind words to say about American mass media discourse. On the abortion issue, at least, it appears to meet the normative criteria for encouraging civic engagement very well. Ferree and Gamson (1999; forthcoming) distinguish two different ways in which abortion discourse is gendered: (1) women as *agents* of decision making, and (2) women as *objects* of state policy needing protection in their vulnerability. In legitimating experiential knowledge and personal narratives, American media coverage opens discursive opportunities for women, presenting them as agents.

Taken as a whole, including prime-time television dramatizations, media discourse on abortion concretizes public discourse and helps to counteract excessive abstraction. It helps to bridge private and public spheres by translating between political policy discourse and the language of everyday life. It helps to integrate experiential knowledge with media discourse. It promotes deliberation and dialogue in a narrative mode rather than through argumentation, and this mode, especially in dramatic form, lends itself more easily to the expression of moral complexity. At least on this issue, storytelling facilitates a healthy, democratic, public life.

Endnotes

1. Sections of this paper appear in Gamson (1999) and Gamson (2000) in different contexts.
2. For the fullest report of this research, see Ferree et al. (2001).
3. Account drawn from Luker (1984:62–5).
4. See Ferree et al. (2001) for methodological details on and full citations of our newspaper sample.

References

Bennett, W. L. 1996. *NEWS: The Politics of Illusion*, 3d ed. White Plains, NY: Longman.

Condit, C. M. 1990. *Decoding Abortion Rhetoric*. Urbana, IL: University of Illinois Press.

Ferree, M. Marx and W. A. Gamson. 1999. "The Gendering of Abortion Discourse: Assessing Global Feminist Influence in the United States and Germany." Pp. 40–56 in *Social Movements in a Globalizing World*, edited by D. della Porta, H. Kriesi, and D. Rucht. New York: St. Martin's Press.

————. Forthcoming. "The Gendering of Governance and the Governance of Gender." In *Recognition Struggles*, edited by B. Hobson.

Ferree, M. Marx, W. A. Gamson, J. Gerhards, and D. Rucht. 2001. *Shaping Abortion Discourse: Democracy and the Public Sphere in Germany and the United States*. New York: Cambridge University Press.

Fraser, N. 1995. "What's Critical about Critical Theory." Pp. 21–55 in *Feminists Read Habermas*, edited by J. Meehan. New York: Routledge.

————. 1997. *Justice Interruptus*. New York: Routledge.

Gamson, W. A. 1999. "Policy Discourse and the Language of the Life-World." Pp. 127–44 in *Eigenwilligkeit und Rationalität sozialer Prozesse (Festschrift in Honor of Friedhelm Neidhardt)*, edited by J. Gerhards and R. Hitzler. Opladen and Wiesbaden, Germany: Westdeutscher Verlag.

————. 2000. "Collective Identity and Mass Media." Chapter in *Minnesota Symposium on Political Psychology*, edited by G. Borgida and J. L. Sullivan. New York: Cambridge University Press.

Gans, H. 1979. *Deciding What's News*. New York: Pantheon.

Gilligan, C. 1982. *In a Different Voice*. Cambridge, MA: Harvard University Press.

Luker, K. 1984. *Abortion and the Politics of Motherhood*. Berkeley, CA: University of California Press.

Merelman, R. M. 1984. *Making Something of Ourselves: On Culture and Politics in the United States*. Berkeley, CA: University of California Press.

Press, A. L. 1991. "Working-Class Women in a Middle-Class World: The Impact of Television Modes of Reasoning about Abortion" *Critical Studies in Mass Communication* 8:421–41.

Press, A. L. and E. R. Cole. 1999. *Speaking of Abortion*. Chicago, IL: University of Chicago Press.

Sanders, L. 1992. "Against Deliberation." Presented at the annual meeting of the American Political Science Association.

Thorburn, D. 1987. "Television as an Aesthetic Medium" *Critical Studies in Mass Communication* 4:161–74.

Tribe, L. H. 1990. *Abortion: The Clash of Absolutes*. New York: W. W. Norton.

Warner, M. 1992 "The Mass Public and the Mass Subject." Pp. 377–401 in *Habermas and the Public Sphere*, edited by Craig Calhoun. Cambridge, MA: MIT Press.

Young, I. M. 1996. "Communication and the Other: Beyond Deliberative Democracy." Pp. 120–35 in *Democracy and Difference*, edited by S. Benhabib. Princeton, NJ: Princeton.

SECTION IV

Storage and Retrieval

Storage and Retrieval:
An Introduction

In the previous three sections, authors explored the ways in which we sense information, classify it, and represent it in the mind. But once processed, where does that information go? In this section we will explore the issue as we examine the ultimate destination of information—the human memory.

For cognitive scientists, the study of memory involves three critical components: determining the structure of memory, understanding the ways in which information is acquired and stored in memory, and discovering the strategies by which information is retrieved from memory. Here I will highlight some of the most central discoveries from this ambitious agenda.

Those studying the structure of memory have identified two types of operating systems: short-term or working memory, and long-term memory.[1] Neurophysicists such as Brenda Milner (1966) have actually charted the structural location of these units within the human brain. Other researchers have documented the very different functions and characteristics of each memory system.[2] According to cognitive scientists, short-term memory contains only that information with which the brain is currently engaged. It allows us to "juggle" several dimensions of experience, shifting our focus from one to another, yet keep each dimension available for ready use. As such, short-term memory is limited in size and can encompass only a small number of entries. (In a classic study of the issue, George Miller [1956] proposed that the short-term memory can hold seven plus or minus two "chunks" of information—although the density of a chunk can vary significantly, encompassing a single word or a complex array of items.) Long-term memory, in contrast, brings longevity to thought; it represents the psychological past, housing all of the information that is acquired over a lifetime. As such, long-term memory is nearly limitless in its information capacity. It is established through a long evolutionary history, one characterized by uneven growth.

The structure of long-term memory can be further divided. Endel Tulving (1985; 1993), a leading scholar in this area, suggests that long-term memory consists of three components: procedural memory, episodic memory, and semantic memory. Procedural memory is the most basic element of long-term memory. It functions to retain information on the "how-tos" of experience—how to ride a bike, fry an egg, or tie one's shoes, for example. Cognitive scientists argue that individuals have no direct access to procedural memories. Rather, the presence of such memories is demonstrated through our actions. Thus the fact that we can ride a bike even though we may not have ridden one for years is considered evidence of procedural memory's active operation.

Episodic memory, the second component of long-term memory, houses information about temporally dated episodes and events and information regarding the relationship between those events. Thus an individual's memories about courtship, marriage, and the birth of one's children constitute episodic pieces that pinpoint and connect key moments in an individual's life. Similarly, one's memories of visits to the home of a good friend both highlight and network significant moments in a relationship. Cognitive scientists conceive of episodic memory as a personal scrapbook, an entity constantly under construction. Thus they believe that only parts of episodic memory stay intact for a lifetime; other parts fade with time or are overpowered by new, incoming episodes.

Semantic memory constitutes the final and most influential component of long-term memory. According to cognitive scientists, semantic memory contains organized knowledge, especially knowledge about words, concepts, rules, abstract ideas, and the relations among them. (Indeed, Tulving [1972] described semantic memory as a mental thesaurus.) One's ability to read, solve a math problem, or understand the premises of a theory rely on semantic memory, for this component allows one to store information on meaning and referents, on the relations between things, and on the rules for manipulating symbols and concepts. As such, semantic memory serves as the analytic center for the brain's massive storage "warehouse."

While Tulving breaks long-term memory into various components, he does not believe that these components function as isolated entities. Rather, he argues that memory components interact to facilitate both the storage and retrieval of information. Further, Tulving contends that such memory work can be tracked, for he envisions direct connections between certain types of memory tasks and specific neural activity. David Rumelhart and James McClelland (1986) make a similar claim in presenting the "Parallel Distributed Process (PDP)" model of memory. They argue that memories exist as a network of multiple linked nodes. For example, one combination of nodes might represent our memory of the concept "funeral." Another network of nodes would comprise our memory of "vacations." And the same nodes, in different combinations, can join to create the memory of other concepts and experiences. As individuals are prompted for specific memories, Rumelhart and McClelland argue, some nodal links are activated while others are shut down. Active nodal networks then promote learning by tying newly acquired information to previously stored knowledge. They also serve as "retrieval paths," allowing the individual to zero in on relevant information.

In addition to identifying the structure of memory, cognitive scientists have explored the processes at work in each memory system. For example, the short-term memory system appears to operate primarily (but not exclusively) by means of an auditory code. Information is effectively entered in short-term memory via a method to which cognitive scientists refer as "auditory rehearsal." Individuals repeat information to themselves, either silently or aloud, as a means of retaining the information in their active working space.[3] (Think, for example, of the last time you requested a phone number. How did you retain the information until arriving at a telephone?) Once information is acquired, short-term memory also appears to be guided by both a "primacy" and a "recency" exposure effect. When individuals are exposed to a series of information inputs, they tend to recall best their earliest exposures (the primacy effect) and their latest exposures (the recency effect). This is because earliest exposures tend to be mentally rehearsed and repeated, thus increasing their strength, while the latest exposures can be remembered with minimal effort.[4]

Long-term memory acquisition is also a patterned affair. Indeed, cognitive scientists have discovered several factors that can greatly facilitate the passage of information into long-term memory. Processing depth represents one such factor. Research shows that "deep processing"—concentration on the meaning of information as it is being acquired—enhances the likelihood that information will be stored in long-term memory. In contrast, "shallow processing"—attention only to surface characteristics—decreases the likelihood of long-term memory storage.[5] Cognitive scientists have also learned that "self-referencing" is related to long-term memory acquisition. Sometime referred to as the "narcissistic trait," research shows that autobiographical information, whether positive or negative, is most likely to be stored and most easily recalled within an individual's memory banks. Finally, ordering information can aid in long-term memory acquisition. Mnemonic strategies, information clustering, and networking are all said to order data referentially, maximizing the available memory space, establishing connections between information bits, and facilitating the process of information retrieval.[6]

Patterns of acquisition are integral to our understanding of memory retrieval, for research suggests an intimate link between the two processes. For example, the memory "goals" we hold at the time of acquisition can impact retrieval capabilities. If we acquire information for the purpose of recall (that is, remembering and reproducing information upon cue), we create neural retrieval paths different from those we would construct if our goal was recognition (that is, identifying previously encountered material upon exposure).[7] Similarly, the "state" of acquisition can impact retrieval. Thus we are most likely to retrieve information successfully if we are tested under the same physical conditions and surroundings as those in which we acquired the information.[8] Retrieval power is also maximized when there is a match between an individual's internal state at the time of acquisition and retrieval.[9] Finally, repeated exposure to a stimulus at the time of acquisition can increase the potential for memory retrieval. With each exposure, the brain is primed to recognize the stimulus in the future, providing a certain fluency in information retrieval.[10]

In studying memory acquisition and retrieval, it is important to note that not all memory is accurate. As the brain acquires new information, it must often be reconciled with data already located in long-term storage. Cognitive scientists tell us that this process can create the potential for confusion. For when faced with an onslaught of incoming information, individuals sometimes lose sight of "real" memories, creating either "distortions" of stored memories or completely "false memories." Sir Frederick Bartlett's book *Remembering* (1932) provides the earliest evidence of distorted memories. Bartlett's experiments required subjects to digest various accounts for remembering. When asked to recall these accounts, Bartlett discovered, subjects would "adjust" the accounts in routine ways. For example, subjects would often replace unfamiliar aspects of the story with components that were more familiar to them. Illogical action was often corrected in ways that seemed more sensible to the subject. Aspects of the story might be omitted, and new information might be used in order to enhance the account in ways agreeable to the subject. In this way subjects retained the "spirit" of the story but transformed it in ways that coincided with their general understandings of the world.

Research shows that a similar logic—the imposition of one's worldview—guides the more radical process of false memory. In a study by William Brewer and James Treyens (1981), subjects were asked to recall the objects contained in settings they had occupied during an experiment. The researchers found that subjects routinely "completed" their memory of certain settings according to their expectations of the setting. They added the objects they believed belonged in the setting, even if those objects were not present, thus forcing the setting to conform to a previously held schema.

Research on distortion and false memory best illustrates the importance of organizational constructs such as schemata in the retrieval process. As noted earlier in this volume, schemata are metaconcepts that summarize patterns of experience. They are highly generalized knowledge structures, abstract guidelines and rules that help human beings infer meaning. When encountering new information about which we have prior experience, we tend to acquire and store in memory those data which coincide with the schemata we hold. This process tends to homogenize our experience, allowing contradictory data to be blended out of a scenario and buried in the deep recesses of the brain. Thus, in retrieving memories, previously stored schemata can shape that which we remember. Schematically linked information is the first and easiest to retrieve. In contrast, nonschematically linked information may fail to be located, thus forcing us to "fill in the blanks" with data from an active schema.[11]

The structure of memory and the neural procedures by which individuals remember and forget are undeniably important for the study of the mind. But missing from such discussions is another critical aspect of memory, namely, its sociocultural foundations. Memory cannot be adequately studied solely as an isolated structure of the brain, for memories are both isolated and shared, both private and public, both harbored and commemorated. What an individual remembers and forgets may well be guided by the neural paths of the brain, previously stored schemata, or the unique tapestry of one's personal experience. But on a larger scale, those things that one remembers and forgets, the schemata activated or deactivated in the process of storage and retrieval, are also guided by the social situations, cultural contexts, and thought communities to which one belongs. In essence, the sociocultural factors of which I speak render memory as much a collective phenomenon as it is a personal one.

Maurice Halbwachs was the first to explicitly centralize the collective aspects of memory. He conceived of memory as the product of minds—not isolated minds, but minds working together in society. "It is in society that people normally acquire their memories," wrote Halbwachs. "It is also in society that they recall, recognize, and localize their memories. . . . [Memories] are recalled by me externally, and the groups of which I am a part at any time give me the means to reconstruct them. . . ." (1992:38). Thus, for Halbwachs, topics such as acquisition, storage, and retrieval supercede the internal mechanics of the brain. Debates regarding the amount of information active in short-term memory, the nodal links initiated in storage and retrieval, or the most effective of mnemonic organizational strategies are as much social issues as they are characteristics of the human brain. Halbwachs preferred to study such activities as group phenomena—jointly executed mental events that are structured by the social contexts and arrangements in which group members' minds are embedded.

Many of Halbwachs's insights are now widely shared by social scientists of memory. Hoping to enhance cognitive science's treatment of the topic, social scientists approach memory as a process more than an entity, but as an ongoing and patterned process that is executed in social space and regulated by normative guidelines as opposed to neural rules. From this perspective, collective memory requires corroboration before it is recognized or validated; it may be revised or enhanced before it is utilized by a group; it is stored discriminately in accord with cultural schemata; it is selectively retrieved and jointly experienced via ritual and commemoration. In essence, collective memory is continually constructed, a common property of a group. It functions as a social tool used for understanding the past and mapping the future. Ultimately, it provides groups with a selective history, one that becomes the basis for intersubjectivity, collective identity, and collective action.

This section attempts to explore more fully the sociocultural aspects of memory. In the chapters to follow, three sociologists, renowned for their work in this area, examine the intricacies of collective memory, the processes by which it is constructed, and its impact on social life. In Chapter 11, Barry Schwartz and MiKyoung Kim focus readers on the role of cultural schemata in memory construction. Just as personal schemata direct the acquisition, storage, and retrieval of personal memories, so too, argue Schwartz and Kim, can cultural schemata direct the acquisition, storage, and retrieval of collective memory. The authors are especially interested in the cultural schemata that represent national identities. With this focus in mind, their study addresses two very different national cultures: the United States and South Korea. Schwartz and Kim note the vastly different images embodied by American and Korean identity schemata. They contend that the American identity schema emphasizes independence, equality, individualism, and populism; it is filled with feelings of perseverance, triumph, dominance, and victory. In contrast, the Korean identity schema emphasizes interdependence, hierarchy, communitarianism, and honor; it is marked by feelings of humiliation, acute self-consciousness, self-separation, and resentment toward foreign powers. How do these two very different schemata of national identity impact remembrances of one's nation? To answer that question, the authors utilize the historical reflections of more than one thousand American and Korean undergraduates. Students in their study were asked to name the events in their respective nations' histories that elicited the greatest pride or invoked the greatest shame. In analyzing students' responses and their reasons for selecting specific events, Schwartz and Kim discover that students' answers are highly patterned in accord with the specific cultural themes that comprise each group's identity schema. Thus the authors argue that national identity schemata function as "priming" schemata, schemata that powerfully direct Americans' and Koreans' memories— their very configurations—of their nations' pasts. In recognizing this influence, the

Schwartz and Kim study aptly illustrates the collective dimension, the sociocultural foundations of memory.

In Chapter 12, Gary Allan Fine continues the focus on collective memory. But for Fine, historical narrative—in particular, the great personages of such narrative—provide the vehicle of study. "Historical narrative," argues Fine, "is comprised of a set of linked reputations . . . a sequential pageant of individuals, each defined as being 'the cause' or engine of events" (Fine, pp. 227). These great figures prove critical to the study of memory, for they represent a special type of mnemonic tool. The great figures of such narratives—the heroes of a culture—become a window on history; they filter the people, places, and events that come to define and redefine a group; they become vehicles by which a collective assesses its past and configures its present. But in underscoring the importance of heroes to collective memory and collective consciousness, Fine notes something more. From his perspective, heroes represent just one part of any collective's story. To examine fully collective memory and its impact on present perception, one must examine the villains of historical narrative as well. Like heroes, evildoers establish behavioral boundaries and thus contribute to collective definitions of moral order. Villains increase collective cohesion as members join in opposition against them. When invoked by a collective, evildoers stigmatize undesirable actions and images. In these ways, argues Fine, villains become a critical dimension in the collective's self-reflective lens, a dimension equal in importance to the great personages of history. To illustrate his point, Fine examines an especially poignant case study of evil. His project explores historical narratives and current assessments of Adolf Hitler, the Nazis, and the Holocaust. In probing scores of accounts surrounding these figures and their historical moments, Fine impressively illuminates the impact of evil exemplars on a collective's memory of the past. Further, his study of evil exemplars sets the stage for a theory that examines the ways in which history and memory are "simultaneously accurate and culturally created" (Fine, pp. 230).

Endnotes

1. These memory types were first identified in the late 1800s. See Ebbinghaus ([1964] 1987); James (1890).
2. For a pivotal work on the structure and function of short-term memory, see Peterson and Peterson (1959); for early work on the structure and function of long-term memory, consult Bower (1975); Bahrick, Bahrick, and Wittlinger (1975); Hebb (1949).
3. See, e.g., Conrad (1963, 1964, 1970).
4. See, e.g., Baddeley and Hitch (1974); Glanzer and Cunitz (1966).
5. See, e.g., Craik and Lockhart (1972); Hyde and Jenkins (1969); Parkin (1984); Zinchenko (1981).
6. See, e.g., Bousfield (1953); Bower et al. (1969); Buschke (1977); Cofer, Bruce, and Reicher (1966); E. E. Smith (1978); Tulving (1962).
7. See Tversky (1973).
8. See, e.g., Balch, Bowman, and Mohler (1992); Godden and Baddeley (1975); Schab (1990); S. Smith (1979).
9. See, e.g., Bower (1981); Fisher and Craik (1977).
10. The notion of priming is linked to a large literature on "implicit memory." For a good review, see Roediger and McDermott (1993).

11. Guided by this reasoning, cognitive scientists argue that unique or first-time experiences tend to be retrieved with greater accuracy than familiar experiences.

References

Baddeley, A. D. and G. Hitch. 1974. "Working Memory." In *Recent Advances in Learning and Motivation*, edited by G. Bower. New York: Academic Press.

Bahrick, H. P., P. O. Bahrick, and R. P. Wittlinger. 1975. "Fifty Years of Memory for Names and Faces: A Cross Sectional Approach." *Journal of Experimental Psychology: General* 104:54–75.

Balch, W., K. Bowman, and L. Mohler. 1992. "Music-Dependent Memory in Immediate and Delayed Word Recall." *Memory and Cognition* 20:21–8.

Bartlett, Sir F. 1932. *Remembering*. Cambridge, England: Cambridge University Press.

Bousfield, W. A. 1953. "The Occurrence of Clustering in the Recall of Randomly Arranged Associates." *Journal of General Psychology* 49:229–40.

Bower, G. H. 1975. "Cognitive Psychology: An Introduction." Pp. 25–80 in *Handbook of Learning and Cognitive Processes*, vol. 1, edited by W. Estes. Hillsdale, NJ: Erlbaum.

———. 1981. "Mood and Memory." *American Psychologist* 36:129–48.

Bower, G. H., M. C. Clark, A. M. Lesgold. and D. Winzenz. 1969. "Hierarchical Retrieval Schemes in Recall of Categorized Word Lists." *Journal of Verbal Learning and Verbal Behavior* 8:323–43.

Brewer, W. F. and J. C. Treyens. 1981. "Role of Schemata in Memory for Places." *Cognitive Psychology* 13:207–30.

Buschke, H. 1977. "Two Dimensional Recall: Immediate Identification of Clusters in Episodic and Semantic Memory." *Journal of Verbal Learning and Verbal Behavior* 16:201–15.

Conrad, R. 1963. "Acoustic Confusions and Memory Spans for Words." *Nature* 197:1029–30.

———. 1964. "Acoustic Confusions in Immediate Memory." *British Journal of Psychology* 55:75–84.

———. 1970. "Short-Term Memory Processes in the Deaf." *British Journal of Psychology* 69:171–95.

Cofer, C. N., D. R. Bruce, and G. M. Reicher. 1966. "Clustering in Free Recall as a Function of Certain Methodological Variations." *Journal of Experimental Psychology* 71:858–66.

Craik, F. I. M. and R. S. Lockhart. 1972. "Levels of Processing: A Framework for Memory Research." *Journal of Verbal Learning and Verbal Behavior* 11:671–84.

Ebbinghaus, H. [1964] 1987. *Memory: A Contribution to Experimental Psychology*. Translated by H. A. Ruger and C. E. Bussenius. New York: Dover Publications.

Fisher, R. and F. I. M. Craik. 1977. "The Interaction between Encoding and Retrieval Operations in Cued Recall." *Journal of Experimental Psychology: Human Learning and Memory* 3:701–11.

Glanzer, M. and A. R. Cunitz. 1966. "Two Storage Mechanisms in Free Recall." *Journal of Verbal Learning and Verbal Behavior* 5:351–60.

Godden, D. R. and A. D. Baddeley. 1975. "Context-Dependent Memory in Two Natural Environments: On Land and Underwater." *British Journal of Psychology* 66:325–32.

Halbwachs, M. 1992. *On Collective Memory*. Translated and edited by L. A. Coser. Chicago, IL: University of Chicago Press.

Hebb, D. 1949. *The Organization of Behavior*. New York: Wiley.

Hyde, T. S. and J. J. Jenkins. 1969. "Differential Effects of Incidental Tasks on the Organization of Recall of a List of Highly Associated Words." *Journal of Verbal Learning and Verbal Behavior* 12:471–80.

James, W. 1890. *Principles of Psychology*. Cambridge, MA: Harvard University Press.

Miller, G. 1956. "The Magical Number Seven Plus or Minus Two: Some Limits on Our Capacity for Processing Information." *Psychological Review* 63:81–97.

Milner, B. 1966. "Amnesia Following Operation on the Temporal Lobes." Pp. 109–133 in *Amnesia*, edited by C. Whitty and O. Zangwill. London: Butterworth.

Parkin, A. J. 1984. "Levels of Processing, Context, and Facilitation of Pronunciation." *Acta Psychologia* 55:19–29.

Peterson, L. R. and M. J. Peterson. 1959. "Short-Term Retention of Individual Verbal Items." *Journal of Experimental Psychology* 58:193–98.

Roediger, H. I. and K. B. McDermott. 1993. "Retrieval Blocks in Episodic and Semantic Memory." *Canadian Journal of Psychology* 3:213–42.

Rumelhart, D. E. and J. L. McClelland. 1986. *Parallel Distributed Processing: Explorations in the Microstructure of Cognition*, vol. 1. Cambridge, MA: Bradford.

Schab, F. 1990. "Odors and Remembrance of Things Past." *Journal of Experimental Psychology: Learning, Memory, and Cognition* 16:648–55.

Smith, E. E. 1978. "Theories of Semantic Memory." In *Handbook of Learning and Cognitive Processes*, vol. 6, edited by W. K. Estes. Hillsdale, NJ: Erlbaum.

Smith, S. 1979. "Remembering In and Out of Context." *Journal of Experimental Psychology: Human Learning and Memory* 5:460–71.

Tulving, E. 1962. "Subjective Organization in Free Recall of 'Unrelated' Words." *Psychological Review* 69:344–54.

———. 1972. "Episodic and Semantic Memory." In *Organisation of Memory,* edited by E. Tulving and W. Donaldson. London: Academic Press.

———. 1985. "How Many Memory Systems Are There?" *American Psychologist* 40:38–398.

———. 1993. "What Is Episodic Memory?" *Current Directions In Psychological Science* 2:67–70.

Tversky, B. 1973. "Encoding Processes in Recognition and Recall." *Cognitive Psychology* 5:275–87.

Zinchenko, P. I. 1981. "Involuntary Memory and the Goal-Directed Nature of Activity." In *The Concept of Activity in Soviet Psychology*, edited by J. V. Wertsch. Armonk, NY: Sharpe.

CHAPTER 11

Honor, Dignity, and Collective Memory

JUDGING THE PAST IN KOREA AND THE UNITED STATES

Barry Schwartz and MiKyoung Kim

"A nation is a soul, a spiritual principle. Only two things, actually, constitute this soul, this spiritual principle. . . . One is the possession in common of a rich legacy of remembrances; the other is the actual consent, the desire to live together, the will to continue to value the heritage which all hold in common." Ernest Renan's ([1887] 1947 I:903) observation reveals much truth, but we need to know more. If nations distinguish themselves by what citizens remember about their past, we need to know how they remember collectively. How do they conceive the virtues—and the sins—of their common past?

This chapter, a comparative survey, places Korean undergraduates' judgments of their nation's past against the background of American students rendering judgments of theirs. Besides naming the three events in which they take greatest pride and the three they deem most shameful, students responded to a series of questions tapping their political values and their attitudes about relevant social issues. These data are important not only for what they tell us about Korean national memory but also for what they add to the broader agenda of collective memory study. Recent collective memory research, especially studies of the politics of memory (Bodnar 1992; Gillis 1994; Hobsbawm and Ranger 1983), often challenge the official versions of historical events, but they tell us little about the way ordinary people judge the past. In the theory of the politics of memory, people are manipulated by the state to adopt flattering views of their nation's history; but is the state always successful? What do people actually think about the unpleasant side of their nation's history?

People everywhere are: (1) retrieving and constructing the past; (2) chronicling and commemorating it; (3) agreeing and disagreeing about it; (4) recognizing the past as a model shaping reality and mirror reflecting it; and (5) appreciating its permanence and change. To understand these matters is to know how images of the past are ignored, distorted, revised, transmitted, and received in specific cultural contexts. Since students of collective memory have shied away from comparative analysis, however, their concerns lead precisely to the relativism they have avoided confronting intellectually. Relativism's consequence, reducing the content of memory to the standpoint of the individuals cultivating that memory, is to be overcome "only by facing directly and fully the diversities of human culture" (Geertz 1973:41). Facing collective memory directly means encompassing the entire range of its content, from the reasonable to the absurd, the pleasing to the repulsive, across nations. To this end, we compare Korean and American conceptions of historical pride and shame.

The cultural context of memory has never been an important part of sociology's agenda. Maurice Halbwachs's pioneering work in the 1920s and 1930s demonstrated how selective remembering and forgetting is induced by social categories and experiences, but his agenda excluded systematic comparative study. Mary Douglas's (1985) assessment of Evans-Pritchard's and Robert Merton's essays on memory is more suggestive than Halbwachs's. Evans-Pritchard was intrigued by the capacity of the Nuer to memorize eleven generations of ancestors' names, Merton, by the inability of scientists to remember recent multiple discoveries. The latter system is weak on memory, according to Douglas, because it is competitive; the former is strong on memory because it is hierarchical and patriarchical. The conclusion is elegantly reasoned but based on only two essays, separately conceived and written, rather than on controlled comparative findings.

Howard Schuman's, Hiroko Akiyama's, and Barbel Knauper's (1998) study of Germany and Japan exemplifies the controlled, cross-national comparison but focuses on generational differences in memory within each society rather than on cultural differences between them. Lyn Spillman's (1997) comparison of centennial and bicentennial celebrations in Australia and the United States, on the other hand, is a rich comparative project but relies expressly on Anglo-Saxon cultural *similarities* in order to isolate the effects of *geopolitical* differences on commemorative repertoires. Spillman, like Douglas, Schuman, Akiyama, and Knauper, addresses important questions about structural factors activating collective memory in different nations, but her questions are only partially relevant to culture's effects on memory. We wish to confront this issue directly by asking how two very different cultures promote remembrance of different kinds of events, and what it is about these events that makes them worth remembering in the first place.

Worldview and Ethos

The cognitive aspect of a culture, its "worldview," is distinguishable from its evaluative, aesthetic, and emotional aspects—its "ethos." The worldview of a people "is their picture of the way things in sheer actuality are, their concept of nature, of self, of society. It contains their most comprehensive ideas of order." The ethos of a people is, in contrast, "the tone, character, and quality of their life, its moral and aesthetic style and mood; it is the underlying attitude toward themselves and their world that life reflects" (Geertz 1973:127). Worldview rationalizes ethos; ethos instills worldview with affect. Worldview and ethos are inseparable and converge in every cultural realm, including philosophy, religion, ideology, political values, mythology, art, and collective memory.

"Collective memory," according to Paul DiMaggio (1997:275), "is the outcome of processes affecting, respectively, the information to which individuals have access, the schema by which people understand the past, and the external symbols or messages that prime these schemata." Schemata, in turn, convert worldviews into everyday thinking, feeling, and action. Koreans' schemata include their conception of themselves as a "single-blood people," their self-imposed separation from outsiders, belief that humiliation is Korea's root experience, acute self-consciousness, and resentment of foreign powers (including political allies). Koreans' schemata provoke self-blame for abuses suffered at the hands of others and shame of their own weakness. Korean and American cultural patterns reflect and interpret unique patterns of historical experience: invasion and defeat, in the Korean case; settlement and dominance, in the American case.

Foreign threat literally defines Korean history. Yoon (1984) counted the number of raids and incursions against Korea from the seas and by neighboring peoples, finding no less than 1 to 1.5 per year during the Koryo (918–1392) and Chosun (1392–1910) dynasties respectively (quoted in S.B. Choi 1987:182). Given a history of attacks by stronger neighbors, victimhood has become a major element in Koreans' collective identity and memory. A Korean middle school textbook tells its young readers: "We have suffered from many invasions by neighboring countries throughout our long history. However, we have never provoked, exploited, or caused any pain to any of our neighbors. In other words, we have always tried to maintain peaceful international relations and preserve a peace-loving tradition" (Korean Ministry of Education 1998:10–11).

Comparison of Korea and the United States would be straightforward if the two countries differed only in economic and military power. An inheritor of the political philosophy of the Enlightenment, American political culture incorporates the ideals of independence, equality, individualism, populism, and individual dignity (Lipset 1979), which leads American people to internalize a democratic worldview steeped in libertarian ideals shared with other postindustrial/postcolonial nations of the West. Korean political culture embodies the ideals of interdependence, hierarchy, communitarianism, and honor, which leads Korean people to internalize an authoritarian worldview shared with the emerging industrial and formerly colonized nations of the East. To date, however, no knowledge exists of how the singularities of Korean and American culture, or Eastern and Western cultures more generally, affect understandings of the past.

Comparisons

Our Korean data consist of 432 Kyungnam University students who completed survey questionnaires and 83 students who participated in 13 in-depth group discussions.

Kyungnam University is located in Masan, a southeastern Korean city with a history of student activism in national conflicts.[1] To Kyungnam's students we administered questionnaires during the 1998 and 1999 school years. Freshmen and sophomore participants totaled 35 percent and 32 percent of the sample; juniors and seniors, 18 percent and 15 percent. Male and female respondents made up 55 percent and 45 percent of the sample, respectively.[2] Furthermore, thirteen groups averaging six students each met twice for two hours to discuss the defining points and meanings of Korean history.[3]

The American data include a sample of 449 students enrolled at the University of Georgia in 1997 and 1998. Residing mainly in the state's metropolitan areas, including Atlanta, these students were 88 percent white, 8 percent black, and 4 percent Asian. Seventy percent of the students were born in the South, 30 percent, outside the South. Seventy-one percent were freshmen and sophomores; the rest, juniors and seniors. Female respondents (60 percent) outnumbered male respondents. The sample approximates the composition of the College of Arts and Sciences, in which most of its members are enrolled.

In contrast to the state's moderately conservative population, the University of Georgia's social science and humanities faculties have instituted liberal academic programs. Besides "hard-left" multicultural course requirements for graduation, the regular course content, as Brigitte Berger would put it, is "soft left" (Hollander 1995:176–77). Vigorously recruiting minority (especially African American) students and faculty and supporting minority study centers and programs, the University of Georgia's progressive agenda is deliberately geared to redeeming the sins of slavery and formal segregation.

Kyungnam and University of Georgia students do not represent Korea's and America's university students, let alone their general populations. We assume, however, that the *difference* between Korean and American students' judgments approximates the *difference* between judgments of all Korean and American adults.

History's Vices

Asked to name the "three events in American history of which you do not merely disapprove, but which, in your opinion, degrade the United States and arouse in you as a citizen (rather than private individual) a sense of dishonor, disgrace, shame, and/or remorse," University of Georgia students named a total of 95 historical events. The most prominent events were slavery, named by 41 percent of the respondents; the Vietnam War, 36 percent, and offenses against American Indians, 32 percent. The next four most commonly mentioned events, named by less than 17 percent of the respondents, were segregation, the Civil War, internment of Japanese-Americans, and use of the atomic bomb. Offenses against minority communities, including African Americans, American Indians, Hispanic and Japanese Americans, and the Vietnamese and Japanese peoples, are condemned frequently by American students. (See Table 11–1.)

Events condemned by Korean students include overwhelmingly the victimhood of the Korean people themselves. The most commonly named event is the 1910 to 1945 Japanese occupation; the second most commonly named, the International

TABLE 11–1
**Frequently Mentioned Sources of "Dishonor,
Disgrace, Shame" in the United States**

Event	Number	Percent Mentioning Event*
Slavery	183	40.8
Vietnam War	160	35.6
Treatment of Indians	146	32.5
Segregation	76	16.9
Internment of Japanese	46	10.2

*Event mentioned as first, second, or third choice as a percentage of all events mentioned.

Monetary Fund (IMF) crisis. The Korean War, a fratricidal conflict in which North and South Koreans fought one another, is the third most commonly mentioned negative event. Wrongdoings of recent Korean presidents, Chun Koo Hwan and Roh Tae Woo, the fourth most frequent response, cover a recent three-year period from 1994 to 1997. The fifth response refers to a series of recent construction failures: fatal collapses of bridges and buildings. The sixth response consists of a distillation of historical experiences involving "Big Powers" undermining Korean interests and dignity. (See Table 11–2.)

To judge a historical event or class of events is to categorize and locate it in one or more moral categories. American and Korean students named different types of events as sources of national disgrace, categorized them in different ways, and assigned them incomparable meanings. Indeed, the very conception of "historical event"

TABLE 11–2
**Frequently Mentioned Sources of "Dishonor, Disgrace, Shame"
in Korea**

Event	Number	Percentage Mentioning Event*
Japanese Colonial Rule (1910–1945)	246	56.9
The IMF Emergency Loan	213	49.3
The Korean War	109	25.2
The Wrongdoings of the Former Presidents (Chun Doo Hwan and Roh Tae Woo)	106	24.5
The Collapses of Sung Soo Bridge and Sam Poong Department Store	91	21.1
"Big Power" Abuses	72	16.6

*Event mentioned as first, second, or third choice.

differed. Koreans are more inclined to see recent, current, and, as we will see, even future events as parts of history, while Americans include a larger percentage of history's significant events, positive and negative, in previous centuries. These differences result not from different historical contents but, as will be shown, from different perceptions of historical time.

Dishonor's Roots

After respondents had identified a negative event on their questionnaires, they were asked to "explain in a few words or a sentence what makes this event shameful or dishonorable." Since more respondents named an event than gave reasons for naming it, we confine our analysis to the events most frequently mentioned. American responses are unsurprising. The most common reasons for naming slavery are depriving a people of their freedom for more than two centuries, forcing them to work while their owners rested, and causing enduring interracial division, whose harm is still visible. The most common reasons for naming the Vietnam War are its pointlessness, the wartime government's ineptitude and deceit, the military's ineffectiveness, the killing of innocent civilians, and the causing of disunity at home. Reasons for naming the maltreatment of American Indians cluster closely around the themes of criminal expulsion and slaughter.

Koreans define a different and, from the American standpoint, puzzling range of historical events as shameful. That victimization and defeat should evoke shame is not inevitable. Many badly defeated and cruelly victimized peoples, including African Americans and Jews, and nations, including Russia and Poland, do not blame themselves for their misfortunes. Koreans are different, and the reasons for the difference do not become coherent until we realize the seriousness with which Koreans identify themselves as the people of *Hahn*. *Hahn* is so widely used and its conceptualization so complex that any translation of the word into a Western language will be controversial. English words approaching the meaning of *Hahn* include mourning, frustration, anger, and resentment. The latter word, "resentment," is the most common, but nonetheless inadequate, translation.

Hahn reflects the complexity of Korea's ethos because it not only aggregates the sentiments of anger against injustice, helplessness over inequality, and bitterness over exploitation (Hyun 1986:39) but also envelops the individual in self-blame. *Hahn*, unlike simple anger against others, is reflexive. Angry people revile their antagonists; people feeling *Hahn* also blame themselves (Y. G. Kim 1989:135, 137). *Hahn*, a schema utilizing self-dialogue to direct responsibility for events, is self-sustaining because the self-blame it generates causes painful events to be all the more clearly remembered. *Hahn*, thus, "gets tied as a knot in the stomach," "nailed into the marrow," "cut deep into the heart," "tangled up like a lump in the throat," "like a purple bruise on the chest" Y. G. Kim 1982, *passim*). The metaphoric construction of *Hahn*'s physiology reveals its emotional significance.[4]

Hahn attaches negative emotion to a historical worldview resting on invasion, defeat, and subjugation. Referring to self-blame and resentment, to the acceptance of the past and the drive to avenge it, *Hahn* articulates the paradoxical Korean experience. Among five categories of reasons students gave for naming the Japanese occupation as a national disgrace, the most common by far was weakness and humiliation: "Japan dared to rule us because they looked down on us as an ignorant people," explained one student. "Division among us invited Japan's invasion," observed another. "Our weakness caused the loss of our nation"; "Our ancestors deserve more blame than even the Japanese"; "We failed to protect ourselves" and were therefore "dishonored internationally."

Overestimation of the world's interest in Korea, a key element in its concept of honor, appears as often in the remembrance of Japan's occupation as of any other event. Japan's harsh occupation of Korea included the forcing of Japanese names on the Korean people and the demeaning of their culture. Humiliation, however, is independent of what the Japanese did and did not do. "A nation's submission to another is itself a source of disgrace." Even Japan's defeat in 1945, ending its colonization of Korea, humiliated Koreans, because "we didn't liberate ourselves" but had to depend on other nations.

The Korean War, too, affirmed Korean weakness. Although recently redefined in America as a significant victory rather than a forgotten war and marked by a major war memorial in Washington, DC, Korean feelings remain negative. Korea was "divided into two by the powerful nations," and the subsequent war seemed to some "a surrogate war between the U.S. and U.S.S.R." Lacking national sovereignty, Korea had become a mere arena for superpower dispute. True, 35,000 Americans died on Korean soil, and South Korea remained free from harsh Communist rule, but what about the "horrendous deeds" of U.S. soldiers now stationed in Korea? "This land does not belong to them; yet they are immune from our laws." The stationing of two divisions of American soldiers in Korea under American control for more than a half-century serves American hegemony, not Korean interests.

Americans offend the Korean people with impunity, but Koreans have themselves to blame: America's very presence reveals "our weakness internationally." "I am unhappy with the fact that we were weak and had to accept such an unfair fate." In addition, Korean women allowing Americans to adopt children fathered by American soldiers, as one respondent put it, "makes me feel truly ashamed, yet compounds my own and my nation's responsibility." One respondent after another insisted that the Korean War was unnatural in a nation whose citizens regard one another as brothers and sisters, that Korea is the last or only divided nation in the world—an unnatural state disgracing everyone. Thus Koreans define their relationship to outside powers not in strict geopolitical terms but as an aspect of their national character (see also S. I. Han 1992).[5]

Koreans' penchant for self-blame is also evident in comments about former presidents' evading taxes and colluding illegally with business leaders, for "we are the ones who sent them to their offices and we deserve the blame for not having known better." The former presidents were arrested and tried, but "we spit on our own face by trying them. It is because we are the ones who elected them." "They were our face" and "they damaged our international reputation and caused foreign nations to despise us."

Foreign opinion is persistent and salient in Korean minds. Sensitivity to this opinion transforms local tragedies, such as the collapse of a bridge or building, into national calamities. The causal linkage, however, is complex. Reasons for structures collapsing only begin with poor materials and engineering; the ultimate causes reach into the nation's soul: "Our way of thinking fundamentally caused these collapses." They "revealed a national character" focused on "the short term only, not the long term." The accidents thus revealed "that our technology is still too backward to be exported." And as these failures accumulate, they "exponentially increase the skepticism towards us as a nation." Since codes of honor work by exaggerating the perception of outsider interest, television accentuates the effect of any tragedy. CNN, in particular, "made the world perceive us as the Republic of Collapse." "We became the world's laughing stock."

Self-blame and dependence on the opinion of others is also evident in references to Korea's recent economic crisis. The Korean government had prepared no recovery plan—itself a source of shame. Our respondents, however, blamed themselves for their leaders' shortcomings. Although "I did not vote for Kim Young Sam, who ignored financial problems during his term in office, I feel responsible for the national woes." True, Korea's leaders betrayed the trust of the people, but the people themselves are imperfect: "We have been overconsuming and wasting resources," according to one of the respondents, while another confessed to "our pursuit of vanities." The people, in short, were ready, if not eager, to be misled: "Ours is a greedy and corrupt culture." Again, Koreans deem their vice so great as to awaken the attention of the world. The inevitable result: "Our overconsumption is publicized internationally." "I am speechless with shame." To this culture of shame, overestimation of outsiders' interest is an essential aspect.

Sovereignty is the ideal around which separate sources of self-disparagement converge. The IMF loan package was a response to economic need, but the Korean government's agreement to abide by the IMF's restrictions seemed like a renewal of Japanese occupation, "because it caused us to lose our sovereignty" and "shows the continuing dependence of Korea on foreign nations." New troubles always result from new weaknesses: "Our weak economic base *invited* another nation's intervention." Foreign assistance is more than a mere loan repayable with interest; it is colonialism reincarnate.

Korea's need for assistance convinced the world to ignore earlier evidence of its self-sufficiency—or, more precisely, apparent self-sufficiency. Yesterday Koreans bragged about their success; today there is only failure. The face of the nation had been utterly disgraced. Crisis subsided, but the humiliation grew. We "begged" for Western loans, and "after we received their loans, we were too meek. . . . Why is the president of a nation so meek before the head of a mere financial organization?" While proud Korea became a beggar nation, Korean attitudes remained split between mutually reinforcing extremes: self-aggrandizement (J. Y. Kim 1984; Y. U. Kim 1987) and self-reproach (N. S. Choi 1913; G. S. Lee [1922] 1967; W. J. Kim 1987), the latter exemplified by the abiding question: "What will the world think of us now?"

Humiliation over historical losses is revealed by both closed and open questions. Asked whether: "On balance, the bad (immoral) parts of Korean [American] history outweigh the good," 44 percent of the Kyungnam University students agreed, compared to 29 percent of University of Georgia students (see Table 11–3). Even students from the former East and West Germany, fully recognizing the nightmare of National Socialism and the Holocaust, hold their nation in no lower esteem than

TABLE 11–3
Responses to Statement: "On Balance, the Bad (Immoral) Parts of History Outweigh the Good." (in Percentages)

	United States (n = 418)	Germany (n = 330)	Korea (n = 414)
Very Strongly Agree	3.8	6.4	7.2
Strongly Agree	5.3	15.0	13.5
Agree	20.1	22.3	23.7
Neutral	18.2	30.7	24.2
Disagree	19.1	15.0	17.6
Strongly Disagree	21.3	6.2	9.2
Very Strongly Disagree	12.2	4.4	4.6
Total	100.0	100.0	100.0

their Korean peers. Only 44 percent of the German students believed the bad parts of the past outweighed the good (Schwartz and Heinrich 1999).

Self-blame also appears in answers to the question of moral responsibility: "I personally feel that my generation is morally responsible for treating the effects of past discrimination against all minority groups." (See Table 11–4.) Although oppression of minority groups (mainly foreign workers) is far less relevant to Korean than to American society, 93 percent of the Korean sample agreed with this statement, compared to 24 percent of the American sample. When German students were asked a very similar question, 84 percent agreed with it. Korean students are the most self-critical.

Difference in Americans' and Koreans' sense of responsibility reflect the ways Koreans and Americans define their relationship to the past. The less connected people are to the past, the more firmly they reject responsibility for the misdeeds of

TABLE 11–4
Responses to Statement: "My Generation is Responsible for Past Mistreatment of Minorities." (in Percentages)

	United States (n = 432)	Germany (n = 342)	Korea (n = 426)
Very Strongly Agree	4.2	52.2	52.5
Strongly Agree	6.2	21.2	26.0
Agree	13.6	10.3	14.5
Neutral	16.4	7.9	5.1
Disagree	10.6	3.0	0.7
Strongly Disagree	14.6	1.8	0.5
Very Strongly Disagree	34.4	3.6	0.7
Total	100.0	100.0	100.0

ancestors; the more connected, the greater their felt obligation to accept responsibility for historical debts.

Temporal Boundaries

Whether one generation of people has the right to bind another depends on the cultural frames defining the relation between the living and the dead. Thomas Jefferson ([1789] 1975:445, 448) believed it to be *"self-evident* that the earth belongs in usufruct to the living: that the dead have neither powers nor rights over it (our emphasis)." To prevent past debts, financial and otherwise, from burdening the present, Jefferson believed, laws must be rewritten every 19 years. How else can citizens liberate themselves from the past? "By the law of nature, one generation is to another as one independent nation is to another." Several decades later, Ralph Waldo Emerson ([1837] 1959) echoed Jefferson's words: "Each age, it is found, must write its own books; or rather, each generation for the next succeeding. The books of an older period will not fit this" (p.67).[6] Nathaniel Hawthorne, too ([1859] 1962), demanded to know: "Shall we never, never get rid of this past? It lies upon the present like a giant's dead body" (p.162). He was referring not to his family's sins, which he wished to redeem, but to public affairs, symbolized by public buildings; these should be made of materials that "crumble to ruin once in twenty years, or thereabouts, as a hint to the people to examine into and reform the institutions which they symbolize" (p.163).

Segregation of present and past endures. When Thomas Cottle (1976) invited his American respondents to order past, present, and future atomistically by drawing *separate* circles, continuously by *touching* circles, or integratively by *overlapping* circles, 60 percent atomized time by making the circles separate; 27 percent made the circles touch, and only 13 percent integrated time by making the circles overlap (Cottle 1976:85–94). "We live in a society that encourages us to cut free from the past," Robert Bellah et al. (1985) observed, "to define our own selves, to choose the groups with which we wish to identify" (p.154). Anthropologist Florence Kluckhohn (1951:103–4) distinguished America from other societies by the disposition of its people to deemphasize and radically disconnect the past from the present. Accordingly, when one of the authors replicated Cottle's test with 99 Kyungnam University students, she found only 9 percent of her respondents separating past, present, and future and only 11 percent conceiving time as continuous. The majority, 80 percent (compared to 13 percent of Americans), integrated the three time spheres. To Korean students, the past and present are equally poignant zones of the temporal realm—the extreme opposite of the American pattern.

The thinness of the wall separating past and present in Korea explains not only why Koreans accept responsibility for their ancestors' misdeeds but also why they include so many recent events in their inventory of historical disgrace. Present and past merge because *Hahn* attaches itself to present and past events, rendering their historical significance comparable. The Korean proverbs, "A frog does not look back on his tadpole days," and "A kettle is quick to boil and quick to cool down" (Guk 1987; G. T. Lee 1991) refer to the frequency with which new memories arise and dominate old ones. But since the former superimpose themselves on the latter rather than replace them, *Hahn* can intensify the relevance and emotional intensity of both (K. K. Han 1999).

National Boundaries

The relevance and emotional intensity of past events are lineaments of ethos. America's ethos of rights includes different criteria for the judgment of history from Korea's ethos of duty. When Americans are asked to name their nation's gravest sins, they include events leading to the denial of rights of others—slavery, oppression of Indians, internment of the Japanese, killing innocent civilians in war, and waging war with insufficient cause. In duty cultures, the needs of the community trump the entitlements of the individual. When Koreans are asked to name their nation's sins, therefore, they include most prominently the events bringing the greatest harm to their own nation. Koreans' misdeeds result not from victimizing others but from allowing themselves to become victims. Injury suffered, not caused, is Korea's shame.

Defining themselves as a one-blood people, Koreans' sense of disgrace is magnified by political separation. The 1945 division of Korea makes this evident: "Our powerlessness led to the powerful nations' decision to divide us up. I feel ashamed of this division of more than fifty years." The 1950 to 1953 Korean War compounded the dishonor: "We, blood brothers, fought against each other."

Since disdain for outsiders is part of blood brotherhood, we asked students in a short questionnaire what came to mind when they heard the word "foreigner."[7] Eight percent believe foreigners are inferior to Koreans: "Unfamiliar, scary, they may stink," and "their difference in appearance makes me feel hostile toward them." Many respondents conflated foreigner and American, but they conceded that American television and film furnished their only information. The most common response to this question, given by 42 percent of the students, expressed both unfamiliarity and curiosity: "They may be very different from me and I feel scared. But on the other hand, they feel like close friends to me"; "Since I cannot communicate with them, I feel alienated"; "I am curious about them, but I do not have the courage to approach them." Twenty percent of the respondents believed foreigners to be "kind, rational, family-oriented"; "They think rationally, they abide by the law, they respect life and individual freedom." Eight percent of the respondents asserted that there are no differences between Korean and foreigners. The data thus make visible a relevant but also permeable boundary, made of velvet rather than steel, a bridge inviting crossing, a mark of positive and attracting difference. Yet this bridge also spans a gap—a cultural gap—of considerable magnitude.

The Good Past

When American students were asked to identify the "three events in American history of which you do not merely approve but which, in your opinion, elevate the United States and arouse in you as a citizen (rather than a private individual) a sense

TABLE 11–5
Frequently Mentioned Sources of Honor, Esteem, and Dignity in the United States

Event	Number	Percentage Mentioning Event*
Founding Events	172	38.6
World War II	115	25.8
Gulf War	80	17.9
Space Achievements	53	15.7
Civil Rights	70	11.9

*Event mentioned as first, second, or third choice as a percentage of all events mentioned.

of honor, esteem, dignity, and self-respect," they named 59 events.[8] (See Table 11–5.) Thirty-nine percent of the students named the American "Founding Moment," which includes events occurring between the start of hostilities with Great Britain in 1775 and the establishment of federal government in 1789. Twenty-six percent of the respondents named World War II; 18 percent, the Persian Gulf War. Civil rights and space achievements are the only other groups of events named by more than 10 percent of the respondents.

Thirty-five percent of the American students chose the Founding Moment most often because of the moral purpose (notably freedom and equality) for which the new nation was established; 25 percent, because it culminated in a just and beneficent Constitution that divided powers and prevented tyranny; 20 percent because it produced the Declaration of Independence, and 13 percent because it guaranteed political rights. The remaining 7 percent named the Founding Moment because it promoted self-respect, cohesion, and unity.

Almost two thirds of American students named World War II because it ended atrocities, saved lives, and affirmed democratic values; 28 percent named it because it established American global power; 10 percent, because it increased national unity. (Twenty percent of these same students named the Gulf War because it helped weaker nations withstand tyranny; 20 percent, because it increased national cohesion, and 10 percent because it enhanced respect for American credibility and power).

To American minds, Korean responses seem strange (see Table 11–6). Koreans' most frequently mentioned source of esteem was not a political event; it was the 1988 Olympic Games. The next most frequently mentioned event was the World Cup competition, scheduled for 2002—an event anticipated, not remembered, yet invoked as an object of memory. The third and fourth choices are the invention of the Hangul alphabet, which liberated Korea from cultural dependence on China, and the indigenous resistance movement that formed during the 1910 to 1945 Japanese colonization. The next group of choices includes the winning of different international sporting competitions, the Gold Collection Drive in response to the IMF crisis, and the period of economic growth that transformed Korea into an important member of the world economy.

TABLE 11–6
Frequently Mentioned Sources of Honor, Esteem, Dignity in Korea

Event	Number	Percentage Mentioning Event*
The 1988 Olympic Games	91	21.0
The 2002 World Cup	32	7.4
The Invention of Hangul	30	6.9
Independence Movement	30	6.9
Winning of International Competition	30	6.9
The Gold Collection Drive (1997–1998)	25	5.8
Economic Growth (1960s–1970s)	24	5.6

*Event mentioned as first, second, or third choice.

The difference between Korean and American conceptions of national virtue became clear when we asked Korean respondents to name the reasons for their choices. Invention of the Hangul alphabet is noteworthy because, in the context of the cultural dominance of China, it provides Korea with its own letters, is difficult to learn, is the most creative and scientific language in the world, promotes Korean dignity and common identity, and, perhaps most importantly, "proves our excellence to the world." Likewise, the economic expansion that began in the 1960s, the Miracle of the Han River, "demonstrated our excellence." In fact: "We can invent new technology in a very short period of time like 30 years, while other countries (e.g., the United States) took about 200 years." Following this short-term achievement came long-term "international recognition."

International recognition is the most common reason for naming the Olympics. Hosting the 1988 Games in Seoul was an honor because: "The world came to see us"; "We are not that weak any more"; "The world now knows of our economic success." Admiration by other nations, not intrinsic satisfaction in hosting the Olympics, characterized the responses: "The Olympics was a good opportunity to show our economic growth and culture to the world"; "We proved our potential to so many advanced and powerful nations"; "We feel dignified because the world now knows we exist." In group discussions, too, students betrayed their obsession with foreign recognition:

> I was so proud throughout the entire event. Even though we were one of the world's developing economies, we managed to win the competition to host the games. And the world evaluates the Seoul Games as the greatest ever.[9]

Every discussant, in some way, elaborated on the relevance of international recognition:

> Before the Seoul Games, people did not know where Korea was. Korea, located between China and Japan, was hard to find. But the games reminded them that Korea exists, and I feel proud because of that.[10]

Success raises expectation as it embellishes rhetoric: the Olympic Games "gave us hope that we can become one of the advanced nations of the world"; "Our success with the games proved our incredible potential."

Sports stars exemplify this potential. Since sports competition is a venue where Koreans can compete fairly, the spectacle of Koreans defeating representatives of oppressor nations is exhilarating and makes sports figures like Park Chan Ho, a Los Angeles Dodgers pitcher, into national heroes.

Sports achievements hardly exhaust the symbolism of Korean historical pride, but they capture its principle: positive impressions made on others. People around the world cannot be as aware of Korean successes and failures as our respondents believe, but concern with this awareness drives their sense of esteem. Thus, the March 1st Independence Movement (1919), involving mass demonstrations against Japanese occupation, failed to affect Japanese imperial policy, but it "reminded the entire world of our true spirit." In fact, few people outside Korea knew about this futile demonstration, but in one way it is more meaningful than the 1945 expulsion of Japan from Korea or the 1950 to 1953 Korean War: "Even though we failed to liberate Korea, it was our own voluntary movement." The imagination of an admiring audience reinforced Koreans' embracing of self-reliance, a trait that in American society makes admiring audiences unnecessary.

Conclusion

The study of collective memory is more than an effort to map variations in the working of the mind; it seeks to provide models of human beings using their minds—symbol-making, conceptualizing, meaning-seeking—to fix the experiences of their lives within the history of their nation. Different combinations of culture and experience, however, lead to different perspectives.

"Perspective," rooted in the experiences and contingencies of life, influences "the manner in which one views an object, what one perceives in it, and how one construes it in his thinking" (Mannheim 1936:272). Since American and Korean students possess "widely differing modes of experience and interpretation," they display "fundamentally divergent thought systems" (Mannheim 1936:57) and construe the past in fundamentally divergent ways. We have tried to show what these differences consist of, how they came about, and how they evolved.

American and Korean judgments of the past are aspects, not products, of the contrasting worldviews and ethos of Korean and American societies. American society rests on political ideals—liberty, egalitarianism, individualism, populism, and laissez-faire (Lipset 1996:31)—rather than common race, ethnicity, or religion. This abstract creed forms the basis of "American exceptionalism," an aspect of American culture that includes the particularities of American memory. Americans take pride in events that exemplify their conception of an orderly, free, and just society, notably the founding era, World War II, the Persian Gulf and Yugoslavia wars; they affirm their shame about events, including slavery and the treatment of the Indian, that violate these ideals. That Americans distinguish themselves from the participants in these events, rarely become passionate about them, rarely accept credit or blame for them, rarely hold themselves responsible for them, reflects the same individualistic/egalitarian values that promote commemoration of the events themselves.

Korean judgments, on the other hand, articulate a culture of honor distinguished by the *Hahn* ethos. In every social sphere, "*Hahn*ful" people, as Koreans call themselves, react to trauma and injustice not only by resentment of the perpetrators but also by self-blame. Since the latter incorporates the belief that unjust suffering proves the victim's virtue and the offender's vice, *Hahn* shapes the victimization theme in Korean folklore: in popular and widely known poems, like "Azalea," wherein a virtuous wife, abandoned by her bored husband, throws flowers in his way (J. O. Kim 1987:37; Y. G. Kim 1982, 1987; M. J. Lee 1986:13–19); in a girl, murdered by a wicked stepmother, turning into a nightingale (Oh 1986:11); in a bride, wrongly condemned for lasciviousness and abandoned by her husband, turning into ashes in her wedding dress while awaiting his return (Y. G. Kim 1982:316);[11] in a mother, already deserted by her husband, freezing to death while awaiting the return of her son imprisoned by the Japanese (Dong Ri's *Rock*); in a young girl, blinded by her stepfather to improve her singing (*Sopynje*), which reminds listeners of the bird's cry (in Korean the bird's sound is a "cry" rather than a "song") (Y. G. Kim 1989:33); in paintings of bleak scenery and objects such as gutters, "representing anger and the land's *Hahn*" while affirming the sanctity of the land, in which all forebears rest (Y. N. Kim 1998:422–34). In each case, suffering is a vehicle for the display of virtue and faith. "*Hahn*," in the words of Noh Gwi Nam (1998:178), "is like dust which people gather over them as they continue to live on. To some people, living is the process of building *Hahn* in them. Some are born with a lump of *Hahn* inside them, and they endure it until the lump finally becomes the nutrient of their existence."

Korean memory is a lump of *Hahn* that admits of contradictory meanings. Korean memory embodies pride, of which international recognition is an essential source, but the need for this recognition reveals the defining tension in Korean self-consciousness: ambivalence toward things foreign, on the one hand, and, on the other, adoption of foreign standards for self-judgment. Resentful of Western countries seeking to impose alien values, Koreans apply these values to themselves. "I sometimes wonder what makes us truly proud and ashamed," said a student in a group discussion. "Are we using our own mirror [standard] or our image reflected in somebody else's mirror in deciding how to feel."[12] All nations rely on international perceptions as a reference point for their own esteem, but Koreans push this tendency much further than most.

Since *Hahn* synthesizes the worldview and ethos of a historically vulnerable nation, it is tempting to compare Korea and ancient Israel—weak nations at the mercy of strong neighbors and surviving only by their cohesion. This comparison is useful because it points up the limits of a purely historical theory of collective memory. Specifically, the Israelites never condemned themselves for their weakness or their tragedies. They regarded themselves as a Chosen People and saw in their suffering God's own plan. Even divine punishment affirmed the holiness of the people, for it increased their sense of legacy and of belonging to God (Douglas 1966, 1975).[13] Taken separately, centuries of victimization can account for Korea's historical consciousness no more than it can Israel's; it is the interpretation of victimization that comprises collective memory, and this interpretation is culturally as well as factually molded. Failure to assess the cultural molding process adequately is the point we have addressed. Douglas's comparison of Evans-Pritchard's and Merton's essays, written in separate times and places, suggests that egalitarian competitive systems are weak on memory, hierarchical systems are strong on memory. However, Korea and the United States (hierarchical and egalitarian cultures respectively) differ not so much in the amount of memory retained as in the kind of events remembered and the way they are interpreted morally. Just so, nationwide samples such as Schuman, Akiyama, and Knauper's (1998) might demonstrate strong generational differences in the content of Korean and American memory, but these differences could not explain why Koreans and Americans of the same generation judge the past so differently. We must not exaggerate the importance of cultural differences. If Korea and the United States were culturally similar, we would still expect the different geopolitical experiences of the two nations to lead to differences in memory—differences no less dramatic than those Spillman (1997) reports in her Australia/America comparison.

Traditional topics of collective memory research include the relation between history and commemoration, enterprise and reception, consensus and conflict, retrieval and construction of the past, models for and models of reality, and intergenerational continuities and discontinuities of memory. These issues are relevant to the American and Korean cases considered separately but shed no light on the nature of their difference. They fail because they are designed to reveal the universals, not the particulars, of collective memory—and not until we examined particulars, close up, did we learn to see American and Korean cultures as constituents, not contexts, of collective memory. Whether collective memory's universal or local elements are "fundamental," in the sense of revealing its most important qualities, is not for us to say. Our sole claim is that one learns about memory differently—not necessarily better, but differently—by studying it comparatively in specific cultural sites rather than through universal dimensions applicable to all sites.

Endnotes

1. The 1959 student uprising against a corrupt presidential election in Masan ignited the nationwide protest that led to the demise of the Syng Man Rhee regime. In 1979, student protests in the Masan-Pusan area led to the assassination of Park Chung Hee, ending his 18-year reign.
2. We had a 95 percent response rate.
3. Students enrolled in "Contemporary Korean Society" (spring semester, 1999) comprised the discussion groups.
4. In Korean, this term is expressed as *"Hahnyi Gasumae Maethyutdah."*
5. A Korean college student presents a labeling theory of Korean self-conception: "I believe others evaluate Koreans as an inferior and defeated people. I am afraid such poisonous ideas about us have been internalized within us as well. Before the beginning of Japanese rule, Koreans were a people of pride and optimism. It is shameful that this colonial legacy lingers on today" (Group discussion, April 14, 1999).
6. In "Self Reliance" ([1840] 1959:159), Emerson added: "All men have my blood and I all men's. Not for that will I adopt their petulance or folly, even the context of being ashamed of it."
7. For a discussion of social distance *among* Koreans, including Korean attitudes toward strangers, see Kobari (1999:30–3; 190–99).
8. The tendency for negative events to outnumber positive ones is evident in both American and Korean responses. Schwartz and Heinrich (1999) have shown this tendency to be evident in German responses to the same questions and to be independent of question ordering. For suggestive comments on the identifying power of negative experience, see Simmel (1950).
9. Group discussion, April 14, 1999.

10. Group discussion, April 8, 1999.
11. In this story, the husband's clothing is caught on a nail as he goes to undress for his wedding night. Assuming that his bride, out of eagerness for sex, is tearing off his clothing, he condemns her and leaves. Without protesting, she endures her fate, remaining where she sat when he left, her wedding costume surviving the decomposition of her body.
12. Group discussion, April 14, 1999.
13. Serbian history, although marked by defeat and subjugation, induces resentment, not self-blame, (Levinsohn 1993).

References

Bellah, R. N., R. Madsen, W. M. Sullivan, A. Swidler, and S. M. Tipton. 1985. *Habits of the Heart.* New York: Harper and Row.
Bodnar, J. 1992. *Remaking America: Public Memory, Commemoration, and Patriotism in the Twentieth Century.* Princeton, NJ: Princeton University Press.
Choi, N. S. 1913. *Haedongyuksah (History of Haedong).* Seoul, Korea: Chosun Gwangmunhoe.
Choi, S. B. 1987. "Hakmunjuk Sadaewa Jajon" (Intellectual Dependency and Self-Reliance). Pp. 180–86 in *Hankukin Hankukbyung (Koreans and the Korean Disease).* Seoul, Korea: Ilnyum.
Cottle, T. J. 1976. *Perceiving Time.* New York: Wiley.
DiMaggio, P. 1997. "Culture and Cognition." *Annual Review of Sociology* 23:263–87.
Douglas, M. 1966. "Abominations of Leviticus." Pp. 39–57 in *Purity and Danger: An Analysis of Concepts of Pollution and Taboo.* London: Routledge & Kegan Paul.
———. 1975. "Self-Evidence." Pp. 276–318 in *Implicit Meanings.* London: Routledge & Kegan Paul.
———. 1985. "Institutions Remember and Forget." Pp.69–80 in *How Institutions Think.* Syracuse, NY: University of Syracuse Press.
Emerson, R. W. [1837] 1959. "The American Scholar." Pp. 63–80 in *Selections from Ralph Waldo Emerson,* edited by Stephen E. Whicher. Boston, MA: Houghton-Mifflin.
———. [1840] 1959. "Self-Reliance." Pp. 147–68 in *Selections from Ralph Waldo Emerson,* edited by S. E. Whicher. Boston, MA: Houghton-Mifflin.
Geertz, C. 1973. *The Interpretation of Cultures.* New York: Basic Books.
Gillis, J. R., ed. 1994. *Commemorations: The Politics of National Identity.* Princeton, NJ: Princeton University Press.
Guk, H. G. 1987. "Hankukineun Wae Seoduruhnungah?" (Why Do Koreans Rush?). Pp. 111–19 in *Hankukin Hankukbyung (Koreans and the Korean Disease).* Seoul, Korea: Ilnyum.
Han, K. K. 1999. "Wieghieui Inryuhak: Hankuk Junjaenggwa Wighieui Whakdae Jaesaengsan" (Anthropology of Crisis: The Korean War and the Expansive Reproduction of the Sense of Crisis). Presented at the 31st Annual Korean Cultural Anthropology Studies Association Meeting.
Han, S. I. 1992. "Mangunuro Dalrinun Ilbonyoldo" (The Insane Blahs of the Japanese Islands). *Shindongah,* April, pp. 180–191.
Hawthorne, N. [1859] 1962. *The House of the Seven Gables.* New York: New American Library.
Hobsbawm, E. and T. Ranger. 1983. *The Invention of Tradition.* Cambridge, England: Cambridge University Press.
Hollander, P. 1995. *Anti-Americanism: Irrational and Rational.* New Brunswick, NJ: Transaction.
Hyun, Y. H. 1986. *Hankuk Munwhawa Gheedokgyo Yunri (Korean Culture and Christian Ethics).* Seoul, Korea: Munhakgwa Jisung.
Jefferson, T. [1789] 1975. "To James Madison." Pp. 444–51 in *The Portable Thomas Jefferson,* edited by Merrill Peterson. New York: Penguin.

Kim, J. O. 1987. "Sowoleui Shijunggwa Wonchojok Ingan" (Sowol's Poetic Sensitivity and Basic Human Emotions). Pp. 34–47 in *Kim So Wol Yon Guh (A Study on Kim So Wol)*, edited by Y. G. Kim and D. W. Shin. Seoul, Korea: Saemunsa.

Kim, J. Y. 1984. *Hankukineui Puri (The Root of Koreans)*. Seoul: Sahoebaljunyonguso.

Kim, W. J. 1987. "Minjok Gaejoroneun Gwayon Tahdanghangah?" [Is the Transformation of National Character Plausible?]. Pp. 18–26 in *Hankukin, Hankukbyung [Koreans and the Koreans Disease]*. Seoul, Korea: Ilnyum.

Kim, Y. G. 1982. *Hahnmaek Wonryu: Hankukin, Maeumeui Ungoriwa Maetchim (The Knot in the Korean Mind)*. Seoul, Korea: Juwoo.

———. 1987. *Hankukin, Guh Maeumeui Ghunwoneul Channundah (In Search of the Essence of the Korean Mind)*. Seoul, Korea: Munhacksahsaengsah.

———. 1989. *Hankuk Munhwaeui Puri (The Root of Korean Culture)*. Seoul, Korea: Iljogak.

Kim, Y. N. 1998. *Yiship Seghieui Hankuk Misul (The Twentieth Century Korean Arts)*. Seoul, Korea: Yegyung.

Kim, Y. U. 1987. *Hankukeui Gheechung Munhwa (The Korean Mass Culture)*. Seoul, Korea: Hanghilsa.

Kluckhohn, F. 1951. "Dominant and Variant Value Orientations." Pp. 97–113 in *Social Welfare Reform*. New York: Columbia University Press.

Kobari, S. 1999. *Kankoku to Kankokujin (South Korea and Its People)*. Tokyo: Heibonsha.

Korean Ministry of Education. 1998. Middle School National History Textbook (sophomore). Seoul: Korean Ministry of Education.

Lee, G. S. [1922] 1967. *Chosuneui Hyunjaewa Mirae (The Present and Future of Korea)*. Seoul, Korea: Gwangmundang.

Lee, G. T. 1991. *Hankukineui Burut: Buhrigoh Shipun Burut (The Korean Habits: Those Needed To Be Discarded)*. Seoul, Korea: Shinwonmunhwasa.

Lee, M. J. 1986. "Jin Dal Rae Goteui Jaim" (The Structure of the Azalea). Pp. 8–20 in *A Study of Kim So Wol*, edited by Y. G. Kim and D. W. Shin. Seoul, Korea: Saemunsa.

Levinsohn, F. 1993. *Belgrade: Among the Serbs*. Chicago, IL: Ivan Dees.

Lipset, S. M. 1979. *The First New Nation: The United States in Historical and Comparative Perspective*. New York: W. W. Norton.

———. 1996. *American Exceptionalism: A Double-Edged Sword*. New York: W.W. Norton.

Mannheim, K. 1936. *Ideology and Utopia*. New York: Harcourt, Brace and World.

Noh, G. N. 1998. "Sorueui Bitgaw Hahneui Reality: Seopyunjaeeui Munhakgwa Youngsang" (The Light of Sound and the Reality of Hahn: The Literature and Film of Seopyungjae). *Munhakgwa Changjak* 29:(1):176–87.

Oh, S. Y. 1986. "Mosangshil Euishikeuroseoeui Hahn" [Hahn as Resentment over an Absent Mother]. Pp. 21–37 in *A Study of Kim So Wol*, edited by Y. G. Kim and D. W. Shin. Seoul, Korea: Saemunsa.

Renan, E. [1887] 1947. "Qu'est-ce qu'une Nation?" *Ouevre Completes*. 2 vols. Paris: Calman-Levy.

Schuman, H., H. Akiyama, and B. Knauper. 1998. "Collective Memories of Germans and Japanese about the Past Half-Century." *Memory* 6:427–54.

Schwartz, B. and H. A. Heinrich. 1999. "Perceiving Atrocity in the United States and Germany: Time Frames of Responsibility." Presented at the Annual Meeting of the American Sociological Association, Chicago IL.

Simmel, G. 1950. "The Negative Character of Collective Behavior." *The Sociology of Georg Simmel*, edited by Kurt Wolff. New York: Free Press.

Spillman, L. 1997. *Nation and Commemoration*. Cambridge, England: Cambridge University Press.

Yoon, T. R. 1984. *Hankukin (Korean)*. Seoul, Korea: Hyunamsa.

CHAPTER 12

Thinking about Evil

ADOLF HITLER AND THE DILEMMA
OF THE SOCIAL CONSTRUCTION
OF REPUTATION

Gary Alan Fine

In the past two decades social scientists have increasingly turned their attention to the process by which members of societies and societal subgroups think about and remember their pasts. Particularly influential in this regard was the translation of Maurice Halbwachs's (1980; 1992) writings into English, leading to a focus on collective memories (Lang and Lang 1990; Schwartz 1987). In the words of Benedict Anderson (1983), societies constitute "imagined communities." Societal histories and narratives are central to this imagination. This approach suggests that the politics of memory is central to the development of a state or community's consciousness: What we believe that we were shapes how we continue to think about ourselves in a mnemonic process (Olick and Robbins 1998; Zerubavel 1997).

However, in practice, history consists not primarily of ideas but of stories. These stories have their own dramatic personae. In a sense, history consists of a sequential pageant of individuals, each defined as being "the cause" or engine of events. These great personages of history constitute one of the key mnemonics by which we recall the past. Historical narrative is comprised of a set of linked reputations.

Two fundamental questions organize how sociologists think of reputation. First is the Durkheimian question: What do reputations do? Or, put another way, what roles do reputations play—as collective representations—for the society that embraces them? Second is the Goffmanian question: How do reputations come about? Whose interest do they serve within the micropolitics of social organization?

Much of the original impetus for the examination of reputation focused on the first question, inquiring about the impact of history's heroes on national consciousness. What does the memory of historical actors do for society? These heroic figures represented our best images of our selves. Thus George Washington, despite all of his faults, is used to symbolize the American republic to citizens. Even though few knew Washington personally, he could be taught and presented in a variety of ways that convinced members of the polity that they did know and, of greater significance, admired him with a passion that could brook no dispute. It is relatively easy to understand how those who are defined as great come to define a people through collective representations.

Further research has examined the process by which reputations are made. Great figures are not "naturally" recognized as great but must be defined so by social agents, or what I have previously termed "reputational entrepreneurs" (Fine 1996). Like the moral entrepreneurs (Becker 1963) who help to create social problems, reputational entrepreneurs attempt to structure how an audience conceives of the images of social actors, both immediately and in historical memory. The legions of "spin doctors" and "PR experts" give testimony to the need for reputation work in contemporary society.

While it is understandable that scholars will have addressed these questions by examining those figures who best represent ourselves to ourselves, figures with a different cast also have reputations that are socially meaningful. As a consequence, during the past decade I have been engaged in an extended research program to understand how we—in this case, we Americans—think about figures whose reputations are not positive: those individuals possessing what I have labeled "difficult reputations." Some of these individuals, such as Benedict Arnold (Ducharme and Fine 1995), are depicted as immoral, others, such as Warren Harding (Fine 1996), are seen as incompetent, and still others, such as John Brown (Fine 1999), are intensely controversial figures with defenders and attackers.

The understanding of difficult reputations provides answers to both sets of questions. As Kai Erikson (1966) noted with regards to Puritan witch trials, such figures serve dramatically to establish boundaries for the moral order and as means of enforcing social control. In extreme cases, these reputations even have a "magical" or numinous quality. The evil that is embedded within our memory of them is so powerful that there are circumstances in which it—like sympathetic magic—can rub off on the identity of one who strays too close to a defense of such figures, causing the loss of moral credibility. For reputational entrepreneurs, negative exemplars have their use to discredit opponents, who can be likened to that discredited figure. Who today wishes to be known as a McCarthyite or a Stalinist?

To examine the potential power of a negative reputation as a boundary marker and as a strategic stigma, it is useful to choose an extreme case: an ideal type. To this end I wish to analyze the significance of that most difficult reputation of all: that of Adolf Hitler. As part of this project I attempt to understand how Americans think about *Der Führer*, the Nazis, and the Holocaust.

When asked: "What is the reputation of Adolf Hitler?," I respond dryly, "not good." Such a response, of course, true in one sense, is inaccurate in another and, in that sense, is fundamentally misleading. Hitler's reputation is far deeper and more robust than the label "not good" suggests. Unlike the reputation of most other historical figures, Hitler still "matters," and one would have to be far, far out on the American political extreme to provide a broad defense of this German dictator, reveling in hostility that such a defense provokes (see Simonelli 1999).

As noted, social memory studies appear to provide some measure of purchase on how the facts of history become socially fixed and how they become mnemonics for reading the present. These research projects for the most part (but see Schwartz 1996) are grounded on the social-constructionist argument, suggesting that memory is fundamentally political and filled with conflict between self-interested parties.

Yet it is in its ability to challenge the more extreme claims of social-constructionist theory that the reputation of Adolf Hitler, the Nazi Party, and the Holocaust become of intense sociological interest. If all history is socially constructed, not grounded in a set of definitive, ascertainable facts, does this claim not apply equally to Germany in the Hitler era, from 1933 to 1945? Such a case study asks, in effect: What, then, are the limits of social-constructionist analyses? If, as the strong, strict, or radical constructionists allege (Schneider 1985; Woolgar and Pawluch 1985; Ibarra and Kitsuse 1993), meaning is always in play, facts can never be known definitively, and interest groups determine our knowledge, what sense are we to make of this historical epoch? Is Hitler's reputation something that we select according to our need?

The examination of the Holocaust makes problematic the premises of the construction project, just as the constructionist project makes problematic the confident assumptions that most Americans share about the Nazi era. Indeed, the more sophisticated Holocaust revisionists or deniers (and what label we bestow on them is surely a social construction) are attuned to the academic claim that facts are inherently provisional and are linked to the interests of those who put them forth. Those who question the existence of Nazi genocide use the social-construction perspective in their writings explicitly or implicitly. Thus Arthur Butz (1992) writes in this vein in his *Hoax of the Twentieth Century: The Case Against the Presumed Extermination of European Jewry*, suggesting that the hoax serves the needs of Jews and Israel, notably in terms of gaining sympathy, foreign support, and financial reparations:

> . . . the political interests involved [in pushing the hoax] are not dead and gone, like those of World War I, but are as contemporary as tomorrow's headlines, for Israel is always in trouble, and will be in trouble as long as it exists as a Jewish state. . . . The almost universal delusions have existed not because of the complexities of the subject but because of political factors in Western society. (pp. 321, 332)

Significantly, a similar argument has recently been made (without the claim that the facts are wrong) by respected University of Chicago historian Peter Novick (1999) in his *Holocaust in American Life*, suggesting that images of the Holocaust have been a strategy used by the Jewish community for its collective ends.

In making these claims, these writers have performed a singular service for social theorists in forcing us to confront the boundaries of facts. As a cautious naturalist or contextual constructionist (Fine 1997; Gubrium 1993), my concern is not to consign constructionism to the dustbin of history, but to employ this case study of the "greatest villain" of the twentieth century to examine the limits of this perspective (Hacking 1999). I do believe, perhaps with a certain desperation, that there exists a set of "facts" that, if they cannot be ascertained "for certain," can be known, in practice, well enough, often enough: facts whose presentation cannot be linked wholly to self-interest.

Social constructionism is grounded on the claim that what we label "knowledge" depends upon two features that have independent standing from what is being depicted. Specifically, constructionist theory forces us to consider the interests and resources of the parties to that "knowledge" and its promulgation.

What one wishes and needs to believe for reasons external to the claims—one's interest—determines (or, minimally, contributes to) how one will interpret a set of persons and events. In extreme cases, these interests may influence one's interpretations of one's own experiences.

Interests are bolstered by resources. Interests represent the goal orientations of individual or collective actors; resources refer to the extent that individuals can make these perspectives "stick" socially. If the discursive arena is inherently political, as constructionists allege, how can one version of reality become consensual? As resource-mobilization theorists have argued forcefully (Jenkins 1983), the amounts and types of resources to which one has access determine the recruitment of allies and the responses of potential foes. With regard to reputations, resources are of two fundamental types: relations and materials. Relations tie claims-makers to those who, because of personal networks, serve as supporters. Those with tight and powerful connections have advantages in proposing reputations. Materials refer to the assets through which one is able to gather and present information. Those, for instance, with the resources that a university position or foundation support provides have considerable advantages over those who lack these resources.

All of this seems plausible—up to a point. Interests and resources are powerful in determining how history and reputation are proposed and subsequently accepted. Yet before we find ourselves without confidence in the existence of the past, we must stop and ask how problematic we wish to make historical knowledge. Where does historical reality reside? As the case of the Holocaust suggests, historical knowledge does, or should, have an obdurate character. The challenge for the sociologist is to conceptualize the ways in which history is simultaneously accurate and culturally created. Put another way, how can the constructionist project, so powerful in so many ways, be made responsible as an intellectual matter in a world in which historical knowledge (and the belief in such knowledge) is consequential? Must we all be Holocaust agnostics?

Constructing Hitler

For many domains of historical memory, what we believe has few consequences, even when those beliefs conflict with others that have been sedimented into historical memory. The case of President Warren Harding (Fine 1996) is instructive in this regard. Harding is remembered—when he is remembered at all—as America's worst president: the lowest-ranking chief executive, according to those polls that historians are so fond of conducting (e.g., Murray and Blessing 1988). Indeed, a historian who specialized in this period joked that a "Harding revisionist" is a historian who believes that Harding was only a below-average president. However, if one were to allege that Harding was a great president, as effective as Lincoln (as, indeed, some at the time of his death seriously argued), one would be looked at somewhat askance, perhaps be mocked or asked to explain one's reasoning, but not treated as immoral. The view of American history that students are taught would not noticeably change if this allegation of Harding's greatness was incorporated into high school textbooks. Even if one were to allege that the widely publicized Teapot Dome "scandal" never occurred, as Harding's disgraced secretary of the interior Albert Fall asserted even after his conviction, one would not be scorned as depraved.

Reactions to Harding revisionism are comparable to discourse surrounding the reputation of most historical figures: allegations about most persons or events do not constitute fighting words. Facing the new millennium, one could say almost anything one chose about George Washington, George III, or even Benedict Arnold, as the vigorous debate about Thomas Jefferson as saint or sinner attests. The situation with Hitler is different, and we need to address why that should be.

Adolf Hitler has a *sticky reputation*. By "sticky reputation" I mean that evaluations of his reputation that reject his sedimented role as the embodiment of evil are often linked by audiences to the moral character of the claimant. For a speaker discussing Hitler to justify him- or herself, the established position of Hitler as thoroughly evil must be upheld. (Humorous discourse provides somewhat more leeway, but only if the point of the humor can in some way be taken as ratifying Hitler's evil). Little tolerance exists for revisionist views, even those that are generally critical but which provide partial defenses of some aspect of Der Führer's rule.

Hitler is perhaps the most "exemplary" holder of a sticky reputation, but he is not the only one. Within the American context, other figures, both positive and negative, exist for whom we enforce a consensual evaluation. Negative figures include Stalin, Joe McCarthy, and Saddam Hussein. On the positive side we imagine Martin Luther King Jr., Winston Churchill, and Abraham Lincoln. Evaluations of these figures are linked to moral discourse; they belong to the pantheon of civil religion. Within the public marketplace of ideas, only one perspective is legitimate. To be sure, these reputations change over time, but change is slow and typically occurs within the basic evaluative parameters.

As a thought experiment, ask what positive things could one say about Hitler and get away with. Biographers of Hitler have certain discursive leeway in this regard, in that they can situate their limited, circumscribed praise in a larger context of defamation, but consider the case of Marge Schott, the controversial owner of the Cincinnati Reds baseball team. Ms. Schott, who had been known for making colorful and controversial remarks, was considered to have gone too far when she said of Adolf Hitler that he was "OK in the beginning. He rebuilt all of the roads. . . . He just went too far." As a direct consequence of these remarks, her fellow baseball owners forced Ms. Schott to relinquish control of her team. For this group of megacapitalists to abrogate the property rights of a colleague suggests a powerful sanction, especially over such a seemingly mild remark, referring to Hitler's reconstruction of Germany's infrastructure. No one accused Ms. Schott of being herself a Nazi or an active supporter of Hitler. Yet many felt that she had crossed a line that should not be crossed.

Similar criticism was directed toward Minister Louis Farrakhan of the Nation of Islam. Farrakhan termed Hitler: "wickedly great." Once again, the claim was not that

Minister Farrakhan was himself a Nazi, yet he strayed too close to a seeming endorsement of some of Hitler's policies, even though he explicitly labeled Hitler "wicked." Most recently, we have witnessed the opprobrium heaped on Patrick Buchanan (1999) for his book about American foreign policy, *A Republic, Not an Empire*, but only for that chapter that reflected on American and European policies in the early years of World War II. Buchanan's writing is unambiguously filled with attacks on Hitler, yet his claim that the Western democracies should not have attacked the Nazis as early as they did, letting Hitler weaken himself by fighting against the Soviet Union, was taken by many opinion leaders as representing his hidden fascist sympathies. Jokes on late-night television paint the conservative commentator and politician as a jackbooted Nazi. It is appropriate to note in each of these three cases that there were other statements that led audiences to consider that these mild remarks stood for a deeper endorsement and that, thus, a context for criticism existed, but still each of the statements were hardly intense endorsement of Nazi policy. It is clear that Adolf Hitler represents the "third rail" of American political discourse.

Let us return to the speculative question of what can one say admiringly about Adolf Hitler and get away with. Can one allege that he had good dental hygiene, that he was a man of vision, that his agricultural policies were worthy of emulation, that he made the trains run on time, that he brought Germany out of the Depression, or that he brought a sense of pride to German (Christian) citizens? Which of these statements, taken by themselves, without being situated in the context of an attack on Hitler's essential character, would constitute legitimate social commentary, and which would tar the speaker with the implications of "admiring" this most evil man? Put another way, what kinds of praise can be given without that praise coming to stigmatize the speaker or to define the core identity of the speaker? The answer, in many ways and in many places, seems to be: not very much. Violating discursive norms about this sacred collective representation is tantamount to rejecting social order. This dynamic represents the power of a sticky reputation.

Holocaust Revisionism and the Stickiness of Deviant History

I turn to the sociologically curious case of Holocaust revisionism/denial. (As noted, the issue of who gets to select the proper label for the group is important to this analysis. For the rest of this chapter, I use the label "revisionism," since that is the label of choice within the group, but it should be emphasized that the label is controversial, meaningful, and, perhaps, misleading). Reading the works by diverse authors that attempt to cast doubt on the received historical wisdom of the Holocaust is an odd experience. While there are significant differences within the group, the fundamental argument is that Jews were not killed as part of a "genocidal policy" deliberately carried out by the Nazi government, even though some, such as Butz (1992:318), recognize that "the Jews were singled out for special persecution by Nazi Germany. Many were deprived of their property, conscripted for labor, or deported east during the war." Still, the standard claim by their critics is that these writers, taken as a group, as they virtually always are, are anti-Semites. The more charitable of these evaluators, even in scholarly discourse, suggest that Holocaust "deniers" are "misfits," "losers," or, in the words of University of Chicago historian

Peter Novick (1999:13), "fruitcakes"—hardly labels of scientific precision, particularly since these critics have no acquaintance with those of whom they are writing.

The designations of "fruitcake" or "misfit" are circular. These men are fruitcakes because they believe that the Holocaust never occurred, and because they are fruitcakes we have no need to take any of their claims seriously. Their beliefs demonstrate their moral depravity or mental illness, rather than the reverse. Yet some of these individuals have received advanced degrees, hold responsible positions, and write books that, at the very least, have the appearance of scholarly tomes, filled with citations and "evidence." It is because of their social standing and those of their supporters that these authors lack the publishing resources to have the works look as professionally compiled as do those with whom they disagree.

As noted above, the more sophisticated among the doubters seem aware of the arguments of social-constructionist analysis and implicitly use this theoretical apparatus to support their assertions, even if they do not cite the theory as such. They claim, plausibly, it must be admitted, that those who write about the Holocaust have interests in defining the "Holocaust" as a crime against humanity (particularly against the Jews) and in depicting Hitler as uniquely evil. These interests include the desire to provide a justification for the establishment of the state of Israel, the diminution of anti-Semitism through sympathy with the oppressed, and the continuation and expansion of reparations.

These claims stand apart from whether Hitler and the Holocaust were indeed as mainstream historians contend. The facts could be as most reputable scholars claim, while the motivations could be as revisionists allege. (This, roughly, is Novick's [1999] argument.) The constructionist argument that emphasizes the power of interests and resources applies whether or not obdurate reality supports the basis of these claims.

Central to the analysis is the question of what the "Holocaust" signifies. The Holocaust is, of course, not a singular event, but the representation and typification of a historical period. As a consequence of the fact that the Holocaust is a set of events rather than a "thing" itself, it is possible to prove that some particular event covered under the rubric of the Holocaust never occurred. For instance, the claim that the Nazis turned Jews into soap is now accepted as a false war-atrocity story; similarly, most now recognize as inaccurate the claim that the Nazis used the skin of Jews for lampshades. The list of disproved claims could be extended. Some of these claims were designed strategically to denigrate the Germans as part of the propaganda of warfare.

How many of these now-denied claims exist, and does the number matter? Mainstream historians gain little credit for debunking stories that make Hitler and the Nazis look bad, and this recognition of a lack of interest in "defending Nazis" from false information provides a space in which Holocaust revisionism can breathe. If some allegations are wrong, can most allegations be wrong? If one Holocaust survivor can be demonstrated to err or lie (and it can be so demonstrated), does it follow that all should be questioned?

A characteristic of Holocaust revisionism is that the practitioners endorse "negative history." These writers are adept at describing those things that they allege did not happen, but have not produced a broad history of the Nazi regime that describes the events that did transpire. Such a history, too, could be picked apart. Thus revisionists criticize the limitations and hypotheses of others, rather than presenting their own historical reconstruction, which could be attacked as a social construction.

Of course, it is not simply the demonstrable presence of false information that empowers the constructionist argument. History is replete with information that, if examined thoroughly, might be questioned. However, the presence of false information *per se* is not sufficient. The constructionist must present an account that suggests that errors are both systematic and symptomatic. That is, the claim must be that the errors serve the interest of some group and that this group has the resources to enforce its beliefs on others.

Without denying the possibility of anti-Semitism or a hatred for Jews on the part of individual authors, some of the impulse behind Holocaust revisionism seems to be grounded in resentment toward elites. As much research has demonstrated (e.g., Novick 1999; May and May 1982), American Jews have an impact far beyond their numbers in American culture.[1] While it is surely inaccurate to suggest that Jews control the media and cultural occupations in a self-consciously conspiratorial vein, Jews as a group share similar *habitus* (Bourdieu 1984), and on issues of segmental importance many hold common beliefs. It is a truism of constructionist analysis from Gusfield (1963) on that group's attempt to shape public beliefs in light of their own interests.

If the issue is whether American attitudes have been shaped by selective information presented by those with an interest in the topic and beliefs in which have consequences for social and political goals (e.g., reparations to Israel or to Holocaust survivors), the answer is clearly affirmative. Indeed, the label Holocaust (or Shoah) is a constructed label, not widely used with a similar meaning during the events themselves, to understand the horror of these events. The figures of six million Jews and, especially, eleven million persons in sum, killed by the Nazis are matters of social construction, as becomes clear when one examines how these seemingly precise numbers emerged from those with political interests in expanding the death toll. Indeed, the standard claims of historians is that fewer than six million Jews were slaughtered—with most estimates in the range of 5.1 to 5.8 million. On some level, these numbers may be "close enough," but these standard numbers point out dramatically that the figure of "six million" killed is simultaneously both reasonable and inflated. There is far less justification for the figure of eleven million in total (Novick 1999:214–16).

However, to make these assertions is not to accept another claim: that the Nazis did not engage in a systematic policy of gassing and shooting of members of groups that they felt were morally and biologically undesirable, notably, but not exclusively, Communists and Jews, and that millions of humans were exterminated in the process. To contend that history is subject to distortions does not and cannot mean that any knowledge is impossible unless we wish to embrace ontological hopelessness. It is not my intention here to discuss the legitimacy of the historical evidence except to note that, with the exception of Hitler himself, who remains silent, at least some members of most other relevant populations (e.g., guards, Nazi officials, camp inmates) seem to agree on the broad outlines of the Nazi genocidal plans. Given the range of claims and the evidence that stands behind them, must constructionists claim that all history of the Nazi era is a social fiction promulgated by those with interests and resources?

I suggest not, and to defend this position, I present three justifications for the assertion that students of social order can put forth claims sufficiently plausible that they should be taken on their face as credible depictions of the past, even if definitive and fully transparent knowledge can be challenged: (1) claims can provide evidence that is good enough in intersubjective terms for understanding a world; (2) claims reflect the techniques by which participants understand their worlds; and (3) claims provide for the development of "testable" theory. Thus claims can be defended intersubjectively, epistemologically, and pragmatically. Given these bulwarks, I contend that historical claims—about the Holocaust and other significant events—do matter.

AN INTERSUBJECTIVE DEFENSE

Even if truth claims are not definitive, they typically serve well enough. After all, most of what we know of history is not experienced, but taught. We settle for consensual claims about the nature of the world. We look for "truths" that serve us well enough often enough. The similarity of claims about the Holocaust coming from survivors, perpetrators, journalists, and historians provide some confidence. One is struck by the fact that, in general, the claims of former Nazis, surviving Jews, and written records and accounts from the period broadly agree, even if some particulars and justifications vary. Further, although professional historians might picture the Holocaust differently; the visions are typically recognizable by each other. The degree of academic consensus on the empirical reality of the Holocaust is remarkable, even despite various heated disputes about conscious and unconscious motivations. Histories of the period make sense both to readers and to participants of the scenes described. In the face of this agreement, a gigantic conspiracy, while possible in theory (almost everything is possible in theory), is difficult to imagine in practice.

Ultimately effective histories gain plausibility by virtue of their intersubjective power. Others read our works and then come to the conclusion—individually and collectively—that our claims are more or less valid. That a recognition exists that we can critique research projects justifies the legitimacy of history.

AN EPISTEMOLOGICAL DEFENSE

The second defense for the legitimacy of historical truth derives from the recognition that how historians learn about the world is precisely how all public actors come to learn about their worlds. The belief that the world has an obdurate quality comes naturally (Fine 1992). Indeed, one wonders whether the world could function if people in their mundane lives adopted a postmodern stance, questioning not only master narratives, but also the shared reality and collective memories that people take for granted. Accepting the world as a given makes sense for anyone who has had to navigate among social actors. Even if it is always possible (and occasionally legitimate) to question the epistemological provenance of a fact, such academic play is legitimate only as an intellectual game. It serves poorly as a means by which lives are ordered. Even constructionists reside—most of the time—in an obdurate world.

In the case of Hitler and the Holocaust, a set of doubts and possible questions about the certainty of claims related to the extermination of the Jews surely classifies as such an intellectual game. Those present at the time know perfectly well what was happening from their own (admittedly limited) perspective. If some few lied and some others were confused or misled, our self-knowledge of a variety of historical events should suggest that experiential knowledge, coupled with documentary traces, is how the world comes to be known. While this defense cannot suggest that this self-knowledge is infallible, without it we face a barren world of epistemological chaos.

A PRAGMATIC DEFENSE

The final defense of realist depiction is pragmatic. Who better than construc-tionists to embrace pragmatic defenses? Putting aside the question of whether a real-ist approach to history is legitimate "in fact," such accounts are surely useful. Realist accounts permit the building of knowledge and community, comfortable in the belief that we can learn about the contours of the world. Truth may be problematic on a deep, epistemological level; however, it is possible to judge knowledge by its results.

Without a belief in shared knowledge, what purpose can history serve? A prag-matic belief in accurate depiction, even if imperfectly realized, is necessary to legit-imate the scholarly enterprise. If external knowledge is impossible, then, after all, what is the point? Let us put aside whether our knowledge of Hitler is "actually" correct; a belief in lessons from what all agree was a dictatorship of immense and brutal proportions serves us well as a lamp by which we can better face our own future challenges. Perhaps we might disagree with all of the lessons of the "Hitler narrative," but a large proportion of the world citizenry would agree that more good has come from this knowledge than ill. Hitler thus may possibly have saved more lives subsequently than were lost under his rule.

Conclusion

In sum, I suggest that historical reputations matter—especially Hitler's, but not only his. In this chapter I have searched for a ground on which constructionism and obdurate reality can embrace. While reputations are always constructed in some measure, based on the interests and relations of those who serve as reputational entrepreneurs, this should not blind us to the reality that reputations have both real effects and real causes. We often agree on reputations, we know them as we know the rest of the world, and we use them for socially validated ends.

The important task for sociologists is to determine the limits of the social con-struction of reputations and the limits of realist claims of truth. Because of the power of their cultural resonance, and because they matter to so many, the figure of Adolf Hitler and the image of the Holocaust are effective, if odd, places to begin the search for the recognition of both facts and accounts in the creation of reputations.

Endnotes

1. The case of Germany, with few Jews, raises different issues, although surely, in certain cases, impact is possible without presence, especially given the presence of those who, for reasons of their own *habitus*, wish to push these beliefs.

References

Anderson, B. 1983. *Imagined Communities*. London: Verso.

Bourdieu, P. 1984. *Distinction*. Cambridge, MA: Harvard University Press.

Buchanan, P. 1999. *A Nation, Not an Empire*. Washington, DC: Regnery Publishing.

Becker, H. 1963. *Outsiders: Studies in the Sociology of Deviance*. Glencoe, IL: The Free Press.

Butz, A. R. 1992. *The Hoax of the Twentieth Century*. Newport Beach, CA: Institute for Historical Review.

Ducharme, L. and G. A. Fine. 1995. "The Construction of Nonpersonhood and Demonization: Commemorating the 'Traitorous' Reputation of Benedict Arnold." *Social Forces* 73:1309–31.

Erikson, K. 1966. *Wayward Puritans*. New York: Wiley.

Fine, G. A. 1992. "Agency, Structure, and Comparative Contexts: Toward a Synthetic Interactionism." *Symbolic Interaction* 15:87–102.

———. 1996. "Reputational Entrepreneurs and the Memory of Incompetence: Melting Supporters, Partisan Warriors, and Images of President Harding." *American Journal of Sociology* 101:1159–93.

———. 1997. "Scandal, Social Conditions and the Creation of Public Attention: 'Fatty' Arbuckle and the 'Problem' of Hollywood." *Social Problems* 44:297–323.

———. 1999. "John Brown's Body: Elites, Cultural Resonance, and the Legitimation of Political Violence." *Social Problems* 46:1–25.

Gubrium, J. F. 1993. "For a Cautious Naturalism." Pp. 89–101 in *Reconsidering Social Constructionism*, edited by J. A. Holstein and G. Miller. Hawthorne, NY: Aldine de Gruyter.

Gusfield, J. 1963. *Symbolic Crusade*. Urbana, IL: University of Illinois Press.

Halbwachs, M. 1980. *The Collective Memory*. New York: Harper.

———. 1992. *On Collective Memory*. New York: University of Chicago Press.

Hacking, I. 1999. *The Social Construction of What?* Cambridge, MA: Harvard University Press.

Ibarra, P. R. and J. I. Kitsuse. 1993. "Vernacular Constituents of Moral Discourse." Pp. 25–58 in *Reconsidering Social Constructionism*, edited by James A. Holstein and Gale Miller. Hawthorne, NY: Aldine de Gruyter.

Jenkins, J. C. 1983. "Resource Mobilization Theory and the Study of Social Movements." *Annual Review of Sociology* 9:527–53.

Lang, G. E. and K. Lang. 1990. *Etched in Memory: The Building and Survival of Artistic Reputation*. Chapel Hill, NC: University of North Carolina Press.

May, L. L. and E. T. May. 1982. "Why Jewish Movie Moguls: An Exploration in American Culture." *American Jewish History* 72:6–25.

Murray, R. and T. H. Blessing. 1988. *Greatness in the White House: Rating the Presidents, Washington through Carter*. University Park, PA: Pennsylvania State University Press.

Novick, P. 1999. *The Holocaust in American Life*. Boston, MA: Houghton Mifflin.

Olick, J. and J. Robbins. 1998. "Social Memory Studies: From 'Collective Memory' to the Historical Sociology of Mnemonic Practices." *Annual Review of Sociology* 24:105–40.

Schneider, J. 1985. "Social Problems: The Constructionist View." *Annual Review of Sociology* 11:209–29.

Schwartz, B. 1987. *George Washington: The Making of an American Symbol*. New York: Free Press.

———. 1996. "Memory as a Cultural System: Abraham Lincoln in World War II." *American Sociological Review* 61:908–27.

Simonelli, F. J. 1999. *American Fuehrer: George Lincoln Rockwell and the American Nazi Party*. Urbana, IL: University of Illinois Press.

Woolgar, S. and D. Pawluch. 1985. "Ontological Gerrymandering: The Anatomy of Social Problems." *Social Problems* 32:214–27.

Zerubavel, E. 1997. *Social Mindscapes: An Invitation to Cognitive Sociology*. Cambridge, MA: Harvard University Press.

SECTION V

Building Bridges

Building Bridges:
An Introduction

In introducing each section of this volume, I have followed a deliberate plan. I have approached each topic with a binary lens, first providing overviews of cognitive scientific knowledge on a subject, and then raising the problems and omissions that cultural sociologists see in cognitive scientists' approach. Initially, my strategy surely underscores the striking differences in these two disciplines. But ultimately, I hope that annunciating such distinctions will create an opportunity for rich interdisciplinary dialogue.

Can such a dialogue realistically ensue? The question seems prudent. For comparing the research foci of cognitive science and cultural sociology conjures an image of two independent, intellectual islands. Cognitive science approaches thought as the product of electrochemical and neural factors; cultural sociology approaches thought as the product of situated interaction. Cognitive science searches for universal mechanisms of information processing; cultural sociology searches for the ways in which social settings particularize such mechanisms. Cognitive science seeks the generalizeable rules that enable the organization and storage of thought; cultural sociologists seek ways in which such rules are differentiated by sociocultural context. Can one identify common ground in these seemingly contrary agendas? Are there intellectual links and parallels sufficient to trigger a fruitful exchange of ideas? In this final section of *Culture in Mind*, three renowned scholars of cognition address these very questions. In so doing, each author proposes new and exciting foundations for interdisciplinary paradigms of cognitive research.

The section begins with a dialogue between cognitive psychologist Jerome Wakefield and cultural sociologist Allan V. Horwitz. Mental illness represents the topic of discussion. In Chapter 13, Wakefield initiates the dialogue, proposing a model that simultaneously applies cognitive science and cultural sociology to the analysis of mental illness. Specifically, Wakefield's model—the "Foucault Sandwich"—considers both the universal and culturally relative aspects of mental disorders. In adopting Wakefield's model, one must begin with "the meat," representing the model's universalistic element. This translates to accepting the concept of "mental disorders" as representative of true dysfunction—a genuine breakdown in natural mental functioning rather than a social or cultural construction.

According to Wakefield, only after acknowledging this essential basis of mental disorders can one move on to the "crust" of the sandwich—the cultural aspects of mental illness. He argues that acknowledging real dysfunction frees one to situate mental disorders in their sociocultural context, a strategy that opens the door to fascinating research questions: Why is the concept of mental disorders salient at a particular time or in a particular culture? Why does this concept rather than another come to organize social attention and action? How is the deployment of the concept of mental disorders manipulated for purposes of power? According to Wakefield, his two-dimensional Foucault sandwich allows one to examine a "natural" phenomenon in its sociocultural context. And only when one engages in such analytic nesting, only when one stands at the intersection of the essential and the constructed, will culture's impact on cognition fully emerge.

In Chapter 14, Allan Horwitz responds to Wakefield's essay; he then proceeds to build on Wakefield's analytic model. Horwitz begins with high praise for Wakefield's universalistic definition of mental disorders. He argues that conceptualizing mental disorders as a harmful internal dysfunction provides both a solid basis for reevaluating and improving current diagnostic techniques, and a standard means for comparing mental disorders across differing cultural contexts. But in reflecting on the universalistic element of Wakefield's Foucault sandwich, Horwitz cites two important addenda that emanate from a cultural sociological perspective. First, he contends that the relationship between symptoms and disorders represents a key aspect of Wakefield's analysis. And he powerfully underscores the fact that symptoms of mental disorders are not direct indicators of underlying dysfunction. Unlike the realm of physical illnesses, where symptoms emerge from the disease, "the symptoms of mental disorders are symbolic representations of underlying vulnerabilities that are structured to fit dominant cultural models of 'appropriate' disorders in particular times and places." In noting this, Horwitz makes the important point that "culture has a critical role in structuring the symptoms through which internal dysfunctions become manifest . . . the symptoms of mental disorders are part of 'cultural tool kits' no less than language, fashion, and musical or culinary tastes" (Horwitz, p. 268).

Horwitz also notes an unintended benefit of Wakefield's universalistic definition of mental illness—and it is a benefit upon which he believes both cultural sociologists and students of mental illness should capitalize. According to Horwitz, conceptualizing mental disorders as a harmful internal dysfunction compliments the cultural sociological perspective "because it does not define as pathological the psychological consequences of stressful social arrangements." In this way, Wakefield's definition broadens the basis of sociocultural inquiry; it directs sociologists to focus on the conditions that Wakefield's analysis excludes—"the psychological consequences that result from the struggles of normal people who must cope with stressful structural arrangements" (Horwitz, p. 272).

Section V concludes with a third proposal for interdisciplinary research. In Chapter 15, cultural sociologist Paul DiMaggio provides readers with a blueprint for interdisciplinary exchange, one that elegantly intertwines current ideas on culture, cognition, and action. DiMaggio begins by selecting several foci of cognitive science research. Specifically, he highlights debates surrounding: (1) the differences in deliberative and automatic cognition—calm, measured thinking invoked with regard to complex issues versus the efficient, scripted, routine form of everyday action; (2) discussions that distinguish "hot" and "cold" cognition—cool and detached versus emotional, passionate thought; and (3) research establishing domain independence— "the relative independence of schematically organized knowledge and dispositions that pertain to different classes of life situations (for example, those related, respectively, to work and family)" (DiMaggio, p. 278). DiMaggio raises these debates because he believes that each one has the potential to advance sociological treatments of culture, especially treatments such as the "tool kit" approach which depict culture as a malleable entity differentially applied across different social situations. His article itemizes the specific contributions of cognitive science in this regard. Further, he suggests ways in which these cognitive science foci might directly feed new sociological theories of action. By specifically delineating the convergence of cognitive science and cultural sociology, DiMaggio outlines a strong foundation for an exciting intellectual collaboration.

CHAPTER 13

Fixing a Foucault Sandwich

COGNITIVE UNIVERSALS AND CULTURAL PARTICULARS IN THE CONCEPT OF MENTAL DISORDERS

Jerome C. Wakefield

The concept of mental disorder has often played a pivotal role in the development of new sociological theories of meaning, ranging from Goffman's (1963) role theory and Scheff's (1966; 1975) labeling theory to Foucault's (1965; 1978) genealogies and various social control theories (Horwitz 1982; 1990). I believe that this concept might be similarly pivotal in creating an account of cognition that encompasses both universalist and social foundations of cognition. In this chapter, I use the concept of mental disorder to illustrate and explore the distinction between universal and social elements in cognition. I start by using some passages from Eviatar Zerubaval's (1997) book, *Social Mindscapes*, to pose the problem of distinguishing the social from the universal and to illustrate how difficult the distinction can sometimes be. Then I present an analysis of the concept of mental disorder as "harmful mental dysfunction," based on earlier work of mine (Wakefield 1992a; 1992b; 1993). I examine my analysis of mental disorder with the issue of the universal versus the social in mind, hopefully drawing some lessons that might be helpful in illuminating the broader conceptual challenges facing sociologists of culture and cognition.

The Natural and the Social in Explanations of Cognition

In the last lines of his seminal book, *Social Mindscapes*, Eviatar Zerubavel suggests that sociological explanations of cognition must be integrated with explanations in terms of universal cognitive design, but that distinguishing the two is none too easy. He writes:

> Highlighting what cognitive individualism and universalism normally ignore is a tough epistemological challenge that resembles driving in a tunnel without bumping into either of its walls. Yet the ultimate goal should be to develop an integrative, multilevel approach to cognition that views us both as individuals, as human beings, and as social beings. Ultimately, only a science that addresses all three levels can provide a truly comprehensive account of how we think. (1997:113)

In insisting on the legitimacy of the universal level of explanation, Zerubavel rejects tired ideological positions that dismiss human nature as a social construction and dismiss the individual as an epiphenomenon of intersecting social practices and discourses. His acknowledgment that sociological explanation is not exhaustive is a strength of his account.

This complex vision presents us with a challenge. First, we must distinguish what varies from what is constant, or what requires explanation in terms of socially mediated factors from what is universal or natural or otherwise explainable independently of social structure. Second, we must integrate the two within one model. Of course, the categorization of a cognitive process as social or universal is not at all a dichotomous matter, even though, for ease of expression, I write as though it is. Most explanations of cognitive processes will contain elements of both the universal and the social. But once one accepts Zerubavel's multitiered explanatory framework, it is no longer acceptable to merely ignore (or "bracket") the problem of the universal and proceed with sociological analysis. The problem with this common strategy is that before one begins one's social analysis, one has already arbitrarily eliminated an alternative substantive hypothesis, namely, how the target meaning came into existence. Thus one is in danger of creating spurious "just so" social explanations. Of course, the universalist hypothesis can often be eliminated on obvious grounds, as when one is analyzing the seven-day structure of the American week. But in other domains, such as mental disorder, one cannot assume from the outset that everything is socially constructed; ignoring possible universalist factors may mean that one's interpretive cleverness in constructing a social explanation is wholly misguided. The challenge, then, is to distinguish what is likely socially mediated from what is not. I hope to show in this chapter that the concept of mental disorder provides an interesting case study in the subtleties of this challenge.

To show how surprisingly difficult it is to respect the natural/social distinction or even to be clear about it, I consider some further passages from Zerubavel's book. Zerubavel presents the semiotic idea of an "indicator" to illustrate how some meanings are not socially constructed:

> The most striking contrast is the one between symbols and indicators, which are distinctively characterized by the intrinsic (and thus inevitable) nature of their association with what they represent. The semiotic relation between an indicator and what it signifies to us is absolutely natural and does not require any artificial mediation in the form of social convention.
>
> Consider medical symptoms, those pieces of physical evidence we regard as "symptomatic," or "indicative," of particular diseases. The mental association of rectal bleeding

with cancer of the colon or of certain blisters and the viral condition we call chicken pox, for example, has absolutely nothing to do with social convention. Nor does the association of smoke with fire, of daffodils with spring, of a fast heartbeat with excitement, or of the height of a mercury column in a glass tube with the temperature. Such connections are certainly not something for which we ourselves are in any way responsible. (1997:70)

Certainly, we are not responsible for the causal links themselves between these various facts. But Zerubavel is saying more than that the causal association between daffodils and spring is not socially explainable. He is saying that the cognitive structure in our mind that represents this natural link (he calls this structure a "mental association," but we can ignore here the likely inadequacy of an associationist account of representation and meaning) is itself a natural and socially unmediated indicator of the daffodil-spring connection. The point is that given the nature of the facts and our exposure to those facts, it is not primarily social structure that explains why we come to represent things the way we do. Rather, the nature of our cognitive processing mechanisms explains why we form such a representation after perceiving certain kinds of evidence. Roughly, spring causes daffodils, and the occurrence of the spring-daffodil causal sequence causes in human observers a mental representation of the causal relationship; neither of these two events necessarily requires social explanation. Of course, social structures can purposely inhibit or otherwise interfere with the naturally designed working of our cognitive apparatus or with our access to the facts. But, active interference aside, more or less any human being from more or less any culture, if put in the right circumstances with normally functioning cognitive processes, will come to have certain kinds of representations after experiencing certain stimuli, and it is this counterfactual—not a survey of actual beliefs—that makes the process universal, not social.

However, there is another view expressed by Zerubavel that appears to be inconsistent with the above picture and more in tune with the current constructivist *Zeitgeist*. This other view is a social-constructivist view of concepts that is wholly at odds with there being any natural or universal mental connections:

We tend to forget that language itself rests on social convention and to regard the mental divisions it introduces as real. When we label our world, we often commit the fallacy of misplaced concreteness and regard the purely conventional mental gaps separating North America from Central America or business from pleasure as if they were part of nature.

It is important, therefore, to avoid the tendency to reify the conventional islands of meaning in which we organize the world in our minds and to remember that the gaps we envision separating them from one another are purely mental. In the real world, after all, there are no actual divides separating the moral from the immoral or the public from the private. Mental divisions as well as the entities they help delineate have no ontological status whatsoever. It is we ourselves who organize reality into separate mental compartments.

Classification, thus, is a process of actively "sculpting" islands of meaning rather than simply identifying already-existing natural ones. (1997:67)

The view of meaning expressed in this passage can be a corrective to a tendency for overreification of socially constructed categories. Nonetheless, this kind of constructivism seems inconsistent with the assertion that there is no social mediation in the connection between smoke and fire, blood and bowel cancer, daffodils and spring. Those are "already-existing natural" connections that have been sculpted by nature, not by us, and thus do have ontological status before we ever represent them. Even if *concepts* are socially deployed structures, that does not imply that *what the concepts refer to in the world* is socially constructed or that our *possession of the concepts* is explained primarily by social construction.

Moreover, granting the validity of Zerubavel's examples of socially constructed categories, still the fact that categories possess fuzzy boundaries does not always imply that what they refer to is not real or natural. There is a real distinction between red and blue, child and adult, death and life, even though there are no sharp boundaries between these pairs. If there are socially unmediated facts, as Zerubavel observes there are, and if our meaning system sometimes represents those facts due to universal cognitive processes that are not socially mediated, as Zerubavel suggests, then our classification system may contain some concepts that represent natural categories even if the distinctions represented are vague and fuzzy ones.

Indeed, the notion that fuzzy boundaries imply that a concept does not refer to a real distinction in nature is probably the most common fallacy in the literature on concepts. The confusion behind the "fuzzy boundary" argument emerges more fully in the following statement by Zerubavel (1997:66) of the same argument:

> Distinctions between "things" are not as sharp as (and the actual transitions among them far more gradual than) we may envision. As one might expect, the categories in which we organize the world in our minds are therefore also not as sharply delineated (that is, as "well-defined") as we may perhaps envision them. Membership in those categories is only a matter of degree, and the transition from member to non-member, therefore, rather gradual. The mental outlines for the categories "light" and "dark," for example, certainly overlap. . . . The transition from "masculine" to "feminine" is likewise gradual (and the differences within each gender, therefore, as significant as those between them), since even the distribution of purely physiological male and female features is rarely ever absolutely bipolar. (Although the female body is, on the average, somewhat less muscular and hairy than the male's, many women happen to have a more muscular and hairy body than many men.)

There has got to be something wrong here, because "light" and "dark" are surely naturally distinct conditions, even though there is a continuum connecting them. This illustrates the point that conceptual distinctions can refer to a real distinction by limiting their references to sets of fairly clear cases on either side and ignoring the continuum of intervening cases. But the more basic problem with this passage's account of concepts emerges in the argument regarding the classification of males and females, which ignores the distinction between superficial properties and underlying realities. It is claimed that the distinction between males and females is a fuzzy one and that membership in these categories is thus a gradual function. To show this, examples are presented of females who have superficial properties more typically associated with males. But the "graded membership" theory embraced in the passage should predict that such women are therefore not clear members of the category "female." The facts are just the opposite. Although it is surely correct that women differ more among themselves than they differ as a group from men, it is still the case that muscular, hirsute women are unquestionably members of the "female" category, as the passage presupposes.

This implies the opposite of what the passage is trying to argue; it implies that superficial properties like hairiness or muscularity ultimately have nothing to do with the criteria for membership in the categories "male" or "female." Beyond the hair, the muscles, and other such superficial traits, there is some conceptual representation—presumably an essentialist representation that postulates unknown, shared, underlying properties—that allows us to classify the described females as clear members of the female category despite the superficial properties. The superficial properties are often used to recognize males or females, but they are so used only as long as we believe that they correlate with deeper properties. And they are abandoned when they do not agree with those deeper criteria, as when we abandon our usual use of clothing as a recognition criterion for maleness or femaleness when we enter an environment in which we know cross-dressing is common. So the vague boundaries of these superficial properties has nothing at all to say about whether the concepts "male" and "female" also have vague boundaries or are natural or constructed.

The passage relies on the popular "prototype" theory of concepts put forward by the psychologist Eleanor Rosch (1973; Rosch and Mervis 1975), which in my view has been amply demonstrated not to work as an explanation of category membership (see Wakefield 1999a; 1999b). If membership in categories was determined by similarity to a prototype, then there could be no red spherical carrots or orange elongated tomatoes—yet I have seen and tasted both. Prototypes and similarity may play important roles in our cognitive processing, but they are not the ultimate basis for category membership judgments.

But Zerubavel, in the quoted passage, is correct to this extent: The fuzzy boundaries between categories—even natural categories—do allow scope for the sociology of cognition to explain how precise boundaries are fixed by societies, if they are. For example, there is a natural difference between a child and an adult, but there is no natural boundary. For various social purposes, we need to establish such a boundary—actually, many different such boundaries for different purposes—and the cut line is conceptually arbitrary in a way that requires sociological considerations to explain.

The social-constructivist version of Zerubavel's account inevitably contradicts the realist version of the account, causing Zerubavel to crash against the universalist wall of his self-described epistemological tunnel. Consider the following:

> Cognitive sociology recognizes the fact that we do not think just as individuals . . . reminding me, for example, that it is not as an individual but as a product of a particular social environment that I dismiss the fundamentalist account of the current AIDS epidemic as sheer nonsense, and that if my ten-year-old son already knows that the earth is round and that the world is made up of atoms it is only because he happens to live in the twentieth century. (1997:6–7)

Without in any way discounting the influence of our culture on our beliefs, it seems to me that this sort of talk is very misleading. If beliefs about daffodils blooming in spring are not socially mediated, why should beliefs about the earth being round be socially mediated? The only argument offered is that other people in other times did not know the earth was round, so the belief is relative to culture. But other people who live in flowerless deserts do not know about daffodils blooming in spring, yet that knowledge is not socially mediated in any interesting sense, according to Zerubavel.

Surely temporal and spatial reasons for lack of access to evidence constitute conceptually the same basic phenomenon. These days, we even have pictures of the earth from space and pictures of atoms, evidence that once you understand it, and assuming no active interference by social processes, more or less inevitably leads to belief, given universal evidence-processing mechanisms. True, people in earlier societies did not know the earth is round. But there is a big difference between something varying socially and something's variation being due to social structure. The elementary principle that correlation does not imply causality applies here; correlation of a belief with membership in certain societies does not imply that the belief is caused by the social structures of those societies.

Perhaps one could argue that some of the evidence for the roundness of the earth or the existence of atoms is based on technology that only certain cultures possess, unlike the daffodil case, where universal perceptual capacities are the only "technology" necessary. For this and other reasons, surely such beliefs do have some social aspects—as noted, the roles of social and universal explanation are a matter of degree that varies with context and with exactly what is being explained. So if the question is whether one's society influences the availability of evidence and thus belief, the answer is obviously "yes." However, if the question is whether possessing the belief given the available evidence (i.e., evidence that itself is not socially constructed in any theoretically interesting sense, even though its availability may be socially determined) is a by-product of social structure or part of a socially constructed belief system, the answer is likely "no." That is, it seems likely that almost any human being from almost any culture who is possessed of species-typical evidence-processing capacities and who is placed in the same relevant evidential position would believe what Zerubavel's son believes, for the same reason that anyone in a certain situation would believe that daffodils bloom in spring. The beliefs that the world is round and that there are atoms thus have relatively little to do with our social structure and much to do with the evidence and our universal cognitive tendencies.

As noted, social structures can of course interfere with the working of universal evidence processing by suppressing the evidence or creating suspicion about the integrity of the evidence or placing various social "spins" on the evidence. But the fact that social structures can interfere with or influence the functioning of a universal mechanism does not mean that when the mechanism works as designed, it is not a manifestation of a natural, universal mechanism. For example, speech capacity is universal in the relevant sense and is not explained by social structures, and this is not in the least disconfirmed by the fact that there are communities (e.g., monasteries) in which manifestations of this universal capacity are suppressed or by the fact that when one speaks and what one says are socially influenced.

Although Zerubavel acknowledges the universal, he suggests that sociology of cognition should be seen primarily as a corrective to excessive universalism, particularly the tendency of societies to see their own conventions as universal traits of human nature:

> Cognitive sociology helps us to avoid the danger of regarding the merely conventional as if it were part of the natural order by specifically highlighting that which is not entirely subjective yet at the same time not entirely objective either. Cognitive sociology tries to promote a greater awareness of our cognitive diversity as social beings. The more we become

aware of our cognitive differences as members of thought communities, the less likely we are to follow the common ethnocentric tendency to regard the particular way in which we ourselves happen to process the world in our minds as based on some absolute standard of "logic" or "reason" and, thus, as naturally or logically inevitable. (1997:9)

This emphasis makes sense in many areas of cognition, where there is a traditional bias in favor of universalism. But in the study of the concept of mental disorder, despite much empirical evidence for universalism, it is social theories that have predominated, from Scheff's (1966) labeling theory and Szasz's (1974) claim that mental disorders do not really exist to Foucault's (1965) genealogical theory. Zerubavel, too, embraces the social-explanatory approach to mental disorder in some brief comments:

> Another striking cognitive difference specifically addressed by the sociology of mind is the one between ordinary, "normal" thinkers and cognitive deviants such as the demented, whom we typically regard as "mentally disturbed" because they focus their attention, frame their experience, classify the world, reckon the time, and reason somewhat differently from the rest of us. The existence of cognitive deviance reminds us once again that the way most of us happen to process the world in our minds is neither naturally nor logically inevitable. It also implies the existence of various cognitive norms that affect as well as constrain the way we think. Like any other social norm, cognitive norms are something we learn. (1997:12)

This passage is puzzling in light of Zerubavel's earlier-quoted distinction between universal and social levels of explanation. It is unclear what Zerubavel's postulated universals of cognition refer to if not to certain capacities for attention and reasoning. Surely our uses of these universal capacities are structured and shaped by society and to that extent are within the scope of sociological explanation. But it is equally clear that there is a level of functional design that is not socially explainable and that is part of universal human nature, that things can go wrong with these universal functions, and that such failures would constitute disorders on at least partly non–socially defined grounds. Thus, given the distinctions provided by his own analytical framework, Zerubavel is unjustified in assuming that cognitive disorders *en masse* consist of violations of learned social norms for cognitive behavior rather than failures of innate cognitive mechanisms.

Zerubavel's lapse here underscores an important point: With respect to mental disorder, the primary need is not to correct excesses of universalist reification but rather to correct excesses of sociological explanation. We need an approach that takes account of cognitive universals in understanding both the concept of mental disorder itself and the conditions that the concept refers to. The trick is to acknowledge the universal without obscuring or abandoning genuine dimensions of social variability.

The Natural, the Universal, and Human Nature versus the Social

Before proceeding, I want to identify some potentially confusing ambiguities of terminology. I use "natural" in two different senses in this chapter. In one sense, the natural refers to what transcends culture or does not depend on cultural structure for its explanation. As in the above discussion, "natural" in this sense is often taken to mean the same as "universal," that is, unvarying across cultures. However, this equation is a bit misleading; if an asteroid hits someone on the head, that is a "natural" occurrence in this sense of "natural," but it is hardly universal. It is "natural" in the sense that it is not mediated by social variables. If a meteor shower hits a particular set of societies, and thus whether a given individual has a chance of getting struck by a meteor covaries with the individual's society, that still does not show that social structure is relevant to explaining either why the meteorites struck those individuals or the nature of the victims' conditions resulting from their being struck. (As above, correlation is not causality.) Similarly, to return to Zerubavel's example, the perception that daffodils bloom in the spring is not really universal, but does not depend in any theoretically interesting way on social structure and so in that sense is "natural" (i.e., not dependent on social structure for its explanation and thus not primarily within the explanatory domain of the sociology of cognition). So the "universal" in this sense need not be literally universal, and the "natural" is just whatever is outside the explanatory domain of the sociology of cognition. As we saw, there is a counterfactual sense in which such natural features and events—even when rare—*can* be considered universal, namely, the explanation *would* be the same and the events *would* turn out the same more or less whatever the social structure of the individuals involved.

The second sense of "natural" concerns "human nature," or the "natural functions" of human mental and physical processes, which will be considered in the remaining sections of the chapter. In this sense, what is "natural" is how people are designed to be. Human nature is, of course, universal to human beings, so this sense of "natural" overlaps with the earlier one; human nature, such as natural human cognitive processing mechanisms, is universal among human beings and is primarily explainable not by social structure but rather by the evolutionary history of the species. However, most natural occurrences in the first sense of "natural" have nothing to do with what is natural in this second sense; meteorites striking the heads of unlucky individuals has nothing to do with human nature.

The distinction between the two senses of "natural" becomes critical when we consider dysfunctions—breakdowns in designed human nature that are often considered disorders. Because they are failures of designed human nature, dysfunctions are the opposite of "natural" in the second sense; neither physical nor mental disorders are natural conditions. However, although dysfunctions are certainly not universal, they may be "natural" in the first sense to the extent that they are not socially constructed. That is, the fact that a condition is a breakdown in natural functioning has little or nothing to do with social structure (or at least, that is what I will argue below). So in this respect the fact that a condition is a dysfunction is, just like a meteor shower, outside the explanatory realm of the sociology of cognition. (Sociological factors may, however, certainly be responsible for causing a dysfunction or for how we react to a dysfunction—see below.) Thus, although dysfunctions are certainly not "natural" in the biological-design sense, they are just as natural as natural design itself in the sense of "natural" that refers to being outside the explanatory domain of the sociology of cognition. Social structure has no role in explaining why a certain condition is a dysfunction, if human nature itself (and specifically the ways people are designed to process information, of which the dysfunction is a failure) can be understood independent of culture.

Obviously, whether an account of a phenomenon does or does not fall under the explanatory domain of the sociology of cognition depends on exactly what one is trying to explain about that phenomenon. If functions and dysfunctions are natural categories, there are still many questions about the relation of social structures to such phenomena that require a sociological approach for their answer. I return to this point at the chapter's end. But now I turn to an examination of the concept of disorder with these distinctions in mind.

Presuppositions of the Conceptual Analysis of "Mental Disorder"

In attempting to analyze the concept of mental disorder, I accept the following provisional assumptions:

1. The point initially is to explain classificatory judgments that are widely shared and are considered clear instances of disorder or nondisorder. Elsewhere (Wakefield 1992a; 1992b; 1993; 1997a; 1997b; 1997c; 1997d), I have argued that no existing account manages to accomplish this basic task. (I do not review that argument here.) Once we have an account that explains our judgments about clear cases of disorder and nondisorder, we can then worry about more controversial cases. In any event, controversies will not necessarily be resolved by a correct analysis of the concept; rather, the analysis may only clarify the source of the disagreement and perhaps help explain why it seems intractable.

2. I take a realist view of concepts to this extent; I assume that a culture shares a mental representation for a concept. I consider the enterprise of conceptual analysis as analogous to a linguist studying the shared judgments of native English speakers about the grammaticality of various possible sentences in English and trying to formulate a theory of what rules of grammar are governing subjects' production of sentences. The conceptual analyst studies community members' shared classificatory judgments in response to actual and counterfactual cases and tries to discern the shared conceptual representation or rule that governs such judgments.

Note that there is no assumption that even widely shared and seemingly clear classificatory judgments are in fact correct relative to the classifiers' own classificatory concepts. There is a gap between possessing a concept and correctly judging that a certain thing falls under that concept, and people can agree on the concept but disagree—or even generally err—on the judgment. A good analysis will help to explain why people make the incorrect judgments they do on the basis of false beliefs that lead them to think that a condition does fall under their concept when in fact it does not.

3. There is no assumption that there is a precise or crisp boundary between disorder or nondisorder. Like most concepts, it is assumed that "mental disorder" has areas of indeterminacy, ambiguity, fuzziness, and vagueness, and that clear cases are accompanied by a penumbra of unclear cases. The function of the analysis is not to resolve artificially such fuzziness but to capture the clear cases and leave the fuzzy cases fuzzy, thus explaining our judgments.

4. I assume until proven otherwise that mental disorders (at least in one widely shared sense of "mental disorder," the one in which I am interested) are instances of disorder in the same sense that physical disorders are disorders. So both mental and physical examples are sometimes relevant to getting at the representational structure of the concept.

Note that this does *not* mean that mental disorders have to be physiological disorders. Although I cannot argue this point here (see Wakefield 1992a), contrary to Thomas Szasz's claims, the medical concept of disorder is itself a functional concept, not an anatomical or physiological concept; a lesion is not a disorder unless it causes functional failure, and functional failure without a lesion is still a disorder. So mental disorders are disorders of mental processes in the same sense that heart disorders are disorders of heart processes, but the logic of that sense is not dependent on there being a physiological lesion. To use the standard cognitive science analogy, there can be failures of the software even if the hardware is working perfectly well (Wakefield 1999c).

5. I focus on the question of what makes a mental condition a mental disorder. I leave aside the equally complex issue of what makes a condition mental versus physical. For present purposes, mental processes are simply those like emotion, thought, perception, motivation, language, intentional action, and other such processes. There is no intended Cartesian implication about any special ontological status of the mental—it is just an identified set of functions and processes. The deeper principle by which mental functions are classified as mental will not be pursued here, but it probably has something to do with the involvement of what philosophers and cognitive scientists call intentionality or representationality. All the mentioned processes have the feature of being about some represented state of affairs.

6. Despite the fact that "disorder" is a technical concept at the foundation of psychiatry and the other mental health professions, I assume until proven otherwise that this is a concept that is shared across the subcommunities in our culture. In particular, I assume that the concept of disorder is shared by laypeople and professionals, and I evaluate examples with this in mind. This assumption goes against recent arguments that "mental disorder" is a purely technical concept defined only by an arcane professional discourse (e.g., Kirmayer and Young 1999). The proof of my assumption that the concept is shared among laypeople and professionals will ultimately lie in the empirical pudding: Do lay and professional judgments work the same way? I comment later on some preliminary evidence that suggests that, in one diagnostic area, they do.

7. I cannot delve into the theory of concepts here in any detail, but one assumption is critical: Concepts are not the same as beliefs or theories about the things that fall under a concept (see Wakefield 1994a). To take a mundane example, two people can share exactly the same concept of "bachelor" but come away from a gathering with entirely different beliefs about which men are bachelors, because of different theories they have about the evidence (e.g., one believes that lack of a wedding ring is a good sign of bachelorhood,

while the other thinks it is not, etc.). Or two scientists can have entirely different theories of a natural phenomenon (e.g., one can theorize that fire is phlogiston release, while another may theorize that fire is rapid oxidation) while having exactly the same concept of the phenomenon itself; indeed, it is only the shared concept that allows the two scientists to have a fruitful dispute over who is right about fire.

Having stated my background assumptions, I turn to the analysis of the concept of disorder.

The Concept of Mental Disorder

So what does the term "mental disorder" mean? I claim but cannot fully defend here (see Wakefield 1992a) that two criteria are central to the definition of a disorder.

First, the condition must be harmful according to social values. "Harm" is construed rather broadly here. For example, the harm can be to the self or to others and can include any condition socially judged as negative. This requirement represents the practical aspect of the concept of disorder; unless a condition is harmful and thus at least potentially warrants attention or action, it is not considered a disorder.

Some analyses of "disorder" stop at this point; they maintain that a mental disorder is simply a socially disapproved mental condition (e.g., Sedgwick 1973; 1982). But there is a vast realm of negative mental conditions that are not considered disorders, for example, ignorance, lack of skill, lack of talent, low intelligence, illiteracy, criminality, bad manners, foolishness, and moral weakness. There are many negative things that can happen to a person, and the category "mental disorder" is defined as one category within the universe of such negative conditions.

Can the distinction be that mental disorder is residual rule-breaking (Scheff 1966)—that is, negative behavior that is not covered by any other existing category, such as crime, bad manners, or illiteracy, as labeling theorists have claimed? No, because many symptoms that can be indicative of mental disorder do fall under one of these categories. For example, criminality may be a symptom of antisocial personality disorder, rudeness may be a symptom of Tourette's syndrome, and illiteracy may be a symptom of reading disorder. Nor can the distinction be that mental disorders are statistically abnormal, for many nondisordered mental conditions are statistically abnormal as well. (Indeed, many physical disorders are statistically normal, such as, in our society, periodontal disease, tooth decay, atherosclerosis, and mild lung inflammation, and in other societies, a host of endemic diseases.) So we need some other way to distinguish disorders from other negative conditions.

I suggest that the second basic intuition underlying judgments of disorder is that something has gone wrong with some part of the organism. So the additional requirement is that to be a disorder, a mental condition must be due to a mental dysfunction, by which I mean that some mental process must be failing to perform its natural function or failing to work as it was designed to work. Note that exactly the same requirement applies to physical disorders. I use the controversial term "design" because, although people are obviously not literally designed, it is the only term that satisfactorily describes the very special features involved here. The designlike features of human beings and other organisms are readily apparent and are perhaps the most remarkable facts about them. It cannot be an accident that our eyes enable us to see, our hands to grasp, and so on. The same observation applies to our mental processes; it cannot be accidental that thinking processes enable us to reason somewhat rationally about how to obtain what we desire, that our thirst and hunger push us to ingest needed water and food, that we often feel fear just when it might save us from danger, and so on. The mechanisms underlying these benefits must have been shaped to provide the benefits, and we call such designed benefits "natural functions." So a mental disorder is a harmful failure of a mental function, such as functions involved in emotion, thought, motivation, language, and so on.

But how can an effect, such as seeing, shape the very feature that causes it, such as the eyes? Although there have been many theories of how such seemingly miraculous and beneficial processes could have come about and could have been shaped by their effects—such as Aristotle's notion of "final causes" and theological notions of God's design—we now know that such designlike features are due to natural selection. But most cultures have not known about evolution. The critical element for formulating a concept of disorder, an element that is shared across millennia and across cultures, is the recognition of natural functions, whatever the preferred explanation for how they came to exist. For example, fundamentalist Christian communities reject evolutionary theory, but they too embrace the notion of designlike human features and they therefore share secular society's notions of dysfunction and disorder.

The term "dysfunction" is used with many different meanings, so why choose the "failure of natural function" sense? The medically relevant sense of "dysfunction" is clearly *not* the colloquial sense in which the term refers to failure of an individual to perform well in a social role or in a given environment, as in assertions such as: "I'm in a dysfunctional relationship" or "Discomfort with hierarchical power structures is dysfunctional in today's corporate environment." These kinds of problems need not be individual disorders. Moreover, the kinds of functions that are relevant are *not* those that result from social or personal decisions to use a part of the mind or body in a certain way. For example, although there is a colloquial sense in which the nose has the function of holding up one's eyeglasses, the fact that an individual's nose does not do a good job of holding up his or her glasses implies nothing in itself about nasal pathology. Nor are natural functions merely the beneficial effects of a mechanism. The language of function is used to indicate that certain effects are so complex, beneficial, and intricately structured that they cannot be accidental side effects of random causal processes. Instead, like the intentionally designed functions of artifacts, certain effects must somehow be part of the explanation of why the underlying mechanisms exist and are structured as they are. We are left, then, with the conclusion that the only functions that are relevant are those that are the "natural functions" of some internal mechanism—that is, those functions that the mechanism possesses in virtue of how human beings are designed. A dysfunction, then, is a failure of an internal mechanism to perform one of the functions for which it is naturally designed.

One might object that what goes wrong in disorders is sometimes a social function that has nothing to do with natural, universal categories. For example, reading disorders seem to be failures of a social function, for there is nothing natural or designed about reading. However, illiteracy involves the very same kind of harm as reading disorders, yet it is not considered a disorder. Inability to read is only considered indicative of disorder when circumstances suggest that the reason for the inability lies in a failure of some brain mechanism to perform its natural function. There are many failures of individuals to fulfill social functions, and they are not considered disorders unless they are attributed to a failed natural function.

If one looks down the list of disorders in the American Psychiatric Association's *Diagnostic and Statistical Manual of Mental Disorders* (DSM; 1994), it is apparent that by and large it is a list of the various ways that something can go wrong with the seemingly designed features of the mind. Very roughly, psychotic disorders involve failures of thought processes to work as designed, anxiety disorders involve failures of anxiety- and fear-generating mechanisms to work as designed, depressive disorders involve failures of sadness and loss-response regulating mechanisms, disruptive behavior disorders of children involve failures of socialization processes and processes underlying conscience and social cooperation, sleep disorders involve failure of sleep processes to function properly, sexual dysfunctions involve failures of various mechanisms involved in sexual motivation and response, eating disorders involve failures of appetitive mechanisms, and so on. There is also a certain amount of nonsense in the manual; however, in the vast majority of categories, a good case can be made that the category is inspired by conditions that even a layperson would correctly recognize as a failure of designed functioning.

When we distinguish normal grief from pathological depression, or normal delinquent behavior from conduct disorder, or normal criminality from antisocial personality disorder, or normal unhappiness from adjustment disorder, or illiteracy from reading disorder, or normal lack of empathy for enemies of one's group from sociopathic lack of empathy for anyone, or normal childhood rambunctiousness from attention-deficit hyperactivity disorder, we are implicitly using the "failure-of-designed-function" criterion. All of these conditions—normal and abnormal—are disvalued and harmful conditions, and the effects of the normal and pathological conditions can be quite similar behaviorally. Yet some are considered pathological and some not. The natural-function criterion explains these distinctions.

It bears emphasis that even biological conditions that are harmful in the current environment are not considered disorders if they are considered designed features. For example, the taste preference for fat is not considered a disorder, even though in today's food-rich environment it may kill you, because it is considered a designed feature that helped us to obtain needed calories in a previous food-scarce environment. Again, higher than average male aggressiveness is not considered a mass disorder of men even though in today's society it is arguably harmful, because it is considered the way men are designed. Feminists sometimes claim that men are suffering from a mass disorder of testosterone poisoning, but this is generally taken to be a joke and not considered a serious classificatory judgment. (Of course, there are disorders of male aggressiveness; here, as elsewhere, individuals may have disordered responses of designed features.)

In sum, a mental disorder is a harmful mental dysfunction. If the harmful dysfunction analysis is correct, then a society's categories of mental disorder offer two pieces of information. First, they indicate some conditions that the society considers negative or harmful. Second, they indirectly reveal what the society thinks about the natural or designed working of the human mind.

"Harmful Mental Dysfunction" as a Universal Concept of Mental Disorder

I now consider what is universal across cultures with respect to mental disorder. I make two claims in this regard.

The first claim is that the concept of mental disorder itself is more or less universal. When I say that the concept of mental disorder is more or less universal, I do not mean what some conceptual relativists mean—that while every society has some concept that classifies as deviant some or all of those whom we would classify as mentally disordered, the actual concepts such societies use might be quite different from our own. One often hears this view expressed in the statement "the concept of mental disorder varies from culture to culture" or "different cultures have different concepts of mental disorder." I think this claim is not merely false but incoherent. To have the concept of mental disorder is to have the concept of a harmful dysfunction, or whatever else it is that we mean by our concept of mental disorder. This is not ethnocentrism but just the logic of the translational situation. Any other concept—such as mental suffering or mental deviance—is not the concept of mental disorder but a different concept. We have or we can create these other concepts as well, so it is hard to see why one would consider another culture's concept of mental suffering, say, as our concept of mental disorder rather than as our concept of mental suffering. Either other cultures do have the concept of mental disorder—that is, the same concept we have—or they have no concept of mental disorder at all, although they may have other concepts that perform some of the same social functions as our concept of mental disorder.

The evidence for the universality of mental disorder has been reviewed by others (e.g., Horwitz 1982), and I do not try to defend this claim here. I have collected some as-yet-unpublished data suggesting that, contrary to common claims, professional and laypeople in our society do seem to share the same concept of disorder, at least as applied to judgments of whether adolescent antisocial behavior is disordered or not, based on symptoms and contextual information. That is, the concept of disorder does seem to be shared across various "cognitive communities" (Zerubavel 1997) in our culture. So, contrary to Kirmayer's (1994; see also Kirmayer and Young 1999) claim, disorder is not defined strictly by a technical discourse. Laypeople do apparently understand how to make disorder judgments. Those who deny that the concept of mental disorder is universal generally confuse other things which do vary, like theories of disorder, with the concept itself, and I discuss these fallacies elsewhere (e.g., Wakefield 1994b).

Rather than reviewing such evidence here, I attempt to illustrate what a universalist explanation would look like, given that the concept is certainly not an innately programmed feature of the mind. Why should this particular concept, which is not innately programmed, arise universally or almost universally in human societies?

Presumably the answer must lie in an interaction between universal cognitive factors and universal human circumstances. The case for universalism might be based on an intersection of the following three claims about human categorization:

First, people are causal theoreticians about almost anything they care about. Because they care about potential harms, they try to classify them by causal sources. Second, people understand notions of design and natural functions and they notice the nonaccidental, designed quality of many human features. They thus understand that some features require functional explanations and that some conditions are failures of functions. Third, human beings are essentialist conceptualizers; they have a tendency to categorize things not in terms of observable features but in terms of inferred, unobservable, and often as-yet-unknown commonalities. In the case of mental disorder, the commonality is unobservable failures of unknown, designed, mental mechanisms, inferred fallibly from surface symptoms and their context. For example, ice and liquid water were recognized to be the same substance long before molecular theory came along, because the fact that they so easily could be transformed one into the other suggested that they are the same essential stuff in different forms. This essentialist tendency is so strong that it is difficult to create a concept that is not so interpreted. For example, if one explicitly and nonessentialistically defines "underclass" as those who have been on welfare for five years or more, people will immediately tend to read into the concept a presupposition that there is some unknown essential property, perhaps a personality configuration, shared by the members of the defined category. At any rate, there is evidence from developmental psychology that all three of the described cognitive tendencies are innately programmed or at least regular and early occurrences. Given that people have these features and they live in an environment where there are in fact disorders, the formation of the concept of disorder is very likely to occur.

Of course, essentialism can mislead us, and essentialism has therefore come in for much criticism. However, a lot of the controversy about essentialism fails to distinguish the bare essentialist logic of our concepts that postulate some underlying commonality from the more politically fraught question of exactly what the essence is and whether inflated beliefs about essences are used as tools of power. For example, one must distinguish the question of whether specific oppressive views of the essence of femaleness versus maleness have been deployed in our society and need to be challenged, from the question of whether the concepts of maleness and femaleness are essentialist concepts defined in terms of some unknown, more minimal, underlying biological properties and whether there in fact might be such properties. Sometimes essentialistically defined concepts lead us astray because there is no essence (e.g., "jade" turns out not to be a substance but really several different similar types of gems), but at other times the concept does successfully pick out a set of things that do share some common underlying property (e.g., water in all its many forms is H_2O; maleness and femaleness are understandable roughly in terms of certain genetic properties). With respect to mental disorders, the common property that we now know is picked out is failure of evolved mental functions, so here the essentialist definition succeeds in picking out a real property.

In any event, if we do tend to be essentialists by nature, then we had better confront that fact. Ann Stoler, an anthropologist and Foucault scholar at the University of Michigan, notes that by failing to take our innate cognitive tendencies seriously, social constructionists may be dodging the uncomfortable question as to whether oppressive ideologies like racism and sexism acquire the weight they do because of the ways in which they build upon universal cognitive properties.

Now, if we put together these three (claimed) universal cognitive tendencies—that is, causal theorizing about sources of harm, functionally explaining designlike beneficial features, and essentialist reference to hidden defining features—then we get the concept of disorder. For the concept of disorder categorizes harms by their cause, and that cause is a failure of a designed, functionally explained feature that usually benefits us. Because we have no surface property that always indicates function or dysfunction, we simply define disorder as any condition that is caused by a failure of the sort of designlike features with which we are familiar from eyes, thirst, and so on.

A second thing about mental disorder that, in an important sense, is independent of social explanation is what conditions are dysfunctions. What are believed to be dysfunctions may vary, and what dysfunctions actually occur locally may vary, but the conditions that would be recognized as dysfunctions under ideal evidential circumstances are the same, namely, genuine failures of human design. That is, dysfunction is an "objective" concept.

Zerubavel notes that certain facts, like the fact that rectal bleeding may indicate colon cancer or the fact that daffodils bloom in spring, are not mediated by social convention, and our mental representations of these processes need not be either if we are in the right evidential position. Similarly, there is nothing social about the fact that certain conditions are dysfunctions. There is, of course, a large measure of universality in beliefs about dysfunctions, because many dysfunctions occur cross-culturally and are obviously recognizable to everyone as dysfunctions. But I am saying something more. We think that a condition is a disorder only if it is truly a failure of how human beings are designed to function. We count ourselves as having been wrong if this does not turn out to be true, and this self-correction process reveals that we are all aiming to identify the same set of conditions. So, to take a physical example, in some isolated societies malaria and hookworm were so endemic that it was believed that they were normal until contact with Westerners revealed that these conditions are interferences with designed functioning, and these societies changed their minds. Or consider the convenient American belief that it is "natural" for babies to cry a lot, which was thrown into question by cross-cultural work showing that in cultures where babies are held more, they do not cry at anywhere near the rate of American babies. We believe that moderate overweight is not a disorder but rather a matter of indulging one's appetites. But if a recent discovery is upheld, one that suggests, in some instances, being overweight results from a virus that disrupts appetite regulation, then we will all change our minds. In sum, we think that a condition is a disorder only if it is truly a failure of how human beings are designed to function, and we count ourselves as having been wrong if this does not turn out to be true. The dysfunction component of the concept of disorder is thus an objective concept referring not to what people happen to believe (in the way that value concepts refer to whatever they happen to value), but to what they would acknowledge to be true under ideal evidential circumstances. And that does not vary cross-culturally.

One weakness of normative or skeptical views of mental disorder, those that ignore the objectivity of "dysfunction," is that they offer no ground from which to mount a critique of psychiatric diagnostic criteria. If all criteria are equally invalid, then there is no hope of improving the criteria to make them valid, and any set of criteria is just as invalid as any other. This is not how most of us think about the situation. For example, we think that the conservative Victorian physicians were just plain wrong to classify masturbation and clitoral orgasm as disorders, that antebellum Southern physicians were just plain wrong to classify runaway slaves as suffering from drapetomania, and that Freud was just plain wrong to classify women who lacked the elusive vaginal orgasm as disordered. But if the normativists are right, then you have to say that relative to the values of their day among those making the diagnoses, these were genuine disorders and perfectly correct diagnoses. Or if the skeptics are right, then you have to say that these diagnoses are no more wrong than are our diagnoses of schizophrenia or panic disorder or manic depression. Either way, the ability to make needed distinctions is lost. The objectivity of "dysfunction" not only allows one to make such discriminations, it enables one to explain *why* various diagnostic practices are incorrect—namely, because they fail to pick out conditions genuinely caused by dysfunctions.

The objectivity of dysfunction limits the cultural relativity of "disorder." Dysfunctions define the space of possible disorders, and cultural values determine which dysfunctions are considered disorders. Disorders cannot be manufactured wholly out of values.

What is Socially Explainable about the Concept of Mental Disorder?

I finally come to the question of variation. Even if the concept of mental disorder itself is shared across cultures, there are still several ways that judgments of disorder and nondisorder can vary.

First, the same dysfunctions may express themselves in different behaviors and symptoms. Due to various cultural factors, for example, the dysfunctions underlying schizophrenia or depression may lead to different behaviors.

Second, the social circumstances of a culture may change the likelihood that a given dysfunction will occur. Just as we do not suffer from hookworm, and many other societies do not suffer as we do from high rates of heart disease, the occurrence of mental dysfunctions may differ as well because of variations in local child-rearing and socialization practices. To take some obvious examples: In cultures where thinness is not held out as an aesthetic ideal, anorexia nervosa is unlikely to occur. In low-stress cultures, anxiety disorders are unlikely to be triggered. In societies without snakes, such as New Zealand, the childhood conditions under which snake phobias develop are unlikely to occur. And in cultures that are more shame-oriented than our own, intense pathological shame responses may occur that do not occur in our society.

A third source of variation is that different cultures possess different values, and as a result some cultures do not classify some genuine dysfunctions as disorders. For example: Inability to learn to read due to a minimal brain dysfunction is harmful in literate societies and thus considered a disorder, but it is not harmful in preliterate societies and thus is not a disorder in those societies. In some cultures where skin shade is important, simple albinism is considered a disorder, whereas in other cultures it is considered a benign anomaly. Someone who has cognitive dysfunctions that make it impossible to hold a job in our society might be capable of work in a society that makes different demands from those we do on cognitive functioning, and might not be considered disordered in that society. And when the phenomenon we label "agoraphobia" occurs in a woman in some non-Western societies, it is not considered a disorder because a woman's place is perceived to be in the home and there is no tension between the desire to stay home and cultural expectations, as there is in our society.

A fourth source of variation is different theories about human nature, leading to different beliefs about what conditions indicate a dysfunction. (However, as noted, such beliefs should not be confused with the question of whether a condition in fact constitutes a dysfunction; cultural beliefs can be wrong on this count and are correctable.) A culture's theory of how the mind is naturally supposed to operate is likely to be influenced by cultural values. For example, the very existence of the DSM category of oppositional-defiant disorder of children implies a theory that it is natural for children to obey their parents and comply with adult directives. It is unclear whether this is an accurate view of child development or a wish-fulfillment fantasy in a culture that leaves little time for working out conflicts with children.

It is certainly easy to project one's values into nature and thus to mistake what is disvalued for a failure of designed functioning. The antebellum Southern view that certain people are designed to be slaves and that runaway slaves suffer from the disorder of drapetomania is one of the more blatant instances of such projection. But one must wonder: When we use DSM criteria to diagnose children as "conduct-disordered" partly on the basis of the fact that they have run away from home, and we do this without considering the quality of the relationship between the child and the parents, are we being just as potentially oppressive to some nondisordered children?

One reason why locally disvalued conditions might appear to be disordered when they are not is that socially valued conditions are likely to be reinforced and thus statistically normal in a culture and may therefore seem functionally normal. Consequently, it may seem as if some special dysfunction is needed to cause deviation from the norm. For example, in a society where disciplined behavior in school is the norm, a child who does not stay in his seat, who is not sufficiently quiet during class, and who is not responsive to the teacher's requests may be seen as suffering from an internal dysfunction and thus a disorder. In fact the child's behavior may be a normal-range response to the constraining conditions of school. Indeed, it may be due to only a massive constriction of normal modes of childhood activity that most children sit quietly in class in the first place.

Some projections of social values take the form of developmental theories that are claimed to describe a designed developmental progression but that in fact simply describe the sequences of psychological changes that lead to the culture's preferred outcomes. Thus, for example, the currently popular theory of attachment and separation, and corresponding accounts of disorders of these processes, may express value assumptions local to our culture, which prizes the ability of children to be autonomous and to separate early and often from parents.

Variations in theories of dysfunction within a culture can also lead to differences in classificatory judgments given the same evidence and the same concept of disorder. For example, some people think that anyone who experiences sexual activity during childhood must suffer from a dysfunction as a result, so they will interpret any negative emotions or behaviors on the part of those who have experienced such activity as indicative of a mental dysfunction caused by the activity, even in cases where other observers would see no evidence of dysfunction or disorder.

A final example: In Victorian times, many conservative physicians as well as laypeople considered a woman who had orgasms during intercourse to be disordered. Now most physicians and laypeople consider a woman who *does not* have orgasms during intercourse to be disordered. How can we understand this disagreement, if we and the Victorians share the same concept of mental disorder? The answer is that the Victorian physicians believed that God designed women not to experience intense sexual pleasure and that the pathological reaction was caused by excessive stimulation. In contrast, recent sexologists theorize that women are designed to have orgasms during intercourse, despite their rejection of the Freudian notion of a vaginal orgasm. Such differences over diagnosis almost always represent a difference in theories of natural function and dysfunction. And, unlike values or social constructs, such beliefs are understood to be factually right or wrong, and are correctable.

The fifth and final reason for cultural variation is that both the harm and dysfunction components of mental disorder suffer from indeterminacy, ambiguity, and vague boundaries. This is no impediment to "mental disorder" being a perfectly good concept that picks out clear instances and noninstances of disorder. But it does mean that different cultures may resolve these ambiguities or draw boundaries in different ways. Moreover, within a culture there may be disputes over how to resolve ambiguities or draw boundaries, with different factions attempting to exploit the concept in ways that serve their interests. Such issues of concept deployment provide material for a Foucauldian analysis of the workings of power through our concepts. Even though "mental disorder" is a universal concept, and functions and dysfunctions are natural—not socially constructed—facts, the social roles of these concepts and the ways they are deployed vary across cultures and require sociological analysis. Thus even universal concepts are suitable targets for what might be dubbed a "sociology of concept deployment." I briefly and very schematically develop this point in the concluding section.

The Foucault Sandwich

As noted earlier, to have an intellectually coherent basis for critiquing the misuse of diagnosis of mental disorder in our society and others (e.g., "runaway slave disease"; the Soviets' diagnosis of political dissenters), one had better first understand what it would be to use the concept of mental disorder correctly. This means acknowledging that there are naturally designed human psychological processes that are not socially constructed and that such processes can go harmfully wrong, and that pretty much universally, such failures are collected under the concept of mental disorder. The understanding of disorder as harmful dysfunction allows one to critique psychiatric criteria based on the very concepts that are presupposed by and lie at the foundation of psychiatry itself. Such a critique is hard for the psychiatric community to ignore.

Only an account of human nature can form an adequate foundation for a compelling social critique, for it is only relative to the needs dictated by human nature that a compelling case can be made that social structures have gone wrong. Having violated this principle, Foucault's resultant difficulties due to his relativism are well known and are often summarized in the phrase: "Where can Foucault stand?" That is, if everything is constructed in accordance with the working of power—including, for example, one's sense of justice and even the preference for pleasure over pain—then what is the independent basis for arguing that any particular social arrangement is better than any other? In the domain of mental disorder, it would seem that analyzing the concept of mental disorder and acknowledging that there really are mental dysfunctions in the literal sense of failures of naturally designed functions give one a place to stand and liberate one to make needed distinctions.

Does this mean that the Foucauldian approach must be rejected when one is examining a universally held concept or a concept referring to socially unmediated phenomena? Not at all. Rather, it means that a Foucauldian critique, in terms of the power sources and implications of the concept, has to be integrated with a prior conceptual analysis in a way that respects the reality of the concept and what it refers to. I have come to call this vision of integration the "Foucault sandwich."

How do you fix a Foucault sandwich? You start by doing a conceptual analysis, where appropriate (this is the filler of the sandwich). You have to understand a concept before you can understand how it is used for purposes of power. But the conceptual analysis is concerned exclusively with the logic of the concept, not with power. The logic of a concept has a power all of its own for shaping thought because of universal human cognitive tendencies.

Although I focus on concepts for ease of expression, note that everything said here about concepts has a parallel in the approach to beliefs and the evidence for them. For example, Foucault is surely right that there is a social-control dimension to psychoanalysis, with roots in the medieval confessional. But that fact does not begin to tell us whether Freud's theories are right or wrong, or whether they are evidentially supported—and evidential support has a power of persuasion all of its own, based on universal human cognitive architecture that transcends social explanation. Thus Foucault's analysis does not tell us to what degree the evidence itself may, via universal information-processing mechanisms, be influencing adherence to psychoanalysis in a given culture at a given time.

The moral is paradoxical and striking in its implications for sociological analysis: To understand psychoanalysis as a cultural phenomenon, one must simultaneously assess the evidence for and against Freud's theories. Similarly, to understand judgments of mental disorder as a cultural phenomenon, one must simultaneously analyze the logic of the concept and assess the evidence that various conditions fall under the concept. To do less is to ignore a possible nonsociological causal pathway to belief and thus to leave one's sociological analysis without *prima facie* credibility.

Once the conceptual analysis is completed, two related Foucauldian analyses of the conceptual structure can be undertaken and fitted around the conceptual analysis. First, there is the question: Why is this concept salient at this time in this culture? This analysis places the concept in a broader historical-social context, perhaps offering a Foucauldian genealogy explaining how one concept rather than another came into prominence and organized thought and action. For example, one might ask why the concept of mental disorder is so important in our culture rather than other related concepts, and why mental disorder more than other sources of suffering is privileged with respect to social resources available for help. So, placing the conceptual analysis in a broader social context, you have the Foucauldian strategic question: Why this concept?

On the other side, the conceptual structure itself is the assumed context for a more detailed Foucauldian tactical question: How is the deployment of this concept in classificatory judgments manipulated for purposes of power? As noted, every concept contains indeterminacy, ambiguity, and boundary vagueness—and these provide ample opportunities for classificatory judgments to be manipulated so as to gain advantage from the deployment of the concept in one way or another. Controversies over application of concepts such as mental disorder are possible because essentialist concepts, especially, are very abstract, and there are a great many intervening steps between the concept itself and concrete classificatory judgments, offering ample room for disagreement. Understanding the logic of the underlying abstract concept is critical in an analysis of such disputes because it is the logic of the concept that explains why certain (perhaps fallacious) inferences might seem to make sense whereas others do not. That is, the concept helps explain the nature and possibilities of the disputes over deployment. Thus, for example, we might ask how new categories of behaviors come to be construed as disorders or reconstrued as nondisorders by the DSM (i.e., introduced into or removed from the manual) and the degree to which the logic of the concept of disorder and the evidence for dysfunction versus other social processes determine such changes. We also might look at what techniques are used to extend "mental disorder" to larger ranges of conditions when the economic interests of drug manufacturers and therapists are at stake—such as the current push to identify depression in general medical practices as a disorder without regard to a contextual understanding of whether the condition is due to a real loss and thus might not be a disorder at all.

The success of the tactical moves made in attempting to deploy a concept will depend on convincing others that the deployment is warranted. The nature and success of such moves will depend very sensitively on the logic of the concept and how its logical features can be exploited. It is thus only by integrating all three of the above analytical levels—that is, by placing the conceptual or evidential analysis between two layers of Foucauldian analysis—that a complete social explanation of a concept and its deployment can be achieved. It is thus surely the case, as psychologist Phoebe Ellsworth has recently noted, that the meeting of human universals and culture is where the interesting questions begin. Indeed, if the above analysis is correct, then only by integrating the universal and the social can a coherent and persuasive investigation of the social occur.

References

American Psychiatric Association. 1994. *Diagnostic and Statistical Manual of Mental Disorders*, 4th ed. Washington, DC: American Psychiatric Association.

Foucault, M. 1965. *Madness and Civilization: A History of Insanity in the Age of Reason*. Translated by R. Howard. New York: Pantheon.

———. 1978. *History of Sexuality*, vol. 1. New York: Pantheon.

Goffman, E. 1963. *Stigma: Notes on the Management of Spoiled Identity*. Englewood Cliffs, NJ: Prentice-Hall.

Horwitz, A. V. 1982. *The Social Control of Mental Illness*. New York: Academic Press.

———. 1990. *The Logic of Social Control*. New York: Plenum Press.

Kirmayer, L. J. 1994. "Rejoinder to Professor Wakefield." Pp. 17–20 in *Controversial Issues in Mental Health*, edited by S. A. Kirk and S. D. Einbinder. Boston, MA: Allyn and Bacon.

Kirmayer, L. J. and A. Young. 1999. "Culture and Context in the Evolutionary Concept of Mental Disorder." *Journal of Abnormal Psychology* 108(3):446–52.

Rosch, E. R. 1973. "Natural Categories." *Cognitive Psychology* 4:328–50.

Rosch, E. R. and C. B. Mervis. 1975. "Family Resemblances: Studies in the Internal Structure of Categories." *Cognitive Psychology* 7:573–605.

Scheff, T. J. 1966. *Being Mentally Ill: A Sociological Theory*. Chicago, IL: Aldine.

———., ed. 1975. *Labeling Madness*. Englewood Cliffs, NJ: Prentice-Hall.

Sedgwick, P. 1973. "Illness—Mental and Otherwise." *Hastings Center Studies* 3:19–58.

———. 1982. *Psycho Politics*. New York: Harper & Row.

Szasz, T. S. 1974. *The Myth of Mental Illness: Foundations of a Theory of Personal Conduct*, Rev. ed. New York: Harper & Row.

Wakefield, J. C. 1992a. "The Concept of Mental Disorder: On the Boundary Between Biological Facts and Social Values." *American Psychologist* 47:373–88.

———. 1992b. "Disorder as Harmful Dysfunction: A Conceptual Critique of DSM-III-R's Definition of Mental Disorder." *Psychological Review* 99:232–47.

———. 1993. "Limits of Operationalization: A Critique of Spitzer and Endicott's (1978) Proposed Operational Criteria for Mental Disorder." *Journal of Abnormal Psychology* 102:160–72.

———. 1994a. "Is the Concept of Mental Disorder Culturally Relative?" Pp. 11–17 in *Controversial Issues in Mental Health*, edited by S. A. Kirk and S. D. Einbinder. Boston, MA: Allyn and Bacon.

———. 1994b. "Theories Are Not Concepts: Reply to Kirmayer." Pp. 9–11 in *Controversial Issues in Mental Health*, edited by S. A. Kirk and S. D. Einbinder. Boston, MA: Allyn and Bacon.

———. 1997a. "Normal Inability Versus Pathological Disability: Why Ossorio's (1985) Definition of Mental Disorder Is Not Sufficient." *Clinical Psychology: Science and Practice* 4:249–58.

———. 1997b. "When Is Development Disordered? Developmental Psychopathology and the Harmful Dysfunction Analysis of Mental Disorder. *Development and Psychopathology* 9:269–90.

———. 1997c. "Diagnosing DSM-IV, Part 2: Eysenck (1986) and the Essentialist Fallacy." *Behavior Research and Therapy* 35:651–66.

———. 1997d. "Diagnosing DSM-IV, Part 1: DSM-IV and the Concept of Mental Disorder." *Behavior Research and Therapy* 35:633–50.

———. 1999a. "Evolutionary versus Prototype Analyses of the Concept of Disorder." *Journal of Abnormal Psychology* 108: 374–99.

———. 1999b. "Disorder as a Black Box Essentialist Concept." *Journal of Abnormal Psychology* 108:465–72.

———. 1999c. "Philosophy of Science and the Progressiveness of the DSM's Theory-Neutral Nosology: Response to Follette and Houts, Part 1." *Behavior Research and Therapy* 37:963–99.

Zerubavel, E. 1997. *Social Mindscapes: An Invitation to Cognitive Sociology*. Cambridge, MA: Harvard University Press.

CHAPTER 14

Culture, Harmful Dysfunctions and the Sociology of Mental Illness

Allan V. Horwitz

A central question in the sociology of mental illness involves how to separate the universal from the culturally specific aspects of mental disorders. As Wakefield notes in his incisive critique of sociological work, sociologists have emphasized the culturally specific side of disorders and have unwisely rejected the notion that there is a universal aspect to the concept of mental disorder.[1] Wakefield accurately argues that a universal concept of mental disorder is necessary for a number of reasons. Without some concept of what a legitimate mental disorder is, sociologists are unable to critique the empirical practices of the mental health professions because they cannot claim that any model of mental illness is any better (or worse) than any other model. In particular, a universal concept serves as a basis for questioning current standards for judging mental disorders, which vastly overestimate the number of people who are mentally ill. The recent Surgeon General's Report on Mental Health, for example, uses community studies to estimate that 50 million people in the U.S. develop mental disorders each year (U.S. Department of Health and Human Services 1999). The lack of a universal concept of mental disorder also precludes the possibility of comparing mental disorders across differing cultural contexts: The study of cross-cultural variation is impossible unless something constant serves as a point of reference for what is being compared. Finally, a universal concept of mental disorder not only indicates what sorts of conditions should be considered valid mental illnesses, but also distinguishes what conditions are *not* legitimate disorders. Sociologists of all perspectives, including constructionists, would be wise to heed Wakefield's call to use a universal concept of mental disorder.

It is virtually impossible to generate consensus about what the most adequate concept of a phenomenon as controversial as mental disorder might be.[2] Nevertheless, in my opinion, Wakefield has provided the best general concept of mental disorder yet developed (see especially Wakefield 1992a; 1992b). He recognizes that the major problem any valid concept of mental disorder must overcome is how to reconcile the universal aspects of mental disorders, which are properties of the human species, with the culturally specific and contextually dependent aspects of disorders, which vary widely across different social groups. His concept of mental disorders as "harmful internal dysfunctions" goes a long way toward resolving what Wakefield calls the central task of sociological analysis: "only by integrating the universal and the social can a coherent and persuasive investigation of the social occur" (see p. 265). This response will not reiterate Wakefield's analysis, which is a model of clarity, but will build on it to derive some implications for the sociological study of mental illness.

Symptoms as Indicators and as Symbols

Readers of this volume might naturally wonder how the study of mental disorders is related to the central issues of concern to the sociology of culture. In this brief section, I argue that culture has a critical role in structuring the symptoms through which internal dysfunctions become manifest. Unlike physical illnesses, where symptoms are usually indicators of underlying disorders, the symptoms of mental disorders are symbolic representations of underlying vulnerabilities that are structured to fit dominant cultural models of "appropriate" disorders in particular times and places. In this sense, the symptoms of mental disorders are part of "cultural tool kits" no less than language, fashion, and musical or culinary tastes (cf. Swidler 1986). A key aspect of Wakefield's analysis is the relationship between symptoms and disorders. Rectal bleeding is an indicator of colon cancer just as the blooming of daffodils indicates that spring has arrived: These phenomena are not socially structured but are universal processes that are, at best, trivially affected by social forces. Wakefield's analysis, however, does not deal with the question of whether the symptoms of mental illnesses are related to underlying disorders in the same way that symptoms such as rectal bleeding are related to underlying cancerous processes. Although the universal concept of harmful dysfunction might be analogous in mental and in physical disorders, the relationships between mental and physical symptoms and the disorders that produce them differ in fundamental ways.

For physical illnesses, symptoms are *indicators* of natural underlying disorders (Zerubavel 1997). That is, they are not arbitrary, random, or culturally shaped symbols, but naturally emanate from the disease. Because of this, diseases of the body have similar manifestations regardless of the cultural context in which they appear. Colon cancer, for example, will have virtually identical manifestations among Kenyans, Japanese, or Americans. In contrast, with some exceptions such as, arguably, the psychotic disorders, the manifestations of mental disorders are not indicators of specific underlying diseases. Instead, the specific sorts of psychological symptoms people

develop are ones that are appropriate in specific cultural contexts, that fit their identities, and that suit the current fashions of the medical and mental health professions.

Culture structures the symptoms of mental disorders in far stronger ways than it
affects the symptom of physical disorders. Some disorders, such as hysteria, were
prominent in earlier time periods but have virtually disappeared today (Micale 1995).
Others, such as eating disorders or dissociative disorders, were virtually nonexistent
in the past but are widely prevalent now (Brumberg 1988; Hacking 1995). The most
common disorders, the depressive and anxiety disorders, take on widely differing
shapes across different cultural contexts (Kleinman 1988). The huge variability in the
manifestations of mental disorders across cultures indicates that culture is related to
the symptoms of mental and of physical disorders in fundamentally different ways.

While biological and psychological as well as social processes affect who is likely to
be vulnerable to developing a mental disorder, culture has a far more prominent role in
shaping the overt manifestation of the symptoms of mental, compared to physical, disorders. This hypothesis does not contradict Wakefield's analysis, which asserts that
harmful internal dysfunctions must underlie any collections of symptoms that are valid
mental disorders. It does, however, call into question whether the symptoms of these
disorders are indicators of an underlying dysfunction or are symbolic manifestations
that are structured to conform to the pool of legitimate symptoms that cultures provide
their members (Shorter 1992; 1994). Cultural sociologists potentially have a major role
in showing how the symptoms of mental disorders emanate from cultural rather than
natural processes, and so vary widely across different historical and social contexts.

Grounding Mental Disorder in Specific Social Practices

Wakefield's analysis is overwhelmingly conceptual. Only at the very end of his paper
does he touch on an issue that is of central sociological concern: How are concepts of
mental disorder grounded in the practices and interests of specific social groups?
While this question need not be of critical concern to philosophers, it is a core issue
for sociologists. Indeed, one of the most fascinating sociological issues about mental
disorders regards the medicalization of many human problems over the course of the
twentieth century (Conrad and Schneider 1992).

For most of human history, mental disorders were isomorphic with notions of
"madness," "insanity," "lunacy," and like terms that seem to be lay analogues to
Wakefield's notion of harmful internal dysfunction. At the turn of the twentieth
century, Freud and the dynamic psychiatrists who followed him created a category of
neuroses that included physical symptoms that stemmed from psychological causes,
anxiety, depression, and psychosexual disorders.[3] Dynamic psychiatry, however,
lumped these disorders as variants of *normal* behavior and distinguished both neurotic
and normal behavior from the psychotic disorders that had previously nearly ex-
hausted the realm of the psychiatric profession. Further, they found the causes of neurotic and normal behavior alike in the same underlying unconscious mechanisms of
repression, sublimation, projection, and the like. No human behavior escaped the psy-
choanalytic gaze: Dynamic psychiatry both pathologized normality and normalized
pathology (see especially Grob 1991; Hale 1995; Lunbeck 1994). This immeasurably
broadened the scope of mental disorder from harmful internal dysfunctions to a wide

variety of human ills. In 1980, the DSM-III—the *Diagnostic and Statistical Manual of Mental Disorders* of the American Psychiatric Association—recreated the cornucopia of human suffering found among the patients of mental health professionals as specific disease entities such as "major depression," "dysthymia," "social phobia," "oppositional defiant disorder," and literally hundreds of others (see especially Kirk and Kutchins 1992). The DSM-III did not increase the range of behaviors that dynamic psychiatry had considered as signs of psychological abnormality, so much as it reclassified these behaviors as specific categories of various mental diseases.

Sociologists will want to move beyond conceptual analysis to ask: What were the social reasons behind the reclassification of the vague neuroses of dynamic psychiatry into the current, sharply delineated, disease entities of modern, diagnostically oriented psychiatry at the end of the twentieth century? Here, I can sketch only a few of the most important reasons, some of which stem from the internal dynamics of the psychiatric profession and others from changes in the external economic and political environments of the profession.[4] Symptom-based, categorical entities allowed research psychiatrists to conduct large statistical studies with reliably measured disorders and thus to gain entry into the prestige system of biomedicine. These discrete disorders also allowed clinicians to obtain reimbursement from a payment system increasingly driven by third-party private and public funders who would fund the treatment of specific diseases but would not pay to treat blurry unconscious mechanisms. In addition, government regulations allowed medications to be marketed only after proof that what they treated were disease entities, regardless of how these drugs actually operated.[5] As well, increasingly powerful lay organizations, composed primarily of parents with mentally ill children, argued that mental disorders were brain diseases, not problems stemming from faulty parenting. The National Institute of Mental Health, in retreat from an activist political agenda in the 1960s, found the study, prevention, and treatment of diseases a wise political strategy in the relatively conservative decades after the 1960s (Kirk 1999). The specific social practices of a variety of groups that had interests in viewing mental disorders as discrete, symptom-based diseases underlie the movement from fuzzy to rigid logics in classifying mental disorders (cf. Zerubavel 1997).

Wakefield's emphasis on "harmful internal dysfunction" as the basis of valid mental disorders provides a lever for a sociological critique of using attributions of mental disorders to account for general human problems. Without a universal concept of mental disorder, sociologists would be able to describe the increasing medicalization of mental disorder over the course of the twentieth century, but they would have no means of critiquing this process. Wakefield's concept allows sociologists to go beyond description to informed questions about whether conditions that are not internal dysfunctions should fall within the legitimate realm of the mental health professions.

Harmful Internal Dysfunctions and the Sociology of Mental Illness

A final issue Wakefield's concept raises may be less relevant for cultural sociologists than for sociologists of mental disorder. By far the most popular sociological style of research about harmful psychological phenomena has been to associate various qualities of stressful social arrangements with resulting states of psychological disturbance.[6] Various studies associate psychological disorders with the occurrence of stressful life events such as bereavement, divorce, unemployment, or natural disasters (e.g., Thoits 1983); with chronic social stressors such as poverty, social isolation, noxious working conditions, or neighborhood disorganization (e.g., Turner, Wheaton, and Lloyd 1995); and with stressful social relationships with, for example, spouses, lovers, or bosses (e.g., Horwitz, McLaughlin, and White 1998).

Wakefield's analysis raises a central but neglected question for the sociology of mental illness. According to him, a valid concept of mental disorder includes only those conditions where a psychological mechanism is *not* functioning appropriately. Mental disorders only arise when something has gone *wrong* in the person. Yet there is nothing wrong with the functioning of people who grieve after the death of a loved one, who become depressed while their marriages dissolve, who drink more than usual during periods of unemployment, or who are anxious while living in an area with much street crime. In other words, the psychological consequences of the acute life events, chronic social conditions, and oppressive social relationships that sociologists typically study are *not* mental illnesses: They are the appropriate responses of normally functioning individuals to stressful conditions.

Wakefield's analysis implies that the field of the sociology of mental illness is wrongly named. Its central area of study ought to be psychological conditions that are not mental illnesses but instead are the expectable consequences of stressful social arrangements. This does not mean that sociological analysis is irrelevant to the study of "valid" mental illnesses: Social and cultural forces have major roles in how mental illnesses are defined, the kinds of symptoms that they feature, how much stigma they evoke, and their courses over time, among many other factors. My point is that the psychological conditions that the field typically studies are not mental illnesses at all but are normal responses to stressful environmental circumstances.

A key problem is that that symptom scales such as the CES-D (Radloff 1977) or diagnostic measures such as the CIDI (Kessler et al. 1994) used to measure mental health outcomes hopelessly entangle psychological symptoms that are appropriate responses to stressful conditions with those that are internal dysfunctions, as Wakefield defines the term. Wakefield's analysis has the important methodological implication that sociologists must explicitly build the contexts and causes of symptoms into the instruments that measure psychological outcomes. Only those symptoms that arise independently of causes that would expectably lead to them, that persist after the causes that have given rise to them have abated, or that are of inappropriate severity and duration relative to their causes should count as possible signs of internal dysfunctions. In contrast, symptoms that emerge because of stressful experiences and that disappear when these experiences have gone away indicate normal, not abnormal, psychological functioning. The implicit message of Wakefield's paper is that adequate conceptual analysis must guide the appropriate measurements of mental disorders.

Conclusion

Sociologists focus on variation rather than universality. But, as Wakefield reminds us, the study of variation cannot proceed without some notion of what is universal. This point, while valuable for any area of sociological investigation, is especially important in the study of mental disorder. The concept of harmful psychological dysfunction provides a reference point to view how cultural processes structure the symptoms of mental disorders into symbolically appropriate forms that vary across particular times and places. Changing social conceptions of mental illness have been especially pronounced in recent decades. Sociological analyses of these changes need some fulcrum, which must be grounded in a universal concept of mental disorder, in order to analyze and to critique these developments.

The concept of mental disorder as harmful psychological dysfunction should also be congenial to sociologists because it does not define as pathological the psychological consequences of stressful social arrangements. Sociologists should be more assertive in approaching these consequences as expectable results of social arrangements and not, as the psychological professions now view them, as forms of mental pathology. Paradoxically, a major contribution of Wakefield's eloquent concept of valid mental disorder is to show that a central focus of sociologists should be on the conditions that this concept excludes: The psychological consequences that result from the struggles of normal people who must cope with stressful structural arrangements.

Endnotes

1. While Wakefield accurately states that sociologists err on the side of cultural particularism, this is surely not the case outside of the social sciences. Both the psychiatric profession and media reporting on mental illnesses swing to the opposite pole of explaining mental illnesses as culture-free, genetically based brain disorders. In this sense, the universalist rather than the particularistic notion of mental disorder is in need of correction at the present time.
2. See especially the *Journal of Abnormal Psychology*, August 1999 issue; it features an article by Wakefield, eight responses, and Wakefield's reply.
3. See Horwitz (2001, chap. 3) for more detail on these processes.
4. See Horwitz (2001, chap. 4) for a more extensive examination of these reasons.
5. For example, many people may use Viagra to enhance their sexual performance, Paxil to overcome their nervousness, or Ritalin to control their children's behavior problems, but the makers of these drugs can only market them for the treatment of "erectile dysfunction," "social phobia," and "attention deficit disorder," respectively.
6. For examples, see any issue of the field's central journal, The *Journal of Health and Social Behavior*.

References

Brumberg, J. J. 1988. *Fasting Girls: The History of Anorexia Nervosa*. Cambridge, MA: Harvard University Press.
Conrad, P. and J. Schneider. 1992. *Deviance and Medicalization*. 2nd ed. Philadelphia, PA: Temple University Press.
Grob, G. N. 1991. *From Asylum to Community: Mental Health Policy in Modern America*. Princeton, NJ: Princeton University Press.
Hacking, I. 1995. *Rewriting the Soul: Multiple Personality and the Sciences of Memory*. Princeton, NJ: Princeton University Press.
Hale, N. G. Jr. 1995. *The Rise and Crisis of Psychoanalysis in the United States: Freud and the Americans, 1917–1985*. New York: Oxford University Press.

Horwitz, A. V. 2001. *The Creation of Mental Illnesses*. Chicago, IL: University of Chicago Press.

Horwitz, A. V., J. McLaughlin, and H. R. White. 1998. "How the Negative and Positive Aspects of Partner Relationships Affect the Mental Health of Young Married People." *Journal of Health and Social Behavior* 39:124–39.

Kessler, R. C., K. A. McGonagle, S. Zhao, C. B. Nelson, M. Hughes, S. Eshleman, H. Wittchen, and K. S. Kendler. 1994. "Lifetime and 12-Month Prevalence of DSM-III-R Psychiatric Disorders in the United States: Results from the National Comorbidity Survey." *Archives of General Psychiatry* 51:8–19.

Kirk, S. A. 1999. "Instituting Madness: The Evolution of a Federal Agency." Pp. 539–62 in *Handbook of the Sociology of Mental Health*, edited by C. Aneshensel and J. Phelan. New York: Plenum.

Kirk, S. A. and H. Kutchins. 1992. *The Selling of DSM: The Rhetoric of Science in Psychiatry*. New York: Aldine de Gruyter.

Kleinman, A. 1988. *Rethinking Psychiatry: From Cultural Category to Personal Experience*. New York: Free Press.

Lunbeck, E. 1994. *The Psychiatric Persuasion: Knowledge, Gender, and Power in Modern America*. Princeton, NJ: Princeton University Press.

Micale, M. S. 1995. *Approaching Hysteria: Disease and Its Interpretations*. Princeton, NJ: Princeton University Press.

Radloff, L. S. 1977. "The CES-D Scale: A Self-Report Depression Scale for Research in the General Population." *Applied Psychological Measurement* 3:249–65.

Shorter, E. 1992. *From Paralysis to Fatigue: A History of Psychosomatic Illness in the Modern Era*. New York: Free Press.

———. 1994. *From the Mind into the Body: The Cultural Origins of Psychosomatic Symptoms*. New York: Free Press.

Swidler, A. 1986. "Culture in Action: Symbols and Strategies." *American Sociological Review* 51:273–86.

Thoits, P. A. 1983. "Dimensions of Life Events That Influence Psychological Distress: An Evaluation and Synthesis of the Literature." Pp. 33–103 in *Psychosocial Stress: Perspectives on Structure, Theory, Life-Course, and Methods*, edited by H. Kaplan. New York: Academic Press.

Turner, R. J., B. Wheaton, and D. A. Lloyd. 1995. "The Epidemiology of Stress." *American Sociological Review* 60:104–25.

U.S. Department of Health and Human Services. 1999. *Mental Health: A Report of the Surgeon General*. Rockville, MD: Center for Mental Health Services.

Wakefield, J. C. 1992a. "The Concept of Mental Disorder: On the Boundary between Biological Facts and Social Values." *American Psychologist* 47:373–88.

———. 1992b. "Disorder as Harmful Dysfunction: A Conceptual Critique of DSM-III-R's Definition of Mental Disorder." *Psychological Review* 99:232–47.

Zerubavel, E. 1997. *Social Mindscapes: An Invitation to Cognitive Sociology*. Cambridge, MA: Harvard University Press.

CHAPTER 15

Why Cognitive (and Cultural) Sociology Needs Cognitive Psychology

Paul DiMaggio

Cognitive sociology is a growing field. Growth leads to differentiation, and cognitive sociology is no exception. Within cognitive sociology, we can distinguish two dimensions. The first dimension (horizontal in Figure 15–1) counterposes work that focuses on how we think to work that focuses on the content of thought. Work on how we think includes much organization theory in the Carnegie School tradition, as well as much of Eviatar Zerubavel's (1997) recent trail-blazing work and much other research on social classification and memory (e.g., Durkheim 1915). Work on *what* we think dominates most of the sociology of culture—for example, research on individualism, on how people make sense of love, on cross-national differences in trust, and so on (e.g., Fine, this volume; Gamson 1992; Mohr 1994; Schwartz 1991; this volume; Swidler 1986; 2001). Clearly, both kinds of work are valuable.

The second dimension (vertical on Figure 15–1) has to do with the strategy one employs for the development of cognitive sociology: Whether we want it to be autochthonous—whether we as sociologists think we can go it alone—or whether we believe it is more productive to build on the work of cognitive and social psychologists (March and Simon 1958; Schuman 1986; White 2000). This dimension does not entail a forced choice any more than does the first. Zerubavel (1997) has demonstrated that a sociological approach can explain a great deal about the "social mindscape": that is, about the ways in which social institutions organize cognitive processes at the "macro"

FIGURE 15–1
The space of cognitive sociology.

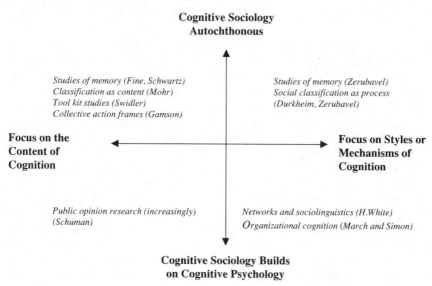

Cognitive Sociology
Autochthonous

Studies of memory (Fine, Schwartz)
Classification as content (Mohr)
Tool kit studies (Swidler)
Collective action frames (Gamson)

Studies of memory (Zerubavel)
Social classification as process
(Durkheim, Zerubavel)

**Focus on the
Content of
Cognition**

**Focus on Styles or
Mechanisms of
Cognition**

Public opinion research (increasingly)
(Schuman)

Networks and sociolinguistics (H.White)
Organizational cognition (March and Simon)

Cognitive Sociology Builds
on Cognitive Psychology

level. Many other scholars have demonstrated the self-sufficiency of the sociological approach in explicating the shifting content of particular ideas or systems of classification.

I would argue that both cognitive psychology and social psychology have become indispensable for sociologists who are interested both in how cultural processes enter into individual lives and how such processes enter into some kinds of collective behavior. Cognitive psychology and social psychology have also become indispensable for sociologists interested in microfoundational theories of action. For these purposes, I believe, familiarity with recent work in these fields is increasingly useful, for such work has become more consistent with sociological intuitions.

Recent work in psychology is helpful to sociologists of culture for several reasons. First, it has the capacity to take debates over presuppositions and render them empirical. I have believed Swidler's "tool kit theory" of culture (1986) from the start, but not until I familiarized myself with recent work on cognition could I defend that preference on empirical grounds (DiMaggio 1997).

Second, work on social cognition helps to fill in the blanks where sociological work is misleading or incomplete. For example, Diane Vaughan's contribution to this volume suggests that Bourdieu underestimates the extent to which intersecting social circles create separate cognitive cultures in different life domains. In another arena, Kathleen Carley (1999) has drawn on cognitive psychology for a microfoundational approach to knowledge organization.

Finally, research on social cognition can help sociologists who study cognition and culture in a less obvious way: by helping us understand the sort of biases that are likely to be built into the way we collect, perceive, and interpret our data. In the rest of this chapter, I try to make these assertions more concrete, first, by describing four generic lessons that psychology can teach sociologists who study cognition and culture, and second, by focusing in somewhat more depth on two of them.

Some Lessons from Psychology

Here, I list four psychological findings that are fundamentally important for cognitive sociology.

1. We retain a huge amount of the information and attitudes to which we are exposed, and that information is stored without tags for either source or truth value (Gilbert 1991; Johnson et al. 1993). As Swidler (1986) has written, we know a lot more culture than we will ever use. Consequently, there is much less internal pressure for consistency than most people have thought. As Martin (2000) argues, pressure for consistency is social, not intrapsychic, and remembering requires active construal, which introduces much contingency into knowledge and belief.

2. Some of the vast store of information, opinion, and attitudes that we retain is organized into schemata: images or representations of objects, actions, or events, and the linkages among these in stereotyped behavioral routines. People have varying degrees of access to these schemata, depending upon their centrality to self-image, their emotional weight, their salience, and the frequency and recency with which the environment has activated them (D'Andrade 1995). Social schemata provide frameworks that help us interpret new information. That is, they represent objects or events and provide default assumptions about their characteristics, relationships, and entailments under conditions of incomplete information. People are more likely to perceive information that is consistent with existing schemata, quicker to recall it, more likely to recall it accurately, and more likely to use it once it is recalled (DiMaggio 1997). In fact, people even recall schematically embedded events that never happened (Freeman et al. 1987). Sociologists of culture who, as most of us do, rely heavily upon interpretations—our own or our informants'—should find this work cautionary. It demonstrates how natural it is to impose interpretive coherence on materials that are not intrinsically related and how important it is for cultural analysts to guard against this tendency.

3. Schemata are themselves organized into relatively independent domains, among which there are not necessarily homologic relations (DiMaggio 1997). Information and schemata about behavior at work may be organized quite separately from information and schemata about behavior at home, and there may be little correspondence between the two. This means that knowledge and dispositions are far less coherent (given the particular way in which we tend to understand coherence) than conventional understandings of culture would have us think.

4. Psychologists have learned that people do at least two very different kinds of cognition: one that is characterized (somewhat variously by different commentators) as deliberate, planful, critical, cool, and/or thoughtful, and another that is characterized as impulsive, constrained, hot, and/or based on stereotypes (Metcalfe and Mischel 1999). This work is significant for sociologists because it provides a microfoundational basis for revisiting the old Parsonian problem of multiple orientations to action (Parsons 1937).

In the next sections, I discuss two of these areas of research in greater detail.

Orientations toward Action

As I mentioned, psychologists' empirical research on modes of cognition permits us to return to Parsons's classic work (Parsons 1937; Parsons and Shils 1951) and base it on a more up-to-date psychology. By this, I refer to a psychology that affirms Parsons's belief that orientations to action are variable, as against popular approaches such as rational-choice theory, ethnomethodology, or even Bourdieu's ([1980] 1990) praxis theory that seem to imply that particular orientations to action are characteristic of human behavior.

Psychologists interpret the two modes of cognition in two rather different ways, but they tend to elide differences between them. One version emphasizes the distinction between *automatic* and *deliberative* cognition—between the efficient, scripted, routine form of everyday action and the calmer, more thoughtful form of thought of which we are capable when facing complex and important issues (Devine 1989). The other version emphasizes the distinction between "hot" and "cold" cognition, focusing on the more passionate, emotional tone of the former and the cooler, more detached form of the latter (Metcalfe and Mischel 1999).

I would suggest that it might be worthwhile to consider the possibility that these are separate continua, that is, that there are two correlated but analytically distinct dimensions, one having to do with degree of affect, the other having to do with degree of planfulness and deliberation. Arraying these two dimensions as they are in Figure 15–2 below gives us a more complex typology of action orientations than psychologists ordinarily describe, but one that is largely consistent with work in this area.

FIGURE 15–2
Space of orientations to action.

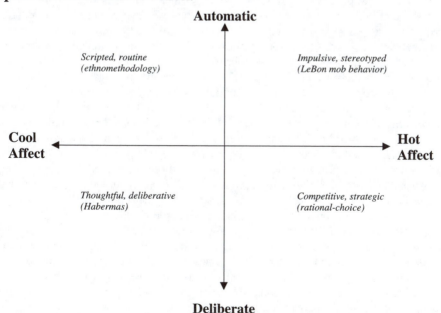

I would not want to spend too much time defending the particulars of Figure 15–2, the value of which is largely heuristic.[1] For example, in ceding the lower left-hand quadrant (cool and deliberate) to Habermas, I smuggle in an additional dimension (collectivity orientation) that is orthogonal to the rest. Moreover, Figure 15–2 limits "rational action" to the lower right-hand quadrant. In fact, I suspect that there are several distinct varieties of rational action, including hot and deliberate, cool and calculating, and (consistent with Bourdieu's [1990] approach) automatic (i.e., strategies embedded in the *habitus*). The important point is that these orientations differ both psychologically and sociologically, and the differences probably matter. This approach invites us to focus on an exceptionally important question that neither psychologists nor sociologists have resolved: Under what conditions do actors switch from one action orientation to another?

Domain Independence

The second lesson that I shall discuss here derives from the principle of *domain independence*, by which I refer to the relative independence of schematically organized knowledge and dispositions that pertain to different classes of life situations (for example, those related, respectively, to work and family).

The phenomenon of domain independence makes people a lot less consistent than we expect them to be. Because our perceptions of behavior are organized schematically, we impose order by perceiving people as more consistent than they are. For cognitive and cultural sociologists in the business of interpreting and attributing meanings, this fact should send chills down the center of one's spine.

To understand this problem better, consider research into the psychology of personality. Shweder (1982) asked groups of experimental subjects to undertake a series of tasks, and also asked observers to rate them with respect to such behaviors as arguing, criticizing, agreeing, reinforcing, and so on. He found that correlations between schematically associated behaviors—for example, arguing and criticizing—were much higher when participants were given global ratings after the fact than when associations were based on their actual observed behavior. Shweder's conclusion: Much clinical research on personality is really about cultural constructions of personhood.

Other studies of personality, based on insights about domain independence, underscore the tendency of both laypeople and social scientists to look for central tendencies in a world of interaction effects (I rely on Mischel and Shoda [1995] for this description). Perplexed by weak-over-time correlations between personality indicators—the so-called "personality paradox"—Bem speculated that people were consistent in traits that they cared about and felt were central to themselves, and inconsistent in traits that were more marginal to their self-concepts (Bem and Allen 1974). If you could only find out what traits people cared about, he argued, you would find that personality traits really are consistent over time.

Taking conscientiousness as his trait, Bem followed Carleton College students around for several months, separated the ones who believed they were consistently conscientious (or consistently irresponsible) from the ones for whom this trait was not very salient, and tested for consistency across situations. Much to his disappointment, he found no difference: Neither group was very consistent.

Some years later, Walter Mischel reanalyzed Bem's data (Mischel and Shoda 1995). Mischel suspected that personality resides in interactions between behavioral dispositions and social situations. In other words, consistency lies *not* in behavior but in *behavior/situation profiles*. His analyses provided striking support—students who believed that they were consistent *were* outstandingly consistent in the way they responded to particular types of situations across time, but not across situations. For example, some were conscientious about relationships but irresponsible about academic deadlines; others were diligent scholars but fickle lovers. Consistent with Bem's original intuition, the students for whom conscientiousness was not a salient characteristic were not consistent at all.

Does sociology have an analog to personality? I would suggest that culture is that analog, and that we often make the same mistake that psychologists did. That is, sociologists often thematize culture as something that varies reliably among groups. In this view, some societies, organizations, or communities are more authoritarian, individualistic, communally oriented, or risk-averse than others. Such differences, so the story goes, are reflected in the distribution of persons with relevant personality traits. And such traits are expressed in behaviors consistent with the assessed personalities.

The problem is that we may look for culture at the wrong level. Rather than having values, groups may have predilections to act in certain ways *in certain situations*. Moreover, they (and we) may tell stories about such predilections that reflect the same person-centered bias that created the personality paradox in psychology, obscuring the fact that culture lies not in central tendencies but in interactions of disposition and domain.

Take for example, differences between people in Japan, who are ordinarily portrayed as communally oriented, cooperative, and trusting, and those in the United States, who are often portrayed as individualistic, competitive, and wary. In a series of comparative studies, Yamagishi and Yamagishi (1994) demonstrated that Japanese and American culture differ not on the traits but *on the interaction of trait and situation*. Japanese people have closer in-group relationships than Americans; but Americans are actually more trusting of strangers than are Japanese. Consequently, they argue, Americans are better at forming new relationships and alliances and better at adapting to change. In other words, our understanding of Japanese and American cultures has been obscured both by the coherence of the stories that we tell ourselves about ourselves and about each other, and by the conflation of *situation-specific dispositions* with global characterizations of cultural traits that obscure the independence of action domains.

Conclusion

Grounding theory in research on social cognition is useful for sociologists who want to study the ways in which culture enters into everyday life. Is it indispensable? Perhaps not for everyone. Sociologists who have challenged the view of culture as a monolithic set of values and dispositions shared across members of a group, who have emphasized the malleability of culture, and who have called attention to framing and narrativity, analogy and code-switching, have moved in parallel with work on cognition in psychology.

Yet I would argue that, as a field, we sociologists of culture and cognition need to engage with psychology. For one thing, all of us who are in the business of interpreting culture need to be inoculated against the perceptual biases hardwired into the way humans make sense of the world. Reflexivity aside, it seems to me that cognitive sociology and cognitive psychology have a lot to learn from one another. The convergence of perspectives is too striking and the complementarity of research questions and research skills too fortuitous to let such an opportunity for multidisciplinary synergy pass unexploited.

Endnotes

1. For a quite different approach that relies on similar insights, see Neuman et al. (1997).

References

Bem, D. J. and A. Allen. 1974. "On Predicting Some of the People Some of the Time: The Search for Cross-Situational Consistencies in Behavior." *Psychological Review* 81:506–20.

Bourdieu, P. [1980] 1990. *The Logic of Practice*. Stanford, CT: Stanford University Press.

Carley, K. 1999. "Culture as Knowledge Level Dynamics." Presented at "Toward a Sociology of Culture and Cognition," November 12, 1999, Rutgers University, New Brunswick, NJ.

D'Andrade, R. 1995. *The Development of Cognitive Anthropology*. New York: Cambridge University Press.

Devine P.G. 1989. "Stereotypes and Prejudice: Their Automatic and Controlled Components." *Journal of Personality and Social Psychology* 56:5–18.

DiMaggio, P. 1997. "Culture and Cognition." *Annual Review of Sociology* 23:263–87.

Durkheim, E. 1915. *The Elementary Forms of Religious Life*. New York: Macmillan.

Freeman L., A. K. Romney, and S. C. Freeman. 1987. "Cognitive Structure and Informant Accuracy." *American Anthropologist* 89:310–25.

Gamson, W. A. 1992. *Talking Politics*. New York: Cambridge University Press.

Gilbert, D. T. 1991. "How Mental Systems Believe." *American Psychologist* 46:107–19.

Johnson, M., K. S. Hastroudi, and D. S. Lindsay. 1993. "Source Monitoring." *Psychological Bulletin* 114:3–28.

March, J. G. and H. Simon. 1958. *Organizations*. New York: Wiley.

Martin, J. 2000. "The Relationship of Aggregate Statistics on Beliefs to Culture and Cognition." *Poetics* 28:5–20.

Metcalfe, J. and W. Mischel. 1999. "A Hot-Cool System Analysis of Delay of Gratification: Dynamics of Willpower." *Psychological Review* 106:(1):3–19.

Mischel, W. and Y. Shoda. 1995. "A Cognitive-Affective System Theory of Personality: Reconceptualizing Situations, Dispositions, Dynamics, and Invariance in Personality Structure." *Psychological Review* 102:246–68.

Mohr J. W. 1994. "Soldiers, Mothers, Tramps and Others: Discourse Roles in the 1907 Charity Directory." *Poetics* 22:327–58.

Neuman, W. R., M. B. McKuen, G. E. Marcus, and J. Miller. 1997. "Affective Choice and Rational Choice." Presented at the annual meeting of the American Political Science Association.

Parsons, T. 1937. *The Structure of Social Action*. New York: McGraw Hill.

Parsons, T. and E. A. Shils. 1951. "Values, Motives and Systems of Action." Pp. 47–275 in *Toward a General Theory of Action*, edited by T. Parsons and E Shils. Cambridge, MA: Harvard University Press.

Schwartz, B. 1991. "Social Change and Collective Memory: the Democratization of George Washington." *American Sociological Review* 56:221–36.

Schuman, H. 1986. "Ordinary Questions, Survey Questions, and Policy Questions." *Public Opinion Quarterly* 50:432–42.

Shweder, R. A. 1982. "Fact and Artifact in Trait Perception: the Systematic Distortion Hypothesis." *Progress in Experimental Personality Research* 2:65–100.

Swidler, A. 1986. "Culture in Action: Symbols and Strategies." *American Sociological Review* 51:273–86.

———. 2001. *Talk of Love*. Chicago, IL: University of Chicago Press.

White, H. C. 2000. "Where Do Languages Come From? Switching Talk." Preprint no. 201, Center for the Social Sciences, Columbia University.

Yamagishi, T. and M. Yamagishi. 1994. "Trust and Commitment in the United States and Japan." *Motivation and Emotion* 18:129–66.

Zerubavel E. 1997. *Social Mindscapes: An Invitation to Cognitive Sociology*. Cambridge, MA: Harvard University Press.

Appendix

Mapping the Field

Karen A. Cerulo

Sensation and Attention

Current literature in cultural sociology suggests a growing interest in the study of sensation and attention. But note that several classic theoretical works form the basis for these contemporary investigations. For example, notions of collective attention and group focus are rooted in the works of Emile Durkheim, Karl Marx, Charles Horton Cooley, and Alfred Schutz. These theorists were among the first to suggest that social structure and cultural circumstance can systematically pattern the objects and events, the beliefs and morals, that enter a collective's awareness. Durkheim's statements on the topic can be found in his writings on collective conscience. Interested readers should consult *The Elementary Forms of Religious Life* (New York: The Free Press, [1912] 1995), and *Suicide* (New York: The Free Press, [1951] 1966). Marx's concept of class consciousness is also relevant here. *The Marx-Engels Reader* provides several essays in which class consciousness is discussed (R. C. Tucker, ed., 2d ed., New York: W. W. Norton, 1978). Cooley elaborates on the phenomenon of collective attention in *Social Organization: A Larger Study of the Mind* (New York: Schocken, [1909] 1962). Finally, Schutz describes the ways in which culturally embedded signals can synchronize the attentions of social members, thus creating a meeting of the minds. See his essay "Making Music Together: A Study in Social Relationship" (*Social Research* 18:76–97, 1951).

In a similar regard, the classics tell us much about the ways in which a collective body can shape individual attention. This point is perhaps most prominent in works addressing topics such as specialization and rationalization. For example, Max Weber's work on bureaucracy demonstrates the ways in which an individual's location in a formal organization can direct that which the individual perceives and that which she or he ignores. Similarly, Weber contends that a formal organization's definition of goals functions to define social relevance and irrelevance for the individuals working within it. Interested readers will find a good collection of Weber's ideas on such matters in *From Max Weber: Essays in Sociology* (H. H. Gerth and C. W. Mills, eds., New York: Oxford University Press, 1946). And it is worth noting that Durkheim makes many compatible points in defining and discussing "organic solidarity" and the specialization that accompanies it. (See *The Division of Labor in Society*, New York: Free Press, [1933] 1964).

The study of inattention can be traced to some classic theoretical works as well. In *Behavior in Public Places*, for example, Erving Goffman explores the systematic patterning of denial and inattention. His discussion of nonperson treatment and civil inattention direct us toward certain sociocultural strategies that allow actors to exclude or release entities from focused interaction. (See Chapter 6 in *Behavior in Public Places*, New York: Free Press, 1963). Similarly, Harold Garfinkel notes the ways in which certain aspects of social life become routine and thus relegated to the background of attention. He also discusses the ways in which routines can be disrupted, thus centralizing certain actions in conscious awareness. Interested readers should consult "Studies of the Routine Grounds of Everyday Activities" (pp. 35–75 in *Studies in Ethnomethodology*, Oxford, England: Polity, [1964] 1967).

During the past two decades, several cultural sociologists have elaborated on these "classic" themes. Some, for example, have explored the vehicles by which collective attention can be synchronized, intensified, and shifted. Symbols and rituals prove central to such inquiries, with scholars documenting the ways in which certain signs and routine practices help to bracket social experience. Several very readable books will help readers familiarize themselves with this ever-growing literature. See, for example, Maurice Agulhon's *Marianne Into Battle* (trans. by J. Lloyd, Cambridge, England: Cambridge University Press, 1981), Karen A. Cerulo's *Identity Designs: The Sights and Sounds of a Nation* (Rose Book Series of the ASA, New Brunswick, NJ: Rutgers University Press, 1995), Roger Friedland's and Richard Hecht's *To Rule Jerusalem* (New York: Cambridge University Press, 1997), Barry Schwartz's *George Washington: The Making of an American Symbol* (New York: Free Press, 1987), and Eviatar Zerubavel's *The Seven-Day Circle: The History and Meaning of the Week* (New York: Free Press, 1985). In a related line of research, scholars of social movements often focus quite prominently on methods of gaining collective attention. Several works address the attention-getting rhetoric adopted by interest groups and political lobbies as they compete for a central position in the foreground of the public mind. Joseph Gusfield offers a pivotal statement in this regard; see *Culture of Public Problems: Drinking-Driving and the Symbolic Order* (Chicago, IL: University of Chicago Press, 1981). Joel Best's *Threatened Children: Rhetoric and Concern About Child Victims* represents another important treatment of the issue (Chicago, IL: University of Chicago Press, 1990). And Bert Klandermans, Hanspeter Kriesi, and Sidney Tarrow provide an engaging collection of studies on the subject; see *From Structure to Action* (vol. 1 of *International Social Movement Research*, Greenwich, CT: JAI Press, 1988).

Those interested in modern treatments of sensation and attention will find several studies of communication media especially relevant. Many scholars have studied the ways in which the introduction of new communication technologies can reorient collective attention and shift collective focus. One of the earliest statements in this regard comes from Marshall McLuhan; see *Understanding Media: The Extensions of*

Man (New York: McGraw Hill, 1964). For other engaging writings on the topic, see Benedict Anderson's *Imagined Communities* (2d ed., London, England: Verso, 1991), Joshua Meyrowitz's *No Sense of Place* (New York: Oxford University Press, 1985), and Elihu Katz's "Broadcast Holidays" (*Sociological Inquiry* 68(2):230–41, 1998).

Finally, note that several contemporary social scientists are exploring the idea of institutionalized perceptual filters. Such works suggest that detection and perception of stimuli are powerfully steered by the specific filters embedded within various contexts of action. The preceding articles by Eviatar Zerubavel and Diane Vaughan (as well as the other books and articles that form their scholarly repertoire—see chapter bibliographies) provide elegant examples of this agenda. Several additional works are worth noting as well. In *The Lenses of Gender: Transforming the Debate on Sexuality*, for example, social psychologist Sandra L. Bem suggests ways in which culturally embedded perceptual filters perpetuate gender inequality (New Haven, CT: Yale University Press, 1993). In another context, Steven E. Clayman demonstrates the ways in which occupational filters can influence that which is considered worthy of attention; see "Defining Moments, Presidential Debates, and the Dynamics of Quotability" (*Journal of Communication* 45:118–46, 1995). Thomas Laqueur describes a similar phenomenon as he traces Western medicine's movement from a "unisex" perspective to the forceful distinction of maleness and femaleness; see *Making Sex: Body and Gender from the Greeks to Freud* (Cambridge, MA: Harvard University Press, 1990). The notion of scientific perceptual filters is further developed by Steven Jay Gould in *The Mismeasure of Man* (New York: Norton, 1996). Gould shows how even the most careful of scientists can be blinded by institutionalized perceptual filters, thus "finding" only those results that confirm her or his established perceptions of the world.

Discrimination and Classification

Within cultural sociology, there is a growing number of works that place discrimination and classification center stage. Such studies problematize the construction of social difference, they track the institutionalization of categorical boundaries, and they probe the ways in which such categories inform behavioral guidelines and social policy.

Contemporary studies of discrimination and classification stem from a long-standing intellectual tradition. Emile Durkheim and Marcel Mauss initiated the dialogue when, in *Primitive Classification* (Chicago, IL: University of Chicago Press, 1963), they suggested a link between classification systems and social organization. Interests in discrimination and classification can also be traced to twentieth-century semioticians. These scholars approached thinking and meaning making as a comparative endeavor—one that requires the individual to locate new data *relative* to other elements of a broader information system. Classic examples of this view include Ferdinand de Saussure's *Course in General Linguistics* (trans. by W. Baskin, New York: Philosophical Library, 1959), *The Collected Papers of Charles Sanders Peirce* (vols. 1–6, edited by C. Hartshorne and P. Weiss, Cambridge, MA: Harvard University Press, 1931–1935), Umberto Eco's *Theory of Semiotics* (Bloomington, IN: Indiana University Press, 1976), and Roland Barthes's *Image-Music-Text* (trans. by S. Heath, Glasgow, Scotland: Fontana-Collins, 1977). Newcomers to the literature will find that John Deely's *Basics of Semiotics* (Bloomington, IN: Indiana University Press, 1990) offers a very readable introduction to the field.

Works such as Mary Douglas's *Purity and Danger* (New York: Praegar, 1966), Barry Schwartz's *Vertical Classification* (Chicago, IL: University of Chicago Press, 1981), and Eviatar Zerubavel's *The Fine Line* (New York: Free Press, 1991) apply Durkheimian and semiotic tenets in macrolevel, cross-cultural explorations of social cognition. These sweeping reviews of sorting and organizational actions illuminate the cultural variations that characterize such activities. The works also demonstrate the very powerful ways in which the clustering and compartmentalizing of objects and experiences direct social action and social organization.

Several prominent cultural theorists have situated the processes of discrimination and classification in issues of power. Pierre Bourdieu's *Distinction: A Social Critique of the Judgment of Taste* (Cambridge, MA: Harvard University Press, 1984), Jacques Derrida's *Disseminations* (Chicago, IL: University of Chicago Press, 1981), and Foucault's *The Order of Things: An Archeology of Human Sciences* (New York: Pantheon, 1971) consider both the symbolic and the political nature of differentiation and boundary construction. Like the semioticians, these writers contend that objects, events, and identities are relationally perceived and defined. Yet, in contrast to earlier literatures, these scholars note that relational definitions are contingent on the power relations among a society's subgroups and sectors.

Over the past two decades, several important studies have empirically documented the creation and maintenance of sameness and difference in specific sociocultural arenas. Paul DiMaggio, for example, traced the development of systems that defined and later maintained distinctions between elite and ordinary art. In "Cultural Entrepreneurship in Nineteenth-Century Boston" (Parts 1 and 2, in *Media, Culture and Society* 4:33–50; 303–22, 1982), DiMaggio ties the emergence of quality standards to the acquisition and classification decisions of nineteenth-century urban elites. Also notable is Viviana Zelizer's work on the public and private uses of money. In *The Social Meaning of Money* (New York: Basic Books, 1994), Zelizer documents the multitude of ways in which social actors differentiate and categorize money, changing its meaning in accord with specific social functions and goals.

Sociological works on classification often problematize the *a priori* status of certain social groups. F. James Davis, for example, explores the discrimination of race in the United States. His book, *Who Is Black: One Nation's Definition* (University Park, PA: Pennsylvania State University Press, 1991), charts the development and application of the "one-drop rule," a metric of racial differentiation. In so doing, Davis's account provides a fascinating perspective on the social construction of racial categories. In a similar manner, other scholars challenge the essentialist dichotomization of gender. Works by R. W. Connell (*Masculinities*, Berkeley, CA: University of California Press, 1995) and Candace West and Don H. Zimmerman ("Doing Gender," *Gender and Society* 1:125–51, 1987) provide provocative excursions on the social construction of gender categories.

Sociologists have also explored the boundary work necessary for reifying and reinforcing social categories. See, for example, David Snow's writings on "identity work" (D. A. Snow and L. Anderson, "Identity Work among the Homeless: The Verbal Construction and Avowal of Personal Identities," *American Journal of Sociology*

92:1336–71, 1987; and D. A. Snow and D. McAdam, "Identity Work Processes in the Context of Social Movements: Clarifying the Identity/Movement Nexus," in S. Stryker, T. Owens, and R. W. White, eds., *Self, Identity, and Social Movements*, Minneapolis, MN: University of Minneapolis Press, forthcoming). Others have explored the ways in which social categories, once created, can shape the rest of our lives. For example, in "Above 'People Above'? Status and Worth among Black and White Workers" (pp. 127–50 in *The Cultural Territories of Race: Black and White Boundaries*, M. Lamont, ed., Chicago, IL: University of Chicago Press, 1999) Michele Lamont uses intensive interviews to explore the varying (and often surprising) metrics by which black and white males in working-class locations compare and differentiate their social worth with reference to members of different ethnic, racial, and socioeconomic groups. (Note that Lamont's collection provides a number of other relevant works on this topic.)

Several social scientists have written about specific strategies of discrimination and classification—analogical thinking, metaphoric thinking—situating these strategies in certain social situations or particular cultural milieus. Bourdieu's work on *"habitus,"* for example, adds a sociocultural dimension to work on analogical thinking. Indeed, *habitus* functions via the successful analogic transfer of culturally acquired schemes, thus permitting the development of patterned social action (see *Outline of a Theory of Practice*, Cambridge, England: Cambridge University Press, 1977). In this way, Ann Swidler's depiction of culture as a "tool kit" explicates a sociocultural basis for analogical thinking as well. The matching of certain strategies and tools with specific social settings (e.g., settled versus unsettled times) suggests the analogic transfer of culturally acquired schemes; see "Culture in Action: Symbols and Strategies" (*American Sociological Review* 51(2):73–276,1986). In *Identity and Control: A Theory of Social Action*, Harrison White's discussion of cultural scripts and repertoires raises similar issues. (Princeton, NJ: Princeton University Press, 1992).

Metaphoric thinking has enjoyed the attention of several social scientists as well. These scholars explore the conceptual metaphors shared by members of a culture. In addition, they map the institutionalization of metaphors and the ways in which such metaphors direct both collective perception and collective action. In *The Argument Culture* (New York: Random House, 1998), for example, sociolinguist Deborah Tannen reviews metaphors of war and conflict, images she identifies as central to modern societies. Tannen argues that the entrenchment of these conceptual metaphors has normalized confrontation and opposition as the primary means of acceptable social interaction. In another arena, Eliza Kitis and Michalis Milapides track dominant cultural metaphors and illustrate the ways in which these metaphors can taint seemingly objective media reports of current events; see "Read It and Believe It: How Metaphor Constructs Ideology in News Discourse. A Case Study" (*Journal of Pragmatics* 28(5):557–90, 1997). Works by Robert L. Ivie ("Metaphor and Campaign '84: Strategic Options on Foreign Policy Issues," pp. 89–105 in *Rhetorical Dimensions in Media*, Dubuque, IA: Kendall/Hunt Publishing, 1991), and Jane Blankenship ("The Search for the 1972 Democratic Nomination: A Metaphoric Perspective," pp. 236–60 in *Rhetoric and Communication*, J. Blankenship and H. G. Stelzner, eds., Urbana, IL: University of Illinois Press), analyze the function of metaphors in press coverage of political campaigns. Students of organizations, too, are becoming increasingly interested in metaphoric thinking, with certain works tracking the role of metaphors in organizational operations. For example, in "Using Metaphor to Read the Organisation of the NHS" (*Social Science and Medicine*, 47(11):1715–27, 1998), Andrea Elkind charts the ways in which social actors use religious, organic, and marketplace metaphors to interpret the ambiguities and paradoxes of organizational life in the British National Health Service. Finally Susan Sontag explores the use of metaphor in the construction of illness; see *Illness as Metaphor* (New York: Farrar, Straus and Giroux, 1978) and *AIDS and Its Metaphors* (New York: Farrar, Straus and Giroux, 1989).

Representation and Integration

Over the past decade, the study of representation and integration has grown central to sociological inquiry. Literature addressing components of these processes—conceptualization, framing, and formatting—proves ever-expanding. This section provides some key entrees to this burgeoning field.

With regard to conceptualization, many sociologists are problematizing longstanding theory dependent concepts in light of changing sociocultural contexts. In the area of deviance and social control, for example, researchers are exploring the ways in which cultural and historical change can influence both medical and legal conceptualizations of deviance. For two fascinating discussions of this topic, see Allan Horwitz's *Creating Mental Illnesses* (Chicago, IL: University of Chicago Press, forthcoming 2002) and Stephen Pfohl's *Images of Deviance and Social Control* (New York: McGraw-Hill, 1994). Similar inquiries can be found in studies of health and technology. Several scholars are considering the ways in which technology and social change have reconfigured conceptualizations of life, death, caregiving, and the very nature of the human body. See, for example, Karen Cerulo's and Janet Ruane's "Death Comes Alive: Technology and the Re-conception of Death" (*Science As Culture* 6(28,3):444–66, 1997), Janet Heaton's "The Gaze and Visibility of the Carer: A Foucauldian Analysis of Discourse" (*Sociology of Health and Illness* 21(6):759–77, 1999), and Renee Fox's and Judith Swazey's *Spare Parts: Organ Replacement in American Society* (New York: Oxford University Press, 1992). In still another topic area, researchers are addressing the ways in which globalization and social change can transform conceptualizations of social groups and social community. Interested readers should consult Robert Wuthnow's fascinating book *Loose Connections: Joining Together in America's Fragmented Communities* (New York: Oxford University Press, 1998), Karen Cerulo's and Janet Ruane's "Coming Together: New Taxonomies for the Analysis of Social Relations" (*Sociological Inquiry*, 68(3):398–425, 1998), James Aho's *This Thing of Darkness: A Sociology of the Enemy* (Seattle, WA: University of Washington Press, 1994), and Niklas Luhmann's "Globalization or World Society: How to Conceive of Modern Society" (*Revue Internationale de Sociologie* 7(1):67–79, 1997).

In problematizing concepts, sociologists have also explored the pitfalls of the conceptualization process itself. In a special issue of the journal *Poetics* (vol. 28, no. 1, 2000), several sociologists (including John Martin, Karen Cerulo, John Mohr, Helene Lee, and Albert Bergesen) explore the problem of "rigid conceptualization," a phenomenon in which strict conceptual parameters confine concepts' analytic power. Across the issue's four very different articles, *Poetics* authors creatively extend and redefine various concepts in ways that make them more flexible and broaden their applicability.

In contrast to rigid conceptualization rests the problem of "hazy conceptualization." Hazy concepts prove imprecise and thus fail to capture adequately that which they represent. Karen Cerulo ponders a specific example of this phenomenon in her article "Specifying the Worst: Issues in Conceptualization" (*Culture* 14(3):1, 6–10, 2000). The essay examines arenas in which "the worst" of people, places, objects, and events are insufficiently defined. Once identifying these areas, the author speculates on the social consequences of such imprecision. In a more general excursion, Eviatar Zerubavel explores in depth the conditions under which conceptual haziness can be both socially functional and dysfunctional; see "The Fuzzy Mind" (chap. 5, *The Fine Line*, New York: Free Press, 1991).

Higher-order representational constructs have also captured sociologists' attentions. Erving Goffman's *Frame Analysis: An Essay on the Organization of Experience* (New York: Harper Colophon, 1974) represents the classic statement on frames. His book proposes a systematic account of the ways in which social actors use expectations to make sense out of everyday life. Note that Goffman drew in part from anthropologist Gregory Bateson's work on the subject. Interested readers should consult "A Theory of Play and Frame" (pp. 177–93 in *Steps to an Ecology of the Mind*, New York: Ballentine Books, 1972).

Since the publication of Goffman's seminal work, the notion of framing has been innovatively developed by a number of cultural sociologists. Students of social movements, for example, have delineated the frame alignment processes that both identify and focus collective action at particular historical moments. Classic works in this field include David Snow's and Robert Benford's "Master Frames and Cycles of Protest" (pp. 133–55 in A. D. Morris and C. M. Mueller, eds., *Frontiers in Social Movement Theory*, New Haven, CT: Yale University Press, 1992), Sidney Tarrow's "Mentalities, Political Cultures, and Collective Action Frames: Construction Meaning Through Action" (pp. 174–202 in A. D. Morris and C. M. Mueller, eds., *Frontiers in Social Movement Theory*, New Haven, CT: Yale University Press, 1992), and Douglas McAdam's *Freedom Summer* (New York: Oxford University Press, 1988). Cultural sociologists have also explored the ways in which the framing of public discourse can mold and shift collective perceptions of reality. Interested readers should consider William Gamson's fascinating excursion on political discourse, *Talking Politics* (New York: Cambridge University Press, 1992) and William R. Freudenberg's and Susan K. Pastor's important article, "Public Responses to Technological Risks: Toward a Sociological Perspective," (*Sociological Quarterly* 33(3):389–412, 1992). More recent and equally inviting treatments include William Bielby's "Framing Sociology in Court: Affirmative Action Discourse and Expert Opinion on Employment Discrimination," (*Research in Social Stratification and Mobility* 17:265–83, 1999), and Rhys Williams's and Timothy Kubal's "Movement Frames and the Cultural Environment: Resonance, Failure, and the Boundaries of the Legitimate" (*Research in Social Movements, Conflict and Change* 21:225–48, 1999).

Closely related to sociological treatments of frames are discussions of information formats. Such literature explores the ways in which the organization of information can influence meaning-making activities. Students of language initiated sociological inquiries on format. Aaron Cicourel's *Cognitive Sociology: Language and Meaning in Social Interaction* provides a good example (New York: Free Press, 1974). See also Erving Goffman's *Forms of Talk* (Philadelphia, PA: University of Pennsylvania Press,

1981). But in recent years, the study of formats has been centered in media studies. In *Deciphering Violence: The Cognitive Structure of Right and Wrong* (New York: Routledge, 1998), for example, Karen Cerulo explores the variety of ways in which media narrators format reports of violence. Her research demonstrates that such format choices are critical, because the sequencing of a violent story's elements (e.g., information on the perpetrator, victim, act, and context) can systematically alter readers' and viewers' tolerance for violent acts. In related research, sociologists have noted that the selection of certain thematic formats can guide audience interpretation. In "Paper Tigers and Video Postcards: The Rhetorical Dimensions of Narrative Form in ABC News Coverage of Terrorism" (*Western Journal of Communication* 56:143–60, 1992), Bethany Dobkin shows that the selection of a melodramatic format in the reporting of terrorism effectively heightens viewers' animosity toward military enemies. Similarly, Joshua Gamson notes that the adversarial format of tabloid talk shows (e.g., Jerry Springer, Ricki Lake, etc.) serves to increase class and cultural tensions between working- and middle-class nonconformists. See *Freaks Talk Back: Tabloid Talk Shows and Sexual Nonconformity* (Chicago, IL: University of Chicago Press, 1998).

In studying formats, several sociologists have documented the ways in which changing social conditions can influence message senders' selection of formats. Reviewing the formatting of etiquette manuals, for example, Jorge Arditi shows that periods of "centered" social relations elicit etiquette formats quite different from those selected during eras of "decentered" social relations; see *A Geneology of Manners* (Chicago, IL: University of Chicago Press, 1998). Similarly, in studying the formatting of national anthems and flags, Karen Cerulo shows that the sociocultural conditions that surround the selection of such symbols—the levels of social disruption experienced by the nation, the nation's economic standing, the cultural diversity of a national population, and so on—are systematically related to the types of formats by which national leaders choose to express their nation's identity; see *Identity Designs: The Sights and Sounds of a Nation* (ASA Rose Book Series, New Brunswick, NJ: Rutgers University Press, 1995).

Storage and Retrieval

The study of memory is most often associated with the field of cognitive science. Yet it is important to note that sociologists have explored the sociocultural dimensions of memory since the early 1900s. Most agree that Maurice Halbwachs triggered this line of inquiry. His book, *Social Frameworks of Memory* (Chicago, IL: University of Chicago Press, [1925] 1992) established memory as something more than a component of the human brain. Halbwachs's work presented memory as a social process, one that could be jointly shared by members of a collective.

Until very recently, sociological works on the collective dimension of memory failed to coalesce as a unified field. Studies of the ways in which collectives build, store, and retrieve memories for use in the present remained compartmentalized, forming subsets of other substantive literatures. Much memory research, for example, was subsumed within nationalism research. In this context, scholars explore the ways in which national symbols, rituals, and commemorative occasions create national histories and identities. Important works in this regard include David Cressey's *Bonfires and*

Bells: National Memory and the Protestant Calendar in Elizabethan and Stuart England (Berkeley, CA: University of California Press, 1989), John Gillis's collection *Commemoration: The Politics of National Identity* (Princeton, NJ: Princeton University Press, 1994), David Lowenthal's *The Past Is a Foreign Country* (New York: Cambridge University Press, 1985), and Yael Zerubavel's *Recovered Roots: Collective Memory and the Making of Israeli National Tradition* (Chicago, IL: University of Chicago Press, 1995). Other scholars specifically address the politics of memory construction. Such authors are especially vocal in noting the ways in which national leaders deliberately manipulate and exploit historical narratives for specific political purposes. In this regard, see Karen A. Cerulo's *Identity Designs: The Sites and Sounds of a Nation* (The Rose Book Series of the American Sociological Association, New Brunswick, NJ: Rutgers University Press, 1995), Peter Novick's *That Noble Dream: The "Objectivity Question" and the American Historical Profession* (Cambridge, England: Cambridge University Press, 1989), and Gerard Noriel's *The French Melting Pot: Immigration, Citizenship, and National Identity* (trans. by G. de Laforcade Minneapolis, MN: University of Minnesota Press, 1996).

The literature on reputations represents another repository for sociological studies of memory. In keeping with the themes of storage and retrieval, scholars working in this area explore the ways in which the images of public figures are initially constructed and maintained; they also probe the ways in which such images are constantly "made over" in accord with the changing needs of social groups. Excellent examples of work in this area include Thomas Brown's *JFK: History of an Image* (Bloomington, IN: Indiana University Press, 1988), Gary Allan Fine's *Difficult Reputations: Collective Memories of the Evil, Inept, and Controversial* (Chicago, IL: University of Chicago Press, 2001), Jaroslav Pelikan's *Jesus through the Centuries: His Place in the History of Culture* (New Haven, CT: Yale University Press, 1985), Barry Schwartz's *George Washington: The Making of an American Symbol* (New York: Free Press, 1987), and "Memory as a Cultural System: Abraham Lincoln in World War II" (*American Sociological Review* 54:359–81, 1996).

Of course, current reviews alert us to the fact that sociological studies of memory supercede any single substantive area. And as we peruse the broader field of memory research, a number of specific themes emerge. For example, some scholars emphasize the specific "sites" of memory construction. Hans Haake's *Framed and Being Framed* (New York: New York University Press, 1975) examines museums as a site of memory building and storage. Elihu Katz's "Broadcast Holidays" (*Sociological Inquiry* 68(2):230–41, 1998), and Kurt and Gladys Lang's "Collective Memory and the News" (*Communication* 11(1):123–40, 1984) engage the media in this regard. Also important is Jay Winter's *Sites of Memory, Sites of Mourning: The Great War in European Cultural History* (New York: Cambridge University Press, 1995). Eviatar Zerubavel provides perhaps the broadest statement on this issue. In *Time Maps: Social Memory and the Topography of the Past* (in preparation), Zerubavel comprehensively explores various sites of mnemonic socialization and carefully studies the formation of mnemonic communities.

Many scholars focus on specific "tools" of memory construction—symbols, narratives, memorials, textbooks, and so on. For example, Frances Fitzgerald examines the role of history books in the building of collective identity; see *America Revised: History Schoolbooks in the Twentieth Century* (New York: Vintage, 1980).

Eviatar Zerubavel's work on calendars and schedules notes the ways in which the tools of time can mark and reconfigure historical eras and events; see *Hidden Rhythms: Schedules and Calendars in Social Life* (Chicago, IL: University of Chicago Press, 1981) and *The Seven-Day Circle* (New York: Free Press, 1985). Other important works in this category include Andreas Huyssen's *Twilight Memories: Marking Time in a Culture of Amnesia* (New York: Routledge, 1995), George L. Mosse's *Fallen Soldiers: Reshaping the Memory of the World Wars* (New York: Oxford University Press, 1990), and Eugene Rochberg-Halton's *Meaning and Modernity: Social Theory in the Pragmatic Attitude* (Chicago, IL: University of Chicago Press, 1986).

Still other scholars dissect the process of commemoration, paying special attention to the cultural "practices" that social actors use both to sustain and to contest collective memory. Stephanie Coontz, for example, examines two hundred years of family life in America, exposing the cultural myths that have sustained images of the perfect nuclear unit; see *The Way We Never Were: American Families and the Nostalgia Trap* (New York: Basic Books, 1992). In *Nations and Commemoration: Creating National Identities in the United States and Australia* (New York: Cambridge University Press, 1997), Lynn Spillman compares centennial and bicentennial celebrations in the United States and Australia, identifying changes and continuities, similarities and differences in the ways in which commemorative practices express nationhood. Other important works in this field include Eric Hobsbawm's "Mass Producing Traditions: Europe 1870–1914" (pp. 203–307 in E. Hobsbawm and T. Ranger, eds., *The Invention of Tradition*, New York: Cambridge University Press, 1983), Jeff Olick's *The Sins of the Fathers: the Third Reich and West German Legitimation* (New Haven, CT: Yale University Press, 1993), and Robin Wagner-Pacifici's and Barry Schwartz's "The Vietnam Veterans's Memorial: Commemorating a Difficult Past (*American Journal of Sociology* 97(2):376–420, 1991).

In pondering the practices of memory, some sociologists explore the "limits" on memory reconstruction. Important works such as Michael Schudson's *Watergate in American Memory: How We Remember, Forget, and Reconstruct the Past* (New York: Basic Books, 1992), Barry Schwartz's "Introduction: The Expanding Past" (*Qualitative Sociology* 9(3):275–82), and Edward Shils's *Tradition* (Chicago, IL: University of Chicago Press, 1981) demonstrate that factors such as the structure of available historical schemata, the strength and popularity of reigning narratives, and cohorts' empirical experiences can limit the ways in which a collective retrieves and applies certain memories.

The sociological study of memory is a fast-growing field. This section highlights only a few of the many existing works. For a wide-reaching summary of this exciting literature, as well as an excellent integration of the field, consult Jeffrey Olick's and Joyce Robbins's fine review article, "Social Memory Studies: From 'Collective Memory' to Historical Sociology of Mnemonic Practices" (*Annual Review of Sociology* 24:105–40, 1998). But in reading any review of the memory literature, it will become clear that there still remains much room for dialogue between cognitive scientists and sociologists. Can the concerns of cognitive scientists translate to sociologists in a meaningful way? For example, do the concepts of "short-term memory" and "chunking" have a meaningful sociological counterpart? Can cognitive scientists' reflections on "long-term memory" enhance the sociological study of collective memory? Clearly, much more work is required if we are to achieve the richest possible sociological treatment of memory as well as a full interdisciplinary dialogue on the topic.

Building Bridges

Forging an interdisciplinary dialogue between cognitive science and cultural sociology may well be a daunting task. Yet the potential fruits of this endeavor make the effort highly worthwhile. The authors of Section V provide three excellent vehicles for intellectual exchange. But readers committed to interdisciplinary dialogue may wish to consult several additional works as well. For example, Paul DiMaggio provides an extensive review of cognitive science research that is especially relevant to the work of cultural sociologists; see "Culture and Cognition" (*Annual Review of Sociology* 23:263–87, 1997). In response to DiMaggio, Norbert Schwartz offers a social psychologist's perspective on cognitive science and speculates on its contribution to the sociological agenda; see "Warmer and More Social: Recent Developments in Cognitive Social Psychology" (*Annual Review of Sociology* 24:239–64, 1998). In a related vein, anthropologist Roy G. D'Andrade traces the development of cognitive anthropology, along with related ideas from psychology and cultural sociology, ultimately providing an explanatory framework that strives to integrate the study of thought, emotion, and action; see *The Development of Cognitive Anthropology* (New York: Cambridge University Press, 1995). Finally, Peter Baumgartner and Sabine Payr construct a stimulating symposium on thought. In *Speaking Minds: Interviews with Twenty Eminent Cognitive Scientists* (Princeton, NJ: Princeton University Press, 1995), the authors interview twenty scholars from a variety of disciplines including anthropology, biology, engineering, linguistics, mathematics, philosophy, political science, psychology, and sociology, providing a truly interdisciplinary look at research on thought.

For more information on the study of culture and cognition, readers are encouraged to visit the Web site of the Culture and Cognition Research Network: http://sociology.rutgers.edu/cultcog/. There one can find bibliographic material and new publications in the culture and cognition field. One can also access announcements of the network's upcoming activities and instructions for subscribing to an online discussion group.

Contributors

David L. Altheide is Regents' Professor and Interim Director in the School of Justice Studies at Arizona State University. His work has focused on the role of mass media and information technology for social control. Two recent theoretical and methodological statements on the relevance of the mass media for sociological analysis are *An Ecology of Communication: Cultural Formats of Control* (Aldine de Gruyter, 1995) and *Qualitative Media Analysis* (Sage, 1996). He is completing a book on the organization and social impact of news media emphasis on fear-as-entertainment.

Karen A. Cerulo is Associate Professor of Sociology at Rutgers University where she specializes in culture and cognition research. Her articles appear in a wide variety of journals and annuals. Her books include *Identity Designs: The Sights and Sounds of a Nation*—winner of the Culture Section's "Best Book Award, 1996" (ASA Rose Book series, Rutgers University Press, 1995), *Deciphering Violence: The Cognitive Order of Right and Wrong* (Routledge, 1998), and *Second Thoughts: Seeing Conventional Wisdom Through the Sociological Eye* (with Janet Ruane, Pine Forge, Sage, 2000).

Paul DiMaggio is Professor of Sociology at Princeton University and Research Coordinator of Princeton's Center for Arts and Cultural Policy Studies. He has written widely on topics in the sociology of culture, organization theory, and economic sociology and is editor of *The 21st Century Firm: Changing Economic Organization in International Perspective* (Princeton University Press, 2001). His current research focuses on cultural conflict in the contemporary United States and inequality in access to the new digital technologies.

Wendy Nelson Espeland is associate professor of sociology at Northwestern University. She is currently writing a book with Mitchell Stevens on commensuration. In 1998 she published *The Struggle for Water: Politics, Rationality, and Identity* (University of Chicago Press). Her research investigates how conceptions of what it means to be rational arise, and how these inform politics.

294

Gary Alan Fine is Professor of Sociology at Northwestern University. He is the author of *Difficult Reputations: How We Remember the Evil, Inept and Controversial* (University of Chicago Press, 2001). His current research on reputation involves issues of the remembrance of Adolf Hitler, and how we recall those charged with sedition.

William A. Gamson is a Professor of Sociology and co-directs the Media Research and Action Project (MRAP) at Boston College. He is the author of *Talking Politics* (Cambridge University Press, 1992) and *The Strategy of Social Protest* (Wadsworth, 2d ed., 1990) among other books and articles on political discourse, the mass media and social movements. He is a past president of the American Sociological Association.

Allan V. Horwitz is Professor of Sociology in the Department of Sociology and Institute for Health, Health Care Policy, and Aging Research at Rutgers University. He has published numerous articles and books in the field of the sociology of mental health and illness including *The Social Control of Mental Illness, A Handbook for the Study of Mental Health* (Cambridge University Press, 1999), and *Creating Mental Illness* (University of Chicago Press, forthcoming).

Nicole Isaacson is a doctoral candidate in sociology at Rutgers University. Her research interests include the cognitive processes of boundary formation, the social construction of prematurity and reproductive practices, and racial disparities in healthcare. Her current work examines the cognitive and cultural processes involved in drawing distinctions between fetuses and infants and the implications of these boundaries for women's reproductive choices.

MiKyoung Kim received a Ph.D. in Sociology from University of Georgia. Her dissertation was entitled "Structure, Culture, Biographies and Women's Resistance: A Case Study of South Korean Women Textile Workers' Labor Resistance, 1970–1979." She has published several articles on labor relations, women, North Korea and race relations in the *Asian Perspective*, *Women's Studies International Forum*, *Nautilus*, the *Korean Journal of Sociology*, and the *Journal of Korean Anthropology*. She is currently affiliated with the U.S. Embassy in Seoul, South Korea, as a country program.

Barry Schwartz is Professor Emeritus of Sociology at the University of Georgia. For the past twenty years, he has studied historians and commemorative agents working independently yet concurrently to represent the past and help shape the historical consciousness of ordinary individuals. He has developed these themes in articles and books, including *Abraham Lincoln and the Forge of National Memory* (University of Chicago Press, 2000), and in studies of the moral judgment of national history in the United States, Germany, and Japan.

Diane Vaughan is Professor of Sociology, Boston College. Her research explores situated action: how culture mediates between institutions, the immediate social setting, and individual action and choice. She is author of *Controlling Unlawful Organizational Behavior* (University of Chicago Press, 1983), *Uncoupling* (Oxford

University Press, 1986), and *The Challenger Launch Decision* (University of Chicago Press, 1996). Currently she is writing *Theorizing: Analogy, Cases, and Comparative Social Organization* and doing field work for *Dead Reckoning: Technology, Culture and Cognition in Air Traffic Control*.

Jerome C. Wakefield is Professor in the School of Social Work, the Institute for Health, Health Care Policy, and Aging Research, and the Center for Cognitive Studies, all at Rutgers University, and Lecturer in Psychiatry at Columbia University College of Physicians and Surgeons. He holds an M.S.W. and D.S.W. in Social Welfare, a Ph.D. in Philosophy, and an M.A. in Mathematics with a specialization in Logic and Methodology of Science, all from Berkeley. His scholarly focus is on conceptual foundations of the mental health professions. Recent writing has concerned the concept of mental disorder and the validity of DSM-IV diagnostic criteria. He is currently working on a book on Freud and philosophy of mind.

Harrison C. White is Giddings Professor of Sociology at Columbia University. He is the author of *Markets from Networks* (Princeton University Press, forthcoming) and *Identity and Control* (Princeton University Press, 1992). In earlier works, he wrote on blockmodels of network roles, vacancy chains, French painting careers, and classificatory kinship. He currently works on the sociolinguistics of grammar.

Robert Wuthnow is the Gerhard R. Andlinger' 52 Professor of Sociology and Director of the Center for the Study of Religion at Princeton University. The author of numerous books and articles on culture and religion, his recent books include *Loose Connections:Coming Together in America's Fragmented Communities* (Harvard University Press, 1998) and *Creative Spirituality:The Way of the Artist* (University of California, 2001).

Eviatar Zerubavel is Professor of Sociology at Rutgers University. His publications include *Patterns of Time in Hospital Life* (University of Chicago Press, 1979), *Hidden Rhythms (*University of Chicago Press, 1981), *The Seven Day Circle* (Free Press, 1985), *The Fine Line* (Free Press, 1991), *Terra Cognita* (Rutgers University Press, 1992), *Social Mindscapes* (Harvard University Press, 1997), and *The Clockwork Muse* (Harvard University Press, 1999). Currently, he is currently completing a book on social memory and the "topography" of the past. Professor Zerubavel is a past Chair of the Culture Section of the American Sociological Association.

Index